The Ancient Liturgy Of The Church Of England, According To The Uses Of Sarum, York, Hereford, And Bangor, And The Roman Liturgy Arranged In Parallel Columns With Preface And Notes

William Maskell, Church Of England, Catholic Church

The ancient Liturgy of the
Church of England

London

HENRY FROWDE

OXFORD UNIVERSITY PRESS WAREHOUSE

7 PATERNOSTER ROW

(m.c.x)

The ancient Liturgy of the Church of England

According to the uses of Sarum York
Hereford and Bangor and the
Roman Liturgy arranged
in parallel columns
with preface
and notes

❦

BY

WILLIAM MASKELL, M.A.

THIRD EDITION.

Oxford

AT THE CLARENDON PRESS

1882

Contents.

Preface.

CHAPTER I.

IN the admonition entitled *Concerning the Service of the Church* which succeeds if indeed it does not rather form a part of the preface to the present book of Common Prayer of the reformed church of England, we find the following :—

"And whereas heretofore there hath been great diversity in saying and singing in churches within this realm ; some following Salisbury use, some Hereford use, and some the use of Bangor, some of York, some of Lincoln ; now from henceforth all the whole realm shall have but one use."

In this passage the word *heretofore* does not relate to the time immediately preceding the last review of the common Prayer book in 1662, for during more than one hundred years (with the exception of the period of the rebellion and the ascendancy of presbyterians and independents) there had been only one use of saying and singing in English parish churches. We must go back to the beginning of the reign of queen Elizabeth, and beyond that again to the year 1549, when the first book of king Edward the sixth having been approved by convocation was put forth and enjoined by the authority of the parliament and the crown. We find in the preface to that book almost word for word the same injunction or admonition.

So, the "Act for the uniformity of publick prayers, and administering the sacraments and other rites and ceremonies, &c. in the church of England" (14 Car. II.) begins: "Whereas in the first year of the late queen Elizabeth, there was one uniform order of common service and prayer, and of the administration of the sacraments, rites, and ceremonies of the church of England." And the act alluded to, the first of Elizabeth, refers in like manner to the last year of Edward the sixth, declaring that then also there was "one uniform order." These statutes, we may therefore say, recognise the previous existence of various allowed forms or uses.

There are certainly some who very imperfectly understand what is meant by these old uses of the church of England; they have often remarked the passage which I have quoted from the preface to the Prayer book, and would be glad to learn something about it.[1] Wheatley and Shepherd, authors generally appealed to, pass over without remark "the Preface:" the latter however[2] in his introduction does say that "it is deserving of notice, that hitherto there had not been in England any one service established by public authority for the general use of the church. In the southern parts of the island the offices according to the use of Sarum, and in the northern those of York, were generally followed. In south Wales the offices of Hereford were adopted, and in north Wales those of Bangor," &c.: and so he passes on. Nor does Dr. Nicholls in his commentary make any remark

---

[1] I leave this passage as it stood in the second edition of this book, in 1846; since that time a good deal has been written and published about the English common Prayer book, giving much evidence of research and enquiry.

[2] Introduction, p. xxxvii.

upon the passage. Bishop Mant in his selection of what he calls "notes" upon the common Prayer has referred to Sparrow and Dr. Burn, who give no further information upon the subject; except indeed that Osmund, bishop of Salisbury about the year 1070, was the compiler of the use of Sarum.

There are many, again, who are better informed but yet have never had an opportunity of examining any copies of the old service books which still exist, whether from living at a distance from public libraries or from some other cause. Nearly forty years ago [1844] in the preface to the first edition of this volume I said my hope was, upon a consideration of the circumstances which I have briefly spoken of above, that an attempt to render accessible these books or portions of them would not be unacceptable. Let me now add [1882], I trust without presumption, that my expectations have been amply realised.

I have alluded to the difficulty of obtaining access to these old books. So rare are they that except in the libraries of the universities of Oxford and Cambridge, and the British museum, it is almost hopeless to expect to find them. Occasionally, in a few instances, we may meet with a single volume, a horæ, or a manual, or it may be even a missal: but one book only will do but little for the student; if he wishes to understand the subject, and to obtain more than a mere smattering of knowledge about it, it can be only after a careful examination and comparison of the many volumes among which anciently the offices of the church of England were distributed.

There are better reasons even than the fact of rarity for making an effort to republish, in some form or other, either all or parts of the old books.

Of late years the demand for them has increased tenfold, and their price has naturally increased with the demand; so as to put them, when they do occur, beyond the reach of men who are nevertheless the most anxious to obtain them. This has been one result of a return to a more sound theological study than had characterised the clergy of an age, which has been emphatically and most justly styled by a late bishop of the diocese of Salisbury[3] in his visitation charge "an unlearned age." And it could not but be so: for a chief object of enquiry, when men began to awake to the need of knowing something of the history, doctrines, and ritual of the middle ages, certainly would be into the faith and practice, into the observances and the worship of their church, before as well as since the sixteenth century. In the pursuit of this, they would be no longer content to rely upon garbled extracts or the unfounded representations of ignorant and prejudiced or slanderous historians.[4]

Before the reformation the public offices of the church of England were not contained, as they now are, in one volume but in many: they were perfectly distinct from each other, and intended for different purposes. There seems to be no necessity to supply here a description of these numerous books, as I have examined at considerable length the whole subject in a dissertation prefixed to another work, the *Monumenta ritualia.* It must therefore be suf-

---

[3] Bishop Denison, in his primary charge.

[4] Attached to this passage in the first edition of "the ancient liturgy" was a note, specifying as an example a writer at that time still living, Mr. Hallam; and I allude to it because I see no reason for altering the opinion which I then expressed, though I do not think it necessary to repeat it. The place referred to is the second chapter of his *Constitutional history of England.*

ficient to refer the reader there, and extract one passage only from an edition of a *Portiforium se-cundum usum Sarum*, published by Grafton and Whitchurch in 1544. This has at the beginning a privilege and licence of the king under his great seal to those printers, that they alone should print certain " bookes of devyne servyce, and praier bookes, that is to say, the masse booke, yᵉ graile, the hympnal, the antiphoner, the processyonale, the manuel, the porteaus, and the prymer." Of these books the " masse booke" or the missal contained the rites and ceremonies and prayers to be used in the celebration of the holy communion. The graile or gradual contained, often with the notation also, the various introits, offertories, communions, graduals, tracts, sequences, and other parts of the service. This volume was of course necessary for the more solemn performance of the liturgy in choir, and with the full attendance of the officiating priest and his subordinate ministers.

Before we pass on, I propose first briefly to discuss what the meaning is of the term " use." Upon this question the chief difficulty seems to be how far, or if at all, we are to include the varieties also which unquestionably existed of music and chanting. How much of ceremonies and rites besides the bare words and order of the prayers ought to be included is another question and rests upon very different grounds : but as regards music, when we speak of the use of the church of Salisbury, or of the church of York, or Hereford, not only need we not include the chants, but rather, if we wish to be precise, altogether exclude the consideration of them.

It has been said upon the other hand by writers who take a different view, that the primary meaning of the passage from the preface to the Common Prayer book, before quoted, "Whereas heretofore," &c., is "with reference only to the various uses of plain-tune in the several cathedral choirs," and it has been doubted "whether there ever was a Lincoln use in any other sense than a different mode and practice of chanting."

When, however, we take up a missal according to the use of Sarum, and another of Hereford, and a third of York or Bangor, or again a breviary or a manual of Salisbury or York and compare them, we find most important and numerous variations. The notation may or may not be contained in them; very often of some portions it is, but subordinate and may or may not differ also. In many office books, the horæ for example, the notation is almost always omitted. As I have just said, there are numberless variations which constitute the use and distinguish the services of one church from those of another; viz. different prayers; different arrangements of them; different ceremonies to be observed in the administration of the sacraments; and whether a particular diocese of England anciently adopted the use of Sarum or the use of Hereford would depend upon the acceptance of its manual and missal and other office books, and have no necessary reference to its mode of intonation. The diocese of Ely, for example, might observe the use of the church of Sarum and nevertheless adopt the music, supposing (that is) that there were material differences between the two, of the church of York. Or it might retain some parts of both styles or modes of singing with other intonations proper to itself: all which would have no influence upon the use, properly so called, observed by the church of Ely. But if, upon the other hand, a part of the

offices of Sarum, and a part of Hereford, and a
part of York, were taken and rearranged, with an
observance of this one and an omission of another; this would constitute a new use, viz. of the
church of Ely. I do not speak of one or two and
trifling differences; for these might allowably fall
under the head of peculiarities.

In an improper and wide sense we may include
under certain circumstances the mode of intonation
adopted and ordered by any church in its use.
Thus, we cannot separate the notation of a noted
manual or missal of the church of Salisbury from
the use of that church at the time when the particular volume, which we may be examining, was
written or printed. But the book would still be
the missal or the manual "secundum usum Sarum"
if there was not one musical note contained in it.
So, again, at different periods during the thirteenth
and fourteenth centuries the music may have varied
very materially, and yet the use of the church of
Salisbury have continued one and the same.

The references which the rubrics, especially of
the manual, frequently make to notation affect not
as it appears to me the question in dispute. Some
cite, as a proof that the music must necessarily be
included within the meaning of the term "use,"
such directions as "omnes orationes dicuntur cum
'Oremus' sub tono prædicto;" or "dicat sacerdos
sub tono consueto;" or "cum cantu sequenti;" or
"dicat sacerdos orationes sequentes sub tono lectionis;" or, once more, "dicat in more præfationis."
But the ecclesiastical tones to which these rubrics
refer either immediately follow or precede them;
or they might be, as especially in the case of the
"tone of the lection" or "the tone of the preface,"
well-known and fixed, yet nevertheless not the same

tone in all the dioceses which adhered strictly to the use of the church of Sarum or of York. These rubrics do not prove in every instance that the same music was necessarily to be followed, as were the integral portions of the public offices which made up the " use."

It may possibly be going too far to deny that the title " secundum usum Sarum," or "ad usum ecclesiæ Eboracensis," or " Herfordensis," prefixed to a breviary, or hymnal, or psalter, signifies sometimes in the printed books not the prayers only but the mode of singing authorised at the time in those dioceses; but then such books must be noted. If they do not contain the music (which is sometimes the case even with psalters and graduals) they would still be quite as properly and with the title also "secundum usum" of this or of that church ; and in its strict sense, relating solely to the variety and arrangement of the prayers, hymns, and psalter, rites and ceremonies.

Some have said that " the hymnarium, the psalter, the gradual, and the pontifical are choral books, and noted," and therefore that we cannot exclude music from the notion of the term "use." But not to speak of the utter absurdity of calling a pontifical a choral book, the others did not necessarily contain the notation. The psalter, for example, according to the use of any church is entirely independent of the tones which may accompany it. Hence, when printing became general we find many examples of the psalter " secundum usum" of whatever church it might be with the lines ruled for the music, which however is not printed also but left to be filled in with manuscript. This of course would seldom happen in earlier ages, when the entire volumes were manuscript; and therefore affords an additional

and not a light proof why we must not argue hastily
from such expressions as "cum tono sequenti"
and "dicatur hic cantus." Yet, in the same way,
we occasionally find in manuscripts the services of
festivals of late institution, such as of St. Osmund,
or of the transfiguration, or of the visitation of the
blessed Virgin, fully arranged and determined upon
"secundum usum;" but the music not written in,
although the proper lines and spaces may be left
for it.

In the sense in which I have above explained it,
we find the term use employed by the ritualists.
It will be unnecessary for me to cite more than one
example, from Gavantus; who, describing what is
meant by the breviary according to the use of the
church of Rome, says it is so called because it contains the prayers authorised by that church: and
immediately before, in a fuller explanation, he parti-
cularises the lessons, the psalms, hymns, legends,
&c., and the rubrics by which each day's office is to
be ascertained; but not one word does he add which
has reference to the music.[5]

Not improbably much of the doubt which has
been thrown over the term "use" has arisen from
the frequent occurrence of the verb *canto*: "cantare
missam secundum usum," &c. But nothing is more
certain than that *canto* does not always, especially
in the earlier writers, mean to sing in the modern
acceptation. To adopt the words of a very eminent
writer: "cantare missam priscorum phrasi illi dicebantur, qui sine cantu et privatim celebrabant."[6]
So again Mabillon after citing a particular canon

---

[5] *Thesaurus sacr. rit.* tom. ii.
p. 10. Compare Mabillon, *Dis-
quisitio de cursu Gallicano*, § 1;
De lit. Gall. p. 379.

[6] Bona, *Rerum liturg.* lib. i.
cap. xiii. 5.

adds : "verbum *canendo* interpretor de privata recitatione, nec aliam interpretationem sequentia pa-
tiuntur."[7] Thus an old "Expositio missæ" edited
by Cochlæus[8] says: "prima autem oratio super
corpus Christi futurum secreta dicitur, et secrete
canitur:" and the margin explains this to be "secreta oratio legitur." Once more, a passage in the
"defensorium directorii" of the church of Sarum is
very much to the point : "item illa duo verba quæ
ponuntur in multis festis, sic: *Invitatorium triplex*,
nihil oneris imponunt sacerdotibus qui dicunt officium suum sine nota : sed solum pertinent ad illos
qui cantant officium cum nota."[9] Here the use
whether with or without music would continue
equally and perfectly the use of Sarum; and no
distinction as regards it either depends upon or is
involved in the addition of a chant.

But there would be no end of accumulating examples of this sort. If the reader wishes to examine the question further I would recommend him,
among other books, especially to read the dissertation of Mabillon *de cursu Gallicano* to which
reference has already been made, and he will be
satisfied that music does not form, except in an
extended and improper sense, any part of what
we ought to understand by the term "use" of a
church.[10]

One word also, before I pass on, upon the expression in the passage in the preface to the com-

---

[7] *De cursu Gallicano*, § 46.
Gerbert, *de musica*, tom. i. p.
326, cites the same canon, and
explains it "de privata horarum
canonicarum recitatione." See
also pp. 355, 559, &c.

[8] *Spec. ant. devotionis*, p. 140.

[9] The reader will find the whole
of that important treatise printed
in the second volume of the
Monumenta ritualia.

[10] See also Perrone, *Prælect.
theol.* tom. 7. p. 383.

mon Prayer book, "the great diversity in saying
and singing," and "now from henceforth all the
whole realm shall have but one use." It is possible
that the reformers, among their multiplicity of plans,
did intend to enforce an uniformity in singing also
throughout the realm: but, whatever they may have
meant by the words just quoted, I think that it is
quite clear that the first common Prayer book
of king Edward was not aimed at the abolition of
varieties of music but of a variety of prayers, and
rites, and ceremonies. This last object was thoroughly
effected. A diversity of singing nevertheless continued, not only in different dioceses but also in
different churches of the same diocese: and at present there does not seem to be any rule, except the
precentor's pleasure, even for the daily singing in
a cathedral. Nevertheless, no one would suppose
that the preface to the common Prayer is evaded
or the act of uniformity is broken by this custom,
whatever may be said of other practices. Merbecke
(as is well known) about a year after the publication
of the first Book tried something of the sort which
the reformers merely hinted at; but his book was
unauthorised, limited in its impression, and so far
as we know never reached a second edition:[11] which
necessarily must have been the case, if the demand
for the book had been great in consequence of some
authoritative order which enjoined it. Elizabeth in
her injunctions, which were supplemental to her act
of uniformity, and so far as they might have had
any authority were grounded upon an especial clause
in that act, attempted to supply the deficiency: yet
these did not insist on a particular or one mode of

---

[11] See the statement of a doubt about this in a note to the disser-tation on service books, *Monumenta ritualia*, vol. i. p. xxv.

singing, but simply that there be "a modeste and destyncte songe used in all partes of the common prayers in the churche."[12]

The portions of the missals which are reprinted and arranged in this edition form but a very small division of their respective volumes; but by far the most important. In examining them the student must bear in mind that although he may have expected to find greater and more numerous variations between them, such variations were not likely to occur, even in so large a proportion, in the ordinary and the canon. These, especially the last, were parts of the Divine Service which were studiously guarded against alterations, additions, or omissions: and even the changes of single words and differences of arrangement which he will find in them constitute, as decidedly as far more considerable differences in other parts of the books would, a variety of use. And I do not hesitate to say that the distinctions of the ancient liturgies of the church of England, compared between themselves or with the Roman use in the ordinary and the canon, are not only as great but greater and more in number, and involving points of higher consequence, than any

---

[12] The forty-ninth of these injunctions declares that "because in dyvers collegiate and also some paryshe churches heretofore, there hath ben levynges appointed for the mayntenaunce of men & chyldren to use synging in the church, by meanes whereof the lawdable science of musicke hath ben had in estimation and preserved in knowledge: the quenes maiestie ... wylleth and commaundeth, that fyrste no alteration be made of such as-signementes of levynge but that the same so remayne. And that there bee a modeste and destyncte songe so used in all partes of the common prayers in the churche: that the same maye be as playnelye understanded, as if it were read without singing."

Injunctions geven by the quenes maiestie. Imprinted by Jugge and Cawood, anno M.D.LIX. Reprinted in Cardwell, *Documentary annals,* vol. i. p. 196.

previous acquaintance with such subjects, before an actual examination of the English missals, would have entitled us to expect.

To attempt even a sketch of the innumerable variations which existed in other parts of the English missals would be far too extensive a subject of enquiry. But take for example some masses near the beginning of the sanctorale according to the uses of the churches of Salisbury and York. The first service is that of the vigil of St. Andrew. In this the psalm, the verse after the gradual, one of the secrets, and one of the post-communions are different. Upon St. Andrew's day, the psalm again differs. Upon St. Thomas's day, the gradual, the offertory, and the post-communion are different. Upon the feast of the conversion of St. Paul, the introit, the psalm, the sequence, and the post-communion. Upon the feast of the purification, the sequence, tract, offertory, and secret.

Or again, compare one or two services from the commune of the missals of Hereford and Bangor. The services " In natali unius martyris et pontificis" agree only in the epistle and gospel. For "many martyrs" different lections, graduals, secrets, and communions are appointed. And, once more, in the service for a confessor and bishop, the tract, offertory, communion and post-communion are different.

The ordinary and the canon therefore occupying (as I have said) only a small part of the missal, the rest of that volume was filled with the various collects, epistles, gospels, sequences, graduals, &c. proper to the great festivals and fasts, the sundays, and to occasions when the Church offered up especial prayers in behalf, for example, of the king or in the time of any dearth or pestilence. These were of course used, at least many of them, only once a year; but the ordinary and the canon were daily said.

In these latter, moreover, were contained those rites which have been held from the earliest times to be essential not only to the valid but to a right or proper consecration of the holy eucharist. The several collections by Asseman, Renaudot and others, of liturgies which have been used in different patriarchates of the catholic church, contain those portions which are edited in the present volume: the other parts of many are altogether lost, and possibly some of the earlier liturgies had little else beside.[18]

---

[18] All that part (says bishop Rattray, speaking of the liturgy of St. James) which precedes the anaphora, both in this and the other ancient liturgies, is a later addition to the service of the church, as appears from the account given thereof by Justin Martyr, from the Clementine liturgy, and from the nineteenth canon of the council of Laodicea. By comparing of which with other ancient authorities, we plainly find that the service of the church began with reading of the scriptures, intermixed with psalmody; after which followed the sermon. Then the ἀκροώμενοι and ἄπιστοι, the *hearers* and *unbelievers*, being dismissed, there followed in order, the bidding prayer of the deacon, and the collect of the bishop, first for the catechumens; then, after they were dismissed, for the energumens; and after they were dismissed for the competentes or candidates for baptism; and lastly, after dismissing them likewise, for the penitents. Then, all these being dismissed, the missa fidelium, or *service of the faithful*, began with the εὐχὴ διὰ σιωπῆς, the *silent* or *mental prayer*, which is the first of the three prayers mentioned in the Laodicean canon; the second and third are said to be διὰ προσφωνήσεως. And these are the εὐχαὶ κοιναὶ καὶ ὑπὲρ ἑαυτῶν—καὶ ἄλλων πανταχοῦ πάντων in St. Justin. Then, after the priests washing their hands, and the kiss of peace and the μῆτις κατά τινος, the deacons brought the δῶρα, the *gifts* of the people, to the bishop, to be by him placed on the altar; and he having prayed secretly by himself, and likewise the priests, and making the sign of the cross with his hand upon his forehead, says the *Apostolical constitutions*, began the anaphora. *Ancient liturgy of St. James*, pref. 3.

As I shall have occasion presently to observe, so here also I may remind the reader, that the sacrament of the eucharist was never, since its institution, administered without the due observance of certain appointed ceremonies and prayers. These of course would be characterised during the first century of the existence of the church by a greater simplicity than in after years: and this, solely because many just reasons for the addition of other prayers and rites had not arisen, or they could not from the violence of persecution be allowed their due weight. But as time went on, and the roll of the saints and martyrs increased, commemorations of them were added, and collects, and hymns, and antiphons were increased in number, and the faithful sought to show their deep reverence for the service itself by a greater solemnity in its performance; all which was well fitting to the church of Christ when she was no longer driven to celebrate her mysteries in secret places, and hurriedly, and with the constant dread of cruel interruption.

CHAPTER II.

THE chief liturgies which have been preserved are those which are called St. James's, St. Mark's, St. Chrysostom's, St. Basil's, the Roman, and preeminent above all these, of an acknowledged greater antiquity than any, the Clementine.[14] As this liturgy of St. Clement is reprinted at the end of the present volume it seems necessary that I should make one or two remarks by which it is to be hoped the reader will be able to form some opinion of its value.

Theological questions and doctrines of the highest importance are involved in enquiries into the origin and relative authority of the ancient liturgies. Some writers upon the subject have boldly argued that the apostles themselves left not merely decisions upon the doctrine of the sacrament of the blessed eucharist but an accurate form of rites and ceremonies and prayers; in short, a liturgy, according to which it should be administered: and that this still exists either in the liturgy of Antioch, or Alexandria, or Rome. Those who hold this opinion chiefly rely upon a passage in a treatise, generally attributed to Proclus bishop of Constantinople in the fifth century, in which the writer states that the apostles whilst they were together at Jerusalem, before their dispersion into various quarters of the world, were accustomed daily to meet and celebrate the holy communion; "et cum multam consolationem in mys-

---

[14] "The liturgy of Clemens, the most ancient of those extant." Bishop Bull, vol. 2. p. 77.

tico illo dominici corporis sacrificio positam reperis-
sent, fusissime, longoque verborum ambitu missam
decantabant."[15]   St. Chrysostom also (cited by cardinal Bona) in his twenty-seventh homily enquires :
"cum sacras cœnas accipiebant apostoli, quid tum
faciebant ? nonne in preces convertebantur et hym-
nos ?"

On the other hand it has been argued that the
founder of each patriarchal church required his converts to observe some certain rites which were essential to the validity of the sacrament, and left
them at liberty to add to these other prayers and
ceremonies as they might think proper.   One thing
is very certain ; that the holy scriptures give us
little information upon the subject : the institution
of the holy eucharist is related by three of the evangelists, and by St. Paul in the first epistle to the
Corinthians.   We are told that our blessed Lord
took bread, and blessed it, and said " This is my
Body," and in like manner that he took the cup, and
blessed it, and said " This is my Blood :" but
whether any more words were used in blessing is
not recorded.

We cannot doubt that there was some form observed in the first communion which was celebrated
by the apostles after the resurrection of their Lord ;
nor, that they who had been partakers and witnesses
at the institution of the sacrament would be very
careful, in their after celebrations, to imitate as far
as possible the Saviour's example.   Indeed, this
was a divine command : what He had done, they
were to do ; what He had said, they were to say ;
what He had offered, they were to offer ; and power

---

[15] See the whole passage cited
in Gerbert, *De cantu*, tom. i. p.
94; and in Bona, *Rerum liturg.*
tom. i. p. 75.

also was given to them, and through them to the whole Church for ever, of altering or adding to or taking away from time to time, either prayers or ceremonies or rites, provided that they were not of the essence of the sacrament, and were intended to meet the requirements of various ages, climates, and countries, or to increase the solemnity of the celebration or to promote the devotion of the people. And it was this power which St. Paul claimed so unhesitatingly, as having been bestowed by our blessed Lord, when in the same epistle before spoken of to the Corinthians, and upon the very subject of the eucharist, he adds "and the rest will I set in order when I come." [16]

There is a famous passage of Gregory the great : in which it has been said that he asserts, and therefore he has been called in to prove, that the apostles used no other prayer or ceremony than the Lord's prayer only. The words of St. Gregory are : "Orationem dominicam idcirco mox post precem dicimus, quia mos apostolorum fuit, ut ad ipsam solum modo orationem, oblationis hostiam consecrarent. Et valde mihi inconveniens visum est, ut precem, quam scholasticus composuerat, super oblationem diceremus, et ipsam traditionem [*forte* orationem] quam redemptor noster composuit, super ejus corpus et sanguinem non diceremus." [17] But all writers

---

[16] Ch. xi. ver. 34. Conf. van Espen, *Jus eccles.* pars ii. sect. i. tit. v, and St. Augustine, *Epist.* liv. § 8. Also the place in Renaudot, " Verba Christi ad apostolos, *hoc facile in meam commemorationem,* præceptum celebrandæ ex instituto Christi eucharistiæ continent : formam qua celebrari deberet non exprimunt. Nemo tamen Christianus dubitavit, quin eamdem edocti fuerint a Domino apostoli, ut alia omnia quæ ad religionem Christianam constituendam pertinebant. Ab apostolis acceperunt illam eorum discipuli," &c. *Dissert.* p. 2.

[17] Lib. ix. epist. 12.

agree (that is, supposing the passage not to be corrupt) either that this assertion of St. Gregory is incorrect or that he himself intended more than the Lord's prayer to be understood. His argument, as it seems to me, is not that the Lord's prayer only was used by the apostles, but that they did not perform the whole service without reciting it. As cardinal Bona observes,[18] with whom agrees Le Brun,[19] at least the words of institution must have been added: "additis procul dubio verbis consecrationis."

That something must be understood to qualify the statement of St. Gregory is clear from the account of a very ancient writer, the author of the *Gemma animæ:* "missam in primis dominus Jesus, sacerdos secundum ordinem Melchisedech, instituit, quando ex pane et vino corpus et sanguinem suum fecit, et memoriam sui, suis celebrare hæc præcepit : hanc apostoli auxerunt, dum super panem et vinum verba quæ Dominus dixit, et dominicam orationem dixerunt. Deinde successores eorum epistolas et evangelia legi statuerunt, alii cantum, et alii alia adjecerunt qui decorem domus Domini dilexerunt."[20] And another, Walafrid Strabo, who lived some centuries earlier and not long after St. Gregory, speaking of the practice of primitive ages " primis temporibus " declares that although the eucharist was then celebrated with more simplicity than afterwards, yet " præmissa oratione dominica, et sicut ipse Dominus noster præcepit, commemoratione passionis ejus adhibita eos corpori dominico communicasse et sanguini, quos ratio permittebat."[21]

---

[18] Tom. i. p. 75.

[19] *Opera,* tom. ii. p. 82.

[20] Lib. i. cap. 86.

[21] *De rebus eccles.* cap. xxii; *Bibl. patrum auct.* tom. i. p. 680.

Or again, the whole place from St. Gregory is made agreeable to every other testimony of antiquity by rendering the word "ad" in the sense of "post;" of which examples might be found in the best writers. The pope would therefore merely intend to say that before the consecration of the sacred elements the apostles were accustomed to repeat only the Lord's prayer, and afterwards consecrate the eucharist. This interpretation leaves the whole question, except as to the ancient position of that prayer in the service, exactly where it was before.[22]

It is not improbable that sometimes during the violence of persecutions when the faithful were forced to meet at night and in places the most obscure, the blessed eucharist was administered with the fewest possible rites, and even the accustomed and almost necessary prayers were abbreviated. These were extraordinary cases which afford no argument against the general tradition up to the apostolic age. Justin Martyr, presently to be quoted, is a sufficient evidence that the earliest form could not have been very short. To this we may add the text from the first epistle of St. Paul to Timothy, which all the best commentators agree relates to the celebration of the eucharist, as another witness: "I exhort therefore that, first of all, supplications, prayers, intercessions, and giving of thanks be made,

---

[22] Muratori, after citing the passage from St. Gregory, adds: "Quum sine tabulis ac testibus id ab eo affirmatum fuerit, consensum minime extorquet a nobis. Et præcipue quod aliter senserint antiquiores ecclesiæ patres." *Dissert. de rebus lit.* col. 10.

We must not fail to remember the cause of the pope's epistle, and that St. Gregory was merely answering a complaint made by some Sicilians as to the position of the Lord's prayer in the canon: whether it ought to be said before or after the consecration of the elements.

for all men; for kings, and for all that are in authority."[23] Neither must we forget that the first Christian disciples, whether jews or gentiles, had been accustomed to the observance of many ceremonies and long prayers. There seems therefore little reason to believe, even if we had no evidence upon the other hand, that the apostles would so far oppose the prejudices of new converts in this respect, as to celebrate the highest and most solemn mysteries only by the bare use of the words, "This is My Body," "This is My Blood;" with the addition simply of the Lord's prayer.

I have delayed to examine at some little length the above assertion of St. Gregory on account of the importance which by many writers has been attached to it; especially by those who are always anxiously on the watch for every shadow of argument by which they can hope to controvert the steady voice of all antiquity, which declares that from the time of the apostles downwards some form, some liturgy, was always used in every part of the catholic Church. The variations in the ancient liturgies scarcely allow us to suppose that the same form was at first enjoined exactly in all the churches; but their constant agreement in substance and their uniform observance in nearly the same order of some particular rites make it certain that the apostles did at any rate require that order and declare that those rites are essential. We cannot trace the establishment of these rules to any canons of councils, nor can we name any age or place in which they were not observed; so that the rule of St. Augustine comes in, with a force not to be resisted: "Quod universa tenet ecclesia, nec a conciliis institutum sed

---

[23] Ch. ii. ver. 1.

semper retentum est, non nisi auctoritate apostolica traditum rectissime creditur."[24]

Hence (manifest interpolations having been removed) there are few differences in the ancient liturgies which may not be attributed to the legitimate power vested in the bishop of each diocese, and more especially in each patriarch, to arrange the public service of the people over whom he was appointed.[25] That there should have been an exact

---

[24] *De baptismo*, lib. iv. cap. 24.

[25] "Etsi nulla supersit cum occidentalium, tum orientalium ecclesiarum liturgia, quæ eamdem omnino faciem retineat, quam primis sæculis Christianæ religionis sortita fuit: certum tamen est, vel ipsis iis sæculis incruentum sacrificium·celebratum semper fuisse, et preces et ritus, hoc est liturgiam adhibitam in actione, quæ omnium præstantissimum mysterium complectitur. Accesserunt sensim aliæ preces, orationes et ritus pro diversa episcoporum pietate et ingenio," &c. Muratori, *Dissert.* cap. ix. 119.

"At nihil simile circa liturgias orientales et occidentales observari potest, cum omnes inter se ita conveniant, ut ab uno fonte, apostolorum scilicet exemplo et præceptis ad omnes ecclesias permanasse certissime agnoscantur. Neque aliunde tanta in sanctissimis mysteriis celebrandis conformitas, quam ex communi et omnibus nota traditione nasci potuit, cum Jacobus, qui antiquissimus eorum est, quorum

nominibus liturgiæ insignitæ sunt, nihil præceperit de vino aqua miscendo, de pronunciandis verbis Christi Domini, de invocando super dona proposita Spiritu sancto, de mittenda absentibus, aut ægrotantibus eucharistia, ut nec de multis aliis, quæ tamen ubique recepta fuisse et usu quotidiano ecclesiarum frequentata negari non potest. Nihil princeps apostolorum Petrus, aut Antiochiæ, aut Romæ scripsisse legitur, nihil Paulus, nihil alii: sed quod acceperant a Domino idem tradebant novis Christianis. Multo minus Basilius et Chrysostomus novas offerendi sacrificii eucharistici formas instituere poterant: ut neque a Gelasio primum aut a Gregorio magno Romana missa, neque ab Ambrosio Ambrosiana, Gothica a Leandro, Gallicana vetus a Gallicanis episcopis factæ sunt. Verum cum nota esset omnibus vetus et apostolica forma, quæ paucis verbis constabat, eam omnes secuti sunt, nec ab ea recesserunt: orationes quæ inter sacra dicebantur, cum multæ essent, selegerunt, novas etiam addiderunt,

agreement, both in words and ceremonies, cannot be expected; but the varieties were not of such consequence nor in so great a number as to affect the unity of the faith: "Multa pro locorum et hominum diversitate variantur" says Firmilian in his epistle to St. Cyprian "nec tamen propter hoc ab ecclesiæ catholicæ pace atque unitate discessum est." They who will not acknowledge any agreement, because in some matters of less consequence they find much variety, might as well expect a sameness throughout the world of civil rights, and customs, and observances. Not so argued one of our own archbishops, St. Anselm: "Queritur vestra reverentia de sacramentis ecclesiæ: quoniam non uno modo fiunt ubique, sed diversis modis in diversis locis tractantur. Utique si per universam ecclesiam uno modo et concorditer celebrarentur; bonum esset et laudabile. Quoniam tamen multæ sunt diversitates, quæ non in substantia sacramenti, neque in virtute ejus, aut fide discordant; neque omnes in unam consuetudinem colligi possunt: æstimo eas potius in pace concorditer tolerandas, quam discorditer cum scandalo damnandas. Habemus enim a sanctis patribus, quia si unitas servatur charitatis in fide catholica, nihil officit consuetudo diversa. Si autem quæritur unde istæ natæ sunt consuetudinum varietates: nihil aliud intelligo, quam humanorum sensuum diversitates."[26]

It is not possible to say whether, if the reformation

---

tandemque ne perturbatio inter fideles nasceretur, quasdam perscripserunt, et hæc origo fuit diversitatis liturgiarum." Renaudot, vol. i. 14.

[26] Ad Waleranni querelas, responsio; *Opera*, p. 139. Compare also St. Augustine, *Epist.* 54; St. Jerome, *Epist.* 28; and Ivo Carnotensis, *Epist.* 2. Also Catalani, prolegomena in *Pontif. Rom.* cap. ii. 6; Azevedo, *De divino officio*, exercit. x; Pinius, *De Mozar. lit.* cap. i. § 1.

had not taken place bringing with it the new common
Prayer book and other changes, we should still have
retained in England the old uses of, at least, Sarum
and York. We cannot be surprised that under the
pressure of the penal laws during the seventeenth
and eighteenth centuries the observance of the older
rituals gradually gave way to the introduction of the
Roman use. We may—and very reasonably—regret
the fact; but a fact it is, and we have lost, probably
for ever, many an ancient rite and ceremony, many
á prayer and litany, which connected the rituals of
queen Mary's reign with the mass said, or the
offices which were celebrated, not only by St. Augustine before king Ethelbert and his people, but
by priests and bishops of the earlier British church.

The love of uniformity and the desire to reduce
everything to a single pattern—let that type or
pattern be ever so excellent in itself—may be carried
to excess. I would adopt the language which Mabillon has used, speaking of a diversity of ritual:
" Ferenda est rituum illa diversitas, vel maxime
propter bonum pacis, immo etiam propter Ecclesiam,
quæ hac varietate decoratur. Nescio enim quo
modo dulcius sapit, quod vario cultu ornatur. Et
hoc quidem primum cavendum est in illis, qui cærimoniarum magistratum gerunt: quorum nonnulli
nunquam quiescunt, nisi omnes ad suos ritus vel
invitos pertraxerint. Alterum incommodum est
eorum, qui vel antiquos novis, vel e contrario novos
antiquis ritus semper præferendos volunt. Neutrum
sine delectu placet. Ubi regnant antiqui ritus, hi
constanter retinendi; ubi novi præ antiquis præva-
luerint, antiquos laudare decet, novos non rejicere.
Vix enim unquam accidit, ut quod usu semel recep-
tum est ac firmatum, absque perturbatione possit
mutari. Et quidem ut rituum varietatem induxit

locorum varietas, ita etiam eorumdem iisdem in locis mutationem aliquando persuasit temporum diversitas. Itaque laudanda in ejusmodi rebus constantia, modo cætera adsint, Ecclesiæ pax atque concordia, et Christiana caritas, cui omnes ritus cedere ac suffragari necesse est. Quod si salva pace et caritate retineri potest antiquitas, quin novitati præferenda sit, nemo sane sapiens negaverit."[37]

This power just spoken of, which from the nature of the office of the episcopate was vested in the bishops of the church, to accommodate the rites of public worship to the requirements of their people was in general very moderately exercised; nevertheless it was fully allowed and in reality unlimited, so long as the essentials of the eucharistic service were preserved and nothing introduced which was obnoxious to the One Holy Catholic Faith. During the first three centuries there were more reasons than in after-years why individual bishops should not hesitate, upon their sole authority, to make if they thought it desirable even considerable alterations in the liturgies. For they could not upon every occasion of doubt or difficulty which arose in the persecutions to which they were exposed ask advice of other of their brethren, much less meet together in a general council. But when they did so meet, it is clear from some canons of two of the earliest councils whose records have come down to us that liturgical and ritual matters were not overlooked. Thus the second, third, and fourth, the eighth, ninth, and forty-first of the apostolical canons, and several also of the Eliberitan council, have reference to such points.

Here we approach another question : in what age

---

[37] *Mus. Ital.* tom. ii. p. cxlj.

were liturgies first committed to writing? Some
have contended that the apostles were themselves
the authors of those several liturgies which claim
their names; but so great is the majority against
them that we may say it is agreed upon that the
apostles were not the authors. There is no account
of any such composition in the works of the first
fathers; and surely, if no others had, Origen or
Jerome would have made some mention of it.
Councils, at least the very early ones, are silent;
and these would have appealed to a written apostolic
liturgy, if they could, against the errors and teaching of heretics. Both Tertullian, when speaking of
the eucharistic rites,[28] and St. Cyprian,[29] upon the
question of mixing water with the wine, appeal to
tradition only; which we can scarcely conceive would
have been the case had they known of any liturgy
written by an apostle. If, once more, such a liturgy
ever existed it would almost certainly have been
among the number of canonical books, and so included in the sixtieth canon of the council of Laodicea.
Any addition to or alteration in it must have been
instantly disallowed; but we know that alterations
were very anciently made, and prayers if not essential left out or inserted in some of the liturgies
claiming to be apostolic.

The date at which they were first written is open
to far more dispute; perhaps, no liturgy was committed to writing for the first two centuries. Renaudot is clearly of this opinion; he says it is beyond
all controversy and cites St. Basil, *de Spiritu sancto*,
cap. 27. The passage is of great importance in more
respects than in its bearing upon this question, and
I shall therefore extract it according to the text of

---

[28] *De corona*, c. 4.   [29] *Epist.* 63, Ad cæcilium.

the Paris edition, 1839: "Οἷον (ἵνα τοῦ πρώτου καὶ κοινο-
τάτου πρῶτον μνήσθω) τῷ τύπῳ τοῦ σταυροῦ τοὺς εἰς τὸ ὄνομα
τοῦ Κυρίου ἡμῶν Ἰησοῦ Χριστοῦ ἠλπικότας κατασημαίνεσθαι,
τίς ὁ διὰ γράμματος διδάξας; Τὸ πρὸς ἀνατολὰς τετράφθαι
κατὰ τὴν προσευχήν, ποῖον ἐδίδαξεν ἡμᾶς γράμμα; Τὰ τῆς
ἐπικλήσεως ῥήματα ἐπὶ τῇ ἀναδείξει τοῦ ἄρτου τῆς εὐχαριστίας
καὶ τοῦ ποτηρίου τῆς εὐλογίας, τίς τῶν ἁγίων ἐγγραφῶς ἡμῖν
καταλέλοιπεν; Οὐ γὰρ δὴ τούτοις ἀρκούμεθα, ὧν ὁ ἀπόστολος
ἢ τὸ εὐαγγέλιον ἐπεμνήσθη, ἀλλὰ καὶ προλέγομεν καὶ ἐπιλέγομεν
ἕτερα, ὡς μεγάλην ἔχοντα πρὸς τὸ μυστήριον τὴν ἰσχύν, ἐκ τῆς
ἀγράφου διδασκαλίας παραλαβόντες. Εὐλογοῦμεν δὲ τό τε
ὕδωρ τοῦ βαπτίσματος, καὶ τὸ ἔλαιον τῆς χρίσεως, καὶ προσέτι
αὐτὸν τὸν βαπτιζόμενον. Ἀπὸ ποίων ἐγγράφων; Οὐκ ἀπὸ τῆς
σιωπωμένης καὶ μυστικῆς παραδόσεως; Τί δέ; αὐτὴν τοῦ ἐλαίου
τὴν χρῖσιν τίς λόγος γεγραμμένος ἐδίδαξε; Τὸ δὲ τρὶς βαπτί-
ζεσθαι τὸν ἄνθρωπον, πόθεν; Ἄλλα δὲ ὅσα περὶ τὸ βάπτισμα,
ἀποτάσσεσθαι τῷ Σατανᾷ καὶ τοῖς ἀγγέλοις αὐτοῦ, ἐκ ποίας ἐστὶ
γραφῆς; Οὐκ ἐκ τῆς ἀδημοσιεύτου ταύτης καὶ ἀπορρήτου διδασκαλίας, ἣν ἐν ἀπολυπραγμονήτῳ καὶ ἀπεριεργάστῳ σιγῇ οἱ
πατέρες ἡμῶν ἐφύλαξαν, καλῶς ἐκεῖνο δεδιδαγμένοι, τῶν μυστηρίων τὸ σεμνὸν σιωπῇ διασώζεσθαι;" Renaudot however
and Le Brun (who even goes so far as to assert
that for four hundred years no liturgy was written)
interpret the words of St. Basil in a sense beyond
what they necessarily mean. His argument in that
part of his treatise is directed solely to the question
of the canonical and sacred scriptures; and it is not
unusual for that father to speak of customs and rites
as unwritten which are not found distinctly insisted
on and explained.

A better argument by which we may conclude
that until the end of the second century liturgies
were not committed to writing is (as Renaudot observes) that although we find frequent mention made
of the scriptures being given up to the heathens
through fear of punishment or death, we have no

instance of any book of ceremonies or public worship; neither would the persecutors have enquired
so cruelly by torture what mode of offering and
sacrifice the Christians observed, if they could have
procured a written liturgy.

Upon the other hand, as I have already said, it
has been argued that liturgies were in all ages
written; and the chief difficulty of unwritten forms
seems to be that the length of them would have
rendered it impossible that, generally, priests should
have been able to celebrate without a book. But
it is not necessary for us to suppose that more than
the solemn portions were preserved and handed
down unwritten; certainly the psalms and lections
from the scriptures, the epistles and the gospels,
and very probably long prayers and thanksgivings
also were not forbidden to be written. We may
therefore conclude that in its strict sense no liturgy
was written for some ages, because certain indispensable and essential rites which constitute a liturgy
were handed down by tradition only. We have a
very remarkable proof how late this disinclination
to commit those parts to writing was cherished in
the western church, from a letter from Innocent I.
early in the fifth century to a bishop, Decentius, who
had applied to him for the Roman use: " sæpe
dilectionem tuam ad urbem venisse, ac nobiscum in
ecclesia convenisse non dubium est, et quem morem
vel in consecrandis mysteriis, vel in cæteris agendis
arcanis teneat, cognovisse; quod sufficere arbitrarer
ad informationem ecclesiæ tuæ, vel reformationem, si
prædecessores tui minus, aut aliter tenuerint."[30]

It was because of a holy reverence that the
Church required her priests thus to celebrate from

---

[30] Cited by Le Brun, *Opera*, tom. ii. p. 18.

memory. Among her doctrines none were so scrupulously concealed, little less from the catechumen than from the unbeliever, as were those connected with the blessed eucharist. She did not seek to hide them from her admitted children, but from men who were her avowed enemies or unproved candidates for her privileges. She knew and remembered her Lord's command, "Give not that which is holy unto the dogs, neither cast ye your pearls before swine, lest they trample them under their feet, and turn again and rend you."

Hence therefore it was that except in the first epistle to the Corinthians St. Paul in all his writings has not made any plain mention of this sacrament; and then there was abundant reason, from the necessity of the case, not only why he should speak but also openly and freely. For the very abuse which he was endeavouring to correct, namely, the permitting unworthy persons and perhaps not even members of the Church to be present at the holy communion, had admitted these already to the knowledge of much connected with the solemnities of the celebration of it. As a learned but very prejudiced writer has observed, "it was not in the apostle's power to conceal the outward part of the mystery from them, who by the countenance of their new teachers had been emboldened to break in upon the eucharist, without being duly qualified; and therefore the only way that he had left to him, to prevent their further contempt and abuse of it, was to let them into the fuller knowledge of it."[81] Such

---

[81] Johnson, *Unbloody sacrifice*, vol. i. p. 57. The same writer has some very forcible remarks upon the omission by St. Paul in the epistle to the Hebrews of any notice of the prefiguration of the Christian sacrifice in the oblation of Melchisedeck. There was apparently, but for some powerful motive, every reason

an exception, as we can see so evidently the cause, confirms the rule which it is not to be denied that St. Paul appears at other times to have invariably observed.

We have further proof how carefully our Saviour's caution was obeyed from the very obscure manner in which the ante-Nicene fathers, when they speak of it at all, speak of the eucharist; so obscure indeed, especially near the apostolic age, that none could understand their import except those who had been fully admitted into the communion of the Church. No article relating to it was inserted into any creed; and the very probable reason has been given, which must occur to every reader, that creeds were forms of faith to be taught the catechumens in order to their baptism. Not so the eucharist; which was considered too sacred to be spoken of in words at length, except to the *perfect* only.[32] Take

---

why he should then enter into it; and this motive, as St. Jerome tells us, was because he thought it not proper to discourse of that sacrament familiarly to people not yet settled in the faith. "Difficultatem rei prœmio" (says that father, in his epistle to Evagrius) "exaggerat dicens, super quo multus est nobis sermo interpretabilis, non quia aposto-lus id non potuit interpretari, sed quia illius temporis non fuerit. Hebræis enim, id est Judæis, persuadebat, non jam fidelibus quibus sacramentum passim pro-deret."

[32] Upon this Johnson has the following (*Unbloody sacrifice*, vol. i. p. 235): "The reasons they had for the concealment of these

mysteries [of the sacraments] were in sum, to show the great esteem they had of them, and which they by this means en-deavoured to imprint upon all that were admitted to the know-ledge and enjoyment of them; and at the same time to guard, and if possible secure them from the flouts and objections of Jews and heathens, and of all whom they thought too light and frothy to be entrusted with things so very weighty and serious, and yet of so peculiar a nature, that there was nothing in the world that could in all respects be com-pared to them. For they justly believed that a Divine power went along with the sacraments, which was reason enough why

also, for example, the famous passage in St. Justin;
in a part of his *Apology* where he is giving an account of the ceremonies of the Christians in their
common worship; how cautiously he speaks, how
anxiously he seems to weigh every word, lest he
should say even upon such an occasion too much.
" Upon the day called sunday" (he tells us) " we have
an assembly of all who live in the towns or in the
country, who meet in an appointed place; and the
records of the apostles or the writings of the apostles are read, according as the time will allow.
And when the reader leaves off, the president [33]
(ὁ προεστὼς) in a discourse admonishes and exhorts
us to imitate such good examples. Then we all

---

they should set the highest value
upon them, and desire that others
should do so too; and yet they
knew the visible signs of these
sacraments to be *beggarly elements*, things in their own nature
very cheap and common; and
they might without the gift of
prophecy easily foresee that the
enemies of Christianity would
always be ringing in the ears of
all that were well affected to
Christianity (as the deists and
quakers are perpetually labour-
ing to persuade our people) that
there can be no such effects of
water, bread, and wine, as priests
of the Christian church would
have them believe. And there is
one thing peculiar to the eucharist, which made it more liable
to scoffs than any other part of
our religion; which is that the
bread and wine were believed to
be the very Body and Blood of
Christ; no wonder if they were
much upon the reserve in this
point; since all must be sensible
that nothing in the Christian
theology could have afforded
more agreeable entertainment to
the drolls and buffoons of the
age; for whatsoever is most extraordinary, and elevated above
the condition of other things,
which seem to be of the same
sort, lies most exposed to pro-
fane wit and mirth, when that
which gives it its worth and ex-
cellency can only be believed
and not seen: and no doubt
Tertullian spoke the sense of
all the learned fathers of his
own and of the succeeding times
in those observable words, ' nil
adeo quod obduret mentes hominum, quam simplicitas Divi-
norum operum, quæ in actu videtur; et magnificentia, quæ in
effectu repromittitur.' "

[33] That is, the bishop; and so
Reeves renders the word. See
his note upon the passage, vol.
i. p. 107.

stand up together and pray; and, as we before said, when that prayer is finished bread is offered, and wine and water. And the president then also, with all the earnestness in his power (ὄση δύναμις αὐτῷ [34]), sends up prayers and thanksgivings. And the people conclude the prayer with him, saying, Amen. Then distribution is made of the consecrated elements; which are also sent to such as are absent by the deacons."

Such is St. Justin's description of the celebration of the eucharist upon the Lord's day or sunday, as the fathers usually call it in their apologies because it happened upon the day which was dedicated to the sun, and therefore best known to the heathens by that name. In the section immediately preceding, he relates in almost the same language the manner in which the newly-baptized was admitted to and received his first communion, in which one circumstance is added, namely, the kiss; and thus, short and obscure as this account must at the time have appeared, we can clearly trace many important parts of the holy service; the general and the eucharistical prayer; the kiss of peace; the oblation of the elements; the mixture of water with the wine; the consecration of the elements, then no longer common bread and common wine [35] but the

---

[34] Compare, from the thanksgiving in the Clementine liturgy, " εὐχαριστοῦμεν σοί, Θεὲ παντοκράτορ, οὐχ ὅσον ὀφείλομεν, ἀλλ' ὅσον δυνάμεθα." This has reference to a written liturgy, and there seems no ground for the opinion of those who would argue from these words of St. Justin for the use of extemporary prayer in the service of the eucharist.

[35] St. Justin, *Apol. I.* 66. p. 83. See also St. Irenæus, *Cont. hær.* b. 4. c. 18: " Ὡς γὰρ ἀπὸ τῆς ἄρτος προσλαμβανόμενος τὴν ἐπίκλησιν τοῦ Θεοῦ, οὐκέτι κοινὸς ἄρτος ἐστὶν, ἀλλ' εὐχαριστία, ἐκ δύο πραγμάτων συνεστηκυῖα, ἐπιγείου τε καὶ οὐρανίου· οὕτως καὶ τὰ σώματα ἡμῶν μεταλαμβάνοντα τῆς εὐχαριστίας μηκέτι εἰσὶ φθαρτά, τὴν ἐλπίδα τῆς εἰς αἰῶνας ἀναστασίως ἔχοντα."

Body and the Blood of Christ; and their after distribution to those present, or communion. Let us not, by the way, pass on without remembering that there would have been no need of so much carefulness to conceal these mysteries from the world, from those who were without, if the eucharist had been indeed nothing more than what later ages have endeavoured to reduce it to, a mere refreshing of our memories, or a renewal of our covenant, or a symbol of mutual love. But from this jealousy arose the evil of unjust accusations against the Christians "latebrosa et lucifuga natio,"[36] which, although terrible, they were content to bear, unprovoked to further explanation, with the bare reply of an indignant and unhesitating denial.

We may delay for one moment upon the important assertion of St. Justin and of St. Irenæus (in the note) that after consecration the elements are no longer to be looked upon as common bread and wine. So speaks St. Ambrose to an objector: "forte dicas: aliud video, quomodo tu mihi asseris quod Christi corpus accipiam? et hoc nobis adhuc superest ut probemus. Quantis igitur utimur exemplis? Probemus non hoc esse quod natura formavit, sed quod benedictio consecravit: majoremque

---

[36] Cardinal Bona says of the heathens, "quia aliquid subobscure perceperant de sacramento corporis et sanguinis Christi, accusabant eos de cæde infantis et epulis Thyesteis. *Dicimur sceleratissimi*, ait Tertullianus apolog. cap. 7, *de sacramento infanticidii, et pabulo, inde et post convivium incesto.* Cæcilius apud Minutium: *Infantis sanguinem sitienter lambunt, hujus certatim membra dispertiunt, hac fœderantur hostia.* Justinus Martyr in dialogo cum Tryphone: *An vos etiam de nobis creditis, homines nos vorare, et post epulum lucernis extinctis nefario concubitu promiscue involvi?* Theophilus ad Autolycum, lib. 3. *Istud præterea et crudelissimum et immanissimum est, quod nobis intendunt crimen, nos humanis carnibus vesci.*" *Rerum liturgic.* lib. 1. 4. 3.

d

vim esse benedictionis quam naturæ : quia benedictione etiam natura ipsa mutatur . . . ipse clamat
Dominus Jesus : *Hoc est corpus meum.* Ante benedictionem verborum cœlestium alia species nomi-
natur, post consecrationem corpus significatur. Ipse
dicit sanguinem suum. Ante consecrationem aliud
dicitur, post consecrationem sanguis nuncupatur,"
&c.[37] Again, in a remarkable place of his homilies
St. Cyril of Alexandria plainly lays down the same
doctrine : "δεῦτε, φάγετε τὸν ἐμὸν ἄρτον, καὶ πίετε οἶνον, ὃν
ἐκέρασα ὑμῖν· ἐγὼ ἐμαυτὸν εἰς βρῶσιν ἡτοίμασα, ἐγὼ ἐμαυτὸν
τοῖς ποθοῦσί με ἐκέρασα."[38] And once more, St. Irenæus
to the same effect : "Quando ergo et mixtus calix,
et factus panis percepit verbum Dei, et fit eucharistia
sanguinis et corporis Christi, ex quibus augetur et
consistit carnis nostræ substantia ; quomodo carnem
negant capacem esse donationis Dei—quæ de calice,
qui est sanguis ejus, nutritur ; et de pane, quod est
corpus ejus, augetur ?"[39]

To the above, which are but very few out of
many places which might be appealed to in the
primitive fathers, I shall add an extract from a rare
book, once highly popular in this country and, in a
sense, authorised by the church of England to be
distributed among the people for their instruction,
namely, "The ordinarye of a Christen man." The
author is speaking of almsdeeds: "The xij. maner
of almesdede spyrytuell is to offre or to make offrynge

---

[37] *De mysteriis*, cap. ix; *Opera*, tom. 2. p. 338. This and one or two quotations which follow are taken from a valuable collection of treatises and extracts from the fathers, to illustrate the thirty-nine articles, printed at the press of the university of Cambridge, and therefore with some kind of authority attached; *Ecclesiæ Anglicanæ vindex catholicus,* Cambr. 1843; vol. 3. p. 266.

[38] *Opera*, tom. v. p. 372 ; *Ecc. Angl. vindex*, vol. 3. p. 332.

[39] *Opera, Adv. hæres.* p. 400 ; *Ecc. Angl. vindex*, vol. 3. p. 299.

to God the fader, the blessyd Jesu cryst his sone, with yᵉ ryght holy sacrament of yᵉ awter; and this almesdede here surmounteth syngulerly in two thynges, all those other good dedes that may be sayd or thought, that is, in dygnyte and in generalyte. . . There is the breed and the wyne, flesshe and blode, yᵉ ryght holy refeccyon of crysten soules." [40]

Besides, from allusions which we find frequently in the fathers, how certain is it that they could not have believed the blessed elements to be any longer common bread and wine. St. Chrysostom, for example : " Μὴ ὅτι ἄρτός ἐστιν ἴδῃς, μηδ' ὅτι οἶνός ἐστι νομίσῃς· οὐ γὰρ ὡς αἱ λοιπαὶ βρώσεις εἰς ἀφεδρῶνα χωρεῖ. Ἄπαγε, μὴ τοῦτο νόει. Ἀλλὰ ὥσπερ κηρὸς πυρὶ προσομιλήσας οὐδὲν ἀπουσιάζει, οὐδὲν περισσεύει· οὕτω καὶ ὧδε νόμιζε (συναναλίσκεσθαι) τὰ μυστήρια τῇ τοῦ σώματος οὐσίᾳ." [41] Or St. Cyril of Jerusalem, in an explanation of the Lord's prayer : " Τὸν ἄρτον ἡμῶν τὸν ἐπιούσιον δὸς ἡμῖν σήμερον. ὁ ἄρτος οὗτος ὁ κοινὸς οὐκ ἐστιν ἐπιούσιος. ἄρτος δὲ οὗτος ὁ ἅγιος, ἐπιούσιός ἐστιν. . . οὗτος ὁ ἄρτος οὐκ εἰς κοιλίαν χωρεῖ καὶ εἰς ἀφεδρῶνα ἐκβάλλεται· ἀλλ' εἰς πᾶσαν σοῦ τὴν σύστασιν ἀναδίδοται, εἰς ὠφέλειαν σώματος καὶ ψυχῆς." [42] Or, once more, St. Ambrose, speaking of the manna in the wilderness, as compared with the eucharist : " Sed tamen panem illum qui manducaverunt, omnes in deserto mortui

---

[40] Sign. O. 4. *b*, edit. Wynkyn de Worde, 4to. 1506.

"Ante consecrationem, nec panis nec vinum, etiam in altari positum, est sacramentum, nec sacræ rei signum. Sed demum post consecrationem tunc est sacramentum. Propterea dicitur sacrificium visibile, sed est invisibile sacramentum, i. sacræ rei signum: unde, ut ibidem sequitur, sacramentum est in-

visibilis gratiæ visibilis forma." Lyndwood, lib. 1. tit. 1, Altissimus, *verb.* non est sacramentum.

[41] *Hom. de pænit., Opera,* tom. 2. p. 413; *Ecc. Angl. vindex,* vol. 3. p. 320.

[42] *Catech. mystag.* v, *Opera,* p. 329; *Eccl. Angl. vindex,* vol. 3. p. 312. And compare the sixth section of the fourth lecture, *Opera,* p. 321.

sunt : ista autem esca quam accipis, iste panis vivus
qui descendit de cœlo, vitæ æternæ substantiam sub-
ministrat ; et quicumque hunc manducaverit, non
morietur in æternum : et est corpus Christi. Con-
sidera nunc utrum præstantior sit panis angelorum,
an caro Christi, quæ utique corpus est vitæ. Manna
illud e cœlo, hoc supra cœlum : illud cœli, hoc Domini cœlorum : illud corruptioni obnoxium, si in
diem alterum servaretur ; hoc alienum ab omni corruptione, quod quicumque religiose gustaverit, corruptionem sentire non poterit." [43]

To return : the eucharistic rites of the Christian
church in the first centuries being in part, that is all
the most solemn and mysterious portions of them,
handed down by tradition only, the earliest written
liturgy which we have is the Clementine. This
forms a part of the eighth book of the apostolical
constitutions, a work which most certainly was not
compiled by those whose name it bears, namely, of
the apostles ; [44] and therefore labours under all the
disadvantages which must attach to writings not
genuine. Still the authority of the constitutions is
very great and will at least reach thus far ; that
though we might hesitate to insist upon any statement, certainly of belief perhaps also of practice,
to be found there only, yet where such statements
are confirmed by incidental allusions or by direct
accounts of the same things in other writers earlier
or contemporary we may then fully rely upon them.
We must remember also that it was not uncommon

---

[43] *De mysteriis, Opera*, tom. 2.
p. 337 ; *Eccl. Angl. vindex*, vol.
3. p. 266.

[44] A conclusion agreed upon
by almost all writers upon the
subject. The constitutions were
probably gathered together from
very much older materials about
the middle of the fourth century.
The tradition may have been
primitive which traced the rites,
not the language, of the liturgy
to St. Clement.

for authors and compilers of that age, the third and
fourth centuries, to recommend their works by as-
cribing them to great saints and teachers who were
departed. This may have been a practice at all
times to be much regretted, and most undoubtedly
it is little according to modern opinions; yet it not
only is not in itself a condemnation of every fact or
doctrine so recommended, but it sprang from a
sense of unworthiness and modesty which has long
been lost, and was based upon a well-grounded presumption that there existed in the people a reverence for their fathers, which has well-nigh been
lost also.

In the apostolical constitutions then is the liturgy
attributed to him whose name is in the Book of
Life, St. Clement.[45] With respect to his name in
particular being attached to it we may well adopt
the words of Zaccaria, in his defence of the liturgy
given to St. James: " Illud tamen doctissimis cri-
ticis lubens concessero, quæ apostolorum nomine
circumferuntur liturgiæ, eas multo recentiores esse
suisque auctoribus suppositas. At nulla id fraude
factum contendo; Jacobum enim, cæterosque apostolos liturgiam quampiam, seu ordinem precum in
sacramentorum administratione, atque eucharistiæ
præsertim immolatione servandum constituisse pru-
dens nemo inficiabitur. Quare cum processu temporis aliqua in illis immutari, demi nonnulla, addi
alia contigerit, apostoli, a quo primum liturgia edita
fuerit, nomen retentum est tum in tantum auctorem
reverentia, tum eorum, quæ ab illo profecta fuerant,
atque etiam tum usurpabantur, ratione."[46]

---

[45] Brett observes in his dissertation, that the language in which
it is written is no more an argument against its genuineness than
against the acknowledged epistle
of St. Clement.

[46] *Bibl. ritualis*, tom. 1. dissert. 2. p. lxxxvj.

Without entering into any unnecessary discussion, it will be sufficient simply to state that the most probable opinion about the Clementine liturgy is this : that although we grant that it was never used exactly in the form in which we now have it in any portion of the Church (neither indeed does it claim for itself any place or country in particular), still it is to be looked upon as accurately representing the general mode prevalent through the Christian world during the first three centuries of administering the eucharist. A reasonable argument in its favour is that where the other liturgies, claiming to be primitive, are agreeable to each other they agree with the Clementine ; and that the Clementine contains nothing, either particularly in its arrangement or generally in its manner of expression, which is not to be found in all the others. The most important omission is that the Lord's prayer forms no part of it : but this may, as has been suggested,[47] have arisen from the negligence of some transcriber in whose copy the first words only might have been written (and those in contraction) ; or it might be readily allowed never to have been used in this liturgy, because although proper to the holy service yet most certainly it is not essential to the consecration of the eucharist. In the other ancient liturgies in which the Lord's prayer occurs it is placed after the consecration is completed ; and this is what I have already attempted to show was what St. Gregory meant in the passage which was before examined, with whom, so explained, agree a number of the earliest writers.[48] Every other liturgy bears

---

[47] Brett, *Dissertation*, p. 204, &c. (edit. 1720). His remarks should be consulted.

[48] "Hieronymus ait lib. 3. *adv.*

Pelag., 'apostolos quotidie orationem dominicam solitos dicere in sacrificio.' Cyrillus Hierosolymitanus *catech. mystag.* 5.

evident marks of the rites and ceremonies which have been added from time to time to the original form; that form seems to stand clearest in the Clementine.[49] How decided is the opinion of a learned writer[50] "that if we had the very words in which St. Peter and St. Paul consecrated the eucharist, it would not differ in substance from that which is contained in this most ancient liturgy:" and of another also:[51] "the eucharistical office in the apostolical constitutions is the standard and test by

---

'Post hæc inquit, nempe post commemorationem fidelium defunctorum, dicimus orationem illam quam Salvator suis discipulis tradidit.'" Bona, tom. 3. p. 320. These, and other authorities, Optatus, Augustine, Cæsar Arelatensis, St. Ambrose, &c., are cited by most of the ritualists.

Mr. Palmer argues from the omission of the prayer the great antiquity of the Clementine liturgy, speaking of it as a remarkable sign. He says: "Without doubt the Lord's prayer was used between the prayer of the deacon and benediction of the faithful, which precedes the form τὰ ἄγια, &c. all through the patriarchate of Antioch in the early part of the fourth century. Yet it does not occur in this part of the Clementine liturgy. Now it is not credible that the author would have omitted this prayer if it had been used long before his time. Yet from the manner and language of Chrysostom and Cyril we perceive that it must have

been used long before *their* time. They both seem to regard this prayer as coeval with the rest of the liturgy: they do not allude to the idea that it had *not* been formerly used in that part of the liturgy. Since then the Lord's prayer was not used, or was but recently used, in the time of the author of the apostolical constitutions, and yet appears to have been long used in the time of Cyril and Chrysostom, we must infer that the apostolical constitutions were written much before the time of Chrysostom and Cyril." *Origines lit.* i. p. 40.

[49] Upon the arguments for high antiquity from what the liturgy of St. Clement does and does not contain, see especially Le Brun, whose admissions from his peculiar opinions upon written liturgies are very valuable in this respect; *Opera*, tom. 2. pp. 23, 24, 30, 208.

[50] Johnson, *Unbloody sacrifice and altar unvailed*, vol. ii. p. 148.

[51] Hickes, *Christian priesthood*, vol. i. p. 141.

which all others are to be tried. And by comparing them with this the innovations and additions in after times, be they good or bad, will appear."

Being then so valuable a record[52] I cannot think that a reprint of it will be out of place in the present volume. We may refer to it as Hickes has recommended; we may look upon it with Johnson as in substance the apostolic form, and so learn to judge more truly than we otherwise might of other liturgies. As such a guide we may regard it, not to the exclusion of the Jerusalem, or Alexandrian, or Roman[53] (as if these had not also sprung from the teaching and example of apostles), but as containing in an earlier form than is supplied by any extant manuscript those rites which are essential to a valid consecration and perfecting of the eucharist, and without which no service, though it may claim the name, can be allowed to be a Christian liturgy.

Subject to the exception of the omission of the Lord's prayer in the Clementine liturgy—as we now have the text of it in the apostolical constitutions— we may agree with Mabillon's statement, that there were some certain rites and ceremonies to be found in all the liturgies, whether of the east or the west.

---

[52] It is scarcely necessary for me to remind the reader that we have also an equally valuable commentary upon it, in the fifth catechetical lecture of St. Cyril.

[53] "That there were ancient liturgies in the Church is evident: St. Chrysostom, St. Basil, and others: and though we find not in all ages whole liturgies, yet it is certain that there were such in the oldest times, by those parts which are extant: as 'Sursum corda,' 'Vere dignum et justum,' &c. Though those which are extant may be interpolated, yet such things as are found in them all consistent to catholic and primitive doctrine, may well be presumed to have been from the first, especially since we find no original of these liturgies from ancient councils." *Answer of the Bishops to the exceptions of the Ministers;* Cardwell, *Hist. of Conferences,* p. 350.

These were, he tells us, lections from the holy scriptures at the beginning of the service, oblation of the bread and of wine mixed with water, consecration by the saying of the very words used by our Lord Himself, the Lord's prayer, and communion with thanksgiving.[54]

We may add to these some two or three other details; such as the reading of the diptychs, whether of the living or the dead, the recital in some shape of a creed or declaration of the one Faith, the kiss of peace, and a preface or "sursum corda."[55]

After the council of Nice, and in the age immediately preceding, additions were unquestionably made to the original forms which had been used in various churches. Some of these are easily to be traced: and the observation of St. Paul to the

---

[54] "Hæc omnibus semper communia, nempe lectiones sacrarum scripturarum initio liturgiæ, psalmorum aliorumque canticorum recitatio; oblatio panis et vini aqua mixti; consecratio utriusque verbis Christi Domini cum benedictione ac signo crucis a sacerdote facto; oratio dominica, et sacra communio cum gratiarum actione." *De lit. Gall.* lib. 1. cap. 2.

[55] A very useful book has lately been published by Mr. Hammond, under the title of *Liturgies eastern and western.* This contains the texts of several of the Greek liturgies, and a careful arrangement of the Roman, Ambrosian, Gallican, and Mozarabic, in parallel columns. Mr. Hammond has drawn up some tables (pp. xxvj, xxix) showing the differences which exist among the liturgies, and (as he truly remarks) "the marvellous *substantial* identity of the eastern and western" families or groups. In the first sentence of his introduction we are told that he includes under the term "ancient liturgies" "all which can trace their descent directly from some known early form." The present communion service in the book of Common prayer of the church of England is not, however, included in Mr. Hammond's tables of comparison. No explanation (I believe) is given of the omission; and we are left to conclude that in its arrangement and contents the English communion service is to be regarded as a composition of the sixteenth century and cannot be traced to any known early form.

Corinthians in his first epistle, where he says " there must be also heresies among you, that they which are approved may be made manifest among you," is as applicable to the public services and rituals of the catholic church as to the opinions of her individual members.[66] During the short space when there was indeed but one mind and one faith there was little need of cautious phrases, and additional safeguards by which the truth might be preserved : very different was the case after the time of Arius, and Macedonius, and Nestorius ; and epithets even became necessary which in purer days would perhaps but have seemed to mar the earnest simplicity of the prayers of the Church.

---

[66] As Vincentius of Lirins says upon this text of St. Paul : " ac si diceret : ob hoc hæreseôn non statim divinitus eradicantur auctores, ut probati manifesti fiant, id est, ut unusquisque quam tenax et fidelis, et fixus catholicæ fidei sit amator, appareat. Et revera cum quæque novitas ebullit, statim cernitur frumentorum gravitas, et levitas palearum : tunc sine magno molimine excutitur ab area, quod nullo pondere intra aream tenebatur." *Adversus hæreses*, § 20.

CHAPTER III.

WE must now pass to the consideration of the particular liturgy from which the ancient uses of the church of England are known and acknowledged to have been immediately derived. The Roman was the earliest and the chief of the patriarchates of the catholic church. The contentions of neighbouring provinces, the irruptions of barbarians, the local influence of her bishops, and above all her anxious and untiring energy in the propagation of the true faith, rapidly strengthened the primacy of the see of Rome. We might naturally therefore expect that in the remains of antiquity which have been spared to us we should find a complete liturgy which she had used from her first foundation, with perhaps also a history detailing exactly the various alterations which it has undergone.

But we know little about it. Writers who lived long ago, and to whom we may have supposed some accounts would have come down, speak in very general terms. Durand[87] contents himself with saying "in primordio nascentis ecclesiæ missa aliter dicebatur quam modo . . . sequenti vero tempore epistola tantum et evangelio recitatis missa celebrabatur : subsequenter Cœlestinus papa instituit introitum ad missam cantari. . . Cætera diversis temporibus ab aliis papis leguntur adjecta, prout Christianæ religionis cultu crescente visa sunt decentius convenire." Going back some four hundred years, Walafrid Strabo tells

---

[87] *Rationale div. off.* lib. 4. cap. i. 5.

us what is still less satisfactory: "quod nunc agimus multiplici orationum, lectionum, cantilenarum, et ˙consecrationum officio, totum hoc apostoli, et post ipsos proximi (ut creditur) orationibus et commemoratione passionis Dominicæ, sicut ipse præcepit, agebant simpliciter."[58]

Hence it is that some who dislike the authority of liturgies have denied to the Roman all claim to any great age; and have ascribed its first beginning as a form to Gregory the great, or to Gelasius, or Vigilius, or Leo, in succession bishops of Rome. Others, on the contrary, have boldly given the Roman liturgy to St. Peter as the sole author, at least of the canon, and assert that it has come down to us in the main points unimpaired.

Those writers from whom I have just made extracts state their full conviction of the truth of this: for example, Walafrid Strabo in the same chapter: "Romani quidem usum observationum a beato Petro accipientes, suis quique temporibus quæ congrua judicata sunt addiderunt." And more expressly an archbishop of our own Anglo-saxon church; Ælfric in his pastoral epistle: "Now was the mass established by our Lord Christ; and the holy apostle Peter appointed the canon thereto, which we call *Te igitur.*"[59] The later ritualists, men of the greatest learning and of unwearied labour in these enquiries, take the same ground. Gavantus declares that St. Clement received the Roman liturgy from St. Peter.[60] Le Brun also: "Romanæ ecclesiæ

---

[58] *De rebus eccles.* cap. 22. Walafrid arrives at this result after premising "quantum invenire potuimus, exponamus." And he then gives much such an account of additions as Durand and other writers.

[59] Cap. 39. Thorpe, *Anglosaxon laws,* &c., vol. 2. p. 381.

[60] *Thesaurus sacr. rituum,* tom. 1. p. 2. Merati in his notes tells us of the altar pre-

liturgia dubio procul ex S. Petro per traditionem derivatur."[61] Georgius again: "Sacrarum cærimoniarum origo, ab apostolicis temporibus ducta, viam nobis stravit ad Romanæ liturgiæ vetustatem, cujus primordia et ordinem beato Petro ecclesia Romana debet."[62] But the chief authorities upon which these opinions rest are of St. Isidore, who lived in the seventh century; and of Innocent I. in the fifth. The first tells us: "ordo missæ vel orationum, quibus oblata Deo sacrificia consecrantur, primum a sancto Petro est institutus," and he adds, what certainly was incorrect, "cujus celebrationem uno eodemque modo universus peragit orbis."[63] Innocent lays down the same, in a passage too long to extract, in an epistle to the bishop Decentius: from which Georgius draws this conclusion: "Heus quanta ex hoc plane aureo S. Innocentii pontificis testimonio hauriuntur! Vides enim Romanam ecclesiam a sancto Petro, ut diximus, ordinem missæ edoctam."[64] Much more sound is the interpretation which cardinal Bona,[65] with whom agrees Pinius,[66] puts upon the last sentence of St. Isidore; and which I would extend to the other early authorities to the same purpose: "hoc de re et substantia, non de verborum tenore et cæremoniis intelligendum est."

For as the truth is unquestionably not with the advocates of the first of the two opinions which I have mentioned, so with some limitations, although it may

---

served at Rome, upon which St. Peter is said to have offered the eucharist; tom. 1. p. 130.

[61] *Opera*, tom. 2. p. 78.

[62] *De lit. Rom. pontif.* tom. 1. p. 9. See also Martene, *de ant. ecc. rit.* tom. 1. p. 98.

[63] *De eccles. officiis*, lib. 1. cap. 15; *Bibl. patrum auct.* tom. 1. p. 188.

[64] Tom. 1. p. 10.

[65] *Rerum liturg.* lib. 1. cap. 7. v.

[66] *De lit. ant. Hispanica*, p. 2.

not be freed from all objection, we may agree with the others. To name as the author of the Roman liturgy any particular apostle is beyond possibility: but the essential rites which are in all ancient liturgies are to be found also in the canon of the Roman catholic church in every age, up to the most early, through which we are able to trace it. We may assert therefore that the Roman liturgy springs equally with the others from an apostolic form; and that it has preserved all essentials with a most jealous care, whilst successive popes and bishops in various countries have exerted their legitimate power and added such prayers and ceremonies as they thought fit. As Muratori says, "canoni certe, in quo tremendi mysterii summa consistit, nihil unquam additum fuit, quod vel minimum substantiam rei mutet."[67]

---

[67] *De rebus liturg.* p. 119. Some writers, of considerable authority, are disposed to argue that in the first years of Christianity at Rome the liturgy was not said in Latin but in Greek. De Rossi, in his *Roma sotteranea cristiana,* is of this opinion. So also dean Milman; but this last writes in too prejudiced a style to be much relied upon, when the facts or doubts which he is stating give rise to or touch upon disputed questions of theology. Speaking with hesitation, I would say that in the total absence of anything which can be regarded as evidence upon the question it seems to be highly improbable that the Roman liturgy in the first century—to say nothing about the second century—was in Greek. Undoubtedly the Greek language was known widely among the higher ranks of Roman people in the time of Nero; but the first converts were chiefly made from the lower classes. Apostles were at Rome: they had inspired authority to decide what the rites and ceremonies of the liturgy should be, and the especial words to be used in the prayers. There would have been no more difficulty, looking at it simply as a mere worldly matter, in drawing up the liturgy in one language than in another. It is scarcely to be believed that St. Peter or St. Paul, having collected a congregation of new Christians, would have allowed them to offer up the most solemn

In attempting to give a most brief account of the Roman liturgy I said in the preface to the first edition of this work (1844) that we could not do better than adopt the words of a careful enquirer, the author of the *Origines liturgicæ.* I should have to appeal to the same sources as himself, and I have found no reason, after further examination, to suppose that any other plan would be more advantageous now. He tells us, "that many of the mistakes into which men have fallen on this matter have arisen from confounding two very different things, the missal and the liturgy. The missal is a large volume containing a number of missæ, or offices for particular days, which were to be added in the canon.⁶⁶ By the liturgy we are to understand the " ordinary and "canon which did not vary, and the number and order of the prayers which were

---

service of their faith in a language which they did not understand. It is quite probable also that the bishops and priests whom they ordained throughout the west were in many instances ignorant of Greek. The objections—such as they may be —which can be brought against the continued and exclusive use in every part of the world of one single eucharistic service in a dead language would have had more force when referred to the first beginnings of the Christian church, and to the wants or requirements of her members then. I make these remarks in the fewest possible words; being precluded from more fully discussing the subject to the extent which it justly demands, because it would of necessity involve questions of controversy, which I am especially anxious to avoid.

⁶⁶ I have no hesitation in adopting Mr. Palmer's account, but we must take the term liturgy in its *most strict sense,* and an unusual one, to exclude the other portions of the missal from it; in the present instance it is allowable if we include, as I doubt not was intended, the ordinary with the canon. It is much to be wished that Mr. Palmer had remembered his own definition; and not upon the other hand extended somewhat improperly the idea of a liturgy, in giving such a title as *Origines liturgicæ* to his whole work.

to be added from the missal. . . . It is acknowledged that Gregory collected, arranged, improved, and abbreviated[69] the contents of the individual missæ, and inserted a short passage into the canon, viz. *Diesque nostros in tua pace disponas, atque ab æterna damnatione eripi, et in electorum tuorum jubeas grege numerari.* He joined also the Lord's prayer to the canon, from which it had previously been separated by the breaking of bread. All this amounts to positive proof that Gregory was the reviser and improver, not the author, of the Roman liturgy."[70] "Seventy years before Gregory, Vigilius in an epistle to Profuturus bishop of Braga in Spain says that he had received the text of the canon from apostolical tradition: he then gives him a description of it, which coincides accurately with the Roman liturgy in subsequent times." "Before him, Gelasius, A.D. 492, ordained prayers or collects, and prefaces, and arranged them in a sacramentary,

---

[69] I would add from Muratori: "Certe vetustis sæculis præfationes complures in usu fuere. Hasce sanctus Gregorius M. ad paucas nunc usitatas redegit. Psalmi etiam integri adhibiti antiquitus, sive cantati in missa fuerunt; idque ex non uno sancti Augustini loco, et ex homiliis sancti Petri Chrysologi constat; verum nostris temporibus versiculus tantummodo ex iis canitur, aut recitatur. Cur autem a sancto Gregorio pontifice breviata fuerit liturgia, id factum suspicari licet ad majus fidelium commodum, atque ut omnes divinis mysteriis interesse possent. Olim quoque multos occupabat cura filiorum, custodia agrorum et bestiarum, servitium dominis præstitum, ut alia impedimenta omittam. Hosce, ut opinari fas est, absterrebat a sacris prolixitas liturgiæ. Idcirco satius visum fuit, eamdem contrahere, et præsertim postquam præceptum invaluit de missa audienda singulis dominicis, aliisque festis solennibus." *De rebus liturg.* p. 14.

[70] So Renaudot observes: "In Latina ecclesia præcipuum locum obtinet canon Romanus, qui, quod a Gelasio papa primum, deinde a Gregorio magno, in eam quam nunc habet formam reductus est Gregorianus vulgo appellatur." *Dissertatio,* vol. 1. p. 8.

which in after ages commonly bore his name."
Again, "a manuscript sacramentary is in existence
supposed to have been written before the time of
Gelasius, evidently referring to the same order and
canon as that used in his time; and is known by
the name of the Leonian sacramentary. Leo the
great is said to have added in 451 certain words,
which also are specified; *sanctum sacrificium, immaculatam hostiam*: so that the remainder of the
canon was in existence before his time." "Some
time again before Leo, Innocentius speaks of the
Roman rites as having descended from St. Peter the
apostle,[71] and there is no sort of reason to think
that they differed materially from those used by
Gelasius at the end of the same century." And we
are brought to this conclusion: "that this liturgy
was substantially the same in the time of Gelasius
as it was in that of Gregory, that it appears to have
been the same in the time of Innocentius at the
beginning of the fifth century, and was then esteemed
to be of apostolical antiquity."[73]

---

[71] Muratori, p. 10, says, "Accipe nunc, quæ de ipsa Romana
ecclesia anno Christi 416, hoc
est tot ante Gregorium magnum
annos, scripserit Innocentius I.
summus pontifex: 'Si instituta
ecclesiastica ut sunt a beatis
apostolis tradita, integra vellent
servare Domini sacerdotes, nulla
diversitas, nulla varietas in ipsis
ordinibus, et consecrationibus
haberetur.' Addit infra: 'Quis
enim nesciat aut non advertat id,
quod a principe apostolorum
Petro Romanæ ecclesiæ traditum est, ac nunc usque custoditur, ab omnibus debere servari.'"
Mr. Palmer gives the same passage from Labbe, *Concil.* 2.1245.

[73] *Origines liturgicæ*, vol. 1.
pp. 111–119. We may hear also
the opinion of a very learned
writer: "Neque enim a Græcis
sacros ritus Romani acceperunt,
sed ab apostolorum principibus."
Muratori, p. 13.

And the very succinct account
which another ritualist gives us:
"Romanæ liturgiæ triplex veluti
ordo seu status considerandus
est. Unus primigenius, ab ecclesiæ nascentis exordio ad Gelasium usque receptus: alter
Gelasianus, auctorem seu am-
plificatorem habens Gelasium
papam ejus nominis primum:

The reader, if he wishes to enquire further into this subject, will find a good account of the various additions and alterations from time to time in the Roman liturgy in a not uncommon book, the *Thesaurus sacrorum rituum* of Gavantus.[73] But he will do well to correct this by the older ritualists, Walafrid Strabo and others; and especially by two ancient histories of the changes made in the Roman service, which have been printed by Georgius in the appendix to his third volume *de liturgia Romani pontificis.*[74] These were found in the celebrated manuscript of the queen of Sweden, now preserved in the library of the Vatican. Before we pass on I cannot but add, as to a single point, the authority of one of our own most celebrated men, the venerable Bede, who was almost a contemporary of him of whom he is speaking, pope Gregory the great: "sed et in ipsa missarum celebratione tria verba maximæ perfectionis plena superadjecit, 'Diesque nostros in tua pace disponas, atque ab æterna dam-

---

tertius Gregorianus, ita dictus ex nomine Gregorii M. qui Gelasianum ordinem correxisse memoratur. Qualis fuerit primigenius ille, non omnino constat. Gelasianus diu desideratus est: sed tandem illum e tenebris eruit vir de ecclesia bene meritus Josephus Thomasius. Gregorianus demum in usu communi est modo apud omnes fere ecclesias, notis et observationibus a Menardo nostro illustratus. Gregoriani a Gelasiano totum discrimen est in varietate et numero earum orationum, quas *collectas* vocant: nam cætera utriusque eædem omnino partes sunt. In Gelasiano duæ aut tres ante epistolam orationes; unica secreta ante præfationem; atque duæ post communionem, quarum una est *supra populum*. At in Gregoriano tres tantum ad singulas missas assignantur orationes, quarum una ante epistolam, altera secreta, tertia post communionem." Mabillon, *de lit. Gallicana*, lib. 1. cap. 2. iv. Compare also Gavantus, *Thesaurus*, tom. 1. p. 5.

[73] I mean the edition to which I refer in these notes, with the excellent commentary of Merati; 3 vols. folio, 1763.

[74] Append. x, xi.

natione nos eripi, et in electorum tuorum jubeas grege numerari.' " [75]

When, however, we speak of additions, these as regarded the ordinary and canon were small both in number and extent : and there can be but little doubt that the Roman liturgy, in its strictest sense, was in the first and second centuries considerably longer than it now is ; which is indeed certain if more than one pope, as it has been remarked, not only arranged but abbreviated it. Therefore it would at that time be more like the other ancient liturgies, and correspond with the account given us by Justin Martyr. Muratori[76] observes that as in the Greek churches prayers were said before the preface for the whole church, for kings, for catechumens, &c., and other prayers again after the consecration for the clergy; so an old Latin writer upon the sacraments, speaking of the eucharist, says " in it praises are offered to God, and prayers for the people, for kings, and others."

We shall probably never know what was the primitive liturgy of the churches of Britain—observed perhaps in parts of the island for many centuries—before the arrival of St. Augustine. It is almost certain that every copy of it which could be identified has been long ago destroyed. Ancient fragments or even complete copies may possibly have been preserved in some monastic libraries until the time of Henry the eighth. The difficulty seems to be acknowledged by very eminent authorities. Azevedo says, "Anglicani autem officii nullum est monumentum, quo cognosci possit ante S. Gregorii ævum, qui evangelii præcones ad Christianam religionem restituendam illuc misit." [77] And Mabillon,

---

[75] *Hist. eccles.* lib. 2. cap. i. 87.   [77] *De divino officio,* exercit. ix.
[76] *De rebus liturg.* p. 14.   p. 47.

to cite no more: "Qualis fuerit apud Britones et Hibernos sacrificandi ritus, non plane compertum est. Modum tamen illum a Romano diversum extitisse intelligitur ex Bernardo in libro de vita Malachiæ, ubi Malachias barbaras consuetudines Romanis mutasse, et canonicum divinæ laudis officium in illas ecclesias invexisse memoratur."[78] Certainly Azevedo is speaking of the offices of the canonical hours rather than of the liturgy; and so Mabillon also, although he begins with speaking of the "ritus sacrificandi:" but there is so great a connexion between the two that any information or suggestion as regards the one throws some light upon the other.

We are equally ignorant as to the persons by whom or at what exact date Christianity was first preached in Britain. The legends about the coming of St. Paul or St. Peter or St. Joseph of Arimathea, and other similar stories, may be set aside as without real foundation. But whilst we do so put them aside, it by no means follows that the true faith was not known in Britain, and that there were no converts, before the second century. Intercourse with the continent was frequent and easy: there were large numbers of Roman soldiers and merchants in the country and many settlers, whose numbers must have rapidly increased as year after year passed by. Christianity must have been heard of, and it is almost impossible but that some, perhaps many, Christians might have had occasion to visit or to reside in the country. On the other hand, there is no evidence of any value that the true faith was introduced by missionaries from Rome.

When we come to the middle of the second century

---

[78] *De lit. Gall.* lib. i. cap. 2. xiv. Compare also Gerbert, *Vetus lit. Aleman.* tom. i. p. 75.

there seems to be firmer ground to rest on : and we may more readily rely on the suggestion that the formal organisation of a church in Britain, with bishops rightly consecrated, is to be traced to the church at Lyons which had been founded by missionaries from Asia. That there were Christians in Britain before the middle of the third century is undeniable; and in the year 314 British bishops are named among those who attended the council of Arles. Still, we have no records to guide us in even guessing at what were the precise forms of liturgy and ritual at that time used. If they had been brought by converts from Lyons they would have a character like that of the Ephesine church; and the changes in them which might have been made from time to time in Gaul would naturally have been introduced also into Britain. The peculiarities and variations of the Gallican liturgy would have been found in the British.

Stillingfleet is not an author whose judgment is to be depended on, so hastily does he seem in his *Origines Britannicæ* to have settled questions of rituals and liturgies, and so much inclined to misrepresent facts. Yet on this particular difficulty we may adopt his language. Speaking of some ancient manuscripts still extant of the Gallican service, he tells us : "from these excellent monuments of antiquity compared together, we may in great measure understand the true order and method of the communion service of that time, both in the Gallican and British churches." Presently he assures us that we may obtain from those records of the Gallican liturgy "a just and true account of the public service then used in Britain."[79]

---

[79] *Origines Britannicæ*, p. 240.

Upon the whole subject I would further refer the student to an important work, recently published, with very learned notes and introduction, by Mr. Warren, of St. John's College, Oxford.[80] I know no book upon the same subject of equal value. The introduction will be found to be especially useful; and following it are gathered together, carefully edited, the fragments which are still extant of any liturgy or ritual which can justly claim a Celtic origin. By the term Celtic church Mr. Warren means "the church which existed in Great Britain and Ireland before the mission of St. Augustine, and to a varying extent after that event, until by absorption or submission the various parts of it were at different dates incorporated with the church of the Anglo-saxons."[81]

The ancient Gallic churches used the same order of prayers in the celebration of the eucharist, although, as appears from three editions published by Thomasius and from a fourth by Mabillon, the prayers themselves somewhat differed. A brief description of their arrangement is given by Martene in his excellent work *De antiquis ecclesiæ ritibus.*[82] He says :—

---

[80] *The liturgy and ritual of the Celtic church.*

[81] Although perhaps unnecessary, it is right that I should guard myself against being understood as consenting to every deduction which Mr. Warren seems to arrive at. He writes on some points as an Anglican naturally would upon certain claims and assertions made by Roman catholic theologians. These passages however occur but seldom; and the author's opinions are expressed in language to which no exception can reasonably be taken. Even with these demerits —if I may venture so to call them —no student of the ancient history and rituals of the old British church will hesitate to acknowledge the obligation which he is under to Mr. Warren for the care and labour which have been taken in the preparation of his book.

[82] Tom. i. p. 98. See also Le Brun, *Opera*, tom. ii. p. 134.

The Gallic liturgy began with an antiphon, which was sung by the choir. This was followed by a preface or sermon to the people, in which the priest exhorted them to come with due reverence to the holy mysteries. Silence being then proclaimed the priest saluted the people, and after their response said a collect which the people heard upon their knees. After the collect the choir sang the trisagium, which was followed by the canticle, " Benedictus Dominus Deus Israel." (These, however, were omitted during lent.) Then came lessons from the prophets and the apostolic writings, after which the hymn of the three children was sung. This was followed by the reading of the gospel; before and after which the trisagium was again sung, and the people gave the response (still continued by a kind of tradition in the English protestant church), "Glory be to Thee, O Lord." Afterwards the bishop either himself preached or, if he was infirm or ill, ordered a homily to be read by a priest or deacon. Then the appointed prayers were said by a deacon for the hearers and catechumens. These latter having been dismissed and silence enjoined the bread and wine were brought in, and an oblation of them made whilst the choir sang an anthem called *sonum*, or more properly, *sonus:* which according to Martene (who is followed by Gerbert[83] and Le Brun[84]) upon the authority of St. Germanus answered to the offertory of later times. Then the sacred diptychs were read, the collect *post nomina* was said, the kiss of peace given, and the collect *ad pacem* said by the priest, after which the canon followed, which was very short. After the con-

---

[83] *De cantu,* tom. i. p. 116.
[84] *Opera,* tom. ii. p. 138.

secration came the prayer *post secreta ;* " postea fiebat confractio et commixtio corporis Christi." In the mean time the choir sang an anthem. This was followed by a collect, the Lord's prayer, and another collect. (It appears that the Lord's prayer was said by both the priest and the people.) Before communion the blessing was given, if by the priest in this form : " *Pax, fides, et caritas, et communicatio corporis et sanguinis Domini sit semper vobiscum.*" During communion the *trecanum* (it is doubtful what this was [85]) was sung by the choir. Then one or perhaps two collects were said, and the people were dismissed. [86]

---

[85] See Martene, *Anecd.* tom. v. p. 90 ; and Gerbert, *de cantu,* tom. i. p. 126. The latter has some important remarks upon the agreement in this part, as well as in others, of the Mozarabic and Gallican liturgies : a subject which would well repay an accurate examination, although we should not probably after a patient comparison come to the same conclusion with Dr. Giles, who, in a life of Bede prefixed to his biographical writing, quietly sets them down as the same : " the Gallican *or* Mozarabic liturgy." (p. xxij.) I regret to be obliged to pass the enquiry over, with only this brief remark : sufficient however, it may be, to excite the further interest of the student. The *trecanum,* as a title, is not found in the service of any other church.

[86] Compare the account also of this liturgy given by Mr. Palmer, *Orig. lit.* vol. i. p. 158. The argument by which he would prove that it was orginally from the east and not from Rome is of considerable weight. See also Le Brun, *Opera,* tom. ii. p. 126.

A very curious point, of no little importance and well worth examination, is the similarity between the most ancient English and Irish manuscripts now extant, and those of the east. The author of a valuable modern publication says, " the collation of many of these manuscripts has also furnished additional (although unlooked for) evidence that the ancient church in these islands corresponded with the eastern churches." Westwood, *Palæographia sacra,* pref. 1. Again, he alludes to an extraordinary similarity between the ornaments in the ancient Syriac manuscript of Rabula, and those in the most ancient Anglo-saxon manuscripts, particularly as regards a very peculiar and common

Such was the use which the existing English churches probably observed in celebrating the holy eucharist until the end of the sixth century. St. Augustine brought with him the liturgy then authorised and followed at Rome; he first landed about the year 597 during the lifetime of pope Gregory himself. After his return to England, as archbishop, he requested the pope to decide some questions; and among them, especially, what service was to be used in the English churches as the Gallican and Roman liturgies were not the same.[87] The answer was, that he might himself choose either; or select the liturgy which he thought most suitable from the various forms in the catholic church, provided only that he had regard to the circumstances

---

pattern formed of several slender spiral lines united in the centre of a circle: and continues, "these apparently trifling circumstances seem to me to prove more forcibly than the most laborious arguments, the connexion between the early Christians in these islands and those of the east, so strongly insisted upon by various writers." Note upon the psalter of king Athelstan. These remarks have not the less weight because they occur only incidentally, in a work directed towards a totally different object.

[87] This is of great importance, and I give the original from Bede: "Secunda interrogatio Augustini. Cum una sit fides, sunt ecclesiarum diversæ consuetudines, et altera consuetudo missarum in sancta Romana ecclesia, atque altera in Galliarum tenetur?

"Respondit Gregorius papa. Novit fraternitas tua Romanæ ecclesiæ consuetudinem, in qua se meminit nutritam. Sed mihi placet, sive in Romana, sive in Galliarum, seu in qualibet ecclesia, aliquid invenisti quod plus omnipotenti Deo possit placere, sollicite eligas, et in Anglorum ecclesia, quæ adhuc ad fidem nova est, institutione præcipua, quæ de multis ecclesiis colligere potuisti, infundas. Non enim pro locis res, sed pro bonis rebus loca amanda sunt. Ex singulis ergo quibusque ecclesiis quæ pia, quæ religiosa, quæ recta sunt, elige; et hæc, quasi in fasciculum collecta, apud Anglorum mentes in consuetudinem depone." *Hist. Eccles.* lib. i. cap. xxvii. 60.

and prejudices of the country, and the glory of God.

The question of the archbishop appears to me to be a very strong proof of the identity of the old British and the Gallican liturgies. If on his first coming he had not found any remnant of the earlier church, or if the liturgy which it still observed was not the same or nearly the same as the Gallican, I do not see why any doubt or hesitation should have risen in his mind as to the immediate introduction of the Roman use.[88] Had there been no prejudices to remove in the case of the British churches which still existed in many, even though perhaps remote, parts of the island; prejudices which the holy missionary knew and felt were to be considered, and if possible to be indulged; if, I say, there had been none such, there does not seem any reason whatever to suppose that he would not have required everywhere the adoption of the Roman liturgy, to which he had been always accustomed. We learn also from the answer of St. Gregory, that although it differed from the Roman yet in his judgment the Gallican or (if we may so conclude it) the British liturgy contained nothing that was objectionable.

Naturally the influence of St. Augustine and his successors led to a very wide adoption, in its main features, of the Roman liturgy: and it has been said that the few manuscripts which have come down to us of the Anglo-saxon age are but transcripts of the sacramentary of St. Gregory.[89] This

---

[88] I do not overlook but rather would remind the reader of the fact, that he might himself consider it, of the bishop and congregation who accompanied queen Bertha into England; and to which I attribute no weight in this enquiry.

[89] *Origines liturgicæ*, vol. i. p. 186.

may be true of the manuscripts which are extant;
but true only in a general way of the facts as they
existed: in the same way, for instance, in which,
about the middle of the eighth century, Egbert
archbishop of York must be understood in one of
the answers of his Dialogue.[90]   I say must, as even
Dr. Lingard, a great upholder of the early and complete introduction of the Roman use into England,
cannot but allow, when he owns that "even at the
close of the eighth century the Scottish liturgy was
in daily, though not exclusive, use in the church of
York."[91]   That is, in Egbert's own cathedral.   What
Dr. Lingard means by "though not exclusive" I do
not comprehend.

About the same time, A.D. 747, a council at Cloveshoo added the sanction of its authority to the observance, as far as the various dioceses would receive them, of the Roman ritual and missal.   We
must be careful not to press beyond such a limi-
tation these canons, as otherwise we should be
plainly contradicted by other records which have
come down to us: and it is not clear that we must
even go to that extent; for the object seems rather
to be directed to an uniformity of time, and the
Roman or Gregorian chant.   I extract the first of
these, which relates to the liturgy: "xiii. *Ut uno*

---

[90] "Nos autem in ecclesia Anglorum idem primi mensis jejunium, ut noster didascalus beatus
Gregorius in suo antiphonario
et missali libro per pædagogum
nostrum beatum Augustinum
transmisit ordinatum et rescrip-
tum .. servamus." "Hoc autem
jejunium idem beatus Gregorius
per præfatum legatum in antiphonario suo et missali, in plena
hebdomada post pentecosten
Anglorum ecclesiæ celebrandum
destinavit. Quod non solum nostra testantur antiphonaria, sed et
ipsa quæ cum missalibus suis
conspeximus apud apostolorum
Petri et Pauli limina." Wilkins,
Concilia, tom. i. p. 85.

[91] *Anglo-saxon church,* vol. i.
p. 299.

eodemque tempore ubique festivitates dominicæ, seu martyrum nativitates peragantur. Tertio decimo definitur decreto: ut uno eodemque modo dominicæ dispensationis in carne sacrosanctæ festivitates, in omnibus ad eas rite competentibus rebus, id est, in baptismi officio, in missarum celebratione, in cantilenæ modo, celebrentur, juxta exemplar videlicet quod scriptum de Romana habemus ecclesia. Itemque ut per gyrum totius anni natalitia sanctorum uno eodemque die, juxta martyrologium ejusdem Romanæ ecclesiæ, cum sua sibi convenienti psalmodia seu cantilena venerentur."[92]

Le Brun mentions a remarkable manuscript which he says proves that for a considerable period the Anglo-saxon church, or at least some part of it, adopted not the Gregorian but the Gelasian sacramentary.[93] Whether this may have been so or not, there can be little doubt but that the canon of the church of Rome, subject to certain variations, was admitted and generally observed by the Anglo-saxon churches long before other portions of the missal, or other rites and ceremonies. Mabillon allows this to have been the case with respect to the Gallic liturgy in France.[94]

Without delaying longer upon this enquiry we may probably conclude, that as Christianity spread among the Anglo-saxons the canon of the church of Rome, as distinguished from the old Gallican, was gradually received by them, and also in the British churches which may still have existed. But it would be the general arrangement only, and not always the exact words. Not merely would ancient pre-

---

[92] Wilkins, *Concilia*, tom. i. p. 96. The other canon, the fifteenth, concerns the daily office of the canonical hours.
[93] *Opera*, tom. ii. p. 91.
[94] *De lit. Gallicana*, p. 46.

judices and ritual peculiarities have influence against
the newer form, but the bishops of the several
dioceses into which England was gradually divided
(it may well be thought) exercised the power of
which I have already spoken to enjoin, within the
limits of their respective jurisdictions, rites and ceremonies and prayers. Possibly this power was not
invariably exercised with due discretion; some
trifling and objectionable practices may occasionally
have been suffered to interfere with the solemnities
of the public service and offices. Yet, after all,
these were to no great extent; and there is ample
proof how careful the rulers of the church were to
prevent such scandals. In fact, when we remember
the rudeness of the manners of the Anglo-saxons,
how little learned many of the most pious and
earnest of the bishops, how numberless the old
heathen superstitions which still existed, we must
own the constant presence and direction of the
Almighty Head, Who alone could preserve a due
and fitting order against the pressure of so many
difficulties.

One abuse the Anglo-saxon church was most
anxious to fight against; although it has been with
superficial writers not uncommon to assert the contrary: namely, the introduction of any pagan rites.
It will be sufficient to quote two examples. The
nineteenth canon of the council of Chalcuith, A.D.
785, at a time when it would have seemed to human
policy most desirable by any way to conciliate the
heathens, enjoins in the plainest terms: "Ut unusquisque fidelis christianus a catholicis viris exemplum accipiat; et si quid ex ritu paganorum remansit, avellatur, contemnatur, abjiciatur. Deus
enim formavit hominem pulchrum in decore et
specie: pagani vero diabolico instinctu cicatrices

teterrimas superinduxerunt."[95]   And again, in the
eleventh century, the fifth of the ecclesiastical laws
of king Canute : "prohibemus etiam serio omnem
ethnicismum."[96]

---

[95] Wilkins, *Concilia*, tom. i. p. 150.
[96] *Ibid.* tom. i. p. 306, A.D. 1033.

CHAPTER IV.

THE eucharistic offices of the Anglo-saxon church may therefore have been, for many years, distinguished from each other by very important variations : and it is probable that throughout England, up to the century preceding the conquest, they differed in some degree or other, to the extent even of the number of the different dioceses. Doubtless they all preserved the essentials of· the service, according to the very brief account which Ælfric gives us in his easter-homily: " Ða apostoli dýdon swa swa Crist hét. þat hi halgodon hláf and wín to húsle eft sýððan on his gemýnde. Eác swýlce heora æfter-gengan and ealle sacerdas be Cristes hæse halgiað hláf and wín to húsle on his naman mid þære apostolican bletsunge."[97] These differences of each diocese from another continued[98] until the civil subordination of the whole land under one head

[97] " Apostoli prout Christus jussit fecerunt; exhinc enim panem et vinum consecraverunt iterum in eucharistiam, in ejus memoriam. Pariter (faciunt) horum successores et omnes sacerdotes, jubente Christo, in nomine ejus panem et vinum in eucharistiam consecrant per benedictionem apostolicam." *Eccles. Anglic. vindex cathol.* vol. iii. p. 348.

[98] There were also varieties observed by the different monastic orders; several of which have been printed in later years. Those according to the uses of the Benedictines, the Cistercians, the Carthusians, the Dominicans, and Franciscans were published before the year 1500. These were upon the one hand forbidden to the secular clergy, see Benedict XIV, *Opera*, tom. ix. p. 408; and on the other were binding upon the members of the respective orders; Azevedo, *de div. off.* exercit. x. p. 55. But compare the order presently about Barking monastery.

and consequent increased facilities of intercourse introduced a greater sameness of practice, better fitted to the unity of faith.

About the year 1085, Osmund, bishop of Salisbury, drew up and promulgated a form which should be used in his diocese:[99] and whether from the known ability and earnestness of Osmund himself, whether from the fame of his new cathedral and the college of learned clergy which he had collected,[1]

---

[99] "At the conquest monasteries had a deep share in the afflictions of the conquered nation; some of the best of their manors were sacrilegiously taken away, their treasuries plundered, and their liberties infringed. Most of the English abbots being deposed for little or no causes, strangers were preferred to the richest abbeys in the kingdom, who introduced several new customs to the grievance of the old Saxon monks.

"The first thing which seemed very hard was the altering their missals; upon this account what great heats were there in the abbey of Glastonbury! when Thurstan, the pragmatical Norman abbot, would have forced the monks to lay aside the old Gregorian service, which had been used there time out of mind, to make use of the new devotions" (i. e. manner of singing) "of William of Fiscamp. These and several other innovations, which were bringing in upon them, were stopped by the pains of Osmund, bishop of Salisbury, who composed a new ritual, afterwards known by the name of the *missale in usum Sarum,* and generally used in England, Scotland, and Ireland." Tanner, *Notitia monastica,* pref. 4. I do not think it necessary to stop to correct the above statement, which the reader may easily do for himself.

Although we must scarcely take the words of Bromton literally, yet his statement shows that the reception of St. Osmund's arrangement was rapidly and widely spread soon after the bishop's death. Bromton wrote about the year 1300, and speaking of St. Osmund says: "Hic componit librum ordinalem ecclesiastici officii quem consuetudinarium vocant, quo fere tota nunc Anglia, Wallia, et Hibernia, utitur." *Chron.* p. 977. The chronicler here uses the term consuetudinary in its wide and less exact meaning, as including what is properly called the ordinal.

[1] "Hoc anno Hermannus obiit, cui successit Osmundus, qui ecclesiam novam ibidem construxit, clericos insignes tam literis quam cantu aggregavit." Henr. de Knighton, *Chron.* lib. 2.

or from whatever cause, this *Use of Sarum* was very generally adopted in the south of England as well as in other parts of the country, and even, it has been said, upon the continent.[2] It did not however altogether exclude the other uses of York, Bangor, Hereford, and Lincoln which were still enforced in their respective districts: these were small perhaps in comparison with the wide reception of the use of Sarum, and neither their exact limits nor their authors can be ascertained: it seems certain that the uses of Lincoln and Bangor were observed in fewer dioceses than those of York and Hereford.

We must not suppose that this extended influence was obtained all at once, or even in less than a long lapse of time, by the liturgy and ritual of the church of Salisbury: nor, again, must we forget that those who testify to its greatest renown lived some three or four hundred years after its original settlement under the direction of bishop Osmund.[3] During that period many severe struggles, of which all

---

[2] We may understand that the use of Sarum was introduced into Ireland upon the authority of a canon of the synod of Cashel, A.D. 1172. "Quod omnia divina ad instar sacrosanctæ ecclesiæ, juxta quod Anglicana observat ecclesia, in omnibus partibus ecclesiæ amodo tractentur." Wilkins, *Concilia*, tom. i. p. 473. Compare also Collier, *Eccles. hist.* vol. i. p. 379. As regards the church of Glasgow in Scotland, see Wilkins, tom. i. p. 741; and the *Monumenta ritualia*, vol. i. p. lij. note 93.

[3] One reason why writers in modern times have perhaps too much exalted the Salisbury, to the disparagement of the other English uses, has probably been because the service books of that church are with few exceptions the only ones which are extant. No perfect book, or even any large fragment, is known to exist of Lincoln; only two manuscripts, namely, the missal in my possession, and the pontifical belonging to the dean and chapter of that cathedral, claim to be of Bangor; and but ten or twelve copies altogether are known of the books of Hereford and York [1848]. During the last thirty years some few other copies of the two last uses have been found.

memorial has been lost, may have occurred; and many difficulties and jealousies which opposed its progress may have been gradually but slowly overcome. In less however than two hundred years after Osmund's death we have a proof how high the character of the Sarum use already was, in the constitutions of one of his successors; who in the year 1256 declares that "like the sun in the heavens, the church of Salisbury is conspicuous above all other churches of the world, diffusing its light everywhere, and supplying their defects." [4]

There are two important cases upon which a few remarks may not perhaps be out of place. And first of the cathedral of St. Paul in London, the chief city of the kingdom. Collier tells us that in the year 1414, and therefore we may conclude not till then, an order was made by bishop Clifford "with the assent of the chapter, that from the first of December following divine service should be performed in his cathedral, secundum usum Sarum: and that the old form and rubric called St. Paul's should be laid aside." [5] With this is quite agreeable the manner of expression in two inventories of the church, printed in Dugdale's history of St. Paul's: in the one made A.D. 1298 books are simply spoken of "de usu S. Pauli;" but in the other, in 1486, we have "vetus missale," "aliud vetus missale secundum usum S. Pauli," and "unum ordinale secundum primariam ordinationem et antiquam ecclesiæ S. Pauli." [6] But we have the best evidence that in the cathedral of St. Paul the use of Sarum was not admitted without also the retaining some of its own

---

[4] Wilkins, *Concilia*, tom. i. p. 715.

[5] *Ecclesiastical hist.* vol. i. p.

649; and Dugdale, *St. Paul's*, p. 22.

[6] pp. 233, 284.

old peculiar ceremonies: I mean that of the author of
the *Defensorium directorii* who says, speaking on a
certain point, "probatur ista assertio esse vera per
venerabiles viros ac patres canonicos ecclesiæ sancti
Pauli Londonensis, qui totum officium divinum in
cantando et legendo observant secundum usum
Sarum ecclesiæ. Sed de cærimoniis vel observationibus ejusdem nihil curantes: sed custodiunt
antiquas observantias in ecclesia sancti Pauli a primordio illic usitatas."[1]

A manuscript is preserved in the library of the
British museum which is called in the catalogue
"missale in usum D. Pauli:"[2] from which we might
have hoped to obtain much information upon this
point: and we doubtless should, had it been a copy
of the old use of that church. But it is later than
1414 and the rubrics throughout speak of and are
according to the use of Sarum: nor do there seem
to be any variations of the slightest importance, with
one exception. Indeed, the only authority why it
has been so called "of St. Paul's" appears to have
been a tradition, and possibly a correct one, that it

---

[1] *Monumenta ritualia*, vol. ii.
p. 360. The practice of the cathedral of St. Paul was, as we
may suppose, of considerable
authority; and the *Defensorium*
appeals in another place to it,
upon a disputed point (p. 342);
where the decision of the "venerabiles cardinales ecclesiæ sancti
Pauli" is given. As Ducange
tells us, there were in many
cathedrals and monasteries some
chief appointed among the
priests, "quibus ex concessione
summorum pontificum licitum
erat, ut soli ad præcipuum altare quod *cardinale* vocabant,
unde *cardinales* dicti solemnem
missam celebrarent." *Verb.* Presbyter. But I think in the present
instance reference is made to the
cardinals of the choir, who were
officers of St. Paul's cathedral,
chosen from the minor canons
by the dean and chapter to have
the direction of the choir. See
some ancient statutes, printed in
Dugdale, *Hist. of St. Paul's*,
appendix, p. 241.

[2] Harleian MS. 2787. This
valuable manuscript is unfortunately imperfect.

formerly belonged to that cathedral. We may accept the tradition, because although like most copies of the missal in that age it has numerous directions which refer to parish churches and not to cathedrals, it has also some rubrics which could relate only to a large establishment of priests and ministers. Nor can there be any doubt but that it was the property of some great church in London : this is clear from the rubric upon the feast of St. Mark, directing the procession upon that day to go to some church in the city or in the suburbs, and return after the celebration of mass to their own church. The exception above spoken of is remarkable : the canon of this manuscript contains the prayer "Agimus tibi Deo Patri gratias ;"[9] and is the only example I remember to have met with, except in the Hereford missal, and in the magnificent manuscript of abbot Litlington at Westminster. · The prayers which precede it are however not according to the Hereford but to the Salisbury use.

We have a proof that the old use of St. Paul's was held in high estimation in an order relating to Barking monastery, in Essex, about 1390 : " Nota quod diversis temporibus intra conventum nonnullæ emanarunt altercationes . . . igitur nos cupientes dictas altercationes et discordias radicitus extirpari præsenti extirpamus edicto secundum antiquas consuetudines istius domus approbatas, quod conventus prædictus tres modos diversos habeat sui servitii dicendi ; primo horas suas dicat secundum regulam sancti Benedicti ; psalterium suum secundum cursum curiæ Romanæ ; missam vero secundum usum ecclesiæ sancti Pauli Londoniarum."[10]

---

[9] See below, p. 179.

[10] Dugdale, *Monasticon Anglic.* vol. i. p. 437. note k. Upon the distinction between the use "Romanæ ecclesiæ" and " Romanæ curiæ," see Azevedo, *de div. off.*

The other case to which I alluded is of Exeter. In the year 1339 bishop Grandisson drew up a body of statutes for his new and most munificent foundation of the collegiate church of St. Mary at Ottery. These enter into minute particulars of the services to be performed by the members of the college; and whilst two or three chapters prove that the Sarum was then the received use of the diocese they no less show a sort of jealousy still existing, and an earnest desire upon the part of the bishop to establish an Exeter use. Thus in the seventh he speaks of the divine office on certain occasions being performed "secundum ordinale et consuetudinarium quæ eis fecimus et extraximus ex Exoniæ et Sarum usibus."[11] Again in the tenth that all the members should attend chapter "saltem in sabbato, ut Exoniæ fit." In the thirty-sixth we have the two uses identified: " Item volumus quod in majoribus festis . . . sicut Sarum et sicut Exon." And, once more, in the seventy-seventh the bishop speaks out very plainly: " Item statuimus quod ubicumque ordinale vel consuetudinarium vel statuta nostra non sufficiant forte in multis faciendis per totum annum, quod tunc recurratur ad ordinale et consuetudinarium Sarum. Ita tamen quod semper omnia per nos disposita firmiter observentur. Nolumus tamen quod allegent vel dicant unquam se usum tenere Sarum, sed magis Exoniæ, vel, ut verius dicant, usum per nos eis traditum proprium et specialem."[12] The extent

---

exercit. ix. p. 33: "Officium curiæ contractum erat, et mutationibus obnoxium ob varias et continuas occupationes summi pontificis, et cardinalium, aliorumque prælatorum, qui ei in sacello diu noctuque interesse solebant."

[11] This ordinal is still extant, and preserved in the exchequer chamber of the dean and chapter of Exeter. See some account of it in the *Monumenta ritualia*, vol. i. p. l.

[12] Oliver, *Monasticon Exon.* p. 268, et seqq.

to which the bishop's wishes were carried in this matter must remain doubtful : we find however, about one hundred years after, in 1436, an order made by the founder of "Godeshous" (a charitable institution for the poor in the same city of Exeter) that the chaplain should say his office " secundum usum Sarum."[13]

We have proof of the acceptance of the use of Sarum in the county of Suffolk from the fact that one of the ordinals of that church in the library of the British museum was one of the service-books of the parish church of Rysbey.[14] It is true that occasionally the Sarum service-books refer to the uses of other English dioceses; as, for instance, to the use of the church of Lichfield on St. Chad's day (March 2nd). We must not however conclude that in other respects the use of Lichfield varied from the Sarum ; but that this particular exception was allowed as a peculiarity retained by that church, upon the festival of its patron. This is quite clear from the constitutions of Lichfield in 1428, where observance of the rules of the ordinal of Sarum is expressly enjoined.[15]

According then to these various uses of Sarum, York, Bangor, Hereford, and Lincoln[16] (various yet

---

[13] *Monasticon Exon.* p. 404.

[14] See *Monumenta ritualia,* vol. i. p. liv. note 89. Other incidental notices might easily be added ; for example, the service books " ad usum Sarum" among the valuables of Edward the third, in the inventory among the exchequer records ; and the statutes drawn up for the hospital of St. Julian at St. Alban's ; Matt. Paris, *Auct.* p. 1164.

[15] *Concilia,* tom. 3. p. 505.

[16] So Asseman reckons five uses, upon the authority doubtless of the preface to the common Prayer book ; *Codex liturgic.* tom. iv. pars iii. 36. And the author of the *Ordinarye of a Christen man* speaks of them in a general way : " That on the holy sondaye and other grete feestes and solempnytees gyuen by comaundemente, after dyuer-

harmonious) the holy eucharist was celebrated in England until the year 1547, the first of king Edward the sixth. Their origin cannot be attributed merely to man's ingenuity and learning, or even piety; but they are to be traced, as has been very briefly shown, through the sacramentaries of Gregory and Gelasius and Leo to the well-spring of all Christian truth, the age of the apostles.

In March, 1548, a form was published to be used in the distribution of the consecrated bread and wine, if any lay persons desired to communicate. By this there was to be no alteration made in the old services, although a very significant hint was given of the intention of the king's advisers;[17] but after the priest had himself communicated, he was to exhort the people to a worthy partaking with him, in almost the words which are still used in the reformed Prayer book; beginning, " Dearly beloved in the Lord, ye, coming to this holy communion, must consider what St. Paul writeth to the Corinthians," &c. This was to be followed by a charge to all open sinners to withdraw, and the invitation "You that do truly and earnestly repent you of your sins," &c.: after which a confession and absolution, and a prayer; and then both the host and the chalice were given, with these words, " The body of our Lord Jesus Christ, which was given for thee, preserve thy body unto everlasting life;" and, " The blood of our Lord Jesus Christ, which was shed for thee, preserve thy soul to everlasting

---

syte of the countre and of the dyoces, euery man ought to here masse entyerly yf he haue no lettyng nor excusacyon reasonable by the whiche he may be excused." Sign. L. iiij. *b*, edit. Wynkyn de Worde.

[17] See the rubric below, at the time of the communion, "until other order shall be provided."

life." Having received, the people were dismissed with a blessing.

Although this form has been more than once re-printed—for example, by Dr. Cardwell in his *Two Prayer books of Edward the Sixth*, and by Wilkins in the fourth volume of the *Concilia*—I have thought it well to include it in the appendix to the present edition, on account of its great historical importance. The original editions are of extreme rarity; scarcely more than five or six copies are known to exist. There are three in the British museum, all in quarto, of the same date, March 8, 1548, and all different; that is, not in the matter or in the variation pro-bably of a single important word but in the setting up of the type.[18] It would require of course more

---

[18] All of those which have any date are said in the colo-phon to be " imprinted " " in the second year of the reigne of our soueraigne lorde, kyng Ed-ward the vi." This is perfectly correct; Edward began to reign in January, 1547. The first common Prayer book which is dated in 1549, and was probably not printed until either the last day of March or after the month of March in that year, is never-theless a legal document of the second year of king Edward. There have lately been very considerable discussion and somewhat heated arguments as to the right meaning of the words in the rubric of the pre-sent common Prayer book that certain things " shall be retained and be in use, as were in the church of England, by the au-thority of parliament, in the se-cond year of the reign of king Edward the sixth." In these discussions more than one writer has asserted that the rubric does not refer to the first Prayer book of 1549, inasmuch as it was un-deniably neither published nor printed until after January 1549; and, therefore, must have had the authority only of the third year of king Edward. But in those days all acts of parlia-ment dated from and took effect from the first day of the session; and the particular parliament referred to in the rubric began in November 1548, that is, in the second year of his reign. It was not possible in the year 1662 rightly to refer to any statute passed during that ses-sion except as " by authority of parliament in the second year." Even if there were any doubt about this we might further in-

than one press to supply the large number which would be wanted. There is a single copy in the Bodleian; and this, again, is a different edition. It is a small duodecimo; and apparently intended for the use of people in the congregation and not for the priest.[19]

---

sist that the Prayer book of 1549 is the first document relating to the public services of the church of England which was ever submitted to the consideration and approval of parliament, or received its "authority." Nothing of the kind can be alleged about any articles of visitation and enquiry, or any injunctions and the like, put forth either by Henry the eighth or Edward. These, including the Order of communion of 1548, rested solely on the "authority" of the crown.

What I have just said falls (in a certain way) within the scope of the subject of this volume, which extends to the final abolition of the old liturgies, however altered or added to, of the church of England. I would ask permission to say one word (whether exceeding my limits or not) on the alleged "authority" of the Advertisements of 1566. Setting aside the extreme difficulty—and after so much labour spent without success, we may say the impossibility—of proving that these Advertisements at any time had the force of law, no legal judgment in the present century seems to be so directly contrary to all the principles which for generations have

been supposed to rule the decisions of our chief courts as that which lately told us that a clause in an act of Parliament plainly referring to the second year of king Edward is to be understood as referring to the seventh year of queen Elizabeth. We can only hope that if reasons of policy or expediency had weight with any of our judges in arriving at this decision, it may be very long before we need be ashamed of another example. Nothing can shake men's reverence in England for legitimate authority more than bringing in "expedience" to overrule the distinct language of an act of Parliament.

[19] There is no date; and no printer's name. It collates in eights to B. iv, with the last leaf blank. If my memory serves me, no copy of the 1548 Order of communion could be found in the Bodleian forty years ago, when I was preparing the first edition of this book; nor (I believe) is there any entry or other record whence this very curious and unique copy came. It has been recently bound; and I think it possible that the late librarian, in his unwearied searchings among the treasures in his charge, may have discovered it mixed up with a number of other tracts.

Alterations in faith and ritual were marvellously rapid in the time of Edward the sixth ; and it might be difficult to decide whether any trace or remnant of the old faith would have been left in the reformed church of England if he had lived to the common age of man. In comparison with the changes made in the five years of his reign the ten centuries which had elapsed since the coming of St. Augustine may be said to have changed almost nothing. For a thousand years the liturgy of the church of England had suffered no omission, had endured no addition, which in the slightest degree affected the doctrine which it taught. The brief space of what might easily be counted as months instead of years swept away the old liturgy, to be replaced by a new Communion service with new prayers and exhortations, new rites and ceremonies.

The observance of "the order of Communion" of 1548 lasted only for a very short time. I must acknowledge that after a careful examination of the rules or rubrics which it contains I am utterly at a loss to understand how it was to be obeyed; nor do I know where to look for any contemporary explanation of the difficulties.

There may not be much in the omission of a direction at what previous service the priest was to give his parishioners the preliminary warning "at least one day before he shall minister the communion." Still it is an omission ; and we have nothing whatever as a guide. Again, was no one to communicate except on those days of which previous notice had been given ? in other words, was the priest forbidden to give communion to a parishioner at any other mass during the week or (it might be) month before ? Once more : the communion of the people is appointed to follow " immediately after that the priest himself hath received the sacrament," without any purification or ablution ; and there is no break in the service until the conclusion, when the priest, still we must suppose at the altar rails, lets the people depart with a blessing. Can anybody explain what he was to do then ? was he to go back alone to the altar, whilst the congregation were leaving the church and say the rest of the service ? were the communion and postcommunion to be left unsaid ? was he to be allowed to return that at least he might remove as reverently as he could the paten and chalice, or was he also to go away with the people ? In a word, what was he to do ?

It is necessary to give some account of the editions which have been used in preparing the following arrangement of the English and Roman liturgies.

The Roman use is printed from the edition by Plantin, Antwerp, 1759, 4to.

The Hereford use has been taken from an edition of that missal in the Bodleian library. It is supposed that the Hereford missal was printed only once. This supposition, however, rests on the fact that we have no evidence of more than one edition. It is rash to argue that books were never printed, merely because copies are not known to exist now. When the second edition of the present book was published, in the year 1846, no other copies were believed to exist than two in the Bodleian library, and one in the library of St. John's college, Oxford. One of the Bodleian copies is on vellum ; both are imperfect, and unfortunately will not between them give us the perfect book. The imperfection is happily of no great extent ; being limited to an erasure in the canon (see p. 179, and the note) ; but, nevertheless, there is an imperfection.

In the year 1855 I had the good fortune to hear of a fourth copy of the Hereford missal; and this, on examination, proved to be perfect; and not merely perfect, but large and sound; in short, a very beautiful copy.[20] This is now in the British museum.

The Hereford missal is a handsome folio, printed at Rouen in 1502. The following are the title and the colophon.

Title: " Anno Incarnationis domini secundo supra quingentesimum atque millesimum, die vero prima mensis Septembris, opera et industria M. Petri oliverii et Iohannis mauditier Impressorum Rothomagi, iuxta sacellum diui apostolorum principis Petri commorantium. Impensa vero Iohannis richardi mercatoris: hoc novum et egregium opus sacri Missalis ad usum famose ac percelebris ecclesie Helfordensis nuper instanti ac peruigili cura visum correctum et emendatum. Necnon auctoritate reuerendi in Christo patris et domini ejusdem ecclesie epyscopi meritissimi, ac dominorum decani et capituli : est in propatulo venale facili precio coram cunctis productum et exhibitum."

Colophon : " Finis Missalis ad vsum celebris ecclesie Helfordensis. summa cura ac vigili opera nuper Impressi Rothomagi cum additione, Accentuarii legentibus in ecclesiis valde vtili. Et hoc impensis Iohannis richardi eiusdem Rothomagi civis non immeriti : iuxta ecclesiam diui nicholai commorantis." The short title at the head of the service for the first sunday in advent is, " Incipit missale secundum vsum Herfordensem."

The York use is taken from an edition of that missal in my possession [1846];[21] 4to. Title : " Mis-

---

[20] *Mon. rit.* vol. i. p. lxxxiv.   [21] Now in the British museum.

sale ad vsum celeberrime ecclesie Eboracensis opti-
mis caracteribus nouissime Impressum cura peruigili
maximaque lucubratione mendis quampluribus emendatum atque in forma portabili marginatum. Ere
et impensis honestorum virorum Guillermi bernard
et Jacobi cousin, bibliopolarum, Rothomagi degen-
tium ante atrium librariorum majoris ecclesie, atque
in ipso atrio e regione curie ecclesiastice. Anno
salutis christiane decimoseptimo supra millesimum
et quingentesimum, die vero vicesimasexta mensis octobris completum." This edition has not a
colophon.[22]

The York missal is a book of extreme rarity;
Sir Harris Nicolas says[23] " it is doubtful whether
any perfect copy exists, except the one preserved
at Cambridge in the library of St. John's college."[24]
This however is incorrect, because copies of five
editions are now known to be extant.[25] In the
British museum is a fragment of a York missal,
which has been long supposed to be of an unknown
edition ; in fact it is a part of the edition of 1516,
Rothom. fol.

The Sarum use is printed from a copy of the
edition of that missal in my possession [1846],[26] of
1492, at Rouen, in folio. This is the only perfect[27]

---

[22] In the first edition I used a copy of the York missal (folio, Rouen, 1516) in the Bodleian library; but, if I am not mis-taken, the two agree in the text.

[23] In his very useful *Chronology of history*.

[24] Paris, Francis Regnault, m.ccccc.xxxiii. 4to.

[25] For an account of the York missals I must refer the reader to the dissertation on service books, *Monum. ritualia*, vol. i. p. lxxxv.

[26] Now in the British Museum.

[27] There is a large fragment of this edition in the Bodleian upon vellum. The imperfections have been supplied from a copy upon paper with the date 1510, printed also at Rouen by Joh.

copy known, and in all respects a very important book. Until a few years ago this was believed to be the *editio princeps* of the Sarum missal, but it is not mentioned by Gough, or Brunet, or Hain ;[28] all of whom speak of the edition of 1494, by John Hertzog, as the first.[29] The title is simply upon otherwise a blank leaf, " Missale secundum vsum ecclesie sarisburieñ." Then follow a calendar and the " benedictio salis et aquæ ;" after which, under a woodcut, begins the service for the first sunday in advent with the usual title, " Incipit missale secundum vsum Sar." Before the canon is a large woodcut (the reverse blank) representing the first Person of the ever-blessed Trinity, with the evangelistic symbols in the corners, and below is a cross. The colophon : " Impensa et arte magr̃i Martini morin civis Rotho- magensis iuxta ĩsignem prioratum sancti laudi eius- dem ciuitatis moram trahentis officium sacrum ad vsum sar. (ut vulgo loq̃mur) missale dictum, sollerti correctionis lima nuper castigatum et impressum : finit feliciter. Anno domini M.CCCC.lxxxxii. die xii. Octobris." Upon the reverse is the printer's device, viz. a negro's head and the letters M.M. within a circle supporting a double cross, with the

---

Richard. Until lately [1846] this vellum part was supposed to be of about the same date and is so entered in the library catalogue.

[28] *Repertorium bibliographi- cum.*

[29] There was one other edi- tion during this century ; printed in England by Julian Notary, folio, with this colophon : "In laudem sanctissime Trinitatis totiusque milicie celestis ad ho- norem et decorem scē ecclesie Sarum anglicane eiusq. deuo- tissimi cleri. hoc missale diui- norum officiorum vigilanti studio emendatum Iussu et impensis præstantissimi viri Winkin de Worde. Impressum Londoñ. apud Westmonasterium per Iulianum notaire et Iohanem barbier felici numine explicitum est. Anno dñi M.cccc.lxxxxviij. xx. die mensis Decembris." Another was soon afterwards printed by Pynson, fol. 1504.

following legend in the border, " Imprime. A. Rouen. Devant. Sainct. Lo.," in gothic letters.[30]

No printed copy of the Bangor use has been discovered. If there ever was an edition it has so far as we know utterly perished, perhaps by the common accidents of time but more probably by means of the eager inquisitors under Edward the sixth. I have arranged the ordinary and canon according to the use of Bangor from a manuscript written somewhere about the year 1400; a large folio, upon vellum. The evidence is not sufficient that it is certainly that use, but I conceive there are some reasonable grounds for supposing it to be so. It is undoubtedly an English missal, and not strictly according to the uses either of Sarum, York, or Hereford. A very slight examination even of the small portion reprinted in this volume will be sufficient to establish this; a point confirmed by variations in the collects and offices throughout the book.

But I would mention particularly the ordo sponsalium. This agrees with the prayers and order in the famous pontifical according to the use of Bangor, still preserved in the cathedral library of that city; to which it was given in the year 1485 by Richard Ednam, the then bishop.[31] That pontifical does not, however, contain the forms of giving troth and at the putting on of the ring; which were anciently in

[30] See for a collation of this edition and a notice of the earlier one printed for Caxton, *Monum. rit.* vol. i. p. lxix.

[31] This volume originally belonged to Anianus, bishop of Bangor from A.D. 1268 to about 1300. It was for some time lost from the cathedral, but with better fortune than happened to the great majority of such books it was preserved, and restored to the library by bishop Humphreys in 1701. I have given a particular description of this very valuable manuscript in the dissertation on service books, to which I must venture again to refer the reader; *Monum. ritual.* vol. i. p. cxxxij.

all the missals, in English; and I cannot think it altogether out of place to give them at length.

In the Salisbury missal the man is directed to say: " I, *N*, take the, *N*, to my weddyd wyf to haue and tho holde from thys day far warde for beter, for wurs, for rychere for porer: in sykenisse and in helthe tyl deth us deperte yf holy chyrche wol it ordeyne, and therto I plyght the my trouth." The woman repeats the same form, adding after the words *and in helthe*, " to be bonour and buxum [32] in bed and at borde." At the putting on of the ring the man says: "With tys ring I the wedde and tys gold and siluer I te geue: and with my body I te worscype and wyth all my worldly catell I the honore."

The York missal directs both the man and woman to say as follows: "Here I take the, *N*, to my wedded *wyfe* or *husband*, to have and to holde at bedde and at borde, for fayrer, for fowler, for better for warse, in sikenes and in hele (or helth) tyll dethe us departe. And therto I plyght the my trouthe." Putting on the ring:[33] " With this rynge I wedde the and with this golde and siluer I honoure the, and with this gyft I honoure the."

The Hereford missal directs the man to say: " I, *N*, underfynge þe, *N*, for my wedded wyf, for

---

[32] There are more meanings than one given to this old English word. In this place it signifies " obedience." The dictionaries do not commonly mention the privative form of the word, which, however, leads us to the true meaning, and occurs in Hylton's *Medled lyfe*, printed by R. Wyer, p. 4: " Also it longeth to all yonge begynnynge men, the which come newe out of worldly synnes to the seruyce of god: for to make them able to ghostly werkynge, & for to breke down the unbuxumness of the body by discrecion."

[33] The old books, both Salisbury and York, say upon the fourth finger " quia in illo digito est quædam vena procedens usque ad cor."

betere for worse, for richer for porer, yn sekenes and in helþe, tyl deþ us departe, as holy churche haþ ordeyned, and þerto y plyȝth þe my trovvþe." The woman repeats the same, with the addition after the word helþe, "to be boxum to þe." Giving the ring the man says: "Wyþ þys ryng y þe wedde, and þys gold in seluer ych þe ȝeue, and vvyþ myne body ych þe honoure."

In my manuscript the form appointed for the man is: "I *N*, tak þe, *N*, to my weddyd wyf to haue and to holde from thys day forward, for bettere for werse, for fayrere for fowlere, for rychere for porere, in syknesse and in helthe tyl deþ us depart ȝyf holy cherche yt wole ordeyne. And therto y plyȝhte the my trewthe." The woman repeats the same, adding after the word helþe, "to be boneere and buxum in all lawfulle placys." The form at the giving of the ring is: "Wyth thys ring I þe wedde and ys gold and syluer I þe ȝefe and wyth my bodi the wourchepe and wyth all my worldli catell I the onore and endue."

I repeat that I am far from saying that such variations [34] prove this missal to be certainly the Bangor use, whilst joined with others they may possibly suggest a doubt whether it is Sarum; and it is certainly neither York nor Hereford. I humbly leave the question to the consideration of men better learned in the subject than myself, trusting that it may at least lead to further enquiry among

---

[34] Nor is it to be forgotten that the canon of the Bangor pontifical (that is, so much of it as that manuscript contains) has scarcely a variation which militates against the claim of the missal to be of Bangor use, whilst there are some remarkable points of agreement which may be taken to strengthen it. Of these the reader will himself be able to judge, by examining them as they are pointed out in the notes below.

English records. There are probably uncollated and neglected manuscripts in our public and cathedral libraries, which may some day decide without doubt what the Bangor use was. The whole question of the ancient English uses is one upon which little labour has been bestowed until very recently.[35]

A note in the handwriting of the age, at the end of the calendar, fixes the book to have belonged to a church in a part of the country where the use of Bangor was probably observed. It is as follows: "This booke was geuen to the hye alter of the paryshe churche of Oswestry by S[r].[36] Morys Griffith prist, To pray for all Christen soules, the yere of oure Lorde god a thowsande fyve hundred fyfty and foure." The book was in all likelihood removed from the church during the troubles of king Edward's time, was carefully preserved, and possibly for a

---

[35] There are unquestionably many imperfect manuscripts and printed editions of missals of various uses in our public libraries, which have been catalogued (and therefore neglected) under the very convenient title of Roman missal. The reprints in the last few years of the York and Hereford missals will probably lead to the discovery of other copies; and so we may hope also to discover even the lost Lincoln use, or assure ourselves of the Bangor.

A small fragment of Lincoln use, from a manuscript in the Bodleian, is printed at the end of the second volume of the York missal, published by the Surtees society. It contains only the offices for the first and second and third sundays in Advent, with those for the weekdays of the same time, and for the wednesday in ember week. The service is with very trivial variations, and excepting the epistles and gospels for one or two of the days, the same as in the Sarum missal. This fragment agrees equally and to the same extent with the missals of York and Hereford.

[36] *Sir* was a common title given in those days to priests and men of certain religious orders, from the Latin Dominus, which also being contracted into Domnus, became Dom or Dan. And hence *Dan Chaucer*, as he is styled by Spenser. This title after its serious use was lost became ludicrous; as, for example, *Dan Cupid*.

short time restored after queen Mary's accession. There was anciently at Oswestry a monastery, the church of which was made the parish church and is described by Leland in his *Itinerary*.[37]

If in the first edition of this arrangement of the ancient liturgies I trusted that it would not be an unacceptable book, I may now perhaps, after an interval of so many years, allow myself to believe that in some measure my hope has been fulfilled. The circumstances of the times in which we live seem to call for a more general knowledge of such subjects, especially among the clergy of the reformed church of England. Studies of this kind must not be looked upon as merely antiquarian, or even historical, but as of the highest importance in their relation to questions involving doctrine. That temper of mind we may trust is rapidly passing away in which English clergymen have feared to come in contact, as with unholy things, with the ancient liturgies and offices (which are indeed the monuments) of the English church. Men were long accustomed to speak slightingly, and with harsh words also, of holy prayers which for a thousand years rose through the aisles of our village equally with our cathedral churches, and of solemn rites by which devotion was not only quickened but directed to its proper end.

It may be said that the original editions of these books are of such extreme rarity as to be completely beyond the reach of all who have not access to public libraries. When therefore men, by one sweeping condemnation, contemptuously passed judgment upon the old services and worship of the church

---

[37] Leland says that the church of St. Oswald at Oswestry was sometime a monastery "caullid the white minster. After turned to a paroche chirch, and the personage impropriate to the abbay of Shreusbyri." *Itinerary*, vol. v. p. 37.

of England, they spoke of matters about which they knew absolutely nothing, and without the slightest discrimination included within one sentence both good and bad, essentials and non-essentials, trivial or sometimes even superstitious rites and holy ceremonies. Nor did they care to recollect that the common Prayer book now used in their church is founded upon and draws its origin from the very sources about which they did not hesitate to utter these opinions. Such a judgment may perhaps be popular, may be widely received, but is worth nothing.

I. Ordinarium Missae.

II. Canon.

Ordinarium Missae.

SARUM.	BANGOR.	EBOR.
Ad missam dicendam [1] *dum sa-*	*Ad missam dicendam executor*	*Quando presbyter lavat manus suas* [2]

---

[1] (*dicendam.* Sar.) The Church of Christ has always insisted upon a diligent preparation to be made by all her members before the reception of the holy communion: much more therefore should he who is about to celebrate offer up earnest petitions to the Almighty for His especial grace; confess his sins, and ask for pardon, and acknowledge his unworthiness. Anciently (independent of the exact confession which was to be made) the following prayer was appointed to be said:—

"¶ *Oratio dicenda ante missam.* Deus qui de indignis dignos, de peccatoribus justos, de immundis mundos facis : munda cor et corpus meum ab omni contagione et sorde peccati, et fac me dignum altaribus tuis ministrum, et concede propitius : ut in hoc altari ad quod indignus accedo, hostias acceptabiles offeram pietati tuæ pro peccatis et offensionibus meis, et innumeris quotidianisque excessibus; et pro omnibus hic circumstantibus, universisque mihi familiaritate et affinitate conjunctis, atque me odio aliquo insectantibus et adversantibus, cunctisque fidelibus Christianis vivis et mortuis : et per eum sit tibi meum votum atque sacrificium acceptabile : qui se tibi Deo Patri obtulit in sacrificium, Jesus Christus, Filius tuus, Dominus noster. Qui tecum vivit et regnat." *Missale Sarum.* edit. 1492. Some editions add (as all doubtless understand) "in unitate Spiritus sancti, Deus." Two or three other prayers are added, to be said at the option of the priest. The York missal has a very long prayer believed to have been written by St. Augustine.

It will be observed that the York use makes no mention of any vestments, and the Hereford speaks only of the amice and the alb. We must remember that though now they are lost, there were formerly numerous other volumes in which complete instructions were to be found for the due vesting of

Ordinarium Missae.

HERFORD.	ROM.
Ad introitum missæ post-quam sacerdos induerit se	*Sacerdos paratus*[3] *cum in-greditur ad altare, facta*

both the celebrant and his assistants : in the missal sometimes they were but alluded to, at other times omitted altogether. There cannot be a shadow of doubt that the full number of vestments was required by the order of the church of Hereford as well as by the church of Salisbury: and if one would argue from this rubric "postquam sacerdos induerit se amictum et albam" that the chasuble (for example) was not also necessary, he might as well attempt to prove from the York rubric that in that diocese the celebrant was not vested at all, and was simply to wash his hands. The following is a canon of an early council: "Nullus presbyter sine amictu, alba, et stola, et fanone, et casula ullatenus missam celebrare præsumat. Et hæc sacra vestimenta mundissima sint, et in nitido loco intra ecclesiam collocentur. Nec presbyter, cum his induitur, extra ecclesiam exeat : quia hoc lex divina prohibet." Regino Prumiensis, *De ecc. discip.* lib. i. p. 57.

[2] (*Lavat manus suas.* Ebor.) I cannot decide whether the ceremonial rite of washing the hands was peculiar to the church of York, as the other English uses omit any mention of it: nor, whether in that and in the church of Hereford the hymn *Veni Creator* and prayers were said at the putting on of the vestments. It is not probable that the washing would be omitted; an observance so universal and one which, although a mere ceremony, almost the light of nature would suggest. Euclio says (as cited by cardinal Bona) "Nunc lavabo ut rem divinam faciam." Apud Plautum, in *Aulularia*, iv. 2. The Christian church has observed it from the earliest ages. St. Paul possibly alludes to it in his epistle to Timothy: "I will therefore that men pray everywhere, lifting up holy hands;" ep. i. c. ii. This, we must remember, just after he has been speaking of the blessed eucharist. Tertullian asks: "Quæ ratio est, manibus quidem ablutis, spiritu

SARUM.	BANGOR.	EBOR.
cerdos induit se sacris vestibus dicat hymnum :	*officii cum suis ministris se induant.⁴ Dum induit*	*ante missam dicat hanc orationem :*

vero sordente orationem obire?" *de orat.* cap. xi. St. Augustine also : " Si erubescimus, ac timemus eucharistiam manibus sordidis tangere, plus timere debemus ipsam eucharistiam intus in anima polluta suscipere." *Ser.* 244.

The "Veni creator" and the prayer "Deus cui omne" or "Largire sensibus" were said in the sacristy before entering the church : from the first antiphon "Introibo" &c. to "Aufer a nobis" below the steps leading up to the altar.

³ (*Sacerdos paratus.* Rom.) "Sacerdos celebraturus missam, prævia confessione sacramentali, quando opus est, et saltem matutino cum laudibus absoluto, orationi aliquantulum vacet, et orationes pro temporis opportunitate dicat. Deinde accedit ad locum in sacristia, vel alibi præparatum, ubi paramenta, aliaque ad celebrationem necessaria habentur : accipit missale, perquirit missam, perlegit, et signacula ordinat ad ea quæ dicturus est. Postea lavat manus, dicens orationem : ' Da, Domine, virtutem manibus meis ad abstergendam omnem maculam : ut sine pollutione mentis et corporis valeam tibi servire.' "

The Roman missal can be procured by any one : I shall therefore refer the reader to it and recommend him to read carefully, if he wishes to understand the subject, the " Ritus servandus in celebratione missæ" at the beginning of the book.

⁴ "Et si episcopus celebraverit tres habeat diaconos et tres subdiaconos ad minus in omni festo ix. lec. et in omnibus dominicis quando ipse exequitur officium divinum. In die vero pentecostes et in die cœnæ, vij. diaconos habeat, et vij. subdiaconos et tres acolytos. In aliis vero duplicibus festis per annum quinque habeat diaconos tantum, et quinque subdiaconos, et tres acolytos. In die vero parasceves unum solum habeat diaconum." Rubr. *Miss. Bangor.*

⁵ (*Signat se signo crucis.* Rom.) "Ante omnem actum manus pingat crucem. S. Hieron. *epist.* 22. ad Eust. c. 16, et manu dextera, *ex Justino martyre ad orthod., resp. ad quæst.* 118, et manu plena, hoc est, quinque digitis ad quinque vulnera Christi significanda : Durand. lib. ii. cap. 46, sed tribus

HERFORD.	ROM.
amictum et albam: stans ante altare incipiat antiphonam:	*illi debita reverentia signat se signo crucis[b] a fronte ad pectus, et clara voce dicit:*

digitis signum crucis exprimendum esse, quia sub invocatione Trinitatis imprimitur, aiebat Innoc. III. lib. ii. cap. 45, et memorat Leo IV. *epist. ad episcopos:* ita ut manus a superiori descendat in inferius, et a dextera transeat ad sinistram: quia Christus de cœlo descendit in terram, et a Judæis transivit ad Gentiles. Quidam tamen, *subdit ille,* a sinistra producunt in dexteram, quia de miseria transire debemus ad gloriam, sicut et Christus de morte transivit ad vitam." Gavanti, *Thes. sac. rituum,* tom. i. p. 170. And so St. Ambrose has said; that we make the sign of the cross upon our forehead, that we may always be bold to confess: upon our breast, that we may remember to love: upon our arm, that we may be ready at all times to work.

Venerable Bede insists strongly upon the necessity of teaching the people to use this sign: he is writing to archbishop Egbert: "Eorum quoque, qui in populari adhuc vita continentur, sollicitam te necesse est curam gerere, ut..sufficientes eis doctores vitæ salutaris adhibere memineris, et hoc eos inter alia discere facias, quibus operibus maxime Deo placere, a quibus se debeant, qui Deo placere desiderant, abstinere peccatis,.. qua divinam clementiam supplicantes debeant devotione precari, quam frequenti diligentia signaculo se dominicæ crucis, suaque omnia adversum continuas immundorum spirituum insidias, necesse habeant munire," &c. Beda, *Op. hist. minora,* p. 221. The archbishop also himself thus writes in his penitential: "Dilecte mi, ego te hortor, ut cogites, &c...Cum mane primum surrexeris, signa te diligentissime, et Deo commenda." Thorpe, vol. 2. p. 227. Ælfric speaks of the sign as "the sign of the rood;" *Homilies,* p. 73.

The sign of the cross has been removed from the order for the Administration of the Lord's Supper, in the common Prayer book, since 1552. The proper use of the holy sign may well be defended upon many grounds, but not a superstitious or improper excess.

Speaking in another place upon this sign of the cross, Merati says in his additions to Gavantus, tom. ii. p. 108,

SARUM. BANGOR. EBOR.

se sacerdos vesti-
bus dicat hunc
hymnum:

VENI Creator spiritus : mentes tuorum visita : imple superna gratia, quæ tu creasti pectora, &c.

℣. Emitte spiritum tuum et crea-buntur.

℞. Et renovabis faciem terræ.

Oratio.

DEUS cui omne cor patet [7] et omnis voluntas loquitur, et quem nullum latet secretum : puri-fica per infusionem sancti Spiritus cogitationes cordis nostri : ut per-fecte te diligere et digne laudare mereamur. Per Christum.

Per Dominum. In unitate ejus-dem.

LARGIRE sensibus nostris omnipo-tens Pater : ut sicut hic abluun-tur inquinamenta manuum, ita a te mundentur pollu-tiones mentium, [6]

"Aliqui illud tribus digitis dextræ manus efformant sub in-vocatione sanctissimæ Trinitatis, alii vero duobus, ad duas Christi naturas et voluntates contra monophysitas et mono-thelitas indicandas."

[6] It frequently happened in large parishes or in cathedrals and churches of monasteries that more than one mass would be said at the same time. These would be of course at different altars, and very seldom would begin together. Un-less I am mistaken, there is no rubric in any English missal referring to this practice, but there is the following in an "Ordo missæ" printed at Rome in 1511 : "Postquam id [In nomine &c.] dixerit non debet advertere quemcunque in alio altari celebrantem etiam si sacramentum elevet ; sed continuate prosequi missam suam usque in finem." We can scarcely doubt that the same rule was observed according to the English uses after the Introibo.

[7] The Hereford and York liturgies did not admit this

I N nomine Patris, et Fi‧
lii, et Spiritus sancti.
Amen.[6]

---

prayer; neither at any time did the Roman. It is now used
at the beginning of the communion service of the reformed
church of England, immediately before the reading of the ten
commandments.

An early translation occurs on a blank leaf between two
treatises in English, forming part of a volume of religious
tracts which seems formerly to have belonged to the Car-
thusian monastery of Mount Grace in Yorkshire: the manuscript is of about the year 1420 :—

"God, vnto whome alle hertes bene opene, and vnto
whome alle wylle spekyth, and vnto whome no prive thing is
hyd, I beseche the for to clence the entent of myn herte w^t
the vnspekeable gift of the holy goste, that I may perfytely
loue the and worthyliche prayse the, and also haue the here
by grace and in heuene be joy euerlastynge. Amen." MS.
Harl. 2373. fol. 23.

⁸ (*Mentium.* Ebor.) My edition has, by a plain typo-
graphical error, *manuum.*

SARUM.	BANGOR.	EBOR.
		et crescat in nobis augmentum sanctarum virtutum. Per.[9]
Deinde sequatur antiph.		*An.*
INTROIBO[11] ad altare.		INTROIBO ad altare.
	Deinde seq.	
Ps. Judica me[12] Deus, et discerne.	*Ps.* Judica.	*Ps.* Judica me Deus, et discerne.

[9] The preceding prayers according to the uses of Sarum, Bangor, and York, having been said in the sacristy, the priest proceeded to the altar. I do not remember any direction as to whether his head should be covered or uncovered. Possibly in the mediæval church of England the earlier practice, observed almost everywhere throughout the west until the tenth century, was still the rule and the priest wore nothing on his head. For many centuries the Roman use has ordered the contrary, and so it is directed by the present rubrics: "Sacerdos omnibus paramentis indutus ... capite cooperto accedit ad altare ... cum pervenerit ad altare, stans ante illius infimum gradum, caput detegit, biretum ministro porrigit, et altari profunde inclinat."

[10] (*Junctis manibus.* Rom.) "In missa semper ita persistit, nisi quidpiam agendum impediat." Le Brun, *Explicatio missæ*, tom. i. p. 51.

[11] (*Introibo.* Sarum.) This antiphon at the beginning of the service was highly appropriate. Some writers have said that St. Ambrose alludes to it, as being used in his time in the church of Milan: but as others, Bona and Gavantus &c.,

HERFORD. ROM.

<table>
<tr><td></td><td>Deinde junctis manibus [10]
ante pectus, incipit antiph.</td></tr>
<tr><td>INTROIBO ad altare.</td><td>INTROIBO ad altare Dei.</td></tr>
<tr><td></td><td>Ministri ℟. Ad Deum qui lætificat juventutem meam.</td></tr>
<tr><td></td><td>Postea alternatim cum ministris dicit sequentem psalmum 42.</td></tr>
<tr><td>Ps. Judica me.</td><td>Judica me Deus.</td></tr>
</table>

have pointed out, that father in the place cited is not treating of the communion but of the newly-baptized, of baptism and confirmation. "His abluta plebs" (are his words) "dives insignibus ad Christi contendit altaria dicens, *Introibo*," &c. There is no doubt however that it was very anciently used in this place, for *Micrologus* says, cap. 23 : "paratus, sacerdos venit ad altare dicens antiphonam."

[12] (*Judica me.* Sar.) From almost the earliest ages of which records remain, we find evidence that the liturgy began with a psalm : but it was not universal; and for the four first centuries at least there was a variety of practice. It is not possible to decide what psalms in particular were appointed, or even whether in the first ages the later practice of a fixed psalm was observed. Durand says, lib. iv. cap. 7, that pope Cœlestin the first originally appointed this particular psalm. This would have been about the year 430. But it would seem from an old ordo Romanus that Cœlestin merely ratified the custom of saying *a* psalm. A French ritualist of little or no authority, Claude de Vert (of some considerable learning, but excessive prejudice towards many peculiar conceits of his

SARUM.	BANGOR.	EBOR.
Totus psalmus dicatur cum Gloria patri.	Gloria patri : sicut erat.	*Cum* Gloria patri.
Deinde dicitur ant.	*Ant.*	
INTROIBO ad altare Dei, ad Deum qui lætificat juventutem meam.	INTROIBO.	
KYRIE eleison. Christe eleison. Kyrie eleison.	KYRIE eleison. Christe eleison. Kyrie eleison.	KYRIE eleison. Christe eleison. Kyrie eleison.
PATER noster. Ave maria.	PATER noster.	PATER noster. Et ne nos. Ostende nobis domine. Sacerdotes tui induantur. Domine exaudi. Et clamor. Dominus vobiscum.

---

own), has laid it down that the custom of saying the psalm *Judica* is not older than the fourteenth century; in which he is confuted by innumerable witnesses to the contrary: and we may conclude that (though we cannot fix it either to the time of pope Cœlestin or of St. Ambrose, to whom also the institution of it has been attributed, yet) for more than five hundred years it had been so used in this part of the liturgy. The Mozarabic liturgy appoints the antiphon, but omits the psalm. The Roman liturgy follows the same rule in masses

HERFORD.	ROM.
Totus psalmus dicatur cum Gloria patri.	*Cum* Gloria patri.
Sequitur Antiphona.	*S. repetit antiphonam.*
INTROIBO ad altare Dei, ad Deum qui lætificat juventutem meam.	INTROIBO ad altare Dei. ℞. Ad Deum qui lætificat juventutem meam. *Signat se dicens* ℣. Adjutorium nostrum in nomine Domini. ℞. Qui fecit cœlum et terram.
KYRIE eleison. Christe eleison. Kyrie eleison.	
PATER noster. Et ne nos. Sed libera. Ostende nobis Domine misericordiam tuam. Et salutare tuum da nobis. Domine Deus virtutum converte nos. Et ostende faciem tuam et salvi erimus. Domine exaudi orationem meam. Et clamor meus ad te veniat. Dominus vobiscum. Et cum spiritu tuo. Oremus.	

for the dead, and during the days between passion sunday and easter eve: at which season the question would be out of place, "Quare tristis es, anima mea: et quare conturbas me?" But the antiphon is not omitted: which is said to be because though the signs of joy are not allowed at such times, yet the reason and the motive may nevertheless be spoken of: and therefore the priest may still say: "Introibo ad altare Dei, ad Deum qui lætificat juventutem meam."

SARUM.	BANGOR.	EBOR.

Oratio.

ACTIONES nostras quæsumus Domine, aspirando præveni, et adjuvando prosequere : ut cuncta nostra operatio et a te semper incipiat et per te cœpta finiatur. Per Dominum nostrum Jesum Christum, qui tecum.

AURES tuæ pietatis, mitissime Deus, inclina precibus meis et gratia sancti Spiritus illumina cor meum: ut tuis mysteriis digne ministrare, teque æterna caritate diligere, et sempiterna gaudia percipere merear. Per Christum.

His finitis et officio missæ inchoato cum post officium Gloria patri incipitur: accedat sacerdos cum suis ministris ad gradum altaris, et dicat ipse confessionem (capite inclinato, Bangor) diacono assistente a dextris, et

Sacerdos introiens ad altare et procedentibus in ordine ministris dicat:

HERFORD.   ROM.

Oratio.

ACTIONES nostras quæsumus Domine aspirando præveni, et adjuvando prosequere, ut cuncta nostra operatio et a te semper incipiat et per te cœpta finiatur. Per.

Tunc sacerdos stans ante gradum altaris dicat:

Deinde junctis manibus, profunde inclinatus facit confessionem:

SARUM.	BANGOR.	EBOR.

subdiacono a sinistris hoc modo in-
cipiendo:

ET ne nos. Sed libera. Confitemini Domino quoniam bonus.
Quoniam in sæculum misericordia
ejus.

Versus.

CONFITE-
MINI Do-
mino quoniam
bonus. Quoniam
in sæculum mise-
ricordia ejus.

Sacerdos dicat:

CONFITEOR [13] Deo, beatæ
Mariæ, omnibus sanctis, et vobis: (quia *Sar.*) peccavi nimis cogitatione, locutione, et opere mea culpa:
precor sanctam Mariam, omnes sanctos Dei,[14] et vos orare pro me.[16]

CONFITE-
OR ·Deo,
et beatæ Mariæ,
et omnibus sanc-
tis et vobis fra-
tres: quia ego

---

[13] "There or he tho messe bigynne,
Wil he meke him for his synne:
Till alle yo folk he shryues him thare,
Of alle her synnes lesse and mare:
So dos tho clerk a gayn to him,
Shryuen hom there of al hor syn.
And askes god forgyuenes,
Or thai bigynne to here tho mes."

The above is taken from a very curious and important manuscript in the museum library, MS. Bibl. Reg. 17. B. xvi. xvij,
consisting of long rubrics and prayers relating to the liturgy,
all in English verse.

In the second edition of this book I referred to this manuscript as the "Museum manuscript;" but the poem has lately
been printed for the early English text society; admirably
edited by the Rev. T. F. Simmons, canon of York, with an excellent introduction and an appendix of very valuable and
learned notes. Canon Simmons calls it "the Lay Folks
mass book:" and by that name I shall refer to the manuscript as we proceed.

[14] (*Precor omnes sanctos Dei.* Sar.) We know from the
sacred scriptures that the Almighty listens graciously to the

HERFORD.   ROM.

CONFITEMINI Do-
mino quoniam bonus.
Quoniam in sæculum mise-
ricordia ejus.

Tunc inclinet se ad altare
junctis manibus et dicat:
CONFITEOR, &c.

CONFITEOR Deo
omnipotenti, beatæ
Mariæ semper virgini, beato Michaeli archangelo,
beato Joanni baptistæ,
sanctis apostolis Petro et

prayers of His saints. In Genesis, Abimelech (we read) was told that if he restored his wife to Abraham the patriarch should pray for him, and he should live. "Now, therefore, restore the man his wife; for he is a prophet: and he shall pray for thee, and thou shalt live;" ch. xx. ver. 7. And again, in the 42nd chap. of Job, ver. 7, Eliphaz and his two friends, against whom the wrath of the Lord was kindled, are directed to "go to my servant Job,.. and my servant Job shall pray for you: for him will I accept."

In the most ancient offices we find forms of confession and absolution before the more solemn part of the liturgy: they are in the liturgy of St. James, which next to the Clementine is acknowledged as the oldest extant. The Gallican liturgy contains them, under another name, *Apologia;* and several forms are in the sacramentary of St. Gregory. The present form in the Roman missal, it will be observed, varies very materially from the Sarum and other English uses. It has been ascribed, that is, in its present state, to pope Damasus: but without any authority; as the best commentators allow. Archbishop Egbert alludes to the English form of confession in his penitential.

[15] Mediæval translations of the Confiteor and Misereatur

SARUM.	BANGOR.	EBOR.
		peccator peccavi nimis, corde, ore, opere, omissione, mea culpa. Ideo precor gloriosam Dei genetricem Mariam, et omnes sanctos Dei, et vos orare pro me.

Ministri respondeant.

MISEREATUR vestri omnipotens Deus, et dimittat vobis omnia peccata vestra, liberet vos ab omni malo, conservet et confirmet in bono, et ad vitam perducat æternam.
Sacerdos. Amen.   ℟. Amen.

MISEREATUR vestri omnipotens Deus: et dimittat vobis omnia peccata vestra: liberet vos ab omni malo, servet et confirmet in omni opere bono et perducat vos ad vitam æternam.

are rare : the following is written in a hand of about 1450 on the flyleaf of one of the prymers in the Bodleian (Douce MS. 246). This is printed also in the *Monumenta ritualia*, vol. 3. p. 304 :—

"I knowleche to god of heuene, and vnto the blessid marye, and vnto alle his halowes, and vnto thee, fadre, that I wreche synner haue synned to moche, in thinkyng, spekyng, delityng, consentynge, in siȝte, worde, and werk : blame, thoruȝ my greatest blame. Therefore I preye the, blessid virgyne

HERFORD.

ROM.

Paulo, omnibus sanctis, et vobis fratres : quia peccavi nimis cogitatione, verbo, et opere, *Percutit sibi pectus ter, dicens;* [16] mea culpa, mea culpa, mea maxima culpa. Ideo precor beatam Mariam semper virginem, beatum Michaelum archangelum, beatum Joannem baptistam, sanctos apostolos Petrum et Paulum, omnes sanctos, et vos fratres, orare pro me ad Dominum Deum nostrum.

Ministri ℞.

MISEREATUR.

MISEREATUR tui omnipotens Deus, et dimissis peccatis tuis, perducat te ad vitam æternam.

Sacerdos dicit, Amen, *et erigit se.*

---

marye, and alle the halowes of god, and thee, fadre, preye for me vnto god, that he haue mercy of me."

"Misereatur. The alle myȝty god haue mercy of thee, and forgeue to thee alle thy synnes: deliuere thee of alle yuele: saue and conferme thee in euery good werk: and lede thee to aylastyng lif. So mote it be. Amen."

[16] (*Percutit sibi.* Rom.) "Tunsio pectoris obtritio cordis." St. Augustine, enar. 2. in psal. 31.

SARUM.	BANGOR.	EBOR.

Et postea dicant:
CONFITE-OR.

Et postea:
CONFITE-OR.
ad sacerdotem:

Quo dicto, dicat sacerdos, Misereatur, *ut supra.*

tunc ministri respondeant:
Amen.

Deinde dicat sacerdos:

Deinde erectus signet se in facie dicendo absolutionem:

ABSOLUTIONEM[18] et remissionem omnium peccatorum vestrorum, spatium veræ penitentiæ, (et, *Sar.*) emendationem vitæ, gratiam et consolationem sancti Spiritus, tribuat vobis omnipotens et misericors Dominus.

Ministri respondeant, Amen.
Deinde (statim, Bangor) dicat sacerdos ℣.[19]

Amen.
Factaque ante gradus altaris confessione ascen-

---

[17] (*Tibi pater.* Rom.) This, even though a bishop or the pope himself be present. "Cum minister, et qui intersunt (etiam si ibi fuerit summus pontifex) respondent *Confiteor*, dicunt *tibi pater*, et, *te pater*, aliquantulum conversi ad celebrantem." *Ritus celebr. miss.* tit. iii. 9.

[18] The student may be reminded that this absolution was never at any time, from the very earliest age, regarded in the church of England as sacramental or as conveying remission of mortal sin. I would venture to refer him to a book which I published many years ago, upon the doctrine of absolution as now allowed to be held in the reformed English church, where he will find the whole matter very fully discussed. I

HERFORD.

ROM.

Deinde ministri repetunt confessionem: et ubi a sacerdote dicebatur, vobis fratres, *et,* vos fratres, *a ministris dicitur* tibi pater,[17] *et,* te pater.

Postea sacerdos junctis manibus facit absolutionem, dicens:

MISEREATUR vestri, &c.

Signat se signo crucis, dicens:

INDULGENTIAM, absolutionem, et remissionem peccatorum nostrorum, tribuat nobis omnipotens et misericors Dominus. ℞. Amen.

ABSOLUTIONEM.

His dictis ascendat gradum dicens:

Et inclinatus prosequitur:

---

would take this opportunity further to add, that upon the general question there considered I still believe the arguments to be correct. Most certainly they never were answered. I believe that every part of the doctrine of the Roman catholic church upon the sacrament of absolution, with the sole exception of its necessity, may—not as in the year 1848 *must,* but may—be taught in the reformed church of England.

[19] "*Et sciendum est quod quicunque sacerdos officium exequatur: semper episcopus si præsens fuerit ad gradum chori dicat:* Confiteor, Misereatur, *et* Absolutionem." Rubr. *Miss. Sar.*

SARUM.	BANGOR.	EBOR.

EBOR.

dat ad altare dicens:

ADJUTORIUM nostrum in nomine Domini. Qui fecit cœlum et terram. Sit nomen Domini benedictum. Ex hoc, nunc, et usque in sæculum. Oremus.

DEUS tu conversus vivificabis nos. Et plebs tua lætabitur in te. Ostende Domine, &c. Sacerdotes tui. Domine Deus virtutum. Domine exaudi orationem meam. Et clamor meus ad te veniat. Dominus vobiscum.

Deinde finitis precibus, sacerdos deosculetur[20] *diaconum et subdiaconum ita dicens:*

Deinde statim sacerdos deosculetur diaconum et postea subdiaconum dicens:

HABETE osculum pacis et dilectionis: ut apti sitis sacrosancto altari ad perficiendum officia divina.

sancto altaris Domini ministerio.

---

[20] This ceremony is peculiar in this place to the Sarum and Bangor churches: nor is it easy to say from whence it was introduced. We know that there was not an exact agreement as to the giving of the kiss in the ancient missals: having sprung from apostolic usage, it varied totally at last

HERFORD.   ROM.

℣. DEUS tu conversus vivificabis nos. ℟. Et plebs tua lætabitur in te. ℣. Ostende nobis Domine misericordiam tuam. ℟. Et salutare tuum da nobis.

Sacerdotes tui induantur justitia. Et sancti tui exultent. Ab occultis meis munda me Domine. Et ab alienis parce servo tuo. Sancta Dei genitrix virgo semper Maria. Intercede pro nobis. Domine Deus virtutum converte nos. Et ostende faciem. Domine exaudi orationem meam. Et clamor meus ad te veniat. Dominus vobiscum. Et cum spiritu.

℣. Domine exaudi orationem meam. ℟. Et clamor meus ad te veniat. ℣. Dominus vobiscum. ℟. Et cum spiritu tuo.

---

from its original design and was appointed to be given sometimes at one time, sometimes at another. The *Apostolical constitutions*, lib. ii. cap. 61, and St. Justin, *Apolog.* 2, attach it to the oblation, which immediately succeeded: so also the nineteenth canon of the council of Laodicea, A.D. 366.

SARUM.   BANGOR.   EBOR.

Et hoc semper observetur per totum annum: nisi tantum in missis pro defunctis et in tribus proximis feriis ante pascha. His itaque peractis: ceroferarii candelabra cum cereis ad gradum altaris dimittant: deinde accedat sacerdos ad altare, et dicat in medio altaris tacita voce inclinatoque corpore et junctis manibus:
Oremus.

Inclinatus ad altare dicat devote et submisse:

Oratio.

AUFER a nobis [21] (quæsumus, *Bangor*) Domine cunctas iniquitates nostras: ut ad sancta sanctorum puris mentibus mereamur (mereamur puris mentibus, *Bangor*) introire. Per Christum Dominum nostrum. (Amen. *Bangor*.)

AUFER a nobis Domine omnes iniquitates nostras, ut ad sancta sanctorum mereamur puris mentibus introire. Per Christum Dominum nostrum.

Tunc erigat se sacerdos et osculetur altare, et hoc in medio, et signet se in sua facie ita dicens:

IN nomine Patris et Filii et Spiritus sancti. Amen.

IN nomine Patris et Filii.

Erectus signet se:

[21] (*a nobis.* Sar.) There seems to be some doubt, say the ritualists, whether this prayer includes the people as well as the priest or whether the assistant deacon only is intended, who alone with the priest goes to the altar. The next prayer in the Roman use concludes in the singular number, "ut in-

HERFORD.　　　　　　　ROM.

Tunc inclinet se ad altare junctis manibus et dicat: Oremus.

Et extendens ac jungens manus, clara voce dicit, Oremus, *et ascendens ad altare, dicit secreto:*

AUFER a nobis Domine cunctas iniquitates nostras, ut ad sancta sanctorum puris mentibus servire mereamur et introire. Per Christum Dominum nostrum. Amen.

AUFER a nobis, quæsumus Domine, iniquitates nostras: ut ad sancta sanctorum puris mereamur mentibus introire. Per Christum Dominum nostrum. Amen.

Hic se erigendo osculetur altare.

Deinde manibus junctis super altare, inclinatus dicit:

ORAMUS te, Domine, per merita sanctorum tuorum, *Osculatur altare in medio,* quorum re-

---

dulgere digneris omnia peccata mea."

Le Brun says: "Si sedulo res perpendatur eum pro se tantum orare perspicitur: et multitudinis quidem numero tantum utitur, quod una cum ipso diaconus quoque ad altare ascendere debet;" tom. i. p. 68.

SARUM.   **BANGOR.**   **EBOR.**

Deinde ponat diaconus thus in thuri-
bulum et dicat prius sacerdoti:
Benedicite.   Benedicite.

---

[22] It was a common practice, as every reader of ecclesiastical history must know, for the primitive Christians to meet for the offering and service of the communion not only in any secret place but especially in those places where martyrs had suffered or where their remains were buried. Hence, after the persecutions ceased and leave was given that churches might openly be frequented, not unnaturally the first churches were built in places near or in which people had already been accustomed to assemble. And thus probably arose the very ancient and general custom that no church should be consecrated without relics of the martyrs. Cardinal Bona endeavours to prove that the rule is as early as before the council of Nice, and there can be no doubt that it is of high antiquity and soon passed into a law. For not to insist upon passages from St. Ambrose (epist. 54), from St. Jerome, and St. Augustine (which are appealed to by most writers upon the subject, and which unquestionably prove how widely the practice was spreading in their respective times), it was ordered by the seventh canon of the second council of Nice that no bishop should consecrate any church or altar on pain of deposition unless relics were placed under it: "ut qui ecclesiasticas traditiones transgressus est."

The Roman pontifical orders: "Sero ante diem dedicationis, pontifex parat reliquias, ponens eas in decenti et mundo vasculo, cum tribus granis thuris; sigillans ipsum vasculum diligenter," &c.

In the year 816, the second canon of the council of Chalcuith is "De modo consecrandi ecclesias:" and orders; "Postea eucharistia, quæ ab episcopo per idem ministerium consecratur, cum aliis reliquiis condatur in capsula, ac servetur in eadem basilica. Et si alias reliquias intimare non

HERFORD.　　　　　　　　ROM.

liquiæ [22] hic sunt, et omnium sanctorum : ut in-
dulgere digneris omnia peccata mea.　Amen.
In missa solemni, celebrans
antequam legat introitum,
benedicit incensum, dicens :

---

potest, tamen hoc maxime proficere potest quia corpus et
sanguis est Domini nostri Jesu Christi." Wilkins, *Concilia*,
tom. i. p. 169.　There is a reference in one of the canons of
a council at Oxford, A.D. 1222, to a custom which also pre-
vailed, viz. of placing corporals under altars : "vetera vero
corporalia quæ non fuerint idonea in altaribus, quando consecrantur, loco reliquiarum reponantur, vel in præsentia archidiaconi comburantur." Wilkins, tom. i. p. 587.　Upon this statute
Lyndwood says, " *Loco reliquiarum.*　Sine quibus altaria consecrari non debent." lib. iii. tit. 26.　But he goes on to say
that they are not of the substance of the consecration : " Unde
licet reliquiæ non sint de substantia consecrationis altaris, ubi
tamen non habentur reliquiæ, solent aliqui apponere corpus
Christi." This is according to the old decree above of the
council of Chalcuith.　But Lyndwood cites several authorities why such a practice was not to be allowed : " Non
decere corpus Domini recondi in altari." (Lyndwood does
not say this, but refers to Hostiensis, *In summa,* and I suppose
it to be the place intended.　See also Durant, *de rit.* lib. i.
cap. xxv.)　" Alia ratio est, quia corpus Christi est cibus
animæ : item, quia non debet servari, nisi ad opus infirmorum :
et non debet poni ad alium usum quam ad eum pro quo institutum est, nam debet comedi. . . Quod tamen corporale vel
ejus pars detur in consecratione altaris loco reliquiarum, non
videtur esse absurdum." From this gloss of Lyndwood, if any
argument could be wanted, we might learn how unfounded is the
remark which Johnson (*Eccles. laws,* vol. i. p. 816) makes upon
the canon of Chalcuith ; that in it " the eucharistic symbols are
set on a level with the relics of the saints, and scarce that
neither." He utterly mistook the object of the canon : which
is to be wondered at in a writer of so great a reputation.

SARUM.	BANGOR.	EBOR.

et sacerdos dicat: *sacerdos respon-*
                     deat.

DOMINUS. Ab ipso benedi-
     catur: in cujus honore cre-
mabitur.   In nomine Patris, &c.
Tunc diaconus ei thuribulum tradens
deosculetur manum ejus. Et ipse sa-
cerdos thurificet [23] *medium altaris, et*
utrumque cornu altaris. Deinde ab
ipso diacono ipse sacerdos thurificetur:
et postea textum ministerio subdia-
coni sacerdos deosculetur. His itaque
gestis in dextro cornu [24] *altaris cum*   *Et in dextro cor-*
diacono et subdiacono,   *nu altaris,*

---

[23] (*Thurificet.* Sar.) The use of incense in the public services of the church is of the most remote antiquity. Incense
was among the few offerings which were allowed to be made
at the altar to be there consumed, as appears from the second
of the apostolical canons. The object of burning incense
seems to be well expressed in the prayer which is found in
the liturgy of St. John Chrysostom, according to the translation in Goar's collection: " Incensum tibi offerimus Christe
Deus in odorem suavitatis spiritualis, quem suscipe Domine in
sanctum et supercœleste ac intellectuale tuum altare, et re-
pende nobis abundantes tuas miserationes, et illas largire
nobis servis tuis." Goar, *Rituale Græc.* p. 62.

[24] In examining the old uses the student, if he takes for
a guide the modern Roman books, will find much confusion
respecting the right and the left corner of the altar. In the
rubric above and in other places of the English liturgies

HERFORD.   ROM.

AB illo bene✠dicaris, in cujus honore cremaberis. Amen.
Et accepto thuribulo a diacono, incensat altare, nihil dicens. Postea diaconus recepto thuribulo a celebrante, incenset illum tantum.

Et tunc accedat ad dextrum cornu altaris et dicat:
ADJUTORIUM nostrum in nomine Domini. Qui fecit cœlum et terram. Sit nomen Domini benedictum. Ex hoc nunc et usque in sæculum.

---

the right means the Epistle side, and the left the Gospel side. The custom was the same in all the old Roman orders up to the end of the fifteenth century; taking it to be the right hand and the left of the officiating priest, as well as of those who were standing by. But in the year 1485 the Roman pontifical, published at Venice, laid down as a rule that the right hand and the left were to be taken from the crucifix upon the altar: by which new arrangement of course the old was entirely reversed. See on this subject especially Sala's notes to Bona, tom. iii. p. 49, and Le Brun, tom. i. p. 77, note. Thus the general rubric of the present Roman missal makes an explanation, which since the adoption of the new rule has been indispensable: "Accedit ad cornu ejus sinistrum, id est, epistolæ; ubi stans, incipit *Introitum*," &c. *Ritus celebr.* tit. iv. 2.

SARUM.	BANGOR.	EBOR.

Officium missæ [25] *usque ad orationem prosequatur: vel usque ad* Gloria in excelsis: *quando dicitur. Et post officium et psalmum repetatur officium: et postea dicitur* Gloria patri et sicut erat. *Tertio repetatur officium: sequatur Kyrie.* [27]

dicat officium. [26] *Et postea incenset altare. Repetatur officium et postea dicitur* Gloria Patri. Sicut erat. *Deinde repetatur of-*

---

[25] " When thou thi crede thus has done,
    Upon thi fete thou stande up sone:
    For bi this tyme als I gesse,
    Tho prist begynnes office of messe:
    Or ellis he standes turnande his boke,
    At tho south auter noke." *Layfolks mass book.*

The museum manuscript reads " When thou thi crede thus has done;" but two others collated by canon Simmons properly read " thy confiteor."

[26] (*Officium.* Ebor.) More commonly called in later years the introit, " Introitus :" as in the Roman use. In the Milan or Ambrosian missal it is called *Ingressa.* For an account of its first institution and other particulars the student should consult Bona, tom. ii. p. 48, and Gerbert, *de musica*, tom. i. p. 100. These introits, as is well known, were retained in the first revised liturgy of king Edward the sixth. They kept their old name of *Introit* long after the real reason why they were so called had ceased ; namely, because they were sung at the entrance or approach of the priest to the altar. Upon which point all the old writers agree. See Micrologus, cap. i, Rupert. *de divinis off.* cap. 28, Raban. cap. 23. It was to the introit that the tropes were added, when they were introduced : " Tropus proprie est quidam versiculus, qui in præcipuis festivitatibus cantatur immediate ante introitum, quasi quoddam præambulum, et continuatio ipsius introitus." Durand, lib. iv. cap. 5.

There is a curious account in the *Concilia* of a royal charter being sealed and confirmed in the presence of the king (Henry the second) at this part of the mass ; tom. i. p. 429.

[27] (*Sequatur Kyrie.* Sar.) " Post repetitionem officii principalis rector chori officium missæ a cantore quærere debet :

HERFORD.	ROM.
Deinde incipiatur officium missæ:	*Deinde celebrans signans se signo crucis incipit introi-*
Repetatur officium et Gloria patri. Sicut erat.	*tum: Quo finito, junctis manibus alternatim cum ministris dicit:*
Tertio repetatur officium:	**K**YRIE eleïson. Kyrie eleïson. Kyrie eleï-

deinde illud socio suo intimare: et postea simul incipere, et similiter kyrie: sequentia: offertorium: sanctus: agnus: et communio quærantur, intimentur, et incipiantur." Rubr. *Miss. Sar.*

In this rubric we have two officers of the choir mentioned; the cantor, and the rector chori. There seems to have been two of the last named: who probably answer to the precentor and succentor of St. Isidore: " Cantor vocatur, quia vocem modulatur in cantu. Hujus duo genera dicuntur in arte musica; præcentor et succentor: præcentor scilicet, qui vocem præmittit in cantu, succentor autem qui subsequenter canendo respondet." Apud Gratian. dist. xxi. c. 1. If there were two of these, they stood each at the end of his own side of the choir, and having received the necessary information from the cantor who, as we shall see, stood in the centre, passed it on to his companions: Amalarius speaks of one præcentor as opposed to the succentores: " Præcentor in primo ordine finit responsorium. Succentores vero eodem modo respondent. Dein præcentor canit versum," &c. *De ord. antiph.* cap. 18; *Bibl. patrum auct.* tom. i. p. 527.

The name "rector chori" appears to have been if not peculiar to England yet chiefly adopted in her churches. Ducange cites but one authority for it, from a Sarum breviary; and explains it to be the same as "cantor:" in which I cannot but believe him to be in error, though I speak with hesitation against so great an authority. But the rubric at the head of this note seems to put the matter beyond a doubt: and I shall add to it the following account of the duties of the cantor. First, from the statutes of archbishop Lanfranc, cap. v; with which agrees almost in word a statute of Evesham monastery, Dugdale, *Monast.* vol. ii. p. 39: " *De cantore.*

SARUM.	BANGOR.	EBOR.
		ficium: Kyrie eleyson *iij.*[28] Christe eleyson *iij.* Kyrie eleyson *iij.*

Quicunque lecturus aut cantaturus est aliquid, si necesse habet ab eo priusquam incipiat debet auscultare. . . Si quis obliviosus non incœperit, cum incipere debet responsorium, aut antiphonam, aut aliud hujusmodi, ipse debet esse provisus, atque paratus, ut sine mora, quod incipiendum erat, incipiat, vel eum, qui fallendo deviaverat, in viam reducat: ad ipsius arbitrium cantus incipitur, elevatur, remittitur; nulli licet cantum levare, nisi ipse prius incipiat. . . Cantor vero, in medio eorum debet esse in choro: . . et in dextro choro semper sit." Lanfranc, *Opera*, p. 279. Again from the manuscript consuetudinary of Sarum, early in the thirteenth century: "Cantoris officium est chorum in cantuum elevatione et depressione regere vel per se, vel per succentorem suum, et in omni duplici festo lectiones legendas canonicis præsentibus injungere, cantores, lectores, et ministros altaris in tabula ordinare. . . Præterea in majoribus duplicibus festis tenetur interesse regimini chori ad missam cum cæteris rectoribus chori. Præterea in omni duplici festo rectores chori de cantibus injungendis et incipiendis tenetur instruere." The same rule is given in a Lichfield consuetudinary of 1294, printed by Wilkins, *Concilia*, tom. i. p. 498.

The cantor was in this sense the same as the præcentor, properly so called; and not (as I have suggested above) as Isidore uses the word, for a rector chori: so that there might be more than one precentor, as we find in an epistle of Hincmar, cited by Ducange, *verb.* præcentor: "præcentores, qui chorum utrinque regunt, sunt duces," &c. But the precentor strictly was "primus cantorum in ecclesia; qui cantoribus præest." The bishop of Salisbury is precentor (or "chaunter" as the old puritan author of "the life of the seventy archbishopp of Canterbury" calls him; sign. D. ij: but the chronicle of Gervase, speaking of the council of 1175, says, "ad sinistram [primatis] sedit episcopus Wintoniensis, quia

HERFORD.

dicto officio sequitur, Kyrie eleyson. Christe eleyson. Kyrie eleyson. *iij.*

ROM.

son. Christe eleïson. Christe eleïson. Christe eleïson. Kyrie eleïson. Kyrie eleïson. Kyrie eleïson.

---

cantoris officio præcellit;" *Script. X.* p. 1429) of the college of bishops : according to Lyndwood : "Habet namque archiepiscopus Cantuariensis in collegio episcoporum episcopos, *Londinensem* decanum . . *Sarisburiensem* præcentorem ;" lib. v. tit. 15, Eternæ, *verb.* tanquam. Compare also lib. ii. tit. 3, *verb.* usum Sarum. It has been supposed that this distinction arose from the fame of the Salisbury use, and of bishop Osmund. Thomas archbishop of York, A.D. 1100, is said to have first appointed a precentor in that cathedral ; Collier, *Eccl. hist.* vol. i. p. 281.

A curious collection of signals by which the cantor made known his will to the choir are given by Gerbert, from some foreign monastic statutes. These are all to be made by various movements of the hand and fingers. *De musica sacra*, tom. i. p. 310, note a.

[28] (*Kyrie eleison. iij.* Ebor.) It appears from the sixth chapter of the eighth book of the *Apostolical constitutions* (quoted by Le Brun, vol. i. p. 80) that the prayer "Kyrie eleison" was used by the faithful in behalf of the catechumens, "that God would be pleased to illumine them with the light of His gospel, and fill them with the grace of His holy Spirit." This prayer of course occurred before the dismissal of the catechumens and the beginning of the solemn part, the canon.

In the ritualists (vide especially Durant) many reasons may be found, some sufficiently fanciful, why these Kyrie were retained in the Greek and not translated into Latin. I shall give the observation of cardinal Bona upon the point : "Dicunt Latini in missa *Kyrie eleison* Græce, dicunt etiam Hebraice *Amen, Allelujah, Sabaoth,* et *Osanna :* quia fortassis sic ab initio ecclesiasticarum precum institutores voces istas usurparunt, ut ostenderent unam esse ecclesiam, quæ ex Hebrais et Græcis primum, deinde ex Latinis coadunata est :

SARUM. BANGOR. EBOR.

His finitis et offi-
cio missæ inchoa-
to, cum post of-
ficium, Gloria
Patri, incipitur:
tunc accedant mi-
nistri ad altare
ordinatim: primo
ceroferarii duo
pariter inceden-
tes; deinde thuri-

---

vel quia mysteria nostræ fidei tribus hisce linguis ab apostolis et evangelistis, eorumque immediatis successoribus conscripta fuerunt : quæ quidem linguæ in titulo crucis quodammodo consecratæ sunt. Sed quæcumque fuerit causa hujus institutionis, certissimum est eam antiquissimam esse." Tom. iii. p. 73.

Sala in his additions offers three reasons for the repetition of the Kyrie nine times : " Novem vicibus hanc precationem repetimus, contra triplicem miseriam ignorantiæ, culpæ, et pœnæ ; vel, ut tres personas in se mutuo inexistere significetur, ac propterea in iis proprietas, et in essentia unitas, et in majestate adoretur æqualitas, et ad imitationem cantus angelorum, qui in novem ordinum choros distincti sunt ; vel, ut contra novem genera peccatorum divina imploretur misericordia, scilicet originale, veniale mortale : cogitationis, locutionis, et operis : fragilitatis per impotentiam, simplicitatis per ignorantiam, malignitatis per invidentiam, hoc est peccatum in Patrem, peccatum in Filium, et peccatum in Spiritum sanctum."

Upon certain festivals these Kyrie were appointed in the English church to be sung with several verses added to the original words. As, for example, upon the double feasts was to be sung either "Kyrie rex genitor;" or, "Kyrie fons bonitatis;" or, "Kyrie omnipotens pater," or two or three others, at the choice of the precentor. Upon the feast of the epiphany was appointed always, "Kyrie fons bonitatis." Upon St. Michael's day "Kyrie rex splendens," which also

HERFORD.   ROM.

---

was appointed for St. Dunstan's day, who is said to have
heard it sung by angels in a dream.   Below are two of these
Kyrie.

I.

Kyrie, rex genitor ingenite vera essentia, eleyson.
Kyrie, luminis fons, rerumque conditor, eleyson.
Kyrie, qui nos tuæ imaginis signasti specie, eleyson.
Christe, Dei forma humana particeps, eleyson.
Christe, lux oriens, per quem sunt omnia, eleyson.
Christe, quia perfecta es sapientia, eleyson.
Kyrie, spiritus vivifice, vitæ vis, eleyson.
Kyrie, utriusque vapor, in quo cuncta, eleyson.
Kyrie expurgator scelerum, et largitor gratiæ, quæsumus
    propter nostras offensas noli nos relinquere, O consolator
    dolentis animæ, eleyson.

2.

Kyrie, omnipotens pater ingenite nobis miseris, eleyson.
Kyrie, qui proprio plasma tuum filio redemisti, eleyson.
Kyrie, adonai nostra dele crimina plebique tuo, eleyson.
Christe, splendor gloriæ, patrisque figura substantiæ, eleyson.
Christe, patris qui mundum præcepto salvasti nobis, eleyson.
Christe, salus hominum vitaque æterna angelorum, eleyson.
Kyrie, spiritus paraclite largitor veniæ nobis, eleyson.
Kyrie fons misericordiæ septiformis gratiæ, eleyson.
Kyrie, indultor piissime procedens ab utroque, chrismatum
    dator largissime, doctor vivifice, clemens, eleyson.

D

SARUM.	BANGOR.	EBOR.

bularii: post, sub-
diaconus: exinde
diaconus, post eum
sacerdos: diacono
et subdiacono ca-
sulis indutis.[29]
Quo facto sacer-
dos et sui minis-
tri in sedibus pa-

---

[29] The rubric goes on into the following particulars: " Scilicet quotidie per adventum : et a septuagesima usque ad cœnam Domini quando de temporali dicitur missa : nisi in vigiliis et quatuor temporibus : manus tamen ad modum sacerdotis non habentibus : cæteris vero ministris, scilicet ceroferariis, thuribulario et acolyto in albis cum amictibus existentibus. In aliis vero temporibus anni quando de temporali dicitur missa, et in festis sanctorum totius anni, utantur diaconus et subdiaconus dalmaticis et tunicis : nisi in vigiliis et quatuor temporibus : et nisi in vigiliis paschæ et penthecostes : et nativitatis Domini si in dominica contigerit, et excepto jejunio quatuor temporum quod celebratur in ebdomada penthecostes :—tunc dalmaticis et tunicis indui debent. In die parasceves et in rogationibus ad missam jejunii et processionibus et in missis dominicalibus et sanctorum quæ in cappis dicuntur, tunc enim albis cum amictibus utantur, ita tamen quod in tempore pasch. de quocunque dicitur missa, nisi in inventione sanctæ crucis utantur ministri vestimentis albis ad missam. Similiter fiat in festo annuntiationis beatæ Mariæ : et in conceptione ejusdem : et in utroque festo sancti Michaelis : et in festo sancti Johannis apostoli in ebdomada nativitatis Domini : et per oct. et in oct. assumptionis et nativitatis beatæ Mariæ : et in commemorationibus ejusdem per totum annum : et per oct. et in oct. dedicationis ecclesiæ. Rubeis vero utantur vestimentis omnibus dominicis per annum extra tempus paschæ quando de dominica agitur : et in quarta feria in capite jejunii : et in cœna Domini, et in utroque festo sanctæ crucis, in quolibet festo martyrum, apostolorum, et evangelistarum extra tempus paschæ. In

HERFORD.   ROM.

Postea in medio altaris extendens et jungens manus caputque aliquantulum inclinans dicit, si dicendum est,[30] Gloria in excelsis Deo.

omnibus autem festis unius confessoris vel plurimorum confessorum utantur vestimentis crocei coloris."

[30] "*Gloria in excelsis* dicitur quandocunque in matutino dictus est hymnus *Te Deum*, præterquam in missa feriæ quintæ in cœna Domini, et sabbati sancti, in quibus *Gloria in excelsis* dicitur, quamvis in officio non sit dictum *Te Deum*. In missis votivis non dicitur, etiam tempore paschali, vel infra octavas, nisi in missa beatæ Mariæ in sabbato, et angelorum : et nisi missa votiva solemniter dicenda sit pro re gravi, vel pro publica ecclesiæ causa, dummodo non dicatur missa cum paramentis violaceis. Neque dicitur in missis defunctorum." *Rubr. generales miss.* tit. viij. 3, 4.

Very anciently, and indeed it has been supposed up to the year 1000, only bishops were permitted to say this hymn, except on easter-day when priests also were allowed. Walafrid Strabo, cap. 22, says, "statutum est, ut ipse hymnus in summis festivitatibus a solis episcopis usurparetur, quod etiam in capite libri sacramentorum designatum videtur." Cardinal Bona, tom. iii. p. 85, cites a very early missal, now in the Vatican, with this regulation (which Strabo appears to mean) at the beginning : "Dicitur *Gloria in excelsis Deo* si episcopus fuerit, tantummodo die dominico, sive diebus festis. A presbyteris autem minime dicitur, nisi in solo pascha." An old anonymous writer, in a book called *Speculum ecclesiæ,* says that this hymn was sung only once in the year, on the day of the Nativity: and further, that in the first service it was sung in Latin, in the second in Greek. Benedict XIV, *Opera,* tom. ix. p. 81.

SARUM.	BANGOR.	EBOR.

ratis se recipiant, et expectent usque ad Gloria in excelsis: *quod incipiatur semper in medio altaris quandocunque dicitur.*[31]

In medio altaris erectis manibus incipiat Gloria in excelsis Deo.

G LORIA in excelsis Deo.[32]   Et in terra pax hominibus bonæ voluntatis.   Laudamus te, Bene-

---

[31]   "On hegh festis, or on haly dayes,
     When-so men outher synges or sayes
     Gloria in excelsis in hor mes,
     Saie thou then als here wryten es.
     Joy be vnto god in heuen,
     With alkyns myrthe, that men may neuen;
     And pese in erth alle men vntille,
     That rightwis are and of gode wille," &c.
                Layfolks mass book.

[32]   This, as is well known, is called the angelical hymn, from the first few words having been sung by the angels at the nativity of our Redeemer. By whom the remainder was added is the subject of much dispute. Some ascribe it to Telesphorus, bishop of Rome about A.D. 130; Innocent, *De mysteriis*, c. 20. Alcuin, *De div. off.* cap. xl, gives it to Hilary of Poictiers, and with him agree Hugo, *de div. off.* cap. xj, and the author of the *Gemma animæ*, lib. i. 87: but against these (and others who may be mentioned) Bona observes that St. Athanasius, a contemporary of Hilary, speaks of the hymn with its additions as well known in his own time. The fathers of one of the councils (iv. Tolet. can. 12) could not err when they cautiously observed, "reliqua quæ sequuntur post verba angelorum, ecclesiasticos doctores composuisse." This hymn is called by the Greeks the great doxology; and is said by them at their morning prayer. In many manuscripts of the Latin church, especially in the most ancient, it is added to the end of the psalter with the Apostles'

HERFORD.   ROM.

                 Et prosequitur junctis ma-
                 nibus. *Cum dicit* Adora-
                 mus te, Gratias agimus tibi
                 et Jesu Christe, *et* Suscipe
Quo dicto eat sacerdos ad   deprecationem, *inclinat ca-*
medium altaris: et elevando   *put: et in fine dicens*, Cum
manus suas dicat. Gloria   sancto Spiritu, *signat se a*
in excelsis Deo.   *fronte ad pectus.*

G LORIA in excelsis Deo.   Et in terra pax hominibus bonæ voluntatis.   Laudamus te, Bene-

---

and the Athanasian creeds, under the title " Hymnus ma-
tutinus."

The Salisbury, Bangor, and Hereford missals add several
interpolations which were appointed to be said at certain
festivals of the blessed Virgin or services in her chapel. They
begin after the " Domine fili unigenite Jesu Christe," and
continue thus : " *Spiritus et alme orphanorum Paraclyte.*...
Filius Patris. *Primogenitus Mariæ virginis matris.* Qui
tollis ... deprecationem nostram. *Ad Mariæ gloriam.*... tu
solus sanctus. *Mariam sanctificans.* Tu solus dominus. *Mariam gubernans.* Tu solus altissimus. *Mariam coronans,*" &c.
The rubric is (after sundry directions for other times) " nisi
quando, &c.... tunc enim dicitur sequens cantus cum sua
farsura, videlicet in choro. Et etiam dicitur cum sua prosa
in quotidianis missis in capella beatæ Mariæ omni sabbato.... In omnibus aliis missis quando dicendum est : dicitur sine prosa." *Rubr. Sar.* Although Clichtoveus in his
Elucidation (p. 137) says that these interpolations were appointed " secundum ecclesiæ catholicæ ritum," it is highly
probable that they were local introductions which by degrees crept into more general observance. Two examples are
given by Pamelius of other similar additions made to this most
glorious hymn ; *Liturg.* tom. xi.

" Gloria in excelsis " (says the old author of the *Gemma
animæ*) " solus sacerdos incipit, et chorus simul concinit : quia
et solus angelus hoc incepit, et militia cœlestis exercitus simul
concinit." Cap. 93.

SARUM.   BANGOR.   EBOR.

dicimus te, Adoramus te, Glorificamus te. Gratias agimus tibi propter magnam gloriam tuam.[33] Domine Deus, Rex cœlestis, Deus Pater omnipotens. Domine Fili unigenite Jesu Christe. Domine Deus, agnus Dei, Filius Patris. Qui tollis peccata mundi, miserere nobis. Qui tollis peccata mundi, suscipe deprecationem nostram. Qui sedes ad dexteram Patris, miserere nobis. Quoniam tu solus sanctus, Tu solus Dominus, Tu solus altissimus, Jesu Christe, Cum sancto Spiritu, in gloria Dei Patris, Amen.[34]

His itaque peractis, factoque signaculo crucis in facie sua, vertat se sacerdos ad populum, elevatisque aliquantulum brachiis junctisque manibus dicat:

Postea conversus sacerdos ad populum dicat:

Walafrid Strabo who suggests Telesphorus as the author of this hymn, and adds (as already quoted) " statutum ab eo, ut ipse hymnus in capite missæ diceretur et in summis festivitatibus a solis episcopis usurparetur," further observes, "quamvis ille hymnus interdum ante missas diceretur, non fuisse tamen, quod jugiter in omnibus missis ab omnibus sacerdotibus ante lectiones poneretur antequam Celestinus antiphonas ad introitum dicendas instituit." See also Mabillon, *Mus. Ital.* tom. ii. p. 17. But by the time when Micrologus wrote, in the eleventh century, the practice had become general for priests to say the hymn as well as bishops. He further gives the reason, namely, that when the Te Deum was to be said at matins the Gloria was to be said at mass; *De ecc. observ.* cap. 46. This is the present rule, according to an order made by pope Pius the fifth.

[33] (*Propter magnam gloriam tuam.*) " 'Gratias agimus tibi propter magnam *gloriam* tuam.' Magnæ Dei gloriæ, potius quam gratiarum actio, procul dubio honor, obsequium, reverentia, ac prostratio debetur: dicendum igitur, quod ibi *Gloriam* usurpetur pro eo attributo, in quo Deus ipse summe gloriatur, scilicet pro ejus misericordia, quæ erga nos exercita semper in ipsius Dei miserentis vertitur gloriam; sæpenumero etiam in sacris scripturis gloria pro misericordia accipitur,

HERFORD.   ROM.

dicimus te, Adoramus te, Glorificamus te. Gratias agimus tibi propter magnam gloriam tuam. Domine Deus, Rex cœlestis, Deus Pater omnipotens. Domine Fili unigenite Jesu Christe. Domine Deus, agnus Dei, Filius Patris. Qui tollis peccata mundi, miserere nobis. Qui tollis peccata mundi, suscipe deprecationem nostram. Qui sedes ad dexteram Patris, miserere nobis. Quoniam tu solus sanctus, Tu solus Dominus, Tu solus altissimus, Jesu Christe, Cum sancto Spiritu, in gloria Dei Patris, Amen.

His itaque peractis, facto-   *Deinde osculatur altare in*
que signaculo crucis in facie   *medio, et versus ad popu-*
sua vertat se sacerdos ad   *lum, dicit,* ℣.
populum elevatisque ali-
quantulum brachiis junctis

---

sicut ex verbis apostoli, ad Romanos, c. 3. *Omnes enim peccaverunt, et egent gloria Dei*, id est, Dei misericordia." Cavalieri, *Opera*, tom. v. p. 20.

[34] " ¶ Post inceptionem *Gloria in excelsis* divertat se sacerdos ad dexterum cornu altaris, et ministri cum eo prosequentes: diaconus a dexteris et subdiaconus a sinistris submissa voce dicant idem.

" ¶ Notandum est quod omnes clerici stare tenentur ad missam nisi dum lectio epistolæ legitur, et graduale, et alleluya, vel tractus cantatur. In duplicibus tamen festis stare tenentur omnes dum a choro alleluya canitur. Pueri vero semper sunt stantes ad missam choro canente. . . . Et notandum est quod omnes clerici conversi ad altare stare tenentur dum ad missam *Gloria in excelsis* inchoatur: quousque chorus cantet. Et in eodem hymno ad hæc verba *Adoramus te* et ad hæc verba *Suscipe deprecationem nostram* et in fine ejusdem cum dicitur, *Jesu Christe cum sancto Spiritu in gloria Dei*, usque ad epistolam. In fine vero grad. vel. tr. vel allel. vel sequentiæ, chorus ad altare se inclinet antequam ad lectorem evangelii se vertat: et ad *Gloria tibi Domine* semper ad altare se vertat lector evangelii, et etiam omnes clerici signo crucis se signent." *Rubr. Miss. Sar.*

SARUM.	BANGOR.	EBOR.

Dominus vobiscum.
Et chorus respondeat:

Et cum spiritu tuo.
Et iterum revertat sacerdos ad altare et dicat:

Oremus.

Deinde dicitur oratio,[36] *sic determinando.*
Per omnia sæcula sæculorum.
Et si aliqua memoria habenda est, iterum dicat sacerdos, Oremus,

Dominus vobiscum.

Et cum spiritu tuo.

Oremus.

Tunc omnes orationes quæ sequuntur.

Dominus vobiscum.

Cum collecta. Nota quod una dicitur propter unitatis sacramentum: et tres exemplo Domini qui ter ante passionem orasse legitur: quinque propter

---

[35] "*Vel, si sit episcopus,* Pax vobis." *Ritus celebr. miss.* tit. v. I.

[36] Or collect, as it is called in the York use. Another ancient name was "benedictio;" as Amalarius says, "Episcopus dicit *Oremus,* ac deinde sequitur benedictio. Utroque nomine benedictionis et orationis vocatur oratio sacerdotis." *De ecc. offic.* lib. 3. cap. ix. Walafrid Strabo explains the meaning of the name collect: "Orationes, quas collectas dicimus, quia necessarias earum petitiones compendiosa brevitate colligimus;" cap. 22.

There has been much controversy on the question by whom and at what time these short and distinct prayers were first added to the liturgy. More than one writer has claimed for

HERFORD.   ROM.

et manibus disjungens eas dicat:

D OMINUS vobis-cum.

D OMINUS vobis-cum.[35]

℞.

E T cum spiritu tuo.

Tunc jungat manus ut prius et revertat se ad altare et iterum disjungendo eas dicat:

Postea dicit,

O REMUS.[37]

O REMUS.

Tunc omnes orationes quæ sequuntur sub uno Per Dominum *et sub uno* Oremus, *dicantur.*

Et orationes, unam aut plures, ut ordo officii postulat.

---

some of them an apostolic authority: but they offer us no proof. A number of those still in use which may be found in the sacramentaries of Gelasius and Gregory are probably of far higher antiquity than their time, and some others may possibly be attributed to one of those popes as the author.

[37] (*Oremus.*) "Numquid ubi audieritis sacerdotem Dei ad ejus altare populum hortantem ad orandum, non respondebitis, Amen?" St. August. *Epist.* 106, ad Vitalem. "In iis horrendissimis mysteriis communia sunt omnia: omnes eandem dicimus, et non sicut in veteri lege partem sacerdos, et partem populus, sed omnibus unum corpus proponitur, et unum poculum." St. Chrysost. *Homil.* 10, in 2 epist. ad Corinthios. See also Durant, *de ritibus ecclesiæ*, lib. ii. cap. 16.

SARUM.	BANGOR.	EBOR.
ut supra. Et quando sunt plures collectæ dicendæ:[38] *tunc omnes orationes quæ sequuntur sub uno* Per Dominum[39] *et uno* Oremus *dicantur: ita tamen quod septenarium numerum excedere non debent.*[40]		*quinque partitam Domini passionem: septem, ad impetrandum septem dona sancti Spiritus: quem numerum nemo excedere ulla ratione permittitur.*[41]

---

[38] (*Plures collectæ dicendæ.* Sar.) "Sacræ synodi approbatione salubriter duximus statuendum, ut per diœcesim nostram in celebratione missarum, præterquam in festis duplicibus, dicantur quinque collectæ: una de pace ecclesiæ, scilicet 'Ecclesiæ tuæ, quas (*sic*, quæsumus?) Domine preces' &c., alia pro domino nostro rege, et regina et eorum filiis, scilicet, 'Deus, in cujus manu corda sunt regum.'" Concil. provinc. Scoticanum, Wilkins, *Concilia*, tom. i. p. 617.

[39] The last words of the conclusion rest upon the authority of St. Jude, who so ends his epistle; and are used in the primitive liturgies of St. James, St. Basil, St. Chrysostom, and the Clementine.

[40] (*non debent.* Sar.) "Notandum quod in omnibus dominicis et in festis cum regimine chori, per totum annum, hoc generaliter observetur, ut ad missam tot dicantur collectæ, quot dicebantur ad matutinas: nisi in die nativitatis Domini. Ita tamen quod ad missam impar numerus ipsarum collectarum semper custodiatur. Nam si duæ vel quatuor orationes habentur: tunc erit tertia vel quinta oratio de omnibus sanctis: scilicet: *Concede, quæsumus omnipotens Deus: ut intercessio,* per totum annum tam per adventum quam in paschali tempore." *Rubr. Miss. Sar.*

The number three, five, or seven, to one of which the number of collects was limited, was symbolical also of the earnest desire of the Church for unity, which is expressed by an uneven number. Anciently only one collect was said, whence

HERFORD. ROM.

*Ita tamen quod septenarum
numerum excedere non de-
bet.*

---

probably the name of it; because in one prayer many were
collected together: in the Gelasian sacramentary the number
is usually three. Afterwards an excess happened in the other
direction, and a rule was made that they should not be more
than seven. See Martene, *de ant. ecc. ritibus*, lib. i. cap. 4,
who quotes Belethus and Durand. The author of the *Gemma
animæ* says: "qui hunc numerum supergressus fuerit, ut
cæcus errabit." Cap. 116.

[41] " Ut evidens habeatur et plena cognitio qualiter orationes
quas collectas vocamus terminandæ sunt: prius notandum
est quod in eis quandoque dirigitur sermo ad Patrem: quandoque ad Filium: quandoque ad Spiritum sanctum: quandoque ad totam Trinitatem. Sed quando ad Patrem, iterum
considerandum est utrum ita dirigatur sermo ad Patrem quod
fiat mentio de Filio et Spiritu sancto vel non. ¶ Et si in
oratione quæ ad Patrem dirigitur, fiat mentio de Filio, refert
an fiat ante finalem partem an in ipso fine: et secundum has
diversitates narrabitur finis. Si vero dirigitur sermo ad Patrem
absque mentione Filii et Spiritus sancti sic finietur: '*Per
Dominum nostrum Jesum Christum Filium tuum: Qui tecum
vivit et regnat in unitate Spiritus sancti Deus. Per omnia
sæc. sæculorum.*' Si vero de Spiritu sancto fiat mentio dicetur:
'*In unitate ejusdem Spiritus sancti Deus.*' Si vero de Filio
fiat mentio ante finalem partem dicetur: '*Per eundem Dominum nostrum Jesum Christum Filium.*' Si vero in fine
fit mentio de Filio, dicetur: '*Qui tecum vivit et regnat.*' Si

SARUM.	BANGOR.	EBOR.

Et semper dum stat sacerdos ad offi-cium missæ: post eum stet diaconus directe in proximo gradu, et sub-diaconus simili modo directe in se-cundo gradu post diaconum: ita ut quoties sacerdos ad populum se con-vertit, diaconus similiter se convertat. Subdiaconus vero interim genuflec-tendo de capsula sacerdotis aptanda subministret.[42]   *Sciendum est autem quod quidquid a sacerdote dicitur ante epistolam in dextro cornu altaris expleatur: præter inceptionem* Gloria

---

autem ad Filium dirigitur oratio sine mentione Spiritus sancti, dicetur: '*Qui vivis et regnas cum Deo Patre, in unitate Spiritus sancti Deus.*'   Si fiat mentio de Spiritu sancto dicetur: '*Qui cum Patre et eodem Spiritu sancto vivis et regnas.*' Item orationes ad Patrem in quibus mentionem de Trinitate faci-mus, sic concludimus: '*In qua vivis et regnas.*'   Illas autem quas ad ipsam Trinitatem dirigimus, sic finimus.   '*Qui vivis et regnas Deus.*'   ¶ Secundum autem Romanam ecclesiam nullam orationem cum '*Per eum qui venturus est judicare,*' concludimus, nisi quando fit exorcismus, in quo diabolum per divinum judicium ut a creatura Dei recedat exorcizamus. Nam in aliis orationibus quas cum *Per Dominum* concludimus, Patrem ut per amorem Filii nobis subveniat imploramus.   In exorcismis autem diabolum per Dei judicium ut aufugiat increpamus: in quo judicio scit se diabolus potentissime damnandum: cujus timore judicii concutitur." *Rubr. Miss. Ebor.*

It is remarkable that this long and important note occurs in the York use, which is distinguished rather by the fewness and shortness of its rubrics.   It gives also examples from various collects of each conclusion, according to the rules laid down.   The *Rubricæ generales miss. Rom.*, tit. ix. 17, have a short notice on the subject which should be consulted.   The points involved are of no small consequence, and concern the

HERFORD.   ROM.

*Et semper dum stat sacer-
dos ad officium missæ: post
eum stet diaconus directe in
primo gradu: et subdia-
conus similiter in secundo
gradu. Ita ut quotiescum-
que sacerdos ad populum
convertit se, diaconus similiter convertat se, subdiaconus vero interim genu-
flectendo de casula aptanda
subministret.*

---

highest doctrines of the Faith. It has been asserted that in
the first four centuries all the prayers at celebration of the
eucharist were addressed solely to God the Father: "ut in
altari semper ad Patrem dirigatur oratio" are certainly the
words of the third council of Carthage, canon 23. Florus
Lugdunensis says, this was because the Christians feared lest
the doctrine of the undivided Trinity might be misunderstood,
and give countenance to the dreadful error of more gods than
One God.

I shall make a short extract from cardinal Bona: "Ad
solum Patrem omnes fere collectæ directæ sunt, paucæ ad
Filium, nulla ad Spiritum sanctum: non quia is donum est,
et a dono donum non petitur, ut nonnulli cum Durando in
suo rationali philosophantur; sed quia missa repræsentatio
est ejus oblationis, qua Christus se Patri obtulit, ac propterea
ad ipsum Patrem liturgicæ precationes diriguntur." Tom. iij.
p. 105. The place in Durand is lib. iv. cap. 15.

[42] (*Subministret.* Sar.) "Et si episcopus celebraverit, omnes
diaconi in gradu diaconorum consistant, principali diacono
medium locum inter eos obtinente. Simili modo in gradu
subdiaconi se habeant: cæteris omnibus diaconis et subdiaconis gestum principalis diaconi et principalis subdiaconi
imitantibus: excepto quod principalis subdiaconus sacerdoti
ad populum convertenti solus subministret." *Rubr. Sar.*

, SARUM.	BANGOR.	EBOR.

in excelsis. *Similiter fiat post per-*
ceptionem sacramenti. Cætera omnia
in medio altaris expleantur: nisi
forte diaconus defuerit. Post introi-
tum vero missæ unus ceroferariorum
panem, vinum [43] *et aquam quæ ad*

---

[43] *Vide* " De defectibus in celebr. missarum occurrentibus"
in the Roman missal, tit. iij, iv. The English church from
the earliest ages reiterated her injunctions as to the care
which is necessary to be observed in providing proper elements
for the holy eucharist. Take, for example: "Sacerdotes Dei
diligenter semper procurent, ut panis et vinum et aqua, sine
quibus nequaquam missæ celebrantur, pura et munda fiant;
quia si aliter agatur, cum his qui acetum cum felle mixtum
Domino optulerunt, nisi vera pœnitentia subvenerit, punien-
tur." This from archbishop Egbert's excerptions (100th),
A.D. 750; Thorpe, *Anglo-saxon laws*, ii. 111. About thirty
years later, the tenth canon of the council of Chalcuith is
headed " ut in missa ... crusta panis non admittatur:" directing, "Oblationes quoque fidelium tales fiant, ut panis sit,
non crusta." Wilkins, *Concilia*, tom. i. p. 147. It would be
almost endless work to quote from the canons of councils
and synods in the seven centuries succeeding. But two examples may be cited: one, from a council at London in 1246:
"celebret sacerdos cum pane ex tritico purissimo." *Concil.*
tom. i. p. 688. Another, in 1287, at Exeter: "Provideant
igitur sacerdotes, quod oblatas habeant confectas de simula
frumenti, et aqua duntaxat: ita quod nihil immisceatur fer-
menti. Sint et oblatæ integre candidæ et rotundæ; nec per
tantum tempus custodiantur, quod in sapore vel aspectu
abominabiles habeantur." *Ibid.* tom. ii. p. 132. I shall only
add further a rule among those which archbishop Lanfranc
drew up for the order of St. Benedict, showing the excess of
care which anciently was taken in this matter: "Ea autem
die, qua hostiæ fieri debent, secretarius et fratres, qui eum
juvare debent, antequam incipiant, manus et facies lavent,
albis induantur, capita amictibus velent, præter eum, qui

HERFORD.   ROM.

---

ferra tenturus, et inde serviturus est. Horum unus super
tabulam mundissimam ipsam farinam aqua conspergat, et
manibus fortiter compingat, et maceret, frater, qui ferra, in
quibus coquuntur, tenet, manus chirothecis habeat involutas.
Interim dum ipsæ hostiæ fiunt et coquuntur, dicant iidem
fratres psalmos familiares horarum, et horas canonicas, et de
psalterio ex ordine quod tantumdem valeat, si ita potius
voluerint." *Opera*, p. 280.

There was no less care taken always with the wine than
with the bread. One quotation must now suffice; from the
constitutions of a synod of the diocese of Sodor and Man,
A.D. 1350: "Summopere præcaventes ne vinum cum quo
celebratur sit corruptum, vel in acetum commutatum, et quod
potius sit rubrum, quam album. In albo tamen bene conficitur sacrum, et non de aceto, cum in aceto mutantur omnes
substantiales vires, et vinum vim amisit. Et aqua in tam
modica quantitate apponatur, ut non vinum ab aqua, sed
aqua a vino absorbeatur." The practice now of the Roman
catholic church is to consecrate white wine, but the reformed
English church uses red wine for her communions. Either
red or white wine may be used: all which is required being
that it should be of the pure juice of the grape. As the
Pupilla says, "materia necessaria calicis est vinum de vite,
id est, non vinum artificiale seu de alio fructu compressum.
Nec refert an sit album an rubeum, spissum vel tenue, dum
tamen sit verum vinum quoad effectum sacramenti; quamvis
vinum rubeum sit præeligendum propter expressionem et
similitudinem sanguinis." Cap. 3. Wine (says the author
just previously) is of necessity "quia sanguis Christi de alia
materia quam de vino vitis confici non potest." The canon
just quoted goes on to speak of the host: "Hostia de

SARUM.   BANGOR.   EBOR.

eucharistiæ ministrationem disponun-
tur, deferat: reliquus vero pelvim

---

frumento sit rotunda et integra, et sine macula: quia agnus extitit sine macula, et os non fuit comminutum ex eo. Unde versus:

> Candida, triticea, tenuis, non magna, rotunda,
> Expers fermenti, non mista sit hostia Christi,
> Inscribatur, aqua non cocta sed igne sit assa."
> <div align="right">Wilkins, <i>Concilia</i>, tom. iii. p. 11.</div>

It is of the highest consequence, affecting the integrity of the sacrament, that the bread should be of wheat and not of almonds or chestnuts or the such-like. But whether it be leavened or not is a subject to be decided by the authority of the Church. The rule is well laid down by the old English canonist just referred to: "Debet panis consecrandus esse azymus, id est, sine fermento, in signum quod Christus fuit sine fermento malitiæ. Unde sacerdos scienter consecrans panem fermentatum, quamvis conficeret, tamen graviter peccaret." *Pupilla oculi*, cap. 3.

Every priest therefore must follow the appointed order: otherwise it will be sufficient, provided only that the bread be of wheat and the wine of the juice of the grape. "Quæ sit species vini parum refert; modo revera sit vinum de vite." Van Espen, pars ii. sect. i. tit. 4. Let us add to all this the judgment of St. Anselm: "Quoniam multæ sunt diversitates, quæ non in substantia sacramenti, neque in virtute ejus, aut fide discordant, neque omnes in unam consuetudinem colligi possunt: æstimo eas potius in pace concorditer tolerandas, quam discorditer cum scandalo damnandas. Habemus enim a sanctis patribus, quia si unitas servatur charitatis in fide catholica, nihil officit consuetudo diversa." These are memorable words: but not less so are those by which they are preceded: "Utique si per universam ecclesiam uno modo et concorditer celebrarentur (i. e. sacramenta ecclesiæ) bonum esset et laudabile." *Opera*, p. 139. Compare also p. 135: "Et azymum et fermentatum sacrificans, sacrificat. Et cum legitur de Domino, quando corpus suum de pane fecit; quia accepit panem et benedixit; non additur, azimum, vel fermentatum."

Occasionally, and possibly not seldom in some of the English colonies at least, a great latitude seems to be allowed in the Anglican communion with regard to the elements of the sacrament of the blessed Eucharist. Two instances may be quoted: and the only remark which I would presume to make on them is, that the one would rely by way of support on the supposed necessity of avoiding all risk of the sin of drunkenness, and that the other appears to have been prompted by an excess of devotion. But neither the one reason nor the other would have been allowed for an instant by the canons of the mediæval English church.

At Tahiti, four or five years ago, a party of English people went to the church of England service there: I say the English church service on the authority of the author, though not stated in the book from which I quote. After the christenings "there was a hymn ... followed by administration of the sacrament, in which cocoa-nut milk took the place of wine, and bread-fruit that of bread. The proper elements were originally used, but experience proved that although the bread went round pretty well, the cup was almost invariably emptied by the first two or three communicants, sometimes with unfortunate results." *Voyage of the Sunbeam*, p. 234.

Dr. Hobhouse, the bishop of Nelson in New Zealand, sent home about the year 1860 the following account of a visit which he made to a dying native: "I came purposely to administer the holy communion; but I looked round in vain for the means—there was no wine nor any bread, but I could not go away without an endeavour to show the 'Lord's death' in some way as near to the Lord's own appointed way as circumstances permitted. I therefore made vessels of the beautiful mussel-shells which abound on the sea-beach, filling one with water and laying on the other a piece of travelling biscuit softened with water, and in this way I proceeded to celebrate the holy Sacrament of the Body and Blood of our sacrificed

E

SARUM.   BANGOR.   EBOR.

cum aqua et manutergio portet. Cho-
rum licet ingredi usque ad completo-
rium primæ collectæ.
Incepta vero ultima oratione ante   *Dum   legitur* [44]
epistolam: subdiaconus per medium   Epistola,[46]
chori ad legendum Epistolam *in pul-*

Saviour, not doubting but earnestly believing that he was pleased to grant to that truthful partaker as full a share in all the benefits of his passion as if a cathedral had been over our heads and golden vessels on the altar."

[44] (*Dum legitur epistola.* Ebor.) "Lectio dicitur, quia non cantatur ut psalmus vel hymnus, sed legitur tantum. Illic enim modulatio, hic sola pronuntiatio quæritur." Amalarius, lib. iii. cap. 11. This is important, as showing that whatever the later practice in a few places might have been it was not then the custom to sing the epistle; in fact in some churches it was even forbidden.

Compare also Rabanus Maurus: "Tunc lector legit lectionem canonicam." *De institut. cleric.* lib. i. cap. 33.

[46] In old manuscripts this was called *Apostolus*, because commonly taken from one of the apostolical epistles. "Quando epistola trahitur e S. Paulo, communiter incipit per verbum *fratres*, quia hic apostolus frequenter illa expressione utebatur; quando autem ex epistolis canonicis, per verba *fratres charissimi*, eo quod sancti Petrus, Joannes et Judas sæpe illis utantur." Romsée, tom. 4. p. 117. The first words when the epistle is taken from the old testament were usually "In diebus illis."

The custom of sitting to hear the epistle read is very ancient. Rupert the abbot, writing in the eleventh century, says, "Morale legis officium agit epistola, tantum distans ab eo, quod in officio missæ præcedit sancto evangelio, quantum servus a domino, præco a judice, legatus ab eo qui misit illum. Quapropter cum legitur, non injuria sedemus: cum autem sanctum evangelium audimus, demissis reverenter aspectibus sicut Domino nostro assistimus." *De div. off.* lib. i. cap. 32.

I take the following from the valuable publication of the *Rites of the church of Durham:* "When the monkes went to say or sing the high mass, they put on their vestments in the

HERFORD.　　　　　　　　ROM.

Deinde legatur Epistola :　*sequitur* Epistola,⁴⁵
super lectrinum ⁴⁶ *a sub-*
*diacono ad gradum chori,*⁴⁷

---

vestrye, both the epistoler and the gospeller. They were
always revest in the same place, and when the office of the
masse began to be sung the epistoler came out of the revestrie
and the other two monkes following him, all three arow, and
there did stand untill the *Gloria Patri* of the office of the
masse began to be sunge, and then, with great reverence and
devotion, they went all up to the high altar... The epistoler,
when he had sung the epistle, did lay by the booke againe
on the altar, and after, when the gospell was sunge, the
gospeller did lay it downe on the altar untill the masse was
done." p. 7.

⁴⁶ (*Lectrinum.* Herf.) "Epistola inscribitur *lectio*, quia
initio quidem tantummodo elata voce sine cantu legebatur,
locusque in quo legebatur, *lectrinum, lectricium, lectorium,
legeolum*, dictum fuit a verbo *legere*." Le Brun, tom. i. p. 99.
This is the same as that of which the false Ingulphus speaks
when relating his dream : "erat enim sancti Andreæ apostoli
vigilia ; et in suo cursu medium iter tunc fere peregerat, cum
post multa precum dictamina tandem dicti sancti apostoli
lecta passione victoriosa, somno subito obrepente, super lectrinum, quod ante stabat, in latus alterum reclinabar." *Hist.
Croylandensis*, p. 75.

⁴⁷ "Et evangelium a diacono super superiorem gradum
converso ad partem borealem. Et gr. et alleluya cum suis
versibus super lectrinum in medio chori. Quod in omnibus
dominicis et festis ix. lec. et iij. lec., commemorationibus, et
feriis observetur per totum annum. Exceptis festis princi-
palibus dupl. et semidupl. Et exceptis dominica in ramis
palmarum, vigilia paschæ et pentecostes : quia in illis diebus
omnia ista in pulpito legantur." *Rubr. Miss. Herf.* The
"lectrinum in medio chori" was probably used also for the
lections at the canonical hours.

⁴⁸ "Dictis orationibus, celebrans positis super librum vel

SARUM.　　　　　BANGOR.　　　　　EBOR.

pitum[49] *accedat. Et legatur epistola*
in pulpito omni die dominica, et quan-
documque chorus regitur per totum
annum: et in die cœnæ et in vigilia
paschæ et penthe. et in com. anima-
rum. In omnibus vero aliis festis et
feriis, et in vigiliis, et in quatuor
temporibus extra ebd. penthe. ad gra-
dum chori legatur tam in quadra-
gesima quam extra quadragesimam.

Iterum vero veni-
ant duo cerofera-
rii cum cæteris
obviam acolyto
ad ostium presby-
terii, ad locum
administrationis

---

super altare manibus, ita ut palmæ librum tangant vel (ut
placuerit) librum tenens, legit *epistolam*, intelligibili voce ...
et similiter stans eodem modo, prosequitur *graduale, alleluya,*
et *tractum,* ac *sequentiam,* si dicenda sint." *Ritus celebr.*
missam, tit. vj. 1.

[49] " Solebant autem antiquitus tam epistola quam evangelium
legi in ambone seu pulpito." Bona, tom. iii. 127. Still it
appears that a difference was observed in the reading of the
two. Thus the one was read upon a lower step; as we see
in the next note was the order of the church of Hereford, and
according to the old "Expositio missæ," *Bibl. patr. auct.*
tom. i. p. 1171 : "Subdiaconus qui lecturus est, mox ut
viderit post pontificem presbyteros residentes, ascendit in
ambonem ut legat. Non tamen in superiorem gradum, quem
solus solet ascendere qui evangelium lecturus est."

There was certainly also a great distinction in many
churches between the place for saying the epistle and gospel
of the service of the holy eucharist, and the lessons of the
other offices. For example, at Durham: "At the north
end of the high altar there was a goodly fine letteron of

HERFORD.   ROM.

et Evangelium *a diacono
super superiorem gradum
converso ad partem borea-
lem: et* Gradale *et* Alleluya *cum suis versibus super lectrinum in medio
chori.*

---

brasse, where they sung the epistle and the gospell, with a
gilt pellican on the height of it, finely gilded, pullinge hir
bloud out hir breast to hir young ones, and winges spread
abroade, whereon did lye the book that they did sing the
epistle and the gosple.... Also ther was lowe downe in the
quere another lettorn of brasse, not so curiously wroughte,
standing in the midst against the stalls, a marveilous faire
one, with an eagle on the height of it, and hir winges spread
a broad, whereon the monkes did lay theire bookes when
they sung theire legends at mattins or at other times of
service." *Rites of the church of Durham*, p. 11.

In some churches there were two flights of steps, the one
used by the reader of the epistle, the other by the reader of
the gospel. The 33rd canon of the council of Trullo cited by
Bona, and by Gerbert, tom. i. 321, &c., condemns a custom
which at one time was again prevailing of laymen taking upon
them the office of reader and ascending the pulpit. The
Ethiopic missal directs the epistle to be read with a loud
voice: "*Postea magna voce dicit epistolam;*" edit. 1550,
sign. G. 3.

SARUM.	BANGOR.	EBOR.

*prædictæ deferen-
te offertorio et cor-
poralibus*[50] *ipsi
calici superposi-
tis: est autem
acolytus in alba
et mentello serico
ad hoc parato, ca-
lice itaque in eo
debito deposito cor-
poralia ipse aco-
lytus super altare
solemniter depo-
nat: itaque altare
in recessu deoscu-
letur, quo facto
ceroferarii cande-
labra cum cereis*

---

[50] (*Et corporalibus.* Bangor.) "Corporale, super quo sacra oblatio immolatur, ex mundissimo et purissimo linteo sit; nec in eo alterius generis materia pretiosior aut vilior misceatur: quia dominicum corpus in sepulcro, non in holosericis, sed tantum in sindone munda fuit involutum. Corporale nunquam super altare remaneat: sed, aut in sacramentorum libro ponatur, aut cum calice et patena in mundissimo loco recondatur. Et quando abluitur a sacerdote, diacono, vel subdiacono, primo in loco et vase ad hoc præparato abluatur, eo quod ex dominico corpore et sanguine infectum sit. Post hæc a lavandario in nitido loco paretur." Regino Prumiensis, lib. 1. p. 51, Ex concilio Remensi. Lyndwood agrees with this: "Corporalia non debent fieri ex serico, sed solum ex panno lineo puro terreno ab episcopo consecrato. Nec debet confici neque benedici *corporale* de panno misso in confectione farinæ, vel alterius rei ad hoc, quod stet rigidum super calicem. . . . Et erit candidum atque mundum, quia significat sindonem in qua Corpus Christi fuit involutum." Lib.

---

iii. tit. 23, Linteamina. Immediately after the corporals follow *pallæ*, which Lyndwood explains to be "vestimenta altaris, sc. sindones et corporalia, quæ quia quadrangulæ sunt, ideo dicuntur *pallæ:* a quodam muliebri pallio quadrangulo." See also Ducange, *verb.* Corporale ; and the authorities which he cites.

Among the churchwardens' accounts of the parish of St. Michael, York, in the year 1521 is an item, "P^d for a pair of mosfits for to wase the corporase." Nichols, p. 309. The editor in a note supposes these *mosfits* to be *mosticks*, which are said in the dictionaries to be the steadying-rods used by painters; and that such sticks or rods were used in the old fashion of washing by what was called *bucking*, and in the *bucking tub.* As the charge occurs amongst parish accounts we may conclude that, whatever the mosfits mean, special attention was paid at that time to the washing of the corporals.

SARUM.	BANGOR.	EBOR.

ad gradum alta-
ris dimittant.

Quando epistola legitur [51] *duo pueri*
in superpelliciis facta inclinatione ad
altare ante gradum chori in pulpi-
tum per medium chori ad Gradale [52]   *et canitur* Gra-
incipiendum se præparent, et suum   dale,
versum cantandum. Dum versus
gradalis canitur duo de superiori
gradu ad Alleluya [53] *cantandum cap-*
pas sericas se induant. Et ad pul-
pitum per medium chori accedant.
Sequatur Alleluya. *Finito* Alleluya,   *et* Alleluya *vel*
sequatur Sequentia. [54]   Tractus [55] *vel*
                              Tropus [56] *sedeat*
                              cum ministris

---

[51] "Episcopus tribus horis missæ sedet, scilicet dum epistola legitur, dum graduale, et alleluya canitur : quia Christus
tribus diebus inter doctores sedisse legitur in templo." *Gemma
animæ,* cap. xij.

[52] (*Graduale.* Sar. &c.) This was a verse or response
which varied with the day, and was so called not, as some
have supposed, from the steps of the altar but of the pulpit
or ambo upon which it was sung. Cassander, from an old
exposition of an ordo Romanus, has put this beyond a doubt :
"Responsorium, quod ad missam dicitur, pro distinctione
aliorum graduale vocatur, quia hoc psallitur in gradibus, cætera vero ubicunque voluerit clerus." *Opera,* p. 44. Durand
says : "Dicitur graduale, vel gradale, a gradibus scilicet humilitatis. Significans ascensus nostros a virtute in virtutem.…
pertinet ad opera activæ vitæ, ut notetur nos operibus respondere eis quæ in lectione audivimus : scilicet prædicationem."
Lib. iv. cap. 19. Some authors suppose (see Cavalierus, tom.
v. cap. x. 13, and Bellarmine, *Controv.* lib. vj. 70) that the
gradual, whose first author is said to have been pope Celes-
tine, was appointed "ne illud tempus, quo diaconus ab
altari recedens, et in suggestum ascendens in silentio ela-

HERFORD.   ROM.

Deo gratias.

Finita epistola dicatur Gra-   Graduale,
dale *cum suo versu :*

et Alleluya *vel* Tractus *se-* Tractus *vel* Alleluia *cum*
cundum quod tempus exigit. Versu *aut* Sequentia *ut*
                         tempus postulat.

---

beretur." This seems a very likely origin, and serves also to account for its name.

[53] (*Alleluya.* Sar. &c.) I need scarcely say that this as well as the tract, sequence, &c. not only varied but was often omitted. There is an order in the penitential of archbishop Theodore which is important, as regards this : "Laicus in ecclesia juxta altare non debet lectionem recitare ad missam, nec in pulpito Alleluia cantare, sed psalmos tantum aut responsoria, sine Alleluia." Thorpe, *Ancient laws and institutes,* vol. ii. p. 58. In the eighth century, the second council of Cloveshoo in its twenty-seventh canon gave some allowance to the same effect. *Vide* Wilkins, *Concilia,* tom. i. p. 99. Gerbert, *de musica,* should be especially consulted ; tom. i. p. 56.

[54] (*Sequentia.* Sar.) Ducange says, " Canticum exultationis, quæ et *Prosa* dicitur :" and there seems to be no doubt that, at least anciently, these terms were applied to the same thing. Compare Bona, tom. iii. p. 141, and Georgius, *Lit. Rom. pontif.* tom. 2. ccvij. They, as also the tropes, were introduced about the tenth century, and in many churches vast numbers were used, so that in some liturgies

SARUM.	BANGOR.	EBOR.

In fine alleluia, vel sequentiæ, vel
tractus diaconus [57] *antequam accedat*   *usque*

---

even every day had its proper sequence. It does not appear
that they were in such excess at any time in the church of
England. The most common opinion as to their author or
rather first introducer of them (for as time went on they had
many authors) is, that the earliest was composed by Notker
abbot of St. Gall in the diocese of Constance, about A.D. 900.
There have not been wanting writers who have not hesitated,
though without a shadow of authority, to attribute to them so
great an antiquity as the age of Gelasius and St. Gregory.
At the revision of the Roman liturgy in the sixteenth century
all the sequences were removed, except four: three are,
Victimæ paschali, at easter; *Veni sancte Spiritus,* at whit-
suntide: and *Lauda Sion salvatorem,* upon Corpus Christi
day. The fourth which was retained is the very famous
Dies iræ, dies illa, in the missa defunctorum. Strictly speaking this last is improperly called a sequence; because in the
office for the dead there ought not to be, neither is there, any
hymn peculiarly of joy. It may very rightly be called a
Prose, a name given as I have said to the sequences, because
though written in a species of rhythm they are not limited by
any of the common rules of metre. I may add, these sequences are said to have been so called because they followed
the epistle. I must again refer the reader to the dissertation
on service books, *Monumenta rit.* vol. i: and if he wishes to
examine the subject fully, he will find an admirable treatise
upon it in Georgius, tom. 2. ccv, &c.

[55] (*Tractus.* Ebor.) "Cantus ecclesiastici species." Ducange. Durand says, "Dicitur tractus a trahendo: quia
tractim et cum asperitate vocum, et prolixitate verborum
canitur." Lib. iv. cap. 21. It was opposed to the Alleluia:
the one being for the seasons of joy and triumph, the other
of sorrow and abasement. Almost all the ritualists agree with
Durand and the earlier writers from whom he derived his
authorities, as to the origin of the name: Merati adds in his
note to Gavantus: "vere dicitur a trahendo: quia revera
continuata serie modulationis unius cantoris non interrupta
responsionibus aliorum intercinentium peragebatur. Hoc

HERFORD.	ROM.
His finitis diaconus ante-quam procedat ad pronunti-	*His finitis diaconus deponit librum evangeliorum super*

autem est discrimen inter responsorium et tractum, quod primo chorus respondet, tractui vero nemo. Tractus totus dicebatur ab uno solo cantore, qui erat diversus ab illo, qui cantabat graduale, sive responsorium." Tom. 1. p. 93.

The custom of saying some response, either gradual or tract or sequence, after the epistle seems to be as old at least as the time of St. Augustine. He says, "Apostolum audivimus, psalmum audivimus, evangelium audivimus." *Serm.* 8. But it would appear that then an entire psalm was sung, a remnant of which ancient practice was preserved in the Salisbury, York, Hereford, and Bangor missals, upon the first sunday in Lent and on Passion sunday. Probably the new mode of a verse or two only became general about the end of the fifth century: because Leo the great speaks of the whole psalm (A.D. 450), but in the sacramentary of St. Gregory (A.D. 600) the shorter gradual or response is found. See Romsée, *Opera*, tom. iv. p. 121.

[56] (*Tropus.* Ebor.) "Est quidam versiculus, qui præcipuis festivitatibus cantatur; et continet tria, videlicet antiphonam, versum, et gloriam. Ita Durandus, *Ration.* lib. iv. c. 5, qui hæc subdit lib. vi. c. 114. Hi autem versus tropi vocantur, quasi laudes ad antiphonas convertibiles: Τρόπος enim Græce, conversio dicitur Latine." Ducange, *Gloss.* It is not easy to say what is meant by the use of the term *trope* in this place; possibly the sequence is intended, for the true tropi were attached to the introit. Even so used they were of late introduction, and did not obtain universal acceptance. No example of one has occurred before the eleventh century. Certainly the monastic uses were more full of them than the diocesan; and we find prayers with such interpolations in some of their missals: in one sense the addition to the *Gloria in excelsis* (of which I have already spoken) may be called a trope. In such a way, the trope here spoken of may be an addition to the tract or sequence. See more upon this in the dissertation upon service books, *verb.* Troparium, *Monumenta ritualia*, vol. i.

[57] (*Diaconus.* Sar.) "Antiquitus etiam evangelium lege-

SARUM.	BANGOR.	EBOR.
ad evangelium pronuntiandum thuri-ficet medium altaris tantum. Nun-quam enim thurificetur lectrinum ante pronuntiationem evangelii.		*ad evangelium le-gendum.*

batur a lectore, ut colligitur ex epistola sancti Cypriani 33, et ex concilio Toletano 1. cap. 2. Hoc postea munus majoris erga evangelium honoris gratia diaconis demandatum fuit, ut habetur ex epistola S. Hieronymi ad Sibinianum. *Evange-lium Christi quasi diaconus lectitabas.* Et ex epistola sancti Bonifacii episcopi Moguntini ad Zachariam pontificem, ubi conqueritur quosdam diaconos, quamvis plures concubinas haberent, adhuc evangelium legere. Apud Græcos etiamnum mos viget, ut evangelium a lectoribus publice legatur, uti refert Smithius in epistola de præsenti ecclesiæ Græcæ statu. pag. 155." Cavalieri, *Opera*, tom. v. p. 30. An interesting enquiry is here opened which this is not the place to pursue, nor can I afford space. One thing seems certain : that the gospel was read only by deacons long before the read-ing of the epistle was in like manner removed from the office of the lector : of which latter duty as attached to the subdeacon we find no trace earlier than about the seventh century.

It was to meet this that an alteration was made in the six-teenth century in the form of ordination of subdeacons, and the following words were added : "Accipe librum episto-larum, et habe potestatem legendi eas in ecclesia sancta Dei." Amalarius in the ninth century expresses his wonder at the new practice which was then gaining ground : "ut subdiaco-nus frequentissime legat lectionem ad missam, cum hoc non reperiatur ex ministerio sibi dato in consecratione commissum, neque ex nomine suo." Lib. 2. cap. xj. Micrologus speaks much in the same way. And even Durand in the thirteenth century enquires, " Quare subdiaconus legit lectionem ad missam, cum non reperiatur hoc sibi competere, vel ex eo nomine, vel ex ministerio sibi concesso?" Lib. ii. cap. 8.

The canons and the pastoral epistle of archbishop Ælfric supply sufficient information as to the practice of the Anglo-

HERFORD.	ROM.
andum evangelium thurifi- cet medium altaris tantum: nunquam thurificetur lec- trinum ante pronuntiatio- nem evangelii.	*medium altaris et celebrans benedicit incensum, ut su- pra: Deinde diaconus genu- flexus ante altare, manibus junctis dicit:*

saxon church in his time. In the first of these, can. 10, he lays down that "seven degrees are established in the Church: one is ostiarius, the second is lector, the third exorcista, the fourth acoluthus, the fifth subdiaconus, the sixth diaconus, the seventh presbyter." In the succeeding canons he explains the offices proper to each: "12. Lector is the reader, who reads in God's church, and is ordained for the purpose of preaching of God's word. 15. Subdiaconus is truly underdeacon, who bears forth the vessels to the deacon, and humbly minis- ters under the deacon at the holy altar, with the housel vessels. 16. Diaconus is the minister who ministers to the mass-priest, and sets the offerings upon the altar, and also reads the gospels at God's ministries." Thorpe, *Ancient laws and institutes*, vol. ii. p. 349. The pastoral epistle is to the same purpose, p. 379, and clearly attaches the reading to the lector, and not to the subdeacon.

And not only the canons and epistle of Ælfric but other very ancient writers attribute the gospel-lection solely to the deacon. Isidore in his second book of Divine offices "inter officia diaconi" includes "evangelizare." Cap. 8. But, in short, as in another place I have spoken, *Monumenta rit.* vol. i, upon the great reverence with which our fathers treated the Book of the gospels (whether the entire gospels or the selections to be read in the liturgy), the Evangelisterium, lavishing upon it all kinds of outward ornament and inside decorations of the pencil, so also the practice began from the same feelings of pious gratitude and devotion, that the reading of the gospel should be committed to none of less degree and order in the Church than deacons: "diaconis tantum, qui ad sacerdotalem dignitatem proxime accedunt." During the reading the laity showed also greater signs of reverence. Staffs were laid aside: Amalarius, lib. iii. 18; *Gemma animæ*, lib. i. 24; Durand, lib. iv. 24, &c. All rose,

SARUM.   BANGOR.   EBOR.

Constit. apostol. lib. ii. cap. 57 : and in some churches listened to it half-kneeling in a stooping posture.

How high was the estimation in which the gospels were held in the middle ages is proved most clearly by the fact that some writers in the eighth century did not hesitate to say that, in a remote sense, the gospel is the Body of Christ. "Et corpus Christi quod manducatur non solum panis et vini, quod super altare offertur, sed et ipsum evangelium Christi est ; et cum evangelium legimus et intelligimus, filii in circuitu mensæ in una conlatione sedemus, et panem nostrum manducamus." Etherius, lib. i. *de Incarnat.*

The laying aside of staffs alluded to just above was not a very early practice : but was introduced about the eighth century (for Amalarius speaks of it) and lasted through the next three or four. It was then the custom for the people to stand during the whole service and, it being long, they rested themselves on their staffs. Their use ceased altogether in the western church when seats and settles were introduced. See Sala's note to Bona, tom. iii. p. 153. We learn from St. Chrysostom, *hom.* 63, that in the Greek church during the reading of the gospel the emperor laid aside his crown.

I must add to this note an extract from a very rare book, written by one as it was then called " of the new learning," about the year 1529 : the full title is, "A worke entytled of the olde god and the newe, of the olde faythe and the newe, of the olde doctryne and the newe, or orygynall begynnynge of Idolatrye." The author is describing some of the ceremonies of the mass. " But what shall I saye of the gospell, when it is song ? Oh, how goodly ceremonies are then done.—

HERFORD.   ROM.

MUNDA cor meum,[58] ac labia mea, omnipotens Deus, qui labia Isaiæ prophetæ calculo mundasti ignito : ita me tua grata miseratione dignare mundare, ut sanctum evangelium tuum digne va-

---

here is borne a banner of sylke and garnyshed with a oodly crosse, in token of the victorious and blessed trymphe whiche Jesu Chryste made of subduing the worlde nto hym selfe by the doctryne of the gospell.—Then afterrardes a preest beareth a sencer of siluer makyng a fumiation and sauour of ensence, as long as the gospell is in eadynge to sygnyfy our inwarde affection towarde christ.— here is also borne aboute the gospell boke rychely couered rith golde and siluer, garnyshyd with precyous stones.—Afterrardes there thundreth a great bell, by which we do sygnyfy ur chrysten preestly and apostolycall offyce :—last of all the ospell is borne about to euery person in the quyer, and ffered forth to be kyssed :—and we do go aboute to gette lorie in the syght of the lay people, to whome the gospell ı not in lyke manner offered to be kyssed." Sign. M. 4. his is an important little book so far as it illustrates the ıen existing practice ; and is written in a lively satirical ;yle, but with very much of that indecent and blasphemous baldry which characterises so many of the books of the reırmers at that time. The author was, it seems from his own ccount, a chaplain or minor-canon of some cathedral, and isappointed at not having obtained better preferment : which ccounts for much of his virulence against others of higher ignity. The "Old god and the newe" was strictly prohibited by a royal proclamation in the year 1530 : see Wilıns, *Concilia*, vol. iii. p. 737. I have quoted the above from copy in my possession.

[58] This prayer, introduced probably about the eleventh cenury, was not adopted in the English uses.

SARUM.　　　　BANGOR.　　　　EBOR.

Deinde accipiat textum, scilicet librum evangeliorum, et humilians se ad sacerdotem stantem coram altari: versa facie ad meridiem ita dicat:

Dum petit diaconus benedictionem:

JUBE domne benedicere.[59]

Sacerdos respondeat:

DOMINUS sit in corde tuo et ore tuo ad pronuntiandum sanctum evangelium Dei. In nomine Patris et Filii et Spiritus sancti. Amen.[60]

respondeat sacerdos dicens:

DOMINUS aperiat tibi os ad legendum et nobis aures ad intelligendum

---

[59] (*Jube domne benedicere.*) This, says Le Brun, was a manner of address formerly much in use, as being a mark of humiliation and respect. So, anciently among the Greeks the deacon, when he warned the faithful who were assembled in their solemn service either to rise or sit, did not say *Rise* or *Sit*, but merely "*Jubete*," as if it were, *command yourselves* to do so and so.

The word *domne* is a contraction from dominus. The latter was appropriated in its strict use to the Deity alone: and *domnus* or *domna* was a title of great respect in the middle ages, and applied only to eminent dead saints or living people who occupied important offices in the church: as, for example, the officiating priest during the celebration of the eucharist. See also Ducange upon the word.

Upon this request and the reply, Peter Damian has well observed: "Lecturus magnæ humilitatis gratia, non a sacerdote, sed ab eo, cui sacerdos jusserit, se postulat benedici dicens: Jube domne benedicere. Sacerdos autem, ut tantæ humilitati vicem reddat, non subjecto cuiquam benedicendi delegat officium, nec per semetipsum benedictionem dare

HERFORD.

ROM.

leam nuntiare. Per Christum Dominum nostrum. Amen.

Deinde accipiat textum scilicet librum evangeliorum: humilians se ad sacerdotem stantem ante altare versa facie, ita dicens:

Postea accipit librum de altari, et rursus genuflexus petit benedictionem a sacerdote, dicens:

JUBE domne benedicere.

JUBE domne benedicere.

Sacerdos respondeat:

DOMINUS sit in corde tuo et in labiis tuis ad pronuntiandum evangelium pacis.

Sacerdos respondet:

DOMINUS sit in corde tuo et in labiis tuis: ut digne et competenter annunties evangelium suum: in nomine

---

præsumit: sed potius, ut a Deo, qui est super omnia benedictus, prærogetur, exposcit." *De Dominus vobiscum*, cap. ii.

When the pope officiates at matins on the day of the Nativity he does not say *Domne* before the ninth lection which he then reads, but *Jube Domine benedicere;* for he is supposed to be addressing not man, but God Himself: and no response is made; for the greater cannot be blessed by the less. The choir answers simply "Amen." Some bishops (and the object of this rule is not easy to understand) in their own churches at matins were addressed by an inferior, "Jube domne benedicere," to which they made the usual reply and benediction, and themselves read the appointed lection. The *Cærimoniale episc.* now orders the same rite to be observed by all bishops as by the pope; unless an archbishop or one of higher rank be present: "Si vero adesset aliquis prælatus major se," &c. Lib. ii. cap. 5.

⁶⁰ " *Si autem sacerdos per semetipsum celebret, dicat privatim:* Jube domne benedicere. *Et postea dicat ipsemet.* Dominus sit in corde meo et in ore meo ad pronuntiandum sanctum evangelium Dei. In nomine Patris," &c. *Rubr. Sar.*

SARUM.　　　　　BANGOR.　　　　　EBOR.

Et sic procedat diaconus per medium
chori, ipsum textum super sinistram
manum solenniter gestando ad pulpi-
tum [61] *accedat, thuribulario et cerofe-*
rario praecedentibus. Quandocumque
enim legitur epistola in pulpito, ibi-
dem legatur et evangelium. Et cum
ad locum legendi pervenerint: textum
ipsum subdiaconus accipiat; et a si-
nistris ipsius diaconi quasi oppositus
ipsum textum dum evangelium legitur
teneat: ceroferariis diacono assisten-
tibus: uno a dexteris et reliquo a si-
nistris ad eum conversis. Thuribu-
larius vero stet post diaconum ad eum
conversus. Et semper legatur evange-
lium versus aquilonem. [63] *Cum autem*
inceperit evangelium: post Dominus

sanctum evange-
lium Dei pacis.
In nomine Patris,
&c.

Et diaconus dicat:
D A mihi, Do-
mine, ser-
monem rectum et
bene sonantem in
os meum, ut pla-
ceant tibi verba
mea et omnibus
audientibus prop-
ter nomen tuum
in vitam æternam.
Amen.

---

[61] This place in some countries from the benediction which
always immediately preceded the advance to it was vulgarly
called the *Jube;* so say Le Brun, tom. i. p. 110, and Micrologus, cap. ix. It was always a high place. " Evangelium in
alto loco legitur, quia in monte prædicasse perhibetur, ideo
etiam in sublimi legitur, quia sublimia sunt evangelica præ-
cepta." *Gemma animæ,* cap. xvi, " De pulpito." Compare
also Alcuin: " Defertur evangelium ad analogium, præceden-
tibus cereis." *De div. officiis. Bibl. patrum. aut.* tom. i.
p. 280. And Amalarius, lib. iij. cap. 17: " Lector et cantor
in gradum ascendunt, in more antiquorum:" and cap. 18:
" Tribunal vocat Cyprianus. gradum. super quem ascendit
diaconus ad legendum."

[62] *Sequentia* was said when the gospel was taken from the

HERFORD.

ROM.

Patris et Filii ✠ et Spiritus sancti. Amen.

Et signet diaconum dicendo:
In nomine Patris, &c.
Et sic procedat diaconus ipsum librum super sinistram manum solemniter gestando, ad pulpitum vel ad lectrinum accedat et dicat:
Dominus vobiscum.

Et accepta benedictione, osculatur manum celebrantis: et cum aliis ministris, incenso et luminaribus, accedens ad locum evangelii stans junctis manibus dicit ℣.

Domínus vobiscum.
℟. Et cum spiritu tuo.

Tunc faciendo crucem super librum cum dextro pollice dicat:
SEQUENTIA [62] sancti evangelii *vel* Initium sancti evangelii.

Et pronuntians:

SEQUENTIA sancti evangelii secundum N. *sive* Initium,

---

middle of one of the four gospels, *Initium* when it happened to be the beginning of either of the four. On the four days of the Great week neither *Sequentia* nor *Initium* was said, but "Passio Domini nostri Jesu Christi." Thus, in *The rites of the Church of Durham*: "Within the abbye church uppon Good Friday, there was marvelous solemne service, in the which service time, after the Passion was sung, two of the eldest monkes did take a goodly large crucifix," &c. p. 9.

[63] There is no little difference in the old books as to the place where and the quarter towards which the gospel should be read. When as was very anciently the custom the men and the women were divided, it would seem that the gospel was always read towards the south side, where the men sat. Amalarius, *de off.* lib. iii. c. 2, distinctly speaks of this arrange-

SARUM.	BANGOR.	EBOR.

vobiscum [44] *faciat signum crucis super librum : deinde in sua fronte, et postea in pectore cum pollice.*

Evangelium secundum N.[45]

ment : and an old ordo Romanus takes it for granted that on entering a church one would have the men upon the right hand or south side, and the women on the north. See also Amalarius, *Ecloga*, cap. xiij, printed in Georgius, appendix, tom. iii. p. 350 : "Diaconus vero stat versus ad meridiem, ad quam partem viri solent confluere."

"Antequam tamen ulterius progrediamur, juvat in transcursu ob oculos ponere formam veterum basilicarum. Pleræque orienti, quædam occidenti obversæ erant. Navis columnis fulta, in qua viri ad austrum, mulieres ad septemtrionem residebant. Sequebatur schola cantorum, nobis chorus appellatus. Ambon sive lectorium unum aut alterum adjunctum erat : quatuor aut quinque hinc inde gradus duplices habens pro ascensu et descensu. Ex quo videas, longe disparem fuisse formam amborum a forma odeorum nostrorum, quorum situs etiam diversus : cum ambones illi plurimum ad septemtrionem positi essent, odea vero nostra ea parte, quæ chorum a navi disterminat." Mabillon, *Mus. Ital.* tom. 2. p. xx.

The original reason why the men were addressed especially appears natural enough ; viz. that they are the chief objects of the Church's teaching in her public offices, and from them the women are to learn at home ; as St. Paul admonishes. Other customs gradually crept in, and a mystical reason was given why the gospel should be read towards the north : as we have seen (note 47) was the custom of the Church of Hereford : "ut per Dei verbum aquilonis, hoc est, dæmonis, pravi noxiique halitus disjiciantur." Le Brun, i. 111. And the *Gemma animæ*, cap. xvj : "Nunc autem secundum inolitum morem se (diaconus) ad aquilonem vertit, ubi feminæ stant,

HERFORD.   ROM.

Et signet seipsum in fronte cum eodem pollice dicens se-cundum N.

pollice dextræ manus signat librum in principio evan-gelii, quod est lecturus, de-inde seipsum in fronte, ore, et pectore: et dum ministri respondent:

G LORIA tibi Domine.

deinde legatur evangelium.   *incensat ter librum, postea*

quæ carnales significant, quia evangelium carnales a spirituali-bus vocat. Per aquilonem quoque diabolus designatur, qui per evangelium impugnatur. Per aquilonem etiam infidelis populus denotatur, cui evangelium prædicatur ut ad Christum convertatur." This last reason is taken from a very old sacra-mentary which says: "Diaconus dum legit, sistat versus ad aquilonem, quia frigidis in fide prædicatur evangelium." Sala, notes to Bona, tom. iii. p. 153: but he does not say what book: "ex quodam libro sacramentorum;" quoting Martene, *Anecdot.* tom. v. 1587.

     I shall only further make an extract from the will of Maud, lady Mauley, dated in 1438: "My body to be buried in the church . . . on the south side of the altar, where the gospels are usually read." *Testamenta vetusta*, p. 235.

     [64] (*Dominis vobiscum.*) It is strange that the York use takes no notice of this salutation: nor is it easy to suggest why it was omitted, being a custom so general throughout the Church. Alcuin speaks of it: "Salutat et populum, dicens: *Dominus vobiscum:* quatenus corda illorum a mun-danis cogitationibus Dominus emundet, et ad suscipienda verba salutifera aperire dignetur." *De div. off. bibl. patr. auct.* i. p. 280. Innocent the third also: "diaconus in ambone con-sistens salutat populum, dicens: Dominus vobiscum, illud observans, quod Dominus jusserat: 'In quamcunque domum intraveritis,'" &c.

     [65] "If thai singe messe or if thai seie,
       Tho pater noster reherce al weie:
       Til deken or prist the gospel rede,
       Stonde up then and take gode hede:

SARUM.	BANGOR.	EBOR.
Lecto evangelio osculetur librum: et accedens subdiaconus statim porrigat ei textum quem ipse diaconus ex directo pectore deferat. Finito evangelio.[87]		*Post lectum evangelium dicat sacerdos secrete:*

For then tho prist flyttes his boke,
North to that other auter noke:
And makes a cross upon tho letter
With his thoume he spedes tho better:
And sithen an other open his face,
For he has mikel nede of grace:
For then an erthly mon shal neven
Tho wordes of Ihū crist, gods son of heuen. . .
At tho bigynnyng tent thou take,
A large cros on the thou make. . .
Whils hit is red speke thou noght,
Bot thenk on him that dere the boght:
Sayande thus in thi mynde,
Als thou shalt after wryten fynde."

Layfolks mass book.

[86] "*In fine evangelii a ministris respondetur,* Laus tibi Christe." Rubr. *Gen. miss.* tit. x. 6. Anciently was said *Amen:* which is still retained in the Mozarabic missal.

[87] (*Finito evangelio.* Sar.) The usual custom was to preach the sermon, if there should be any, at this part of the service; but there was no strict rule observed in all churches. Sometimes the sermon was preached after the creed; and sometimes after the offertory: as in 1476 on a special occasion at Winchester in honour of the relics of St. Swithun: "antistes Wintoniensis missam celebrabat. Lecto evangelio et offertorio finito, episcopus Cicestrensis sermonem habuit ad populum in vulgari." *Concil.* tom. 3. p. 611. Or again, on the authority of Chaucer, we might suppose that a break in the service at the offertory was by no means unusual. Speaking of the Pardoner, he says:—

" He was in chirche a noble ecclesiast,
    Wel coude he rede a lesson or a storie,

HERFORD.	ROM.
	prosequitur evangelium junctis manibus.
Lecto evangelio deosculetur librum :	*Quo finito*[66] *subdiaconus defert librum sacerdoti, qui osculatur evangelium dicens :*

But alderbest he sang an offertorie :
For wel he wiste, whan that song was songe,
He muste preche, and wel afile his tonge,
To winne silver, as he right wel coude :
Therfore he sang the merier and loude."

Prolog. l. 712.

Very anciently more than one sermon was delivered : the priests first, each in order, gave a short exhortation, and if he were present the bishop last. *Apost. const.* lib. ii. c. 58. In the next chapter of the same book particular directions are given that priests coming from another parish should be pressed to preach, "for a stranger's words are always acceptable and very useful, according to that in St. Matt., *no prophet is without honour save in his own country.*"

"Deinde episcopus sermonem ad populum facit." *Gemma animæ*, cap. 25. This custom of preaching during the liturgy has been established and never omitted during the whole existence of the Christian Church. From the time of Justin Martyr we can trace a multitude of authorities, down to our own day. It has always moreover been held to be one of the peculiar duties of the bishops of the Church : as St. Paul exhorted Timothy that he should " preach the word ; instant in season and out of season."

We find in the earliest records which remain of the English Church evidence of the anxiety which was always felt to enforce this great duty of preaching. The sixth of the excerpts of Egbert orders every priest diligently to instruct his people : the third explains the time when this is to be done : "Ut omnibus festis et diebus dominicis unusquisque sacerdos evangelium Christi prædicet populo." Thorpe, vol. ii. p. 98. Passing over some hundred years, we have the following among the canons of Ælfric : "The mass-priest shall on

SARUM.	BANGOR.	EBOR.
		Benedictus qui venit in nomine Domini.
		Postea osculetnr textum.
incipiat sacerdos in medio altaris:		*Statim sacerdos in medio altaris symbolum fidei incipiat excelsa voce:*

CREDO in unum Deum.[69] Patrem omnipotentem. Factorem cœli et terræ: visibilium omnium et

sundays and mass-days tell to the people the sense of the gospel in English, and concerning the pater-noster and the creed also, the oftenest that he can. . . . Let the teacher warn against that which the prophet says: *canes muti non possunt latrare.* We ought to bark and preach to the laymen, lest, for want of teaching, they should perish." Thorpe, p. 352. Once more, for there would be no end of accumulating directions of this sort during succeeding ages: "The mass-priest shall rightly preach the true faith to men, and recite sermons to them; and visit sick men," &c. Ælfric's *Pastoral epistle*, p. 385. Stillingfleet speaking of the frequency of preaching in the church of England before the reformation has made the strangest statements, and drawn (against the direct evidence of his own authorities) the most outrageous conclusions. The well-known passage from Sozomen (on which he and other protestant controversialists have relied) does not refer to preaching, generally, at Rome—for it is the city of Rome alone to which the historian alludes—but to the introduction of a sermon always at mass; which is not distinctly ordered in the earliest sacramentaries. *Orig. Brit.* p. 236. Cf. van Espen, pars ii. sect. i. tit. v. cap. 2, and synod. Trent. sess. 22. cap. 8.

In masses for the dead when, as was frequently the custom, sermons relating to the character of the deceased were to be preached, or indeed any sermon at all, it was not until the service was entirely finished, and the preacher (if also the

HERFORD.

ROM.

Per evangelia dicta dele-
antur nostra delicta.
*Deinde sacerdos incensatur
a diacono.*

*Et sacerdos stando in medio
altaris manibus junctis aliquantulum levatis dicat vel
cantet: et jungat manus
prosequendo:*

*Deinde ad medium altaris
extendens, elevans, et jungens manus, dicit, si dicendum est, et prosequitur junctis manibus:*[68]

CREDO in unum Deum. Patrem omnipotentem.
Factorem cœli et terræ: visibilium omnium et

---

celebrant) had laid aside the chasuble and maniple and put
on a cope. See upon this Gavantus, tom. i. p. 301 ; Bauldry,
cap. 20 ; Castaldus, lib. ii. 9, and the *Cær. episcop.* lib. ii.
cap. 11.

After the gospel indulgences were proclaimed, and excommunications, and banns of marriage : in some churches
other solemnities, such as the reconciling and readmitting of
penitents. Vide Martene, *de ant. ritibus ecc.* lib. i. cap. 4.
Legates also explained the object of their legation. With
the conclusion of the sermon the missa catechumenorum also
ended : and they, with the unreconciled and unbelievers, were
dismissed and the doors shut, and persons stationed there to
prevent any from coming in. St. Augustine says, *serm.* 49,
"Ecce post sermonem fit missa catechumenis, manebunt fideles." Much information upon all this portion of the liturgy
in the earliest ages may be found in Bingham's *Christian
antiquities ;* on later practice, in Bauldryus, *Manualis sacr.
cærim.* cap. x.

[68] "Cum dicit, *Deum,* caput cruci inclinat : quod similiter
facit cum dicit, *Jesum Christum* et *simul adoratur.* Ad illa
autem verba, *Et incarnatus est,* genuflectit usque dum dicatur,
Et homo factus est. In fine ad *Et vitam venturi sæculi,*
signat se signo crucis a fronte ad pectus." *Rubr. Miss. Rom.*

[69] "Incipit missa fidelium." Bona. "Missa sacramentorum." Ivo Carnotensis, *epist.* 219.

The first words only, according to the Sarum rubric, were

SARUM.   BANGOR.   EBOR.

invisibilium. Et in unum Dominum Jesum[70] Christum, Filium Dei unigenitum. Et ex Patre natum ante omnia sæcula. Deum de Deo, lumen de lumine, Deum verum de Deo vero. Genitum non factum, consubstantialem Patri: per quem omnia facta sunt. Qui propter nos homines, et propter nostram salutem descendit de cœlis. Et incarnatus est de Spiritu sancto ex Maria virgine: et homo factus est. Crucifixus etiam pro nobis sub Pontio Pilato: passus et sepultus est. Et resurrexit tertia die secundum scripturas. Et ascendit in cœlum: sedet ad dexteram Patris. Et iterum venturus est cum gloria judicare vivos et mortuos: cujus regni non erit finis. Et in Spiritum sanctum, Dominum et vivificantem: Qui ex Patre Filioque procedit. Qui cum Patre et Filio simul adoratur et conglorificatur: Qui locutus est per Prophetas. Et unam

---

to be sung by the celebrant at high mass: it continues, "Deinde cantetur a choro, non alternatim sed a toto choro."

"Hæc sunt festa quibus dicendum est *Credo* secundum usum Sarum. Omnibus dominicis diebus per totum annum ad magnam missam, sive de dominica agitur, sive non. In missis tamen vigiliarum et sanctorum trium lectionum, et in missis defunctorum quæ in capitulo in dominicis dicuntur, non dicitur. Sed si missa dominicalis in capitulo dicitur, tunc dicitur *Credo in unum.* Dicetur etiam per octo dies nativitatis Domini, paschæ, et penthecostes: et in omni duplici festo per annum: et in omnibus festis apostolorum et evangelistarum: et in utroque festo sanctæ crucis: et in festo sanctæ Mariæ Magdalenæ: et in utroque festo sancti Michaelis: et in missa sponsalium. Dicetur etiam ad missam de sancta Maria, quando ad missam de die dicendum est per totum annum: et in festo alicujus sancti, in cujus honore dedicatum est altare vel ecclesia, ad altare ejusdem sancti tantum." *Rubr. Miss. Sar.* With this agrees the Bangor rubric: the York adds; "in festo sancti Petri ad vincula, et in die octavarum. Et in cathedra ejusdem. Et in utroque festo sancti Johannis baptistæ. In festo Corporis Christi. Et in festo omnium sanctorum. Et

HERFORD.   ROM.

invisibilium. Et in unum Dominum Jesum Christum,
Filium Dei unigenitum. Et ex Patre natum ante omnia sæcula. Deum de Deo, lumen de lumine, Deum
verum de Deo vero. Genitum non factum, consubstantialem Patri : per quem omnia facta sunt. Qui
propter nos homines, et propter nostram salutem descendit de cœlis. (*Et fiet genuflexio dum dicitur.* Herf.
Hic genuflectitur. Rom.) Et incarnatus est de Spiritu
sancto ex Maria virgine : et homo factus est. Crucifixus etiam pro nobis (*Et tunc fiet levatio.* Herf.) sub
Pontio Pilato : passus et sepultus est. Et resurrexit
tertia die secundum scripturas. Et ascendit in cœlum :
sedet ad dexteram Patris. Et iterum venturus est cum
gloria judicare vivos et mortuos : Cujus regni non erit
finis. Et in Spiritum sanctum, Dominum et vivificantem : Qui ex Patre Filioque procedit. Qui cum Patre

---

in festo reliquiarum. Et in festo sancti Willelmi in matrici
ecclesia tantum. Et in festis quatuor doctorum, scilicet *Gregorii, Ambrosii, Augustini,* et *Hieronimi.*" The Hereford
adds : " in festo sancti Ethelberti : in festo sancti Thomæ
Herfordensis : et in festo sancti Augustini Angliæ apostoli."
For the Roman order, see *Rubricæ generales miss.* tit.
xi. i.

[70] On bowing at the name of Jesus, and at the Gloria
Patri, see among others two constitutions in Wilkins, *Concilia,*
tom. iii. p. 20. This reverent practice was insisted on after
the reformation. In 1561 the following canon was published
in the diocese of St. Asaph : " Item, that yn tyme of servyce
red or songe yn the churche, so often as the name of Jesus
beyng our sauyor shall be rehersed and pronounced, dew
reverence be made of all persons yonge and olde with lowly-
ness of curtesy, and entendyng of mens heds." *Concil.* tom. 4.
p. 229. So, also, the canons of 1604. Nevertheless the reverence gradually died away in practice during the eighteenth
century, but of late years in some parishes has been revived.
At the Gloria Patri I believe the reverence of bowing has long
ceased to be observed in parish churches.

SARUM.   BANGOR.   EBOR.

sanctam Catholicam et Apostolicam Ecclesiam. Confiteor unum baptisma in remissionem peccatorum. Et expecto resurrectionem mortuorum. Et vitam venturi sæculi. Amen.[71]

Post inceptionem Credo in unum Deum *reversis ministris de pulpito ad altare, diaconus librum evangelii sacerdoti porrigat deosculandum, vel alias textum accipiens de manu subdiaconi, ipsum sacerdoti porrigat in dextris ejus osculandum; deinde acolyto ministrante subdiacono, subdiaconus ipsi diacono. Postea sequatur :*	*Post credo dicat sacerdos convertendo ad populum :*	*Dumcanitur* Credo *subdiaconus cum textu, et acolytus cum thuribulo chorum circumeant. Post conversus sacerdos ad populum dicat :*
DOMINUS vobiscum.[72]	**D**OMINUS vobiscum.	**D**OMINUS vobiscum.

[71] " Som-where bisyde when hit is done,
     Thou make a cros, and kys hit sone.
     Men oen to saie tho crede som tyme,
     When thei saie hore, loke thou saie thyne :
     This that folouse in englishe letter,
     I wold thou sayde hit for tho better : . . .

HERFORD.   ROM.

et Filio simul adoratur et conglorificatur: Qui locutus est per Prophetas. Et unam sanctam Catholicam et Apostolicam Ecclesiam. Confiteor unum baptisma in remissionem peccatorum. Et expecto resurrectionem mortuorum. Et vitam venturi sæculi. Amen.

Quo finito vertat se sacerdos *Deinde osculatur altare, et*
ad populum et dicat: *versus ad populum dicit* ℣.

D OMINUS vobis-cum.   D OMINUS vobis-cum.

        ℞. Et cum spiritu tuo.

Here to loke thou take good hede,
For here is wryten thin englyshe crede."
      Layfolks mass book.

[72] (*Vobiscum.*) "Non enim hic digne numerus personarum sed ecclesiasticæ potius unitatis attenditur sacramentum: ubi scilicet, nec unitas excludit multitudinem, nec multitudo violat

SARUM.	BANGOR.	EBOR.
Et:	*Iterum ad altare converus dicat:*	*Reversus dicat:*
O REMUS.[73]	O REMUS.	O REMUS.
Deinde dicitur Offertorium.[75]	*Offertorium.*[74]	*Et canat cum suis ministris Offertorium.*

---

unitatem : quia et unum corpus per multa membra dividitur, et ex diversis membris unum corpus impletur. Nec in unitate corporis membrorum multitudo confunditur : nec in pluralitate membrorum unius corporis integritas violatur." Petr. Damian. cap. xiij.

[73] Some writers seem to make this the beginning of the Missa fidelium. See Le Brun, tom. i. p. 136, and Gerbert, *de musica*, tom. i. p. 431, with others. But this is not really opposed to the opinion of the great ritualists cited above: and depends upon whether the creed be said or not, either at certain seasons as in the majority of churches, or as in others not at all.

[74]   "After that, fast at hande,
    Comes tho tyme of offrande :
    Offer or leeue whether ye lyst,
    How thou shulde praye I wold thou wyst."
               Layfolks mass book.

[75] (*Offertorium.*) The verse is so called which was sung just before the oblation of the elements by the priest. Anciently at this time the people made their offerings. The custom is still observed in all parochial masses in Roman catholic churches. Another name, but not a common one, was "Sacrificium." Very much information (I need scarcely remind the reader) respecting the ancient oblations of the people, the manner of offering, the quality, the restrictions, &c., is to be found in the writers both ancient and modern who have treated on the subject. Indeed so much, that in the compass of a note I am scarcely warranted in entering at all upon it ; but I must extract a short passage from Walafrid Strabo : "Offertorium, quod inter offerendum cantatur, quamvis a prioris populi consuetudine in usum Christianorum venisse

HERFORD.   ROM.

Postea dicit:

O REMUS.   O REMUS.

Deinde dicat Offertorium.   *Et Offertorium.*

---

dicatur, tamen quis specialiter addiderit officiis nostris, aperte non legimus : . . . cum vere credamus priscis temporibus patres sanctos silentio obtulisse, vel communicasse, quod etiam hactenus in sabbato sancto paschæ observamus. Sed sicut supradictum est, diversis modis, et partibus per tempora decus processit ecclesiæ, et usque in finem augeri non desinet." *De reb. eccles.* c. 22. A remark to the same effect occurs in Radulp. Tungr. *de canon. observ.* prop. xxiij, and I shall add that the custom of singing at this time is as old as the age of St. Augustine, who speaks of it in his *Retract.* lib. 2. c. xj.

It is not easy to say whether the most ancient practice was for the people to approach the altar ; probably not : certainly not in the Greek Church : and there are various canons of the western which forbid women, after permission was given to men. Theodulph Aurelian, *Capitular.* cap. 6. And the sixth of the Anglo-saxon ecclesiastical institutes is directed to this point : " We also command that at those hours in which the priest sings the mass no woman approach near the altar, but let them stand in their places, and the mass-priest will there receive from them the offering which they desire to offer to God. Women should bear in mind their infirmities and the tenderness of their sex, and therefore they shall dread to touch any of the holy things belonging to the services of the church." Thorpe, *Ancient laws and institutes,* vol. ii. 407.

The rule in the primitive ages was that nothing should be offered but what was proper also to be consumed at the altar, or at least in the service of the Church : and to this the apostolical canon is directed, can. 3. Afterwards this was further limited to bread and wine and water, only, by

SARUM.	BANGOR.	EBOR.

Post offertorium vero porrigat dia-conus sacerdoti calicem cum patena et sacrificio : et osculetur manum ejus utraque vice. Ipse vero accipiens ab eo calicem : diligenter ponat in loco suo debito super medium altare : et inclinato parumper elevet calicem utraque manu offerens sacrificium Domino, dicendo hanc orationem.

Postea lavet ma-nus et componat hostiam[76] *super corporales pannos et dicat :*

---

the people : and all else when offered was not looked upon as for the sacrifice, but in a lower respect : as first-fruits and pious gifts for the use of the Church and her ministers.

An old ordo Romanus cited by Bona, lib. 2. cap. ix. § 1, thus describes the manner of offering : " Cantores cantant offertorium cum versibus, et populus dat oblationes suas, id est panem et vinum, et offerunt cum fanonibus candidis, primo masculi, deinde fœminæ. Novissime vero sacerdotes et diaconi offerunt, sed solum panem." These *fanones* as Cassander explains were napkins. The *offertorium cum versibus* relates to a period when not only verses but even whole psalms were added to the offertory proper ; and sometimes, for the col-lecting took much time, these were sung and repeated again and again.

It is not known when the old custom of offering bread and wine ceased : the author of the *Gemma animæ* is a witness that money was given instead in his day, the eleventh century :

HERFORD.

Quo dicto ministret ea quæ necessaria sunt sacramento: scilicet panem, vinum et aquam in calicem infundens: benedictione aquæ prius a sacerdote petita hoc modo:

BENEDICITE.

Sacerdote sic dicente:

DOMINUS. Ab ipso sis benedicta, de cujus latere exivit sanguis et aqua. In nomine Patris, &c. Amen.

Et postea sumat patenam cum hostia et ponat super calicem, et tenens calicem

ROM.

Quo dicto, diaconus porrigit celebranti patenam cum hostia: quam offerens, sacerdos dicit:

---

and he states a reason for the change, "quia populo non communicante non erat necesse panem tam magnum fieri, statutum est, eum in modum denarii formari; et ut populus pro oblatione farinæ denarios offerret." Cap. 58. He adds: "qui tamen denarii in usum pauperum qui membra sunt Christi cederent, vel in aliquid quod ad hoc sacrificium pertinet."

This part of the liturgy is sometimes called the "Missa omnium offerentium." Pinius, *de lit. ant. Hisp.* p. 91.

[76] This is the same as that which is called "sacrificium" in the Sarum and Bangor rubrics, and in its own succeeding prayer "Acceptum sit:" doubtless, as being that which is about to be consecrated, and offered to the Almighty Father as the Body of his Son. Speaking of this oblation, Amalarius says: "facit eam transire per suam secretam orationem ad nomen hostiæ, sive muneris, donive, vel sacrificii, seu oblationis." *Præf. 2. de eccles. off.*

G

SARUM.　　　　　BANGOR.　　　　　EBOR.

Oratio.

SUSCIPE, sancta Trinitas, hanc oblationem quam ego (miser et, Ebor.) indignus peccator offero in honore tuo et beatæ Mariæ, et omnium sanctorum tuorum, pro peccatis et offensionibus meis: pro salute vivorum et requie (omnium, Sarum) fidelium defunctorum. In nomine Patris, et Filii, et Spiritus sancti, Amen.

Item calicem cum vino et aqua [79] *et dicat:*

ACCEPTUM sit omnipotenti Deo hoc sacrificium novum.[78]

ACCEPTUM sit omnipotenti Deo, sacrificium istud: in nomine Patris et Filii et Spiritus sancti. Amen.

Dicta oratione reponat calicem, et cooperiat cum corporalibus: ponatque panem super corporalia decenter, ante calicem vinum et aquam continentem, et osculetur patenam et reponat eam a dextris super altare sub corporalibus, parum cooperiendo.

Qua dicta

---

[77] (*Immaculatam.*) A word found only in the Roman use: and can be used solely with reference to the all-pure Body, which it is about to be.

[78] These few words were accidentally omitted in the second edition: and I am indebted to my friend canon Simmons for pointing out the mistake. See his note, in the *Layfolks mass book*, p. 331.

HERFORD.

ROM.

in manibus suis, dicat de-
vote:

SUSCIPE, sancta Tri-
nitas, hanc oblatio-
nem quam tibi offero in
memoriam passionis Do-
mini nostri Jesu Christi, et
præsta, ut in conspectu tuo
tibi placens ascendat, et
meam et omnium fidelium
salutem operetur æternam,
per Christum.

SUSCIPE, sancte Pa-
ter, omnipotens æterne
Deus, hanc immaculatam[77]
hostiam, quam ego indig-
nus famulus tuus offero
tibi Deo meo vivo et vero,
pro innumerabilibus pecca
tis et offensionibus et neg-
ligentiis meis, et pro omnibus circumstantibus, sed
et pro omnibus fidelibus
Christianis vivis atque defunctis: ut mihi et illis proficiat ad salutem in vitam
æternam. Amen.

Qua dicta reponat calicem,
et cooperiat eum cum corpo-
ralibus: ponatque panem
super corporalia decenter,
ante calicem vinum et aquam
continentem, et osculetur pa-
tenam: et reponat eam a
dextris super altare sub cor-

Deinde faciens crucem cum
eadem patena, deponit hos-
tiam super corporale. Dia-
conus ministrat vinum, sub-
diaconus aquam in calice:
et aquam miscendam in ca-
lice sacerdos benedicit, ✠ *di-*
cens:[80]

---

[79] During the mixture, in the Ambrosian missal, there was
appointed to be said: "De latere Christi exivit sanguis et
aqua pariter."

[80] This and the following prayers before the Secret were
added to the Roman use about the year 1050, and are still
omitted in some of the monastic missals.

SARUM.   BANGOR.   EBOR.

---

[81] The use of *Offerimus* and not *Offero*, as before in the oblation of the bread, is very remarkable; nor is Bona's note less important : "Regredior ad sacerdotem, qui calicem aqua mixtum Deo offert dicens, *Offerimus*, &c., cumque in panis oblatione singulariter dixerit *Offero*, hic pluraliter ait *Offerimus*, quia nimirum Romano ritu eandem orationem simul cum sacerdote in missa solemni recitat diaconus, qui antea

HERFORD.   ROM.

poralibus, parum cooperi-
endo.

DEUS, qui humanæ substantiæ dignitatem mirabiliter condidisti, et mirabilius reformasti : da nobis per hujus aquæ et vini mysterium, ejus divinitatis esse consortes, qui humanitatis nostræ fieri dignatus est particeps, Jesus Christus Filius tuus Dominus noster : qui tecum vivit et regnat in unitate Spiritus sancti Deus, per omnia sæcula sæculorum. Amen.

Postea accipit calicem, et offert, dicens :

OFFERIMUS [81] tibi, Domine, calicem salutaris, tuam deprecantes clementiam : ut in conspectu divinæ Majestatis tuæ, pro nostra et totius mundi salute cum odore suavitatis ascendat. Amen.[82]

---

vinum calici infudit, et olim sanguinem populo ministrabat. Neque obstat, quod privatæ missæ sine diacono celebrantur, et nihilominus sacerdos dicit *Offerimus,* quia formulæ pro solemni missa institutæ in privata non mutantur." Tom. iii. p. 217. Compare Sala's note upon this passage.

[82] After this prayer, the subdeacon (at high mass) is ordered by the *Ritus celebr. missam,* tit. vij. 9, to receive the paten from

SARUM.   BANGOR.   EBOR.

---

the deacon and, standing behind the priest, hold it covered with the veil until after the *Pater noster*. I mention this as it seems to be a relic of a very ancient custom; and now observed, merely through a tradition, without any particular object. When the people were in the habit of making large oblations, and these were to be offered upon the paten, this latter was of course proportionably large: and having thus answered its purpose was for a time removed, in order that it might not incommode or interfere with the priest in the discharge of his office.

[83] "Quamvis ergo in hac convocatione nec Spiritus sanctus

HERFORD. · ROM.

Deinde facit signum crucis cum calice, et illum ponit super corporale, et palla co-operit; tum junctis mani-bus super altare, aliquan-tulum inclinatus dicit:

IN spiritu humilitatis, et in animo contrito sus-cipiamur a te Domine: et sic fiat sacrificium nostrum in conspectu tuo hodie, ut placeat tibi, Domine Deus.

Erectus expandit manus, easque in altum porrectas jungens, elevatis ad cœlum oculis, et statim dimissis, dicit:

VENI[83] sanctificator, omnipotens æterne Deus:

benedicit oblata, prosequen-do:

et bene ✠ dic hoc sacrifi-cium tuo sancto nomini præparatum.

_____

expressis verbis nominetur, et nonnullæ voces insint, quæ Deum Patrem designare videntur: unum tamen verbum, *Veni,* palam facit ecclesiam ad Deum Patrem se non convertere, quippe quæ ex sacræ scripturæ loquendi more, non nisi Per-sonarum duarum alterutrum quæ missæ fuerunt, aut Filium scilicet, aut Spiritum sanctum invocare consuevit. Quinimmo cum ad Patrem refertur oratio, dici solet: mitte Spiritum sanctum; seu quoad Filium, mitte redemptorem, agnum mitte, qui mundi peccata delet. Cum autem hoc loco intel-ligi nequeat precem ad Filium spectare, necessaria conse-cutione fit Spiritum sanctum designari." Le Brun, tom. i. 160.

SARUM.   BANGOR.   EBOR.

Hoc peracto accipiat thuribulum a diacono et thurificet sacrificium: videlicet ultra ter signum crucis faciens, et in circuitu et ex utraque parte calicis et sacrificii: deinde locum inter se et altare. Et dum thurificat dicat:

DIRIGATUR Domine ad te oratio mea, sicut incensum in conspectu tuo.

---

[84] The deacon is here directed to say, "ministrante naviculam, *Benedicite pater reverende.*" *Ritus celebr.* tit. vij. 10. The plural is used according to a custom which became general from about the sixth century of thus addressing persons of dignity, or those to whom from their peculiar offices reverence was due. This was certainly later than the age of St. Jerome or of St. Augustine, who writing to the bishops of

HERFORD.   ROM.

Postea[84] *benedicit incensum dicens:*

PER intercessionem beati Michaelis archangeli stantis a dextris altaris incensi, et omnium electorum suorum, incensum istud dignetur Dominus bene ✠ dicere, et in odorem suavitatis accipere. Per Christum Dominum nostrum. Amen.

Et accepto thuribulo a diacono, incensat oblata, dicens:

INCENSUM istud a te benedictum, ascendat ad te Domine, et descendat super nos misericordia tua.

Deinde incensat altare dicens: Ps. 140.

DIRIGATUR, Domine, oratio mea sicut incensum in conspecto tuo : elevatio manuum mearum sacrificium vespertinum. Pone, Domine, cus-

---

Rome say, "tua beatitudo," "sanctitas tua," and the like. But on the contrary, "beatitudo vestra" and "reverentia vestra" are common in the epistles of St. Gregory at the end of the sixth century. The term "sanctitas vestra" is to be found applied to a council about A.D. 390; Concil. Carthag.

SARUM.	BANGOR.	EBOR.

Postea thurifice-
tur. ipse sacerdos
ab ipso diacono:
et subdiaconus de-
ferat ei textum de-
osculandum: de-
inde acolytus thu-
rificet chorum.[85]
His itaque peractis: eat sacerdos ad   *Interim lavet ma-*
dextrum cornu[86] *altaris, et abluat*   *nus et dicat:*
manus[87] *dicens:*

---

[85] "Incipiens a rectoribus chori. Deinde superiorem gradum ex parte cantoris. Eodem ordine secundas, exinde
primas formas: ita quod ipse puer singulos clericos incensando
illis inclinet: subsequente illum diacono cum textu ab omnibus deosculando. Si episcopus celebraverit et duplex festum
fuerit, duo venient cum thuribulis, et duo subdiaconi cum
duobus textibus vel reliquiis. Si autem episcopus non celebraverit, et duplex festum fuerit: textum deferat acolytus ex
parte cantoris. Primo autem thurificandus est cantor qui stat
in medio chori cum cæteris rectoribus chori, scilicet in festis
majoribus duplicibus tantum: deinde principales rectores
chori ex utraque parte sunt, exinde duo rectores secundarii,
postea chorus more solito eodem quoque ordine sequantur

HERFORD.   ROM.

todiam ori meo, et ostium
circumstantiæ labiis meis :
ut non declinet cor meum
in verba malitiæ, ad excu-
sandas excusationes in peccatis.

*Dum reddit thuribulum
diacono, dicit :*

ACCENDAT in nobis
Dominus ignem sui
amoris, et flammam æter-
næ charitatis. Amen.

*Postea incensatur sacerdos
a diacono, deinde alii per
ordinem.*

*Et postea eat ad abluendum
manus suas. Et in eundo
dicat totum hymnum :*

*Interim sacerdos lavat ma-
nus dicens : Ps. 25.*

textus. Quando vero non dicitur *Credo*, tunc immediate post
Oremus et *Offertorium* accedat diaconus et offerat sacerdoti
calicem cum patena, et cætera solito more expleantur : et
thurificet totum sacrificium more solito. Sed chorus non
thurificetur. Nunquam enim incensatur chorus post evangelium ad missam, nisi quando dicitur *Credo*, sed tunc semper."
Rubr. Miss. Sar.

[86] The reader will find some remarks above, note 24, as to
which side is here meant. In almost all churches, I believe,
we find the piscina upon the epistle side of the altar. St. Cyril
testifies to the antiquity of this observance during the holy
Service, and teaches us its meaning: "Ye saw then the
deacon give to the priest water to wash, and to the presbyters

SARUM.	BANGOR.	EBOR.

L AVABO in-
ter inno-
centes manus me-
as: et circumdabo
altare tuum, Do-
mine.
Et hymnum:
V ENI crea-
tor spiritus,
mentes tuorum.

M UNDA me Domine ab omni
inquinamento mentis et corporis: ut possim mundatus implere
opus sanctum Domini.

---

who stood round God's altar.　He gave it, not at all because
of bodily defilement; no; for we did not set out for the
church with defiled bodies.　But this washing of hands is a
symbol that ye ought to be pure from all sinful and unlawful
deeds: for since the hands are a symbol of action, by washing
them we represent the purity and blamelessness of our conduct.　Hast thou not heard the blessed David opening this
mystery, and saying, *I will wash my hands in innocency, and
so will I compass thine altar, O Lord?* The washing therefore
of hands is a symbol of immunity from sin." *Catechetical lect.*
Oxf. trans. p. 273.

So also we are told in the *Apostolical const.* b. viii. c. 11.
The water which at this time is poured upon the priest's
hands " is a sign of the purity which befits a soul consecrated
to God."

HERFORD.

ROM.

LAVABO inter inno-centes manus meas, &c.: *usque in finem: Cum Gloria Patri et* Sicut erat.

VENI creator, *excepto versu,* Dudum sacra-ta. *Cum versu,* Emitte spi-ritum tuum, et creabuntur. Et renovabis faciem ter-ræ.

Oratio.

URE igne sancti Spi-ritus renes nostros et cor nostrum, Domine, ut tibi casto corpore ser-viamus et mundo corde placeamus. Per Christum Dominum nostrum.

---

[87] "Saye pater noster, get up standande,
Al tho tyme tho prist is wasshande:
Til after washing tho priste wil loute
Tho auter, and sithen turne aboute:
Then he askes with stille steven,
Ilk monnes prayers to god of heuen.
Take gode kepe vnto the prest,
When he him turnes knoc on thi brest,
And thenk then for thi synn
Thou art noght worthe to pray for hymm,
But when thou prayes god lokes thi wille;
If hit be gode forgetis thin ille;
For-thi with hope in his mercie,
Answere tho prest with this in hie."
Layfolks mass book.

SARUM.	BANGOR.	EBOR.
Deinde revertat se, et stans ante altare inclinatoque capite et corpore, junctis manibus dicat orationem:	*Diaconus interim ipsum altare in sinistro cornu thurificabit et reliquias more solito in circuitu. Ablutis manibus sacerdos revertat se ad altare ad divinum servitium exequendum: diaconus et subdiaconus suis gradibus supradicto modo se teneant. Deinde sacerdos stans ante altare inclinato capite et corpore, junctis manibus dicat:*	*Postea ante medium altaris inclinatus dicat:*

IN spiritu humilitatis et in animo contrito suscipiamur, Domine, a te: et sic fiat sacrificium nostrum (in conspectu tuo: *Sarum*) ut a te suscipiatur hodie, et placeat tibi Domine Deus. (meus. *Ebor*.)

---

[88] Micrologus says, cap. xi, that in his time there was little authority for the use of this prayer: "Deinde inclinatus ante altare dicat hanc orationem, non ex aliquo ordine sed ex ecclesiastica consuetudine." It does not occur in either of the English uses. Micrologus is speaking of some peculiarity of the Gallican churches. There is reason to suppose also from the way in which he writes that in his time the prayer ended with the word "ascensionis." The date of its introduction into the Roman liturgy is doubtful.

HERFORD.

Postea revertatur in me-
dium altaris, stando et in-
clinando se ad altare con-
junctis manibus, et dicat:

ROM.

Deinde aliquantum inclina-
tus in medio altaris, junctis
manibus super eo, dicit:

IN spiritu humilitatis et animo contrito suscipiamur a te, Domine: et sic fiat sacrificium nostrum ut a te suscipiatur hodie, et placeat tibi Domine Deus.

SUSCIPE[88] sancta Trinitas, hanc oblationem, quam tibi offerimus ob memoriam passionis, resurrectionis, et ascensionis Jesu Christi Domini nostri: et in honore[89]

---

[88] " Difficultas a nonnullis movetur, quomodo sacrificium quod soli Deo debetur, in honorem sanctorum offerri potest. Equidem sacrificium soli Deo offerri potest, et ideo infra offertorium sermonem ad illum solum dirigentes dicimus, *Suscipe, sancte Pater, offerimus tibi, Domine,* sed hoc non impedit quominus aliquo modo cedat in honorem sanctorum; quod ut intelligatur, sciendum est omnes sanctos unum corpus cum Christo componere: unde dum Christus in sacrificio se offert, et sancti se cum eo per eum se Deo simul offerunt.

SARUM.	BANGOR.	EBOR.

Et erigens se deosculetur altare a dextris sacrificii: et dans benedictionem ultra sacrificium, postea signet se dicens:

Et inclinando et ingrediendo osculetur altare, et signet sacrificium dicendo:

S IT signatum ✠ ordinatum ✠ et sanc-

Porro talis associatio et oblatio est sanctis grata et honorifica, et sic sacrificium quod directe tendit in laudem Dei, indirecte etiam sanctos honorificat." Romsée, *Opera lit.* tom. 4. p. 176. The author writes as if the words were "in honorem;" but the right reading is, as in the text above, "in honore." It must be remembered that occasionally mediæval writers used with the same meaning "in honore" and "in honorem."

A somewhat similar prayer is in some of the Greek liturgies, and Sala in his additions to cardinal Bona's work says that it occurs "iisdem fere terminis" in the Ambrosian missal. He does not quote the prayer, and his remark is not strictly

HERFORD.

ROM.

beatæ Mariæ semper virginis, et beati Joannis baptistæ, et sanctorum apostolorum Petri et Pauli, et istorum et omnium sanctorum : ut illis proficiat ad honorem, nobis autem ad salutem : et illi pro nobis intercedere dignentur in cœlis, quorum memoriam agimus in terris. Per eumdem Christum Dominum nostrum. Amen.

Tunc erigat se, et osculetur altare in dextra parte calicis. Deinde teneat manus suas junctas supra calicem et dicat:

Postea osculatur altare, et versus ad populum,

VENI sanctificator, omnipotens æterne Deus.

Tunc signet calicem dicens:

BENE ✠ DIC et sanctifica hoc sacrificium, quod tibi est præparatum.

---

correct. The Ambrosian prayer is : "Et suscipe, sancta Trinitas, hanc oblationem, quam tibi offerimus pro regimine et custodia atque unitate catholicæ fidei et pro veneratione quoque beatæ Dei genetricis Mariæ omniumque simul sanctorum tuorum : et pro salute et incolumitate famulorum famularumque tuarum . . . ut te miserante, remissionem omnium peccatorum et æternæ beatitudinis præmia in tuis laudibus fideliter perseverando percipere mereantur, ad gloriam et honorem nominis tui, Deus misericordissime rerum conditor. Per."

SARUM.　　　　BANGOR.　　　　EBOR.

tificatum ✠ hoc
sacrificium nos-
trum.

I N nomine Patris, et Filii, et Spiritus sancti.　Amen.

Deinde vertat se sacerdos ad popu-
lum, et tacita voce dicat:

Post versus ad po-
pulum dicat:

O RATE fratres [90] et sorores [91]
pro me: ut meum pariterque
vestrum [92] acceptum (aptum, Bangor)
sit Domino Deo (nostro, Bangor)
sacrificium.

O RATE fra-
tres et so-
rores pro me pec-
catore : ut meum
pariterque ves-
trum Domino
Deo acceptum sit
sacrificium.

Responsio cleri　*Responsio chori*
privatim:　　　　*privatim:*

Chorus secrete re-
spondeat:

---

[90] (*Fratres.*)　Cæcilius in the dialogue of Minucius Felix
complains that the Christians made use of this term in addressing one another, taking it in the abominable sense in
which the pagans abused it : to which Octavius replies :
" Sic nos quod invidetis fratres vocamus, ut unius Dei parentis
homines, ut consortes fidei, ut spei cohæredes." See this
argument well treated in a tract by Kortholtus, " de calumniis
paganorum in veteres Christianos sparsis." p. 168.

[91] (*Orate fratres et sorores.* Sar.)　" Se quidem sacerdos
comparat, ut in *sancta sanctorum* pedem inferat, et, ut ita
dicam, fidelibus vale dicit, quos non ante visurus est, quam
sacrificium consummaverit." Le Brun, tom. i. p. 182.　The
custom of saying " et sorores ". is to be found in some very
ancient missals ; but does not seem to have been at any time
adopted into the Roman use.

[92] (*Ut meum pariterque vestrum.*)　The fifth chapter of

HERFORD.   ROM.

Et signet seipsum:

IN nomine Patris, et Filii, et Spiritus sancti. Amen.

Deinde vertat se ad populum et dicat:

ORATE fratres ad Dominum, ut meum pariter et vestrum in conspectu Domini acceptum sit sacrificium.

extendens et jungens manus, voce paululum elevata, dicit:

ORATE fratres: ut meum ac vestrum sacrificium acceptabile fiat apud Deum Patrem omnipotentem.

Minister, seu circumstantes respondent:

---

part 2. sect. 1. of van Espen's *Jus ecclesiasticum universum* concerns the "Honorarium," a payment in money *extra missam* which took the place of the old offerings, and which of course could only be made in primitive times by those who were present and communicants. After a disquisition upon the benefit which can be procured by purchasing of masses, he concludes: " et licet sacerdos etiam pro absentibus orare et sacrificium offerre queat, nihilominus indubitatum est: et constat ex precibus, quæ tempore sacrificii dicuntur, missam specialiter pro circumstantibus, sive præsentibus offerri: ipsosque fideles præsentes una cum sacerdote offerre; adeo ut ipse sacerdos conversus ad populum dicat: 'Orate fratres: ut meum,' &c. Hinc ecclesia a suis primordiis rigide mandavit fidelibus, diebus dominicis festisque missarum solemniis devote assistere: at nullibi mandavit, ut quis missam pro se celebrari curet."

SARUM.	BANGOR.	EBOR.

SPIRITUS sancti gratia illumi- net cor tuum et labia tua, et accipiat Dominus digne hoc sacrificium laudis de manibus tuis, pro peccatis et offensionibus nostris.[93]

EXAUDI- AT[94] te Dominus in die tribulationis: *usque* Memor sit omnis sacrificii tui.

Et reversus ad altare sacerdos[95] *secretas orationes*[96] *dicat juxta numerum antedictarum et ordinem ante epistolam,*

Post versus ad altare dicat secretas: et concludat:

---

[93] "In missis vero pro defunctis, post ablutionem manuum sacerdotis, statim incipiat sacerdos junctis manibus in medio altaris, conversus ad altare, dicens, *Hostias et preces, Domine, offerimus.* Et chorus cantando respondeat, *Tu suscipe pro animabus illis, quarum hodie memoriam agimus: fac eas, Domine, de morte transire ad vitam.* Et interim dicat sacerdos, *In spiritu humilitatis.* Deinde statim dicat, conversus ad populum, tacita voce, *Orate, fratres et sorores, pro fidelibus defunctis.* Responsio clerici cantando. *Requiem æternam dona eis, Domine, et lux perpetua luceat eis, quam olim Abrahæ promisisti et semini ejus.*

"Notandum est quod in omnibus missis pro corpore præsenti, et in anniversariis cujuscunque fuerint, et in trigintatibus, dicitur *Hostias et preces* cum versu *Requiem æternam* et *Quam olim.* In omnibus vero aliis missis pro defunctis non dicuntur, nec in die animarum." *Rubr. Sar.*

The Hereford missal does not supply the answer which the people were to make in obedience to the "orate" of the priest: but we can scarcely suppose that no response was looked for. Possibly, though not likely, the response was left to their own devotion, as might be recommended in the occasional prayers added to the prymers or horæ of the diocese. The last clause in the Sarum response is

HERFORD.

ROM.

SUSCIPIAT Dominus sacrificium de manibus tuis ad laudem et gloriam nominis sui, ad utilitatem quoque nostram, totiusque ecclesiæ suæ sanctæ.

Sacerdos submissa voce dicit,

Amen.

Tunc reversus ad altare secrete dicat: Oremus. *Deinde dicat sub silentio secretas eodem modo et ordine*

Deinde, manibus extensis, absolute sine Oremus[97] *subjungit orationes secretas.*

---

scarcely to be reconciled with the use of the term "sacrificium laudis."

[94] Ps. xix. 1, 2, 3.

[95] "Then tho prest gos to his boke,
His preuy prayers for to loke:
Knele thou doun and say then this,
That next in blak wryten is:
It wil thi prayere mykel amende,
If thou wil holde up bothe thi hende:
To god with gode deuocion,
When thou sayes this oresoun."

Layfolks mass book.

[96] These secrets varied with the day, as did the collects or gradual, &c.: and were sometimes one only, sometimes more. In ancient MSS. we commonly find these prayers called "super oblata," and although Amalarius, lib. 3. cap. 20, with others of no less authority, decides that the name secreta was given because they were said *secreto,* yet it is not improbable that the name arose "a secretione donorum et oblationum." These prayers are entitled in the Sarum, York, and the other English missals, sometimes *secretum,* but the usual way of speaking of them is the "secretæ," i.e. orationes.

[97] (*Sine Oremus.* Rom.) This seems a remarkable variation

SARUM.	BANGOR.	EBOR.

ita incipiens:
OREMUS.[98]

ita dicens:
OREMUS.

PER Dominum nostrum Jesum Christum filium tuum: qui tecum vivit et regnat in unitate Spiritus sancti Deus.
Et dicat:
PER omnia sæcula sæculorum.
Cum alta voce.

Quibus finitis dicat sacerdos aperta voce:
PER omnia[99] sæcula sæculorum.
Cum præfatione.[1]

Et cum pervenerit ad ultimum Per dominum *dicat usque ad* Per omnia sæcula sæculorum, *quod aperta voce incipiat legere sive cantare cum præfatione.*

Manibus non levatis donec dicitur Sursum corda. *Et tunc accipiat sub-*

Et sequatur præfatio.

---

from the English rubrics. The reason of it is said to be, because according to the Roman use all the prayers which come between the offertory and the secret have been considered (since they were introduced) as a part of that prayer; and to be included in the *Oremus* before the offertory.

[98] "Loke pater-noster thou be sayande,
Iwhils tho preste is priuey prayande;
Tho prest wil after in that place,
Remow him a litel space,
To he come til yo auter myddis,
Stande vp thou, als men ye biddis,
Hert and body and ilk a dele,
Take gode kepe and here him wele."
Layfolks mass book.

[99] "Then he begynnes per omnia,
And sithen sursum corda:
At tho ende sayes sanctus thryse,
In excelsis he neuens twyse:

HERFORD.   ROM.

quo collectæ dictæ fuerunt
ante epistolam.

Quibus dictis,   *Quibus finitis, cum perve-*
nerit ad conclusionem, clara
voce dicit :

P ER omnia sæcula sæ-
culorum.

ponat manus super altare   *Cum præfatione. Præfatio*
et dicat præfationem.   *incipitur ambabus manibus*

Als fast as ever that he has done,
Loke that thou be redy sone :
And say these wordis with stille steven,
Priuely to god of heuen."

Layfolks mass book.

[1] Proper prefaces were appointed according to Sarum use
for the Nativity, the Epiphany, Ash-wednesday, Easter-day,
the Ascension, Whitsunday, Trinity sunday, feasts of apostles
and evangelists, and of the holy cross; the conception, the
nativity, the annunciation, the visitation, the veneration, and
the assumption of the blessed Virgin. The common preface
is that printed in the text: "Sequens præfatio est quotidiana, et dicitur quotidie ; nisi in festis et per octavas in
quibus propria habeatur : ita tamen quod omnes præfationes
totius anni sub hoc tono dicuntur, sive propriæ habeantur sive
non, tam in feriis quam in festis secundum usum Sarum."
Rubr. Sar.

The York use added another for the days between Passion

SARUM.	BANGOR.	EBOR.

diaconus offertorium (sudarium, Bangor.) *et patenam, de manu diaconi,
ipsam patenam tenendam quousque*
Pater noster *dicitur: quam acolyto
offertorio coopertam committat in
gradu, scilicet post diaconum interim constituto.*

Hoc modo incipiantur[2] *omnes præfa-*   *Præfatio commu-*
tiones[3] *ad missam per totum annum,*   *nis.*
tam in feriis quam in festis:

---

sunday and easter. The Hereford appointed the same preface from palm-sunday to easter.

  [2] (*Incipiantur.*) Properly the "per omnia sæcula sæculorum " is not the beginning of the preface but the conclusion of
the secret. But from the custom of the priest's raising his
voice here, and the preface immediately succeeding, the words
not unnaturally though incorrectly would be looked upon as
belonging to the preface.

  [3] (*Præfationes.*) So called, as being an introduction to the
Canon or most solemn part of the service. In the Greek
church only one preface is used: anciently in the west there
was a greater number than at present: about the twelfth
century they were reduced to ten. Pope Pelagius (in a letter
to the bishops of Gaul, quoted by almost all the ritualists)
enumerates nine prefaces only, proper to certain days. These
are mentioned in the Leofric missal, preserved in the Bodleian

HERFORD.

ROM.

positis hinc inde super altare: quas aliquantulum elevat, cum dicit Sursum corda. *Jungit eas ante pectus, et caput inclinat, cum dicit,* Gratias agamus Domino Deo nostro. *Deinde disjungit manus, et disjunctas tenet usque ad finem præfationis: qua finita, iterum jungit eas, et inclinatus dicit,* Sanctus. *Et cum dicit,* Benedictus qui venit, *signum crucis sibi producit a fronte ad pectus.*

Ad dicendam vel cantandam præfationem, erigat se sacerdos honeste, et ponat manus super altare ex utra-

Sequens præfatio dicitur per annum in omnibus festis et feriis quæ propriam non habent:

---

library, and I shall quote the passage, on account of the celebrity of that volume :—

" *Epistola Pelagii papæ.* Pelagius sanctæ Romanæ ecclesiæ episcopus novem præfationes tantum modo mandat esse observandas. Unam in natale Domini. Quia per incarnati verbi. Aliam in quadragesima. Qui corporali jejunio. Tertiam in pascha. Te quidem omni tempore. Quartam in ascensione Domini. Quintam in pentecoste. Sextam de sancta Trinitate. Septimam de sancta cruce. Octavam de apostolicis. Nonam pro defunctis."

To these a tenth was afterwards added, in honour of the blessed Virgin, which is mentioned as to be used also in the English church, by the fourteenth canon of the synod of Westminster, A.D. 1175; quoting, but not as in the Leofric MS., the epistle of Pelagius. This (like the canon mentioned

SARUM.   BANGOR.   EBOR.

PER omnia sæcula sæculorum.
Amen. Dominus vobiscum.[4]
Et cum spiritu tuo. *Hic elevet sacerdos manus dicens:* Sursum corda.[5]
Habemus ad Dominum. Gratias
agamus Domino Deo nostro. Dignum et justum est.

PER omnia
sæcula sæ-
culorum. Domi-
nus vobiscum.
Sursum corda.
Gratias agamus
Domino Deo
nostro.

---

immediately below) prohibits any unauthorised addition.
Wilkins, *Concilia*, tom. i. p. 478.

As to the epistle of Pelagius, just cited, I must observe that
cardinal Bona doubts its authenticity: his observations should
be consulted; lib. ii. cap. 10. And the very learned Stephen
Baluze agrees with Bona: to which we must add that the
epistle is rejected by Labbe and Cossart, *Conc.* tom. v. p. 931.
In some of the most ancient manuscripts which are extant (for
example, the famous one formerly queen Christina's of Sweden
and now in the Vatican) the preface is called *Immolatio*, and
sometimes *Contestatio missæ* because, says Bona, "in ea sacerdos audita voce populi, vel cleri, sive ministri asserentis
dignum et justum esse Deo gratias agere, contestatur veram
esse hanc populi assertionem: tum solemni gratiarum actione
se et fideles disponit ad tremenda mysteria, quibus Christi
corpus immolatur." It is styled in the Mozarabic missal
Inlatio; of which there appears to be no satisfactory interpretation.

The preface is of such great antiquity, occurring in the
liturgy of St. James, and being spoken of by St. Cyprian, St.
Cyril, and other fathers as of common use in their time, that
we cannot attribute its introduction to any age later than the
apostolic.

The twenty-fifth of the canons made at Westminster or
Canterbury in 1173 orders, "Non dicantur præfationes præter
ea, quæ statuta sunt." *Concil.* tom. i. p. 475.

HERFORD.   ROM.

*que parte calicis, et dicat
hoc modo :*

PER omnia sæcula sæculorum. Amen. Dominus vobiscum. Et cum spiritu tuo. Sursum corda. Habemus ad Dominum. Gratias agamus Domino Deo nostro. Dignum et justum est.

---

[4] There is no direction here; probably the old custom of the church of England was not to turn at this "Dominus vobiscum," as at other such salutations, toward the people but continue still to face the altar. I mention it on account of the reason having by some been referred to the very ancient practice of the Greek churches of shutting in the sanctuary at this time, and enclosing the priest within the curtains and a veil: which, of course, would so far account for it, as he and the people could not for a time see one another. *Vide* Cavalieri, *Opera*, tom. v. p. 65, and Le Brun, tom. i. p. 186. But compare also Amalarius, lib. iii. cap. 9, who gives other reasons for the exception in this case.

[5] (*Sursum corda.*) This invitation is to be found in all the liturgies both of the eastern and western churches; and we may believe is of apostolical authority. St. Cyprian especially alludes to it in his treatise *de oratione Dominica, Opera*, p. 213: "Sacerdos ante orationem præfatione præmissa parat fratrum mentes dicendo, *Sursum corda,*" &c. And St. Augustine: "Tenetis sacramenta ordine suo. Primo post orationem admonemini sursum habere cor. Ideo enim cum dicitur, Sursum cor, respondetis: Habemus ad Dominum. Sequitur episcopus vel presbyter qui offert, et dicit, Gratias agamus Domino Deo nostro; et vos attestamini, Dignum et justum est." *Serm.* 217, edit. Benedict. In some of the old sacramentaries the canon begins with the words "Sursum corda:" as in the Gelasian; Thomas. *codex sac.* pag. 196.

SARUM.　　　　　　BANGOR.　　　　　　EBOR.

*Hæc præfatio est
quotidiana.*

VERE dignum et justum est, æquum et salutare, nos tibi semper, et ubique gratias agere : Domine sancte, Pater omnipotens, æterne Deus : per Christum Dominum nostrum.　Per quem Majestatem tuam laudant Angeli, adorant Dominationes, tremunt Potestates. Cœli, cœlorumque virtutes, ac beata seraphin, socia exultatione concelebrant.　Cum quibus et nostras voces, ut admitti jubeas deprecamur, supplici confessione dicentes :

Sequitur Sanctus.[6]　*Dum sacerdos dicit* Sanctus, sanctus, *erigat parumper brachia sua et jungat manus suas, usque ad hæc verba* In nomine Domini : *tunc semper signet se in facie sua.*

---

[6] This is the seraphic hymn; and called "Epinicion" or triumphal by the Greeks.　It is not possible to say at how early a period it was added to the liturgy; most probably from the very first.　Some have attributed its introduction to pope Sixtus the first.　He did not however introduce it, but ordered that it should be begun by the priest and continued by the people with him.　The fact, which is stated also by Baronius, A. D. 142, proves the very great antiquity of the use of the hymn.　See Bona, and Cavalieri, tom. v. p. 66.　This hymn, as also the "Gloria in excelsis," was in some churches defaced by interpolations : it is to these that archbishop Lanfranc alludes in his statutes, cap. 5, where he orders all to bow towards the altar during its recitation "nisi versus interponantur."　*Opera*, p. 279.　See also Gerbert, *de musica*, tom. i. p. 445.

Goar, in his notes to the liturgy of St. Chrysostom, reckons four liturgical hymns.　1. Gloria in excelsis; 2. the cherubic, "Qui cherubin mystice," &c., which is sung before the great

HERFORD.   ROM.

VERE dignum et justum est, æquum et salutare, nos tibi semper, et ubique gratias agere: Domine sancte, Pater omnipotens, æterne Deus: per Christum Dominum nostrum. Per quem Majestatem tuam laudant Angeli, adorant Dominationes, tremunt Potestates. Cœli, cœlorumque virtutes, ac beata seraphin, socia exultatione concelebrant. Cum quibus et nostras voces, ut admitti jubeas deprecamur, supplici confessione dicentes:

HERFORD.	ROM.
Tunc sacerdos elevans aliquantulum brachia junctis manibus dicat: Sanctus, *et signet seipsum dicens,* Benedictus qui venit in nomine Domini.	*Sacerdos inclinatus dicit:* Sanctus. *Et cum dicit* Benedictus qui venit, *signum crucis sibi producit a fronte ad pectus.*

---

introit; 3. "Sanctus Deus, Sanctus fortis," daily sung by the Greeks, and once a year upon Good Friday in the Latin church; and 4. the Epinicion, "Sanctus, sanctus, sanctus." Page 136.

Sala, in his additions to Bona, remarks that the words "Osanna . . . in excelsis" are added by the authority of the Church to this hymn: as if (quoting Natalis Alexander) "ostendatur adventum Domini in carne non solum humani generis in terra, sed et angelorum in cœlis esse quodam modo salutem: quia dum nos redempti ad superna perducimur, eorum numerus Sathana cadente imminutus impletur." Micrologus also observes, cap. xj: "presbyter post finitam secretam orditur præfationem in canonem, in qua supernorum civium ordines merito connumerantur, quia iisdem mysteriis, quæ ibi conficiuntur, juxta attestationem sanctorum patrum, interesse creduntur, unde et angelicum trisagium subjungitur."

SARUM.   BANGOR.   EBOR.

SANCTUS, Sanctus, Sanctus,[7] Dominus Deus Sabaoth. Pleni sunt cœli et terra gloria tua: osanna in excelsis. Benedictus qui venit in nomine Domini: osanna in excelsis.[8]

Deinde confestim manibus junctis et oculis elevatis incipiat Te igitur clementissime Pater: *corpore inclinato donec dixerit.* Ac petimus.

---

[7] The rest of this passage, "Dominus Deus Sabaoth . . . osanna in excelsis," omitted in the Leofric missal.

[8] "*In omnibus festis beatæ Mariæ virginis ac etiam commemorationibus ejusdem, dicitur sic:* Benedictus Mariæ filius qui venit in nomine Domini, osanna in excelsis." *Rubr. miss. Ebor.*

[9] There are some other ancient missals in which interpolated prayers of this kind may be found. The present example is cited by cardinal Bona from "Petrus ab Opmeer *in assertione missæ,* p. 362," but with this addition at the beginning: "Domine Jesu Christe Fili Dei vivi adjuva infirmitatem

HERFORD.	ROM.

SANCTUS, Sanctus, Sanctus, Dominus Deus Sabaoth. Pleni sunt cœli et terra gloria tua·: osanna
(Hosanna, Rom.) in excelsis. Benedictus qui venit in
nomine Domini : osanna (Hosanna, Rom.) in excelsis.

*Postea sacerdos adorans cru-
cifixum dicat :*

ADORAMUS te,'
Christe, et benedi-
cimus tibi, quia per sanctam crucem tuam redemisti
mundum. Miserere nobis,
qui passus es pro nobis.

---

meam, et conforta me nunc in hac hora : quia imperfectum
meum vident oculi tui. Adoramus," &c. Micrologus, cap.
xij, attempts to prove that such interpolations are objectionable (as certainly they are, but not) because they were never
allowed to be made in the canon without the highest authority. For certainly the canon cannot be said to begin until
the " Te igitur." As I mention presently, the canon was
not only to be said *secreto* but was also called *secretum;*
whereas the prefaces are said " clara voce ;" and there is no
special direction to the contrary as regards this prayer in the
Hereford use.

Canon Missae.[1]

SARUM.   BANGOR.   EBOR.

Junctis manibus[2]
sacerdos inclinet se
dicens:[3]

TE igitur, clementissime Pater,[4] per Jesum Christum Filium tuum Dominum nostrum supplices rogamus ac petimus:

---

[1] (*Canon missæ.*) "Oratio quæ incipit, *Te igitur*, quamque sequitur *Pater*, dicitur canon, quippe quæ tanquam regula in sacrificio offerendo servanda, nunquamque mutanda præscripta fuerit." Le Brun, tom. i. p. 197.

To ask by whom the canon of the mass was drawn up, or who may rightly be called the author of it, is an idle enquiry. Subject to some few verbal variations, the canon has remained the same from the end of the sixth century to the present time. Very probably it was the same up to the third century, with the exception of slight additions made from time to time. We shall never probably know the exact form and words of the Roman liturgy, during the first three hundred years of the Christian æra. But we may be sure that in the spirit of its arrangement and in the character and general language of its prayers and ceremonies the canon of the mass up to the apostolic age did not differ from the canon as it was observed for nearly a thousand years in the church of England before the reformation, and as it still is in the Roman catholic church throughout the world. We may use the words of Walafrid Strabo who wrote in the ninth century: "Ipsam actionem, qua conficitur sacrosanctum corporis et sanguinis Dominici mysterium (quam quoque Romani canonem, ut in pontificalibus sæpius invenitur, appellant) quis primus ordinaverit, nobis

Canon Missae.

<table>
<tr><td>HERFORD.</td><td>ROM.</td></tr>
<tr>
<td>Hic inclinet se sacerdos ad altare junctis manibus dicendo:</td>
<td>Sacerdos extendens et jungens manus, elevans ad cœlum oculos, et statim demittens, profunde inclinatus ante altare, manibus super eo positis, dicit:</td>
</tr>
</table>

TE igitur, clementissime Pater, per Jesum Christum Filium tuum Dominum nostrum supplices rogamus ac petimus:

---

ignotum est. Auctam tamen fuisse, non semel sed sæpius, ex partibus additis·intelligimus." *De rebus ecc.* cap. 22. Nor need we hesitate to accept the statement of pope Vigilius, who writes of the liturgy in his epistle to Eucherius, " ex apostolica traditione succepimus;" or of a pope earlier even than Vigilius, "quis enim nesciat aut non advertat id, quod a principe apostolorum Petro Romanæ ecclesiæ traditum est, ac usque nunc custoditur, ab omnibus debere servari?" *Innocent. epist. ad Decentium.*

The whole canon of the mass was sometimes called *Secretum:* as, for example, in the third decree of the synod of York, 1195, which respects the correctness of the manuscripts used in the public services and begins: "Quia secretum missæ frequenter invenitur aut scriptorum falsitate, aut librorum vetustate corruptum, ita ut legi distincte non possit," &c. Wilkins, *Conc.* i. 501.

The title *Canon* as applied to this part of the service is as old certainly as at least the time of Gregory the great; who speaks of himself having directed the Lord's prayer to be said "*mox post canonem.*" Mabillon, however, says that the term cannot be traced further back than the time of that pope: "precem illam canonem primus, aut inter primos, absolute vocat Gregorius M." *Mus. Ital.* 2. p. xlviij. Strictly

I

SARUM.   BANGOR.   EBOR.

(*Hic*, Sarum et Bangor.) *erigens se* (*sacerdos*, Ebor.) *osculetur altare a dextris sacrificii dicens*:

---

the canon ends before the Lord's prayer; and in many manuscripts a different style of writing then begins again.

But it may not be improper to mention some other titles which have been given to this portion of the liturgy. "*Precem* vocat Innocentius I. in epist. ad Decentium: et Vigilius p. Profuturum, *canonicæ precis textum.*" Gerbert, tom. i. p. 122. Again, the same author, p. 446, quoting Amalarius: "ab illo loco, ubi secretam dicit episcopus usque ad AGNUS DEI, totum illud vocat Augustinus *Orationes.*" And Gavantus has collected several others. *Regula ecclesiastica*, from St. Ambrose. *Legitimum*, Optatus. *Secretum*, St. Basil. *Ordo precum*, Isidore. *Actio* and *Regula*, by Walafrid Strabo. (*Thesaurus sacr. rit.* tom. i. 105.)

To these I must not omit to add Lyndwood's explanation: "Licet quidam simplices sacerdotes intelligant canonem, quidquid est in secreto missæ: et stricte intelligendo canonem, puto quod *Hostiensis* dicit verum, est namque canon idem quod regula. Missa vero proprie dicitur eucharistiæ consecratio. Alia autem omnia, quæ vel sacerdos dicit vel chorus canit, gratiarum actiones sunt, vel certe obsecrationes. Unde canon missæ vere dicitur regula illa, per quam eucharistia consecratur: large tamen intelligendo canonem missæ juxta communem intellectum simplicium sacerdotum, denotat totum secretum missæ post præfationem." Lib. i. tit. 10, Ut archidiaconi, *verb.* Canon.

[2] (*Junctis manibus.*) In this the English uses agree, differing from what has been the rule of the Roman missal "*manibus extensis.*" It would seem however that very anciently this last was the custom in some parts at least of this country also. For we read of St. Dunstan: "eo quippe inter sacrosancta missarum solemnia sacras manus extendente, et Deum Patrem omnipotentem, ut 'ecclesiam suam catholicam pacificare, custodire,' &c. interpellante, nivea columba de cœlo descendit." *Vita S. Dunstani*, cap. xxxij.

Micrologus says: "Notandum autem, per totum canonem Dominicæ passionis commemorationem potissimum actitari,

HERFORD. ROM.

Hic osculetur altare, et eri- Osculatur altare:
gat se dicendo:

---

juxta Domini præceptum in evangelio: *Hæc, quotiescunque feceritis, &c.* Unde et ipse sacerdos per totum canonem in expansione manuum, non tam mentis devotionem, quam Christi extensionem in cruce designat, juxta illud: *Expandi manus meas tota die.*" Cap. 16. So also Radulph. Tungr. prop. 23. But the later ritualists take a different view.

[3] There is no doubt that for many centuries before the reformation the Church of England, according to her different uses, yet agreed in all of them with the rest of the western Church in this point: that the whole of the canon, from the *Te igitur* to the *per omnia sæcula sæculorum*, was said *secreto*, or *submissa voce.* It is a stupid error to suppose that by *secreto* is meant no utterance at all, or even what is commonly called *mumbling:* for there are many orders of the English Church (which I shall have occasion to cite presently) which prove that a distinct pronunciation was required of every word no less than in those parts of the liturgy which were repeated aloud. The present *Rubricæ generales* prefixed to the Roman missal explain well this point: "Quæ vero secrete dicenda sunt, ita pronuntiet, ut et ipsemet se audiat, et a circumstantibus non audiatur." Tit. xvi. 2.

So the provincial constitution of Walter Reynold, in 1322: "Verba canonis, in his præsertim quæ ad sanctum sacramentum pertinent, plene, integre, et cum summa animi devotione proferantur. Non tamen sit ita morosus sacerdos in præmissis, quod fastidium ingerat auditoribus, et officium suum privet devotionis pinguedine: quia muscæ morientes perdunt suavitatem unguenti, id est, pinguedinem devotionis." *Concil.* tom. 2. p. 513. Lyndwood glosses thus: "*Devotione.* Ut scilicet mentis intentio firmiter applicetur ad Deum, et ad pronunciationem verborum. Intentio namque semper est necessaria, vel specialis, vel generalis: et non solum requiritur intentio consecrantis, sed etiam intentio istud sacramentum instituentis. *Morosus,* i.e. tardans. *Auditoribus.* Qui ut plurimum solent ex prolixitate orationis, vel alias officii divini anxiari; cum tamen brevis oratio, facta cum

SARUM.   BANGOR.   EBOR.

U TI accepta habeas, et benedicas hæc ✠ dona,
hæc ✠ munera,⁵ hæc ✠ sancta sacrificia illibata : ⁶

---

animi devotione, melior sit quam oratio prolixa cum anxietate
cordis."   Lib. 3. tit. 23, Linteamina.

But the subject of chief importance, upon which one or two
brief remarks are necessary, is as to the time when this practice began of repeating the canon so that no one but the officiating priest might hear what was said.   There seems to be
no question that in the primitive ages the faithful heard the
whole and answered at the end, *Amen.*   Very probably there
was a variety of tone; but not to such an extent that the
priest was inaudible.   Cardinal Bona is decisive upon this :
speaking of the use of the Greek Church, that its liturgy is
said aloud, he adds : "eumdem morem servabat olim ecclesia
occidentalis, omnes enim audiebant sanctissima et efficacissima
verba, quibus Christi corpus conficitur."   And he further gives
it as his opinion that no change took place in this respect
until the tenth century.

In the twelfth century, the author of the *Gemma animæ*
not only speaks of secret utterance as then the usual practice
but gives three reasons for it : "Una est, quia cum Deo lo-
quimur, cui non ore sed corde clamare præcipimur.   Secunda
est, ne populus tam prolixa declamatione attædiatus abscedat,
vel sacerdos tam longo clamore voce deficiat.   Tertia est, ne
tam sancta verba tanti mysterii vilescant, dum ea vulgus per
quotidianum usum in inconvenientibus locis dicat."   Cap. 103.
If these were the reasons which led to so great a departure
from primitive use they can scarcely be regarded as sufficient.
Amalarius offers some of greater weight : "non est necessaria
vox reboans" he says, *de off. eccles.* lib. 3. cap. 20 : and again,
"ut impudentis est clamoribus strepere, ita contra congruit
verecundo, modestis precibus orare."   Cap. 23.   He wrote
before the tenth century, and it is not certain that he intends
more than a proper modulation and lowering of the voice.

Modern ritualists and theologians do not agree why the
canon should be said *secreto.*   Some say that the mystery
should be concealed ; some, that greater reverence is to be
the effect of it ; some, that the canon and especially the

HERFORD.   ROM.

U T I accepta habeas et benedicas :

---

verba consecrationis should not be made common. As to this last it can have little if any weight, though most relied on : because not only are there and always have been an infinity of books which the laity may use, but parish priests are strictly enjoined to make known to their people the meaning and complete knowledge of this service, by catechisms and sermons, &c. The words of a learned writer on the subject are, "ut perfectam populo christiano tradant hujus mysterii notitiam." Romsée, *Opera*, tom. iv. p. 200. And the Catechismus ad parochos declares that all those points "a pastoribus diligentissime exponenda erunt, quæ ejus majestatem magis illustrare posse videantur." Edit. Aldus, 1566, p. 130. Of which teaching, as there exemplified, the *verba consecrationis* form the chief part. The council of Trent decrees : " Si quis dixerit ecclesiæ Romanæ ritum, quo submissa voce pars canonis, et verba consecrationis proferuntur, damnandum esse ; . . . anathema sit." *Sess.* 22. *can.* ix.

Against Bona and the other great writers who agree with him Le Brun wrote a long dissertation, in which he collected all the authorities which in any way seem to prove the greater antiquity of saying the canon in an audible voice. It is to be found at the end of the fourth volume of his works.

I shall extract some constitutions of the English Church which are directed to the saying of the canon : and shall leave to the judgment of the reader whether they decide clearly or not, at least the earlier of them, that the then custom in this country was that the priest should not be heard by the people. In one thing they are decisive enough ; that *secreto* did not exclude but rather directed, distinct pronunciation.

The first canon of the council of London, A.D. 1200, orders : " Cum in divinis officiis non sine periculo corporum et animarum erretur, salubri provisione concilii prospeximus, ut a quolibet sacerdote celebrante, verba canonis rotunde dicantur, nec ex festinatione contracta, nec ex diuturnitate nimis protracta." Wilkins, *Concilia*, tom. i. p. 505. In the year 1222

SARUM.	BANGOR.	EBOR.
Factis signaculis super calicem, ele-	*Finitis his tribus signaculis super*	*Hic elevet manus dicens:*

---

a council at Oxford decreed, canon vi: "Verba vero canonis, præsertim in consecratione corporis Christi plene et integre proferuntur." Wilkins, p. 586. One of the synodal constitutions of Gilbert bishop of Chichester, A. D. 1289, would be of importance if we could allow that the canon of the mass is included among the "divina officia" there meant. "Presbyteri sint seduli ad divina officia horis competentibus et statutis in suis ecclesiis celebranda, ne desidia vel negligentia argui sive puniri debeant a prælatis. Quæ autem legunt vel cantant, distincte proferant et aperte, non transiliendo, neque transcurrendo, vel syncopando, sed cum debita reverentia, ut ad devotionem excitent mentes seu animos auditorum." Wilkins, tom. ii. p. 170. Once more, a provincial constitution of Walter Raynold archbishop of Canterbury, A.D. 1322: "Item verba canonis, præsertim in his, quæ ad substantialia sacramenti pertinent, plene, integre, et cum summa animi devotione proferantur." Wilkins, tom. ii. p. 513.

This last statute may be seen in the *Provinciale,* and Lyndwood gives the other constitution of archbishop Stephen Langton (A.D. 1222) in which is the same injunction: "Verba canonis . . . plene et integre proferantur." Lib. iii. tit. 23, Ad excitandos. His gloss is not of great importance to the present point, as he seems to limit the canon chiefly to the words of consecration: which is an improper interpretation of it. *Plene,* he says, means *absque omissione.* In the constitution of archbishop Raynold he refers "cum summa animi devotione" to the intention: "ut sc. mentis intentio firmiter applicetur ad Deum, et ad pronunciationem verborum. Intentio namque semper est necessaria, vel specialis, vel generalis."

I do not think it necessary to enter here upon the subject of Intention; by it (I would remind the reader) is meant the deliberate purpose or will to do or perform something, say, a sacrament; and it is commonly defined to be "volitio efficax finis, unde differt intentio a simplici volitione, seu complacentia finis, sive boni alicujus, quia simplex voluntas, seu compla-

---

centia respicit finem sine habitudine ad consecutionem. Intentio autem est volitio efficax tendens in finis consecutionem."
Gavanti, *Thesaurus*, tom. i. p. 337. Upon the doctrine of the
Roman catholic church in this matter; how intention may
be either actual, or virtual, or habitual, or interpretative; how
these differ from each other and affect the validity of a sacrament, the student will do well to consult Quarti in *Rubr. Miss.*
part. 3. tit. vij; Benedict XIV, *Opera*, tom. ix. lib. iii. cap. 10;
and Billuart, *summa S. Thomæ*, dissert. 3. vj, and 5. vij.

Returning to the order of secret recitation, the only exception at present to the universal rule is at ordinations of
priests; when, as Benedict XIV says, "Ordinandi circa altare
in genua provoluti disponuntur, et episcopus, quasi eos doceat
missam celebrare, lente ac paullulum elata voce secretas
profert, non eas ut populus audiat, sed ut sacerdotes novissime
initiati cum eo possint eas recitare, et verba consecrationis uno
eodemque tempore cum episcopo pronunciare; ad exemplum
Christi qui voce, quæ ab apostolis audiri potuit, in ultima
cæna panem et vinum consecravit, ut eos, quos tunc sacerdotio
initiabat, doceret consecrandi modum legitimumque ritum
ad consummationem usque sæculi duraturum." *Opera*, tom.
ix. p. 248.

[4] "Cum altari assistitur, semper ad Patrem dirigatur oratio."
Excerpt. Egbert., *Concil.* tom. i. p. 104. This would refer to
the canon, from "Te igitur" to the Lord's prayer.

[5] (*Hæc dona, hæc munera.*) "Hæc dona, hæc munera. Quod
superior inferioribus, creator creaturis, rex subditis donant, id
donum dicitur; quod autem subditi principi, inferiores superi-
oribus, iisque exhibent, quibus debent, *munus* appellatur.
Panis et vinum quæ super altari sunt, dicuntur dona quoad
Deum, a quo omne bonum in nos derivatur, sunt autem
munera quoad homines, qui Deo eadem exhibent." Le Brun,
tom. i. p. 200.

See also some verses by Hildebert, quoted by Durant, ii. 33.

[6] (*Illibata.*) This is not to be referred to the sacred elements but rather to the purity both of soul and body which is

SARUM.   BANGOR.   EBOR.

vet manus suas   *calicem, elevet ma-*
ita dicens: *nus suas, dicens:*

IMPRIMIS (In primis, Bangor. et Ebor.) quæ tibi offerimus pro ecclesia tua sancta catholica : quam pacificare, custodire, adunare, et regere digneris toto orbe terrarum, una cum famulo[7] tuo papa nostro N. et antistite nostro N. (*id est proprio episcopo tantum :* Sarum) et rege nostro[8] N. (*et dicuntur nominatim,* Sarum) et omnibus orthodoxis, atque catholicæ et apostolicæ fidei cultoribus.

Hic oret pro vi-   *Hic oret cogitan-*   *Hic oret pro vi-*
vis. In qua ora-   *do pro vivis:*   *vis:*

---

fitting to the priest. By the use of the term the celebrant commends (according to the best ritualists) his own singleness of heart and sincerity to God.

Upon the variety in using the sign of the cross here see St. Anselm, *Opera,* p. 139; *ad Waleranni querelas, resp.* cap. 2.

[7] "Una cum beatissimo famulo tuo." *Missal. Leofr.* Probably the first canon of any council on this point is the fourth of the council of Vaisson, A. D. 529 : "Nobis justum visum est, ut nomen domini papæ, quicunque apostolicæ sedi præfuerit, in nostris ecclesiis recitetur."

[8] (*Et rege nostro.*) "Sacrificamus pro salute imperatoris," says Tertullian (*ad Scapulam,* c. 2) quoted by cardinal Bona ; and we know from Eusebius how strictly this duty was fulfilled even in the case of the emperors Gallus, Valerian, and Gallienus ; *hist. eccl.* lib. vii. cap. 1.

St. Paul in the second chapter of the first epistle to St. Timothy must have alluded to the eucharist and the prayers then to be offered up in behalf of kings. There can be no *giving of thanks* in its usual sense to God for His permitting of a persecuting king. But as Theophylact says "*their safety is our peace.*"

In the ecclesiastical laws of king Ethelred, A.D. 1012, the

HERFORD. ROM.

hæc ✚ dona, hæc ✚ munera, hæc ✚ sancta sacrificia illibata:

Tunc erigat sursum bra- *Extensis manibus prosequi-*
chia et dicat: *tur:*

IN primis quæ tibi offerimus pro ecclesia tua sancta catholica: quam pacificare, custodire, adunare, et regere digneris toto orbe terrarum: una cum famulo tuo papa nostro N. et antistite nostro N. (et rege nostro N. Herf.) et omnibus orthodoxis, atque catholicæ et apostolicæ fidei cultoribus.

Commemoratio pro vivis.

---

third chapter contains express directions that a certain prayer should be said daily for the king and his people: " Et præcipimus, ut in omni congregatione cantetur quotidie communiter pro rege et omni populo suo una missa ad matutinalem missam, quæ inscripta est, contra paganos," &c. Wilkins, *Concilia,* tom. i. 295. Here the word *missa* is used in a rather unusual sense, to signify a collect: but other examples may be found; especially the passage in the second council of Milevia, cap. xij : " Placuit ut preces, vel orationes, seu missæ, quæ probatæ fuerint in concilio ab omnibus celebrentur." The words " et fiant missæ" in the rule of St. Benedict must be taken to mean the same. Other significations of missa, such as for any ecclesiastical office, for lections, &c., before the term became limited to its more proper sense, may be seen in Ducange. And the same laws of king Ethelred afford another example of its use to signify collects; cap. ij : " Et super hoc cantet omnis presbyter xxx. missas, et omnis diaconus et clericus xxx. psalmos," &c.

In the printed missals is frequently inserted, sometimes before the canon, sometimes at the end of the volume, a mass or prayers to be said for the king. The reader will find in the Additional Note an example of these taken from an edition of the Salisbury missal, in 1516.

SARUM.	BANGOR.	EBOR.

tione, ordo debet attendi propter ordinem caritatis. Quinquies orat sacerdos; primo pro seipso; secundo pro patre et matre, carnali videlicet et spirituali, et pro aliis parentibus; tertio pro amicis specialibus, parochianis et aliis; quarto pro omnibus adstantibus: quinto pro omni populo Christiano: et potest hic sacerdos omnes suos amicos Deo commendare. Consulo tamen, ut nullus ibidem nimis immoretur; tum propter cordis distractionem, tum propter immissiones quæ possunt fieri per angelos malos, tum propter alia miracula.

MEMENTO,[9] Domine, famulorum famularumque tuarum [10] N. (et N. Sarum) et omnium circum-

---

[9] At this period of the service the diptychs were recited,

HERFORD.   ROM.

M EMENTO, Domine, famulorum famularumque
tuarum, (N. et N. Rom.)

·that is, the names contained in them : hence in many ancient

SARUM.　　　　BANGOR.　　　　EBOR.

stantium (atque omnium fidelium Christianorum,[11] Bangor. et Ebor.) quorum tibi fides cognita est et nota devotio : pro quibus tibi offerimus, vel qui tibi offerunt hoc sacrificium laudis pro se, suisque omnibus,[12] pro

---

liturgies this prayer is entitled *Oratio super diptycha.* These diptychs were plates of wood or ivory, folded often latterly into three parts : upon the first of which were inscribed the names of great saints, apostles, and martyrs ; upon the second, of those among the living who were illustrious for rank and station or had deserved well of the Church ; and in the third were the names of those who had died in her communion. There was in some Churches a custom of reciting here also the names of those who had offered any oblation previously ; but this could only have been some selected from the many and, I presume, not the same names always or the first and chief ; but taken promiscuously from the whole number. For much information upon the diptychs, see Ducange, verb. Diptycha ; Mabillon, *de lit. Gall.* lib. iii. 11 ; Bingham, *Orig. eccles.* vol. v, and a very learned treatise by Salig, *de diptychis veterum,* 4to. 1731.

[10] The Leofric missal adds, "*illorum et illarum,* et omnium," &c.

[11] This addition in the Bangor and York missals is exclaimed against by Bona : "Post illa verba *et omnium circumstantium* addunt quidam libri *omniumque fidelium :* sed omnino rejicienda hæc additio tanquam superflua : nam in fine præcedentis orationis præmissa est pro omnibus fidelibus deprecatio illis verbis, *et omnibus orthodoxis.*" Tom. iii. p. 256. The reason for the addition seems originally to have been that the clause " et omnibus orthodoxis " was not invariably inserted ; and then this latter reference was necessary : which was not removed from the York and Bangor uses when they adopted the *et omnibus,* &c. See Micrologus, cap. xiij, who on the other hand says that the first clause is the superfluous one. There can be no doubt that both are not required. The last is omitted in the Leofric manuscript.

[12] In this sentence the word *vel* must be taken not in a disjunctive but a conjunctive sense : as Menard shows in his

HERFORD.	ROM.
Hic oret pro vivis in corde suo et postea dicat:	*Jungit manus, orat aliquantulum pro quibus orare intendit: deinde manibus extensis prosequitur:*

---

notes to the sacramentary of St. Gregory. Compare with it the prayer above: "Orate, fratres, ut meum pariterque vestrum sacrificium," &c. There is a very famous place in Tertullian which bears upon the question involved in this passage: he is answering an objection, and whatever else his words may mean, they must be interpreted primarily not only with reference to that, but that the writer probably was not strict in weighing every word: "Vani erimus, si putaverimus quod sacerdotibus non liceat, laicis licere. Nonne et laici sacerdotes sumus? scriptum est, regnum quoque nos et sacerdotes Deo et Patri suo fecit. Differentiam inter ordinem et plebem constituit Ecclesiæ auctoritas, et honor per ordinis confessum sanctificatus adeo ubi ecclesiastici ordinis non est consessus, et offers et tinguis et sacerdos es tibi solus. . . . Igitur si habes jus sacerdotis in temetipso ubi necesse est, habeas oportet etiam disciplinam sacerdotis, ubi necesse sit habere jus sacerdotis." *De exhort. cast., Opera*, p. 522. Now, it might be sufficient to remember in reply to the argument which some would be inclined to draw from this what the fate of Tertullian was, and how unsound many of his peculiar opinions were. But, as Rigalt observes in his note, much more blame than is justly due has been thrown upon Tertullian in regard of this passage, from not properly considering in what sense that ancient author uses the terms oratio, sacrificium, oblatio, and sacramentum: which, he says, may be collected from the index to his works. Not only again does Tertullian use the word *offerre* and not *consecrare*, but he could not have been ignorant of the universal practice of his day to send portions of the blessed eucharist to the sick and to those in prison, of which there would have been no need if every layman was a priest in the more strict and true sense of the word.

The Church has always held that those who are present at the holy communion offer with the priest: and this, either

SARUM.　　　BANGOR.　　　EBOR.

redemptione animarum suarum: pro spe salutis et incolumitatis suæ: tibique reddunt vota sua æterno
Deo, vivo et vero.

---

because they do so by his ministry, or because they unite
with him in the prayers which he puts up to the throne of
grace, or because they actually do make offerings either necessary (as of old) to the due performance of the service itself,
or as alms to be used for the benefit of the Church in any
way. But she has never allowed that a lay-person can, in its
proper sense, consecrate the elements, even in cases of necessity. The conduct of Frumentius a layman who, as Theo-
doret relates, *Hist.* lib. i. cap. 23, went from Alexandria to
Ethiopia, and having there converted many proceeded to
collect them into congregations and desired them to perform
the divine offices, proves nothing although not unfrequently
appealed to: for he went with others amongst whom probably
were priests, and he was chiefly named as the promoter of
the mission: as we learn from Socrates, *Hist.* lib. i. cap. 49,
he came back himself to Alexandria and was consecrated
the first bishop of the Church which he had planted. See
Mosheim, book ii. part i. chap. i. § 20.

I shall have occasion presently to refer to the address of
St. Laurence to pope Sixtus and shall here also speak of
it, because from the received text in that place of the Benedictine edition of St. Ambrose it may be argued that deacons
might consecrate the chalice. But as the very learned editors
say in their note, tom. ii. p. 55, the term consecration is sometimes to be taken "pro ejusdem effectu, i.e. jam peracta consecratione." In this sense a sermon of Guerricus, an abbot,
speaks of the *people* consecrating. And, if so: "sane diacono competit non tanquam uni e fidelium conventu, sed
tanquam primario consecrantis sacerdotis ministro illius actioni
cooperari per modum cujusdam, ut sic loquamur, concelebra-
tionis:" and some authorities are cited in support of this
interpretation. Again: "Secunda consecrationis acceptio,

HERFORD.   ROM.

E T omnium circumstantium, quorum tibi fides cognita est, et nota devotio: pro quibus tibi offerimus, vel qui tibi offerunt hoc sacrificium laudis, pro

---

nimirum pro rei consecratæ distributione, omni prorsus caret offendiculo, maximeque nobis arridet: quia vox commisisti aliquid jam perfectum signat," &c. We must after all remember that dispensationem is the common reading.

I shall add from an old writer: " *Qui tibi offerunt,* &c. In quibus verbis patenter ostenditur, quod a cunctis fidelibus, non solum viris, sed et mulieribus sacrificium illud laudis offertur, licet ab uno specialiter offerri sacerdote videatur. Quia quæ ille Deo offerendo manibus tractat, hæc multitudo fidelium intenta mentium devotione commendat. Quod illic quoque declaratur ubi dicitur, 'Hanc igitur oblationem servitutis nostræ, sed et cunctæ familiæ tuæ, ut placatus accipias.' Quibus verbis luce clarius constat, quia sacrificium, quod a sacerdote sacris altaribus superponitur, a cuncta Dei familia generaliter offeratur. Hanc autem ecclesiæ unitatem apostolus manifeste declarat cum dicit, 'unum corpus, unus panis, multi sumus.'" Petrus Damian. cap. viij.

Although "vel" may be rightly interpreted without difficulty, it is possible that originally the word crept into the prayer, as it were, by mistake. Many early manuscripts omit the clause "pro quibus tibi offerimus," and we may easily understand how when the words were first added it was with an intention that there should be a discretionary decision by the priest whether he would use them or the earlier and succeeding words only, "qui tibi offerunt." Some manuscripts are still extant in which the "vel" is written in red. At what time the addition "pro quibus tibi offerimus" was made is uncertain: some say it may be referred so far back as the sixth or seventh century. But there seems to be no doubt that the words are to be found in all manuscripts written after the eleventh century.

*Sequitur infra
canonem.*[13]

COMMUNICANTES, et memoriam venerantes:
In primis (Imprimis, Sar.) gloriosæ semper virginis Mariæ, genitricis Dei et Domini nostri Jesu
Christi: sed et beatorum apostolorum ac martyrum
tuorum,[14] Petri, (et, Sar.) Pauli, Andreæ, Jacobi,

---

[13] (*Sequitur infra canonem.* Bangor.) This rubric was inserted to remind the officiating priest that on certain days
another form was to be used instead of the usual one here
given.

In the Roman use the "*infra actionem*" means the same
thing: and in the most ancient manuscripts the terms are used
indiscriminately, "propterea quod (says Le Brun) in hac
missæ parte fit consecratio corporis Christi, actio scilicet omnium maxima." *Infra,* he continues, is but another word for
intra; and many examples of its use are to be found in
councils, liturgies, and rituals. *Infra octavam* is commonly
found for *intra octavam.*

But, on the other hand, the *Gemma animæ* tells us: "Hic
(i. e. canon) etiam *actio* dicitur, quia causa populi in eo cum
Deo agitur." Lib. i. cap. 103. And compare Radulph.
Tungrensis, *de canon. observant.* prop. xxiij, *Bibl. patr. auct.*
tom. i. p. 1160.

[14] (*ac martyrum tuorum.*) None are here commemorated
by name who are placed in the Church lower in rank than the
martyrs. The blessed Virgin although she departed at last
in peace is entitled (as St. Jerome has said) to that rank also,
having indeed suffered all the pains of it according to Simeon's
prophecy.

Upon this point we may remember the fourth stanza of a
very ancient English hymn to the blessed Virgin:—

"Heyl mayden, heyl modur, *heyl martir trowe,*
Heyl kyndly i knowe confessour,

HERFORD. ROM.

se, suisque omnibus, pro redemptione animarum suarum, pro spe salutis et incolumitatis suæ : tibique reddunt vota sua æterno Deo, vivo et vero.

Infra actionem.

COMMUNICANTES, et memoriam venerantes:
In primis gloriosæ semper virginis Mariæ, genetricis Dei et Domini nostri Jesu Christi : Sed et beatorum Apostolorum ac Martyrum tuorum, Petri, (et, Rom.) Pauli, Andreæ, Jacobi, Joannis, Thomæ, Jacobi,

---

Heyl evenere of old lawe and newe,
Heyl buildor bold of cristes bour,   .
Heyl rose higest of hyde and hewe,
Of all ffruytes feirest fflour,
Heyl turtell trustiest and trewe,
Of all trouthe thou art tresour,
Heyl puyred princesse of paramour,
Heyl blosme of brere brihtest of ble,
Heyl owner of eorthly honour,
Yowe preye for us thi sone so fre. AVE, &c.
Warton's *Hist. of English poetry*, vol. ii. p. 152.

The reason why confessors are not added is either because the recital of the names was always in this great service strictly limited to those whose blood was poured out unto death, after the pattern of our blessed Lord Himself; or because this part of the canon is older than the third century, when the practice began of honouring the memory also of confessors. In the ninth century for a short time in some of the Gallic churches the names of a few confessors " erga quos major erat fidelium pietas " were introduced, but it was only for a short time. Le Brun, tom. i. p. 259. It is said that all those who are here commemorated suffered either in or near Rome. But there is a little difficulty about Cosmas and Damian, which has been met by the assertion that there were no less than three pairs so named; two in Asia, and the third in Rome. It will be seen below that the *Golden legend* says that they were Arabian martyrs.

K

SARUM.   BANGOR.   EBOR.

Joannis, Thomæ, Jacobi, Philippi, Bartholomæi, Matthæi, Simonis et Thaddæi: Lini, Cleti, Clementis, Sixti, Cornelii, Cypriani, Laurentii, Grisogoni,[15] Joannis et Pauli,[16] Cosmæ et Damiani:[17] et omnium Sanctorum tuorum: quorum meritis precibusque concedas, ut in omnibus protectionis tuæ muniamur auxilio. Per eundem Christum Dominum nostrum. Amen.[18]

Hic respiciat sacerdos hostiam cum magna veneratione dicens:

Hic respiciat hostiam cum veneratione dicens:

HANC igitur oblationem servitutis nostræ, sed et cunctæ familiæ tuæ, quæsumus Domine, ut placatus accipias: diesque nostros in tua pace disponas, atque ab æterna damnatione nos eripi, et in electorum tuorum jubeas grege numerari.[20] Per Christum Dominum nostrum. Amen.

---

[16] (*Grisogoni.*) A noble Roman citizen who, according to the *Golden legend*, suffered martyrdom near Aquileia in the persecution under Diocletian. His day in the calendar is Nov. 24th. *Golden legend*, edit. Wynkyn de Worde, 1527.

[16] (*Joannis et Pauli.*) Brothers who were beheaded by order of Julian the apostate. The history of these saints is given in the *Golden legend*. Their day is June 26th.

[17] (*Cosmæ et Damiani.*) These two, says the *Golden legend*, were " of Arabye," also brothers, " *lerned in the arte of medycyne and of leche crafte; and heled all maladyes and languours for y⁰ loue of God, without takynge of ony rewarde.*" They were put to death about A.D. 284. Their day is September 27th.

[13] *Amen* is omitted in the Leofric copy: it is an addition to the *Communicantes* which does not appear before the twelfth century. Hugo speaks of it as in use in some places in his time, about 1250; in his work called *Speculum sacerdotum:* and Durand also, lib. iv. cap. 38. The interpolation gradually crept in until, though we can scarcely explain how, it was

HERFORD.   ROM.

Philippi, Bartholomæi, Matthæi, Simonis et Thaddæi : Lini, Cleti, Clementis, Xysti (Sixti, Herf.), Cornelii, Cypriani, Laurentii, Chrysogoni (Grisogoni, Herf.), Joannis et Pauli, Cosmæ et Damiani : et omnium Sanctorum tuorum : quorum meritis precibusque concedas, ut in omnibus protectionis tuæ muniamur auxilio. (*Jungit manus*, Rom.) Per eundem Christum Dominum nostrum. Amen.

Hic inclinet se[19] *parum   Tenens manus expansas su-*
versus hostiam dicens: per oblata, dicit:

H ANC igitur oblationem servitutis nostræ, sed et cunctæ familiæ tuæ, quæsumus Domine, ut placatus accipias : diesque nostros in tua pace disponas, atque ab æterna damnatione nos eripi, et in electorum tuorum jubeas grege numerari. (*Jungit manus*, Rom.) Per Christum Dominum nostrum. Amen.

---

universally adopted : none of the ancient missals admit it, nor indeed the word *Amen* in any part of the canon until the termination.

[19] This practice again the English uses continued to observe long after another (*the hands expanded*) had been adopted in the Roman missal. Both Amalarius, cap. xxx, and the old *Ordo Romanus* (edited by Hittorpius) prescribe that the priest should incline "usque *jubeas numerari:*" Micrologus also ; "Cum dicimus, *Hanc igitur oblationem*, usque ad altare inclinamur ad exemplar Christi, qui se humiliavit pro nobis usque ad mortem crucis." Cap. xiv. Once more, the *Gemma animæ:* "Cum sacerdos, *Hanc igitur oblationem* dicit, se usque ad altare inclinat : quia ibi passio Christi inchoatur, qui se usque ad aram crucis obediens Patri pro nobis inclinaverat." *De ant. rit. miss.* cap. 38.

Upon the practice now of the Roman catholic church, see Gavantus, tom. i. p. 246.

[20] The student will observe how strong an argument against

SARUM.   BANGOR.   EBOR.

Hic iterum respiciat hostiam dicens: *Supra calicem:* [21]

QUAM oblationem tu Deus omnipotens in omnibus, quæsumus,

bene ✠ dictam, adscrip ✠ tam, ra ✠ tam, rationabilem, acceptabilemque facere digneris, ut nobis

Cor ✠ pus et San ✠ guis fiat dilectissimi Filii tui Domini nostri Jesu Christi.

Hic erigat sacerdos manus et conjungat: (et, Sar.) postea tergat digitos, et elevet hostiam, dicens:

QUI pridie quam pateretur,[22] accepit panem in sanctas ac venerabiles manus suas: et elevatis oculis in cœlum,[23]

    Hic elevet oculos suos

---

the blasphemous heresy of Calvin and his followers in the sixteenth century is supplied by this very ancient prayer. The Church knows nothing of a predestination such as he feared not to invent; but has followed the teaching of St. Augustine, of the fathers before him, and of St. Peter that we should "give diligence to make our calling and election sure." *Epist.* 2. cap. i. 10.

    [21] "Loke pater-noster thou be sayande,
        To tho chalyce he be saynande;
        Then tyme is nere of sakring,
        A litell bell men oyse to ryng,
        Then shal thou do reuerence,
        To jhesu crist awen presence,
        That may lese alle baleful bandes,
        Knelande holde vp bothe thi handes."
                Layfolks mass book.

    [22] Some editions of the Sarum manual which give the

HERFORD.   ROM.

QUAM oblationem tu Deus in omnibus, quæsumus,

Hic faciat tres cruces su-   Signat ter super oblata:
pra calicem dicendo:

bene ✠ dictam, adscrip ✠ tam, ra ✠ tam, rationabilem,
acceptabilemque facere digneris : ut nobis

Hic faciat crucem super   Signat semel super hostiam,
hostiam dicens,   et semel super calicem,

Cor ✠ pus (*Hic faciat crucem super calicem*, Herf.) et
San ✠ guis fiat dilectissimi Filii tui Domini nostri Jesu
Christi.

Hic sumat sursum hostiam,
et dicat :

QUI pridie quam pateretur (*accipit hostiam*, Rom.),
accepit panem in sanctas ac venerabiles manus
suas :

Erigat oculos sursum :   Elevat oculos ad cœlum :

---

canon of the mass have here the following rubric : " Hic
erigat sacerdos manus et conjungat et postea tergat digitos,
et elevet hostiam parumper, ita quod non videatur a populo,
et sic debet tenere quousque dixerit verba consecrationis ; quia
si ante consecrationem elevetur et populo ostendatur, sacerdotes sicut fatui faciunt populum idolatrare, adorando panem
purum tanquam corpus Christi, et in hoc peccat. Et sacerdos
debet præcipue in hoc loco congregare seipsum ad se ; scilicet
cor ad verba diligenter attendendum et os ad distincte pro-
ferendum, ut ab hoc loco, videlicet, *Qui pridie* usque ibi
Unde et memores, nullæ aliæ rei attendat, nullaque dictio
nullaque syllaba evadat, nihil de forma verborum vel signo-
rum omittat vel diminuat."

[23] (*In sanctas . . . et elevatis oculis.*) These particulars and
some following are not expressly stated in the gospels, but
are to be found in the liturgies of St. Clement, St. James,
St. Basil, and St. Chrysostom.

SARUM. BANGOR. EBOR.

ad te Deum Patrem suum omnipotentem,
*Hic inclinet se et postea elevet (hos-
tiam, Bangor.) paululum, dicens:*

tibi gratias agens, bene✠dixit, (ac, Ebor.) fregit:
Hic tangat hostiam [24] *dicens:*
deditque discipulis suis dicens: [25] Accipite et manducate ex hoc omnes.

*Hæc sunt verba
consecrationis:*

HOC est enim Cor-pus meum. [26]	HOC est enim Cor-pus meum.	HOC est enim Cor-pus meum.

*Et debent ista verba proferri cum
uno spiritu et sub una prolatione,
nulla pausatione interposita.* [27] *Post*

---

[24] "Hic non debet tangi hostia modo fractionis, sicut aliqui fatui tangunt et male faciunt. Videtur tamen ex ordine verborum quod prius debet frangi quam consecrari cum dicat, *benedixit, fregit:* per hæc verba videtur quod prius est fractio quam consecratio. Sed ecclesia prius consecrat quam frangit: sic aliter facit ecclesia quam Christus fecit; et sic ecclesia videtur errare et per consequens delinquit. Solutio. Dicendum est, quod ecclesia non. delinquit; quia Christus post consecrationem et benedictionem fregit; licet ordo verborum aliter sonat." *Manuale Sarum.*

The elevation of the host at this time, before consecration, was a rite peculiar to the churches of Sarum, Bangor, and York. The Hereford rubric does not order an elevation; nor has it been admitted into the Roman use. There is a very proper and obvious reason why elevation should not be ordered before consecration; ill-taught people among the laity might naturally fall into the error of untimely adoration.

[25] "Dedit discipulis suis." *Miss. Leofr.*

[26] "Hæc conjunctio *enim* non est de substantia formæ, sed

HERFORD.   ROM.

et elevatis oculis in cœlum, ad te Deum Patrem suum omnipotentem, tibi gratias agens,

signet hostiam: *signat super hostiam:*

bene ✠ dixit, (ac, Herf.) fregit, deditque discipulis suis, dicens, Accipite et manducate ex hoc omnes.

Inclinet se ad hostiam, et distincte dicat:

Tenens ambabus manibus hostiam inter indices et pollices, profert verba consecrationis secrete, distincte, et attente:

H OC est enim Corpus meum.

H OC est enim Corpus meum.

Et debent ista verba proferri tam sub uno spiritu quam sub una prolatione,

Prolatis verbis consecrationis, statim hostiam consecratam genuflexus ado-

---

de bene esse, unde non debet omitti. Aliud namque est forma necessaria ; aliud est forma debita." Lyndwood, lib. 3. tit. 23, Ad excitandos, *verb.* consecratione.

· [27] Very anciently both in the eastern and the western churches these words were pronounced so that the people, at least those who were near, might hear and answer, *Amen.* This is according to the doctrine of the apostle, 1 Cor. xiv. 16, and is acknowledged by all the ritualists of any authority whatever. St. Ambrose says: "Ante consecrationem aliud dicitur, post consecrationem sanguis nuncupatur. Et tu dicis *Amen,* hoc est, verum est." *Liber de mysteriis,* cap. ix. 54 ; *Opera,* tom. ii. p. 340. Cardinal Bona cites this and another place from Florus (*Expositio missæ*), a writer of the ninth century: after which time he supposes the practice fell into disuse "quia post Florum, ejus mentionem non reperi apud ævi posterioris scriptores." Tom. iii. p. 276. Georgius, *de liturg. pontif.* tom. iii. p. 68, adds some further authorities upon the point, Tertullian, St. Augustine, and Paschasius Radbert : which he allows are clear for the custom

SARUM.   BANGOR.   EBOR.

hæc verba[28] (*inclinet se sacerdos ad hostiam et,* Bangor.) *elevet*[30] *eam su-*

---

in those ages of the Milan, African, and Gallican churches; but does not admit that according to the Roman use the words were said otherwise than secretly, or that "Amen" was answered (as I have remarked above) until the end of the canon.

[28] "In many of the later editions, after *hæc verba*, there is added '*inclinat se sacerdos ad hostiam, et.*' After the reconciliation with Rome in the reign of queen Mary there is a further addition in the missal, as printed in 1554—for the first time in any service book printed in England—of the words 'et capite inclinato illam adoret.'" Canon Simmons, *note to Layfolks mass book,* p. 283.

[29] "Whenne they here the belle rynge,
To that holy sakerynge,
Teche hem knele downe bothe yonge and olde,
And bothe here hondes vp to holde,
And say thenne in thys manere,
Feyre and softely wyth owte bere [noise],
Jhesu, lorde, welcome thow be
In forme of bred as I the se," &c.
            MS. Cotton. Claudius A. 2. fol. 130.

In the year 1556 one of the injunctions issued by cardinal Pole was directed against the neglect of old practices, and the consequent irreverence which had spread amongst the people during the wild times of Edward the sixth: "Item, that all parisheners shall at the time of elevation reverentlie knele in souche places of the churche, where they maie both see and worshippe the blessed sacrament, not lurking behinde pillars, or holdinge downe their heads, or otherwise unreverently behavinge themselves at that time in especiall." *Concil.* tom. iv. p. 147.

Among the innumerable questions which theologians have discussed relating to the blessed eucharist is this: whether the bread is consecrated and becomes the Body of Christ without any consecration of the chalice. It has been decided by the greatest authorities that the bread is validly consecrated, "forma enim consecrationis panis neque quoad signi-

HERFORD.

ROM.

nulla pausatione interpo- *rat:*[29] *surgit, ostendit po-*
sita. Tunc elevet corpus *pulo, reponit super corpo-*

ficatum, neque quoad efficaciam pendet a forma consecrationis
vini." But such a consecration, though valid, is not lawful:
and a priest who so consecrates "magno se peccato astrin-
geret." Benedict XIV. tom. ix. p. 318, who cites Andreas
Zuccherius, Suarez, Aquinas, and Sylvius. He quotes also
the following from St. Bernard, ep. 69, whose argument does
not appear however to be convincing, because our blessed
Lord did not consecrate bread only and we can have no right
to theorise upon the supposition that He did. St. Bernard's
words are: "Puto enim, quod si Dominus post factum de
pane suum corpus, vini consecrationem placuisset aliquandiu
intermittere, aut certe penitus omittere: nihilominus corpus
mansisset quod fecerat, nec factis facienda præscriberent.
Nec nego panem et vinum aqua quidem mixtum simul debere
apponi: quin potius assero, haud aliter debere fieri. Sed
aliud est culpare negligentiam, aliud negare efficaciam. Aliud,
inquam, est quod causamur non bene quidpiam fieri, et aliud
quod mentimur nec fieri." This epistle was written upon
an occasion of the chalice not being consecrated through
negligence.

[30] (*Elevet.*) No mention of the elevation is made by the
early ritualists, Alcuin, or Amalarius, or Walafrid Strabo, or
Micrologus; nor is there any allusion to it in the old ordines
Romani, or the sacramentaries of Gelasius or Gregory. It
is commonly said that the first order was based upon the
decree of the council of Lateran (about transubstantiation)
under Innocent III. But there is no doubt that in some
churches elevation was already the practice. It is not proved
by the passage from Ivo Carnotensis which cardinal Bona
cites, lib. 2. xiij. 2, because Ivo does not even speak of it:
but the following canon seems clear which Georgius, *de liturg.*
pont. tom. iii. 72, has brought forward. A council at Paris,
A.D. 1188, ordered thus: 'Præcipitur presbyteris, ut cum in
canone missae incœperint, *qui pridie quam pateretur*, tenentes
hostiam, ne elevent eam statim nimis alte, ita quod possit ab
omnibus videri a populo, sed quasi ante pectus detineant,
donec dixerint, *Hoc est corpus meum;* et tunc elevent eam,

pra frontem,[31] *ut possit a populo videri:*[32] *et reverenter illud (eam,* Ban-

---

ut possit ab omnibus videri." The same author cites one or two others of about the same date. See also Durant, *de ritibus*, lib. ii. cap. 40, and Durand, lib. iv. cap. 41, and Sala's notes to Bona, tom. iii. p. 283.

The canon of the council of Paris, above, has reference to a practice which about the thirteenth century was common in some places, for the priest to elevate before he had finished the words of consecration. The synod of Exeter, A.D. 1287, has a canon upon this point: "Quia vero per hæc verba, *Hoc est enim corpus meum*, et non per alia, panis transubstantiatur in corpus Christi, prius hostiam non levet sacerdos donec ista plene protulerit verba, ne pro creatore creatura a populo veneretur." The canon goes on to explain what is to be done immediately after the consecration: "Hostia autem ita levetur in altum, ut a fidelibus circumstantibus valeat intueri; per hoc enim fidelium devotio excitatur, et fidei meritum suscipiat incrementum." Then follows a caution, which would not be always out of place now-a-days, against a style of exaggerated reverence which is rather an irreverence: "parochiani vero solicite exhortentur, ut in elevatione corporis Christi non irreverenter se inclinent, sed genua flectant, et creatorem suum adorent omni devotione et reverentia." *Concilia*, tom. ii. p. 132.

At this time the sacring bell was rung: how much oftener in the service in mediæval times it is not possible to decide. The English canons refer only, so far as I remember, to the ringing after the consecration. For example, a synod at Worcester in 1240: "Cum autem in celebratione missæ corpus Domini per manus sacerdotum in altum erigitur, campanella pulsetur." *Concil.* tom. i. p. 667. The usual practice of the Roman catholic Church in England is to ring thrice at the sanctus, once at the words "Hanc igitur oblationem," three times at the elevation of the host, three times at the elevation of the chalice, and three times at the *Domine non sum dignus.*

The bell to be rung according to the order of archbishop Peckham's constitution was the bell which was fixed outside

HERFORD.   ROM.

Christi in altum ut vide-   rale, iterum adorat: et
atur ab omnibus. Nec ni-   non disjungit pollices et

---

the church, commonly over the gable of the chancel: "In elevatione corporis Christi ab una parte ad minus pulsentur campanæ; ut populares, qui celebrationi missarum non valeant interesse, ubicunque fuerint, sive in agris, sive in domibus, flectant genua." On which Lyndwood observes: "*Campanæ.* Non intelligas de pluribus illo tempore simul pulsandis in una ecclesia, quia sufficit unam sonari. Et hæc pulsatio fieri debet de campanis illis quæ longius possent audiri, quod satis patet per rationem quæ sequitur;" lib. iii. tit. 21, *verb.* campanæ. We might probably conclude from this that Lyndwood objected to the use of the small bell over the chancel if there were larger bells in the tower. But the practice, almost beyond doubt, would be against his objection; and for one very common reason, namely, the tone of the "sacring bell" would be well known and the purpose of ringing it easily recognised.

In the British museum among the Harleian manuscripts (no. 955) is a volume of occasional prayers, collects, antiphons, &c. There are in it many indulgences granted to the monastery of Sion, to which the book formerly belonged; and one of them is this: "*Also he that saith at sakering time this prayer:* Ave verum corpus natum ex Maria virgine: vere passum, immolatum in cruce pro homine: cujus latus perforatum vero fluxit sanguine: esto nobis prægustatum, mortis in examine. O clemens: O pie: O dulcis Jesu fili Mariæ, nobis peccatoribus quæsumus miserere. Amen. *he schall haue .CCC. daies of pardon.*" Lyndwood tells us that he used this prayer.

The reader cannot but observe that the above is in a rhyming metre: but I have not altered the arrangement of the manuscript. It is a famous antiphon: and sometimes is found with variations, especially,

"Cujus latus perforatum,
Unda fluxit et sanguine."

[31] "Et caveat ne nimis diu teneat eam, nec aliquo modo corpus Christi osculetur, nec super oculos ponat, sicut solent quidam stulti facere, nec aliquam partem corporis ullo modo tangere debet, nisi tantum digitis ad hoc specialiter consecratis." *Manuale Sar.*

SARUM.	BANGOR.	EBOR.

gor.) reponat ante calicem in modum crucis per eandem factæ. Et tunc discooperiat calicem et teneat inter manus suas non disjungendo pollicem ab indice: nisidum facit benedictiones tantum, ita dicens:

Hic discooperiat calicem, et teneat inter manus suas non disjungendo pollicem ab indice:

Simili modo posteaquam cœnatum est,

accipiens et hunc [33] præclarum calicem in sanctas ac venerabiles manus suas: item tibi, *Hic inclinet se dicens,* gratias agens,

---

[32] "Moneantur laici, quod reverenter se habeant in consecratione eucharistiæ, et flectant genua; maxime in tempore illo, quando, post elevationem eucharistiæ, hostia sacra dimittitur." *Concilium Dunelmense,* A.D. 1220. "Cum autem in celebratione missæ corpus Domini per manus sacerdotum in altum erigitur, campanella pulsetur, ut per hoc devotio torpentium excitetur, ac aliorum charitas fortius inflammetur." *Constit. W. de Cantilup. Wigorn. episc.* A.D. 1240. "Sacerdos vero quilibet frequenter doceat plebem suam, ut cum in celebratione missarum elevatur hostia salutaris, se reverenter inclinet." *Stat. synod. Norvic. episc.* A.D. 1257. "In elevatione vero ipsius corporis Domini pulsetur campana in uno latere, ut populares, quibus celebrationi missarum non vacat

HERFORD.

mis diu teneat elevatum: sed statim reponat illud in locum suum. Nec aliquo modo corpus Christi osculetur: nec ab aliqua parte corpus Christi tangi debet: nisi tantum digitis ad hoc specialiter consecratis. Et ex tunc illos digitos cum quibus levavit corpus Christi teneat junctos usque ad ablutionem, nisi cum necesse fuerit. Post hæc cum aliis digitis discooperiat calicem, et teneat eum per medium et dicat:

SIMILI modo postea-quam cœnatum est,

ROM.

indices, nisi quando hostia tractanda est, usque ad ablutionem digitorum. Tunc detecto calice, dicit:

SIMILI modo post-quam cœnatum est, *ambabus manibus accipit calicem,*

accipiens et hunc præclarum calicem in sanctas ac venerabiles manus suas: (*erigat sursum oculos dicens,* Herf.) item tibi gratias agens,

---

quotidie interesse, ubicunque fuerint, seu in agris, seu in domibus, flectant genua." *Constit. Joh. Peckham.* A.D. 1281. "Hostia autem ita levetur in altum, ut a fidelibus circumstantibus valeat intueri." *Synodus Exon.* A. D. 1287. These are but a few out of many orders to the like effect which might be collected from the *Concilia.* See also Lyndwood, *Provinciale,* lib. iii. tit. 23, Altissimus.

[33] "Adde etiam, quod unus idemque calix est, quem Christus post cœnam consecravit, et quem nunc ecclesia consecrat: nisi enim unus idemque foret, in canone (ait Odo Cameracensis) non diceretur, *Simili modo . . . et hunc præclarum calicem,*" &c. Angelo Rocca, *Opera,* tom. i. p. 16. Compare also the *Gemma animæ:* "Idem calix est in mys-

SARUM.　　　　　BANGOR.　　　　　EBOR.

bene ✠ dixit,[34] deditque discipulis suis,[35] dicens: Accipite et bibite ex eo omnes.
Hic elevet sacerdos parumper calicem,
ita dicens:

H IC est enim calix Sanguinis mei, novi et æterni testamenti: mysterium fidei: qui pro vobis et pro multis effundetur in remissionem peccatorum.

| *Hic elevet calicem dicens:* | *Hic elevet calicem usque ad pectus vel ultra caput dicens:* | *Hic elevet calicem usque ad caput dicens:* |

---

terio, quem Christus in manibus tenuit, quamvis in materia metalli alius sit;" cap. 106.

[34]　" And so tho leuacioun thou be halde,
　　For that is he that iudas salde,
　　And sithen was scourged and don on rode,
　　And for mankynde there shad his blode,
　　And dyed and ros and went to heuen,
　　And yit shal come to deme us euen."
　　　　　　　　　　　Layfolks mass book.

[35]　" dedit discipulis suis." *Miss. Leofr.*

[36]　(*et cooperiendo.* Herf.) There was a variety of practice as to elevating the chalice, covered or uncovered. It would seem that the use of the English church was to elevate uncovered. Durand says: "Et est notandum, quod quædam ecclesiæ duas habent pallas corporales, et ibi elevatur calix coopertus cum altera earum. ... Aliæ vero ecclesiæ unam tantum habent pallam, et ibi elevatur discoopertus absque velamine;" lib. iv. cap. 42. 30. St. Anselm speaks upon the question in his reply to Walerannus: who had complained of the usage contrary to that of his own church (Newemburgh). "Quod vero nonnulli" (says the archbishop of Canterbury) "ab initio calicem operiunt, quidam corporali, alii panno complicato propter cus-

HERFORD.

signet calicem dicens:

ROM.

sinistra tenens calicem, dextera signat super eum,

bene✠dixit, deditque (dedit, Herf.) discipulis suis, dicens, Accipite et bibite ex eo omnes.

Elevet aliquantulum calicem et aperte dicat:

Profert verba consecrationis secrete super calicem, tenens illum parum elevatum.

HIC est enim calix sanguinis mei, novi et æterni testameriti: mysterium fidei: qui pro vobis et pro multis effundetur in remissionem peccatorum.

Tunc elevet calicem in altum ut videatur ab omnibus, et statim reponat calicem in locum suum, et cooperiendo[36] *eum dicat:*

Prolatis verbis consecrationis, deponit calicem super corporale, et dicens secrete:

---

todiam immunditiæ; nec nudum dimittunt calicem, sicut Christus nudus crucifixus est, ut sicut significatis, ostenderet se mundo revelatum: non magis intelligo eos debere reprehendi propter nuditatem Christi, quæ non significant (*sic*) ab illis in sacrificando; quam quia non demonstrant in eodem sacrificio, eum esse crucifixum extra civitatem, extra domum, et sub nudo cœlo.... Neque conjectare possum cur potius curandum sit, ne panno operiatur sacrificium, quia Christus nudus passus est; quam ne sub tecto, vel intra civitatem fiat, quoniam Christus sub nudo cœlo extra civitatem passus est. Si autem usus non habet, ut extra tectum fiat propter perturbationes aeris: simili causa videtur ut calix in sacrificando non discooperiatur, propter quasdam quæ contingere possunt incommoditates. Tutius itaque et diligentius puto ut calix, ne aut musca, aut aliquid indecens in illum cadat (quod sæpe contigisse cognovimus) operiatur: quia discoopertus contingentibus immunditiis exponatur." *Opera*, p. 139. Hence it would seem that in St. Anselm's time the custom of England was different from that of after-years, unless the church of Canterbury varied in this respect from the churches of Salisbury, York, &c. But we must not forget that the archbishop was not deciding the question.

SARUM.   BANGOR.   EBOR.

HÆC quotiescumque feceritis, in mei memoriam facietis.

Hic reponat calicem [87] (*super altare in*   *Deponat calicem :*
locum suum, et cooperiat, Bangor.) *et*
elevet brachia (sua extendendo, Bangor.) *in modum crucis, junctis digitis*
usque ad hæc verba de tuis donis :
                    dicens hoc modo :

UNDE et memores, Domine, nos servi tui, (tui servi,[38] *Bangor. et Ebor.*) sed et plebs tua sancta, ejusdem[39] Christi Filii tui Domini Dei nostri tam beatæ passionis, necnon et ab inferis resurrectionis, sed et in cœlos gloriosæ ascensionis, offerimus præclaræ majestati tuæ de tuis donis ac datis,

Hic signet ter ul-
tra hostiam et ca-
licem simul :

HOSTIAM pu✠ram,[40] hostiam sanc✠tam, hostiam imma✠culatam : (*Hic hostiam tantum :* Bangor.)

---

[87] " Et fricet digitos suos ultra calicem propter micas, et cooperiat calicem." *Manuale Sar.*

[38] " tui servi." *Miss. Leofr.*

[39] *Ejusdem :* omitted in *Miss. Leofr.*

[40] The number of crosses made during the mass, according to the rubrics of the old English uses, was somewhat large : and they are as many, at least, in number according to the present use of the Roman catholic church. Beyond question there were not so many in primitive times nor in the centuries which immediately followed. They gradually increased ; and we ought to believe that, equally beyond question, none was added without what was supposed to be a proper reason and sufficient symbolical meaning. Amalarius, writing in the ninth century, says, " Cæterum de crucibus, quas solemus diverso modo facere super panem et vinum non est quid dicam, cur tali et in tali loco figantur, vel quare

HERFORD.   ROM.

HÆC quotiescumque feceritis, in mei memóriam facietis.

Tunc extendat brachia sua in modum crucifixi et dicat:

Genuflexus adorat, surgit, ostendit populo, deponit, cooperit, et iterum adorat. Deinde disjunctis manibus dicit:

UNDE et memores, Domine, nos tui servi, (servi tui, Rom.) sed et plebs tua sancta, (ejusdem, Rom.) Christi Filii tui Domini (Dei, Herf.) nostri tam beatæ passionis, necnon et ab inferis resurrectionis, sed et in cœlos gloriosæ ascensionis, (*Tunc teneat brachia ut prius et dicat,* Herf.) offerimus præclaræ majestati tuæ de tuis donis ac datis,

signet calicem ter:[40]

jungit manus, et signat ter super hostiam et calicem simul,

HOSTIAM ✠ puram, hostiam ✠ sanctam, hostiam ✠immaculatam.

---

plures in aliquo vel pauciores in aliquo. Si Dominus quando benedixit panem fecisset crucis signaculum, ipsi norunt qui præsentes fuerunt, præsertim cum nondum erat erectum vexillum sanctæ crucis." *De eccl. off*. lib. 3. cap. 24. The editor puts in the margin as a side-note, "de crucibus cur et quot fiant in sacrificio, non est curiose disceptandum." Amalarius presently continues: "Videtur mihi, si semel fuerit facta crux super panem et vinum posse sufficere, quia Dominus semel crucifixus est. Non ab re est si bis figatur, quia pro duobus populis fixus est Christus."

In examining early manuscripts the absence of many of the crosses which are found in missals of the fourteenth and fifteenth centuries must often be remarked. Whether some others were signed, nevertheless, in the actual celebration—the priest recollecting what should be done instead of referring to his book—must remain doubtful. It cannot be

SARUM.   BANGOR.   EBOR.

Panem sanc ✠ tum vitæ æternæ, et ca ✠ licem salutis perpetuæ.

*Hic respiciat sa-
crificium dicens:*

SUPRA quæ [41] propitio ac sereno vultu respicere digneris: et accepta habere, sicuti accepta habere dignatus es munera pueri tui justi Abel, et sacrificium patriarchæ nostri Abrahæ: et quod tibi obtulit summus sacerdos tuus Melchisedech, sanctum sacrificium, immaculatam hostiam.

*Hic sacerdos corpore inclinato [42] et
cancellatis manibus dicat:*

                                      *Hic corpore incli-
nato et cancellatis
manibus dicat:*

SUPPLICES te rogamus, omnipotens Deus: jube hæc perferri per manus sancti angeli tui [43] in sublime altare tuum, in conspectu divinæ majestatis tuæ: ut quotquot,

---

denied that the further we go back the shorter and fewer are all the rubrics, and the priest left more in dependence on his memory of the proper rites or ceremonies.

[41] "Hæc oratio est antiquissima; reperitur enim in liturgiis SS. Petri et Basilii, necnon in opere auctoris quæstionum novi et veteris testamenti, quod inter opera S. Augustini recensetur. Ultima tamen verba 'sanctum sacrificium, immaculatam hostiam' sunt institutionis recentioris; tribuuntur enim Leoni magno, qui floruit sæculo v." Romsée, *Opera lit.* tom. 4. p. 260.

[42] (*Corpore inclinato.*) Upon this gesture all the liturgies agree; and the old ritualists speak of it as to be observed before a prayer which was always looked upon as full of mystery. Amalarius says: "Sacerdos inclinat se, et hoc, quod vice Christi immolatum est, Deo Patri commendat;"

HERFORD.

signet solum Corpus:

ROM.

*signat semel super hostiam,
et semel super calicem:*

PANEM ✠ sanctum vitæ æternæ, (*signet calicem,
Herf.*) et calicem (✠ *Rom.*) salutis perpetuæ.

*Tunc erigat brachia sua ut
prius et dicat:*

*Extensis manibus prosequi-
tur:*

SUPRA quæ propitio ac sereno vultu respicere
digneris: et accepta habere, sicuti accepta habere
dignatus es munera pueri tui justi Abel, et sacrificium
patriarchæ nostri Abrahæ: et quod tibi obtulit summus sacerdos tuus Melchisedech, sanctum sacrificium,
immaculatam hostiam.

*Tunc cancellatis brachiis in
modum crucis inclinet se devote sacerdos ad altare, dicendo:*

*Profunde inclinatus junc-
tis manibus et super altare
positis, dicit:*

SUPPLICES te rogamus, omnipotens Deus: jube
hæc perferri per manus sancti angeli tui [48] in
sublime altare tuum, in conspectu divinæ majestatis
tuæ: ut quotquot,

---

lib. iii. cap. xxv. So also Honorius, lib. i. cap. xlvj; Innocent III, lib. v. cap. v; Hugo Victorinus, lib. ii. cap. xxxiv,
and many others.

Compare the prayer in the Clementine liturgy, beginning
Ἔτι καὶ ἔτι δεηθῶμεν, κ.τ.λ.

[48] (*Per manus sancti angeli tui.*) There is a great variety
of opinion upon the meaning of this passage in this very
ancient prayer. Pope Innocent has said well: "tantæ sunt
profunditatis hæc verba, ut nulla acies humani ingenii tanta
sit, ut ea penetrare possit." And again, according to another
great pope, quoted also by the ritualists: "quis enim fidelium
habere dubium possit in ipsa immolationis hora ad sacerdotis vocem cœlos aperiri, in illo Jesu Christi mysterio angelorum choros adesse, summis ima sociari, terrena cœlestibus
jungi," &c.

SARUM.	BANGOR.	EBOR.
Hic erigens se osculetur altare a dextris sacrificii dicens:		*Osculetur altare a dextris sacrificii:*

ex hac altaris participatione, sacrosanctum Filii tui cor✠pus et san✠guinem sumpserimus:

omni (*hic signet se in faciem dicens,* Sar.) bene✠dictione cœlesti et gratia repleamur. Per eundem (Christum, Sar. et Bangor.) Dominum nostrum. (Amen. Sar.)

Hic oret pro mortuis:	*Hic oret cogitando pro mortuis dicens hoc modo:*	*Hic oret pro mortuis:*

MEMENTO[44] etiam, Domine,[45] (animarum, Sar.) famulorum famularumque tuarum (N. et N.[46] Sar. et Bangor.) (N. Ebor.)[47] qui nos præcesserunt cum signo fidei, et dormiunt in somno pacis.

---

[44] "When thou has made this orison,
Then shal thou with deuocion,
Make thi prayeres in that stede,
For alle thi frendes that are dede:
And for alle cristen soules sake,
Swilk prayere shal thou make."
Layfolks mass book.

HERFORD.

ROM.

Erigat se, et osculetur altare dicendo:

Osculatur altare:

ex hac altaris participatione, sacrosanctum Filii tui,

Signet corpus,

COR✠PUS,

jungit manus, et signat semel super hostiam, et semel super calicem,

signet calicem,

et sangui ✠ nem sumpserimus,

COR✠PUS et san- ✠ guinem sumpserimus,

signet seipsum,

seipsum signat,

omni bene ✠ dictione cœlesti et gratia repleamur.   Per eundem Christum Dominum nostrum.   Amen.

Erigat brachia et dicat:

Commemoratio pro defunctis.

MEMENTO etiam, Domine, famulorum famularumque tuarum (*Hic oret pro defunctis in corde suo et postea dicat,* Herf. N. et N. Rom.) qui nos præcesserunt cum signo fidei, et dormiunt in somno pacis.

Jungit manus, orat aliquantulum pro iis defunctis, pro quibus orare intendit, deinde extensis manibus prosequitur:

---

[45] The Bangor pontifical also omits "animarum."

[46] "Hic oret sacerdos cogitando pro defunctis." *Manuale Sar.*

[47] "*illorum et illarum.*" *Miss. Leofr.*

SARUM.   BANGOR.   EBOR.

I PSIS [48] Domine, et omnibus in Christo quiescentibus, locum refrigerii, lucis et pacis, ut indulgeas,
deprecamur. Per eundem Christum Dominum nostrum. Amen.

Hic percutiat pectus suum (semel, Sar. et Bangor.*) dicens:*

N OBIS quoque peccatoribus famulis tuis, de multitudine miserationum tuarum sperantibus, partem aliquam et societatem donare digneris cum tuis
sanctis apostolis et martyribus: cum Joanne, Stephano,[50] Matthia, Barnaba, Ignatio, Alexandro, Marcellino, Petro, Felicitate, Perpetua, Agatha, Lucia,
Agnete, Cæcilia, Anastasia, et[51] (cum, Sarum et Ebor.)
omnibus sanctis tuis: intra quorum nos consortium,
non æstimator meriti, sed veniæ, quæsumus, largitor
admitte. Per Christum Dominum nostrum.

*Hic discooperiat
calicem dicens:*

P ER quem hæc omnia, Domine, semper bona creas,

*Hic sacerdos ter
signet calicem di-
cens:*

*Hic signet ter ca-
licem coopertum
dicens:*

---

[48] "Ipsis et omnibus, Domine, in Christo," &c. *Miss.
Leofr.*

[49] The English rubrics do not specify this alteration of
voice, which applies only to the first three words, but it was
very anciently observed as Micrologus, cap. xvij, and Amalarius, lib. iii. cap. 26, both remark. Bede, whose testimony
is important, alludes to it as the usual practice in his day in
the English church; *tract. in Luc.* Pope Innocent, lib v.
Myster. missæ, cap. xij, and Durand, lib. iv. cap. 46, mention
the striking the breast.

[50] (*Cum Joanne, Stephano, &c.*) The martyrs, whose names

HERFORD. ROM.

IPSIS Domine, et omnibus in Christo quiescentibus, locum refrigerii, lucis et pacis, ut indulgeas, deprecamur. Per eundem Christum Dominum nostrum. Amen.

Hic tundat pectus dicendo: *Manu dextera percutit sibi pectus, elata parum voce[51] dicens:*

NOBIS quoque peccatoribus famulis tuis, de multitudine miserationum tuarum sperantibus, partem aliquam et societatem donare digneris cum tuis sanctis apostolis et martyribus: cum Joanne, Stephano, Matthia, Barnaba, Ignatio, Alexandro, Marcellino, Petro, Felicitate, Perpetua, Agatha, Lucia, Agnete, Cæcilia, Anastasia, et (cum, Herford.) omnibus sanctis tuis: intra quorum nos consortium, non æstimator meriti, sed veniæ, quæsumus, largitor admitte. (*Jungit manus*, Rom.) Per Christum Dominum nostrum. (Amen, Herf.)

PER quem hæc omnia, Domine, semper bona creas,

Faciat signacula ter dicendo: *Signat ter super hostiam et calicem simul, dicens:*

---

are especially commemorated here, are not of one but of several classes. Evangelists, deacons, apostles, disciples, bishops, popes, priests, exorcists, the married and the virgin states, are all included. The only name which requires a remark is that of St. John: many ritualists explain that it refers to St. John the baptist, who is especially commemorated in this place in the liturgies of St. Basil and St. Chrysostom. On the other hand the opinion given in the *Gemma animæ* (lib. i. cap. 107) seems the most reasonable, that the evangelist St. John is meant.

[51] " Et cum omnibus." *Miss. Leofr.*

SARUM.　　　　BANGOR.　　　　EBOR.

S ANCTI✠FICAS, vivi✠ficas, bene✠dicis, et
　 præstas nobis.

*Hic sacerdos discooperiat calicem et
faciat signaculum crucis cum hostia
quinquies: primo ultra calicem ex
utraque parte, secundo calici æquale,
tertio infra calicem, quarto sicut
primo, quinto ante calicem:* [52]

P ER ip✠sum, et cum ip✠so, et in ip✠so

est tibi Deo Patri omnipo✠tenti, in unitate Spiritus✠
sancti omnis honor et gloria.

*Hic cooperiat sa-
cerdos calicem, et
teneat manus suas
super altare us-
que dum dicitur*
Pater noster, *ita
dicens :*

P ER omnia sæcula sæculorum. [53]　(Amen, Sarum.
　 Oremus, Bangor. et Ebor.) [54]　Præceptis salutaribus moniti, et divina institutione formati, audemus dicere : [55]

---

[52] "Interim vero diaconus a dextris sacerdotis assistat,
manibus prius lotis, eique in corporalibus sustinendis subministret, et in recessu deosculetur altare et humerum sacerdotis dextrum, sacerdote sic dicente." *Man. Sar.*

[53] " Loke pater noster thou be prayande,
　　　 Ay to thou here tho priste be sayande,

HERFORD.

ROM.

SANCTI✠FICAS, vivi✠ficas, bene✠dicis, et præstas nobis.

Tunc detegat calicem et teneat eum cum sinistra manu: et signet eum quater cum corpore Christi hoc modo. Primo faciat largam crucem supra calicem dicendo:

PER✠ipsum: *æqualem calici:* et cum✠ipso: *infra calicem:* et in✠ipso: *iterum largam ut primo:* est tibi Deo✠Patri omnipotenti, *ante calicem,* in unitate Spiritus✠sancti omnis honor et gloria.

Tunc reponat corpus in locum suum et cooperiat calicem: et ponat manus super altare et dicat:

Discooperit calicem, genuflectit, accipit sacramentum dextera, tenens sinistra calicem: signat cum hostia ter a labio ad labium calicis, dicens:

PER ip✠sum, et cum ip✠so, et in ip✠so, *bis signat inter calicem et pectus,* est tibi Deo Patri ✠omnipotenti, in unitate Spiritus✠sancti, *elevans parum calicem cum hostia, dicit:* omnis honor et gloria.

Reponit hostiam, cooperit calicem, genuflectit, surgit, et dicit:

PER omnia sæcula sæculorum. Amen. Oremus. Præceptis salutaribus moniti, et divina institutione formati, audemus dicere:

Per omnia sæcula, al on hight,
Then I wolde thou stode up right:
For he wil saie with hegh steuen,
Pater noster to god of heuen:
Herken thou with gode wille,
And whils he saies, hold the stille:

SARUM.   BANGOR.   EBOR.

Hic accipiat diaconus patenam, eam-
que a dextris sacerdotis extento bra-
chio in altum usque Da propitius
discoopertam[56] *teneat. Hic elevet*
manus sacerdos dicens.[57]

PATER noster, qui es in cœlis : sanctificetur nomen tuum : adveniat regnum tuum : fiat voluntas tua, sicut in cœlo, et in terra. Panem nostrum
quotidianum da nobis hodie : et dimitte nobis debita
nostra, sicut et nos dimittimus debitoribus nostris. Et
ne nos inducas in tentationem. (*Chorus respondeat,*
Sar.) Sed libera nos a malo.

     Bot answere at temptacionem,
     Set libera nos a malo, amen."

Layfolks mass book.

[54] " R. Amen. Oremus." *Miss. Leofr.* " Amen. Oremus."
Bangor pontifical.

[55] " De oratione dominica in missa recitata adeundi Augustinus (*Epist.* lix) ; Hieronymus adversus Pelagianos (lib. iii.
pag. 543, Paris) ; Cyrillus Hieros. (*Catech. mystag.* v), et Gregorius Turonensis (lib. ii. *de miraculis S. Martini,* cap. xxx,
et *de Vitis. PP.* cap. xvj)." Georgius, *Liturg. Rom. pontif.*
tom. iii. p. 109. The same author adds : "ritus dominicæ
precationis dicendæ ex S. Gregorio fuit, ut a solo celebrante
ea pronunciaretur. Alta voce recitari solebat, ac hujus ritus
rationem reddit Amalarius (lib. iii. cap. xxix). In Galliis mos
fuit, ut a populo oratio dominica repeteretur (Mabillon, *de lit.*
Gallic. lib. i. v. 22). Hic idem ritus apud Græcos etiam ser-
vabatur. In missa Mozarabum ad singulas fere petitiones
populus respondebat, *Amen.* Hugo Victorinus auctor est
(lib. ii. xxxix) verba, *Sed libera nos a malo,* a choro dicta
fuisse. De voce *Amen,* in fine orationis dominicæ veter-
rima expositio missæ apud Martenium (tom. i. p. 451) hæc
adnotat : *Amen,* inquit, signaculum orationis dominicæ po-
suere, ubi fideliter possumus dicere, sequentem : *Libera*
nos," &c.

HERFORD. ROM.

Hic sacerdos elevet sursum   Extendit manus.
brachia sua:

PATER noster, qui es in cœlis: sanctificetur nomen tuum: adveniat regnum tuum: fiat voluntas tua, sicut in cœlo, et in terra. Panem nostrum
quotidianum da nobis hodie: et dimitte nobis debita
nostra, sicut et nos dimittimus debitoribus nostris. Et
ne nos inducas in tentationem. (℟. Rom.) Sed libera
nos a malo.

---

[56] (*Discoopertam.*) Vide note 82. p. 85. The reason why
it was now held uncovered is stated in the rubric of the modern
Paris missal that the people might know that the time of
communicating was close at hand. One of the prayers in the
Salisbury pontifical at the consecrating of a paten refers to
this especial use of it: "Consecrare digneris hanc patenam in
administrationem eucharistiæ." See the office in the *Monumenta ritualia*, vol. i. p. 175.

[57] Very anciently the people joined with the priest here in
repeating aloud the whole of the Lord's prayer. This is clear
from a passage in St. Gregory of Tours: "factum est autem
cum dominica oratio diceretur, hæc aperto ore cœpit sanctam
orationem cum reliquis decantare." He is relating a miracle
worked in the case of a deaf woman; *de mirac. S. Martini*,
l. ii. c. 30. This continued in the Gallic churches up to about
the eleventh century: for Ivo Carnotensis observes that by
these words "Præceptis salutaribus," &c. the priest exhorts
the people to repeat this prayer with him. In the earliest
ages the use of the Lord's prayer was allowed only to those
who had been baptized: and in the old Ordo Romanus it was
taught upon the fourth day after the fourth sunday in lent
to all who were about to be admitted to communion on the
easter eve. See Bona, tom. iii. p. 324.

SARUM.	BANGOR.	EBOR.

Sacerdos priva-
tim:

Sacerdos dicat:

A MEN.[58]   A MEN.   A MEN.

et statim:

L IBERA nos, quæsumus Domine, ab omnibus malis, præteritis, præsentibus et futuris: et intercedente (pro nobis, Ebor.) beata et gloriosa semper (semperque, Sar.) virgine Dei genitrice Maria, et beatis apostolis tuis Petro et Paulo, atque Andrea, cum [59] omnibus sanctis (tuis, Bangor.).[60]

Hic committat diaconus patenam sacerdoti deosculans manum ejus: et sacerdos deosculetur patenam:[61] *postea ponat ad sinistrum oculum:*

---

[58] *Amen:* omitted in *Miss. Leofr.*

[59] In many ancient missals and sacramentaries other names of saints are to be found added here. The order edited by Pamelius adds (for example) Cyriacus and Martinus. From what Micrologus says we may conclude that in his time such additions were allowable at the pleasure of the priest, or according to the use of the particular church: "aliorum sanctorum nomina annumerare non debemus, nisi quos in canone invenimus antiquitus descriptos, excepto post *Pater noster,* in illa oratione ubi juxta ordinem quorumlibet sanctorum nomina internumerare possumus." *De ecc. observ.* cap. xiij. The prayer as it stands in the text is the same as in the Gregorian and Gelasian sacramentaries.

[60] This also is the reading of the Bangor pontifical.

[61] "When þe prest taketh the patent, and toucheth þe hoost,

HERFORD.

ROM.

Sacerdos secrete dicit :

AMEN.

AMEN.

Deinde accipit patenam inter indicem et medium digitos, et dicit :

LIBERA nos, quæsumus Domine, ab omnibus malis, præteritis, præsentibus et futuris : et intercedente (pro nobis, Herford.) beata et gloriosa semper virgine Dei genitrice Maria, et (cum, Rom.) beatis apostolis tuis Petro et Paulo, atque Andrea, cum (et, Rom.) omnibus sanctis (tuis, Herford.).

Tunc sumat patenam cum dextera manu, et tangat ambos oculos suos cum ea et osculetur eam dicendo :

Signat se cum patena a fronte ad pectus, et eam osculatur :

---

and kysseth it & saith, *Da pacem*, remember þe pease betwen God & man which our saviour did meryte for us in his gloriouse deth, reconsilynge us to his eternall father ; and þᵗ is signifyed by the kysse of þe prest : and here note, the prest kisseth thre tymes ; first the patent of þe chalice, as it is seid, signifyeng þe pease bitwen gode and man ; second, the chalice betokenyng þe pese in mannes soule ; thrid the pease [i.e. the pax] signifyeing þe pease bitwen man and man : and lyk as in the deth of our savyour thies thre peases wor given to man, so by þe meryte of þe seid deth in every oblacion of þe masse, every person that disposeth hymself therto may have the seid thre graces of þese : þerfor remytt & forgive all displesures and dispose yourself at every masse at þis tyme in a charitable, contrite, and clene hart, to receive your lorde spiritually by his grace." MS. Harl. 494. f. 69.

SARUM.	BANGOR.	EBOR.

deinde ad dexte-
rum: postea fa-
ciat crucem cum
patena ultra ca-
put: et tunc re-
ponat eam in lo-
cum suum dicens:

DA propitius pacem in diebus nostris: ut ope
    misericordiæ tuæ adjuti, et a peccato simus sem-
per liberi, et ab omni perturbatione securi.

Hic discooperiat calicem, et sumat cor-
pus cum inclinatione, transponens in
concavitate calicis, retinendo inter pol-
lices et indices, et frangat [62] *in tres*
partes, [63] *(prima fractio,* Bangor.*)*
dum dicitur:

---

[62] (*Et frangat.*) i.e. *Corpus;* as it is expressed with equal
plainness in the Hereford use. The Ambrosian missal has
a form still stronger than the old rubrics of the English
church: "Corpus tuum frangitur, Christe, calix benedicitur."
These expressions undeniably touch upon some of the most
mysterious of all Roman catholic doctrines connected with
the blessed eucharist; and at one time efforts were made to
alter the wording of the Milan liturgy. But no less undeniable is the truth as expressed in the well-known hymn,
Lauda Sion salvatorem:—

      "Fracto demum sacramento,
        Ne vacilles, sed memento
        Tantum esse sub fragmento
          Quantum toto tegitur.
      Nulla rei fit scissura:
        Signi tantum fit fractura,
        Qua nec status, nec statura
          Signati minuitur."

The "hostiam" of the Roman rubric means and can only
mean exactly what is meant by "corpus" in the old English

HERFORD.　　　　　　　　ROM.

DA propitius pacem in diebus nostris: ut ope misericordiæ tuæ adjuti (*signet se cum ea et osculetur eam iterum dicendo*, Herford.), et a peccato simus semper liberi, et ab omni perturbatione securi.

Tunc reponat patenam super altare, et discooperto calice, sumat corpus Christi reverenter in manibus suis, et supra calicem frangat illud per medium dicendo:	*Submittit patenam hostiæ, discooperit calicem, genuflectit, surgit, accipit hostiam, frangit eam super calicem, per medium, dicens:*

rubrics. The explanation of the terms is given by Benedict XIV. in his work upon the mass: namely, that by "frangitur corpus Christi" we are to understand "franguntur species;" lib. ii. cap. 23.

Compare the rubric in the Sarum office for Good Friday; when, after the bringing back to the altar the host which had been reserved in the sepulchre, the priest is thus directed: "*Deinde dicat,* Libera nos, quæsumus, *et* Da propitius. *In qua oratione dum dicitur per eundem, frangat corpus Domini sicut solet fieri cæteris diebus.*"

⁶³ (*Et frangat in tres partes.*) Upon this rite which Bona calls as it indeed is "antiquissimus," and which may be traced up to perhaps the apostolic age, I would recommend the reader to consult the authors whom he cites; also Bingham, book xv. cap. iii, with Sala's reply, in his notes upon cardinal Bona, tom. iii. p. 328. The Greek Church divides into four parts, and the Mozarabic missal orders division into nine portions: to which separate names are given, having reference to the life, passion, and glory of our blessed Saviour.

SARUM.	BANGOR.	EBOR.

PER eumdem[64] Dominum nostrum Jesum Christum Filium tuum.

secunda fractio: *secunda fractio:*

QUI tecum vivit et regnat in unitate Spiritus sancti Deus.[65]

Hic teneat duas fracturas in sinistra manu: et tertiam fracturam in dextera manu in summitate calicis, ita dicens aperta voce:

PER omnia sæcula sæculorum.[66] Amen.   PER omnia sæcula sæculorum.

---

[64] *Eumdem:* omitted in *Miss. Leofr.*

[65] *Deus:* omitted in *Miss. Leofr.*

[66] After this and before the "Pax domini" the ancient episcopal benedictions were given. An account of them may be seen in the ritualists, although they no longer are used in the Roman catholic church: I would refer the reader also to my Dissertation on the service books, *Monumenta ritualia*, vol. i, under the title "Benedictionale."

According to the Mozarabic missal priests were allowed to give this benediction: and the eighteenth canon of the fourth council of Toledo insists on their doing so: "Nonnulli sacerdotes post dictam orationem dominicam statim communicant et postea benedictionem populo dant: quod deinceps interdicimus: sed post orationem dominicam, benedictio in populum sequatur." Mabillon says that the same permission existed very anciently in the Gallic liturgy; *De lit. Gall.* lib. i. 4. 13. The reader will find one or two examples of these episcopal benedictions in the Additional Notes, which will enable him to judge of their general character.

HERFORD.

ROM.

PER eundem Dominum nostrum Jesum Christum Filium tuum.

Et illam partem in dextera manu frangat per medium dicendo:

Partem, quæ in dextera est, ponit super patenam. Deinde ex parte, quæ in sinistra remansit, frangit particulam, dicens:

QUI tecum vivit et regnat in unitate Spiritus sancti Deus.

Remaneant duæ partes in sinistra manu: et tertia in dextera, et dicat:

Aliam mediam partem cum ipsa sinistra ponit super patenam, et dextera tenens particulam super calicem, sinistra calicem, dicit:

PER omnia sæcula sæculorum. Amen.

PER omnia sæcula sæculorum. ℟. Amen.

The episcopal benedictions during mass are not unfrequently alluded to in ancient documents. For example: in the year 1309 a solemn mass was celebrated before the opening of the council of London: "Et est sciendum quod Norwicensis, qui celebravit missam, dedit solemnem benedictionem in missa." Wilkins, *Concilia*, tom. ii. p. 304. Again, in the account of the mass before a provincial synod in the same year we read: "In fine vero missæ, ante *Agnus Dei*, prædictus episcopus Norwyc. de præcepto et licentia speciali Cantuar. archiepiscopi solennem benedictionem super populum fecit. Expleta missa archiepiscopus benedictionem populo dedit." *Concilia*, tom. ii. p. 312.

At this period of the service denunciations of excommunications, and prayers, sometimes were also to be said: some examples of which are given by Bona, and by Angelo Rocca *de campanis*. To those I would add from Wilkins: "Advertentes insuper præsentium turbationum pericula, quæ veraciter ex nostris excessibus et delictis causari creduntur,

M

SARUM.　　　　BANGOR.　　　　EBOR.

　　　　　　　　　　　　　　Hic faciat ter sig-
　　　　　　　　　　　　　　num crucis di-
　　　　　　　　　　　　　　cens :

---

ad quorum inde remedium opportunum decet et expedit divinum implorare subsidium : vobis cæterisque coepiscopis antedictis injungimus, ut psalmos et orationes pro pace, antequam dicatur 'Pax Domini,' intra missas et processiones publicas, prout jamdudum mandabamus, dici ac fieri faciatis, et faciant diligenter." *Concilia,* tom. ii. p. 222, A.D. 1296.

The following, again, from the oath of an abbot of Westminster for fulfilling the will of king Henry the seventh : "Item I shall cause every monke singing and sayeing in the chapitre masse in the said monasterie . . . to sing and sey deuoutly for the same kyng, at euery such masse after the fraccion of the holy sacrament, and before the holye prayer of Agnus Dei, all such special psalms, orations and prayers for the same kyng, as be conteigned in the same indentures." Dugdale, *Monast. Anglic.* vol. i. p. 279.

To this part of the service are also to be referred the *Preces in prostratione,* which are commonly found in the printed editions of the Sarum missal according to the rubric : "et sciendum est quod in omni missa quando de feria dicitur fiat prostratio a toto choro statim post *Sanctus* usque *Pax Domini,* per totum annum : nisi a pascha usque, *Deus omnium.*" These prayers consisted of three psalms, *Deus venerunt gentes, Deus misereatur nostri,* and *Domine in virtute tua ;* followed by some verses and responses, and three collects, viz. "Oremus. Deus qui admirabili providentia cuncta disponis, te suppliciter exoramus : ut terram quam unigenitus Filius tuus proprio sanguine consecravit, de manibus inimicorum crucis Christi eripiens restituas cultui Christiano, vota fidelium ad ejus liberationem instantium misericorditer dirigendo in viam pacis æternæ.

"*Oratio.* Rege quæsumus, Domine, famulum tuum pontificem nostrum : et intercedente beata Dei genitrice semperque virgine Maria, cum omnibus sanctis tuis, gratiæ tuæ dona in

HERFORD.	ROM.
Deinde cum parte hostiæ quam tenet in manu dextera fiant tres cruces supra calicem, dicendo:	*Cum ipsa particula signatter super calicem, dicens:*

---

eo multiplica: ut ab omnibus liberetur offensis: et temporalibus non destituatur auxiliis: et sempiternis gaudeat institutis.

" *Oratio.* Da, quæsumus omnipotens Deus, famulo tuo regi nostro salutem mentis et corporis: ut bonis operibus inhærendo, tuæ semper virtutis mereatur protectione defendi. Per eundem Christum Dominum nostrum. Amen. *Sequatur.* Pax Domini," &c. The first of these at least is to be traced to the time of the crusades.

A similar office is appointed in the other English missals; but they vary as to the days on which it may be said. Thus, the York use appoints two different arrangements of psalms and prayers; the Bangor has one only; and so the Hereford. The order of this last is as follows :—

" *In missa de die vel de pace vel pro familiaribus: dicantur preces hoc modo... Quando sacerdos hanc missam celebrans, postquam* Pater noster *dixerit et* Per omnia sæcula sæculorum: *antequam dicat* Pax Domini, *dicantur hi psalmi a sacerdote cum ministris, et similiter a choro sub silentio: videlicet, ps.* Domine in virtute tua. Deus misereatur. *ps.* Lætatus sum. *Dictis psalmis: dicatur* Kyrie eleyson," &c. Then follow verses and responses as in the Salisbury use: after which these three collects :—

" *Oratio.* Da quæsumus, Domine, famulo tuo," as above.

" *Alia oratio.* Miserere quæsumus, Domine, populo tuo: et continuis tribulationibus laborantem propitius respirare concede. Per Dominum.

" *Alia oratio.* Deus, a quo sancta desideria, recta concilia et justa sunt opera: da servis tuis illam quam mundus dare non potest, pacem, ut et corda nostra mandatis tuis dedita, et hostium sublata formitudine tempora sint tua protectione tranquilla. Per Dominum nostrum Jesum Christum Filium tuum, qui tecum vivit et regnat, in unitate Spiritus sancti Deus, per omnia sæcula sæculorum. Amen."

SARUM.   BANGOR.   EBOR.

PAX Do✠mini sit sem✠per vo✠biscum.

Chorus respon-   *Chorus   respon-*
deat: *deat aperta voce:*

ET cum spiritu tuo.

*Ad Agnus Dei dicendum [67] accedant
diaconus et subdiaconus ad sacerdotem
uterque a dextris: diaconus propior,
subdiaconus remotior, et dicant privatim:* [68]

AGNUS Dei, qui tollis peccata mundi, miserere
nobis. [69]

---

[67] See a very learned disquisition in Gerbert, *de musica*,
tom. i. p. 454, &c., as to the ancient custom of singing or
saying this, and whether the people joined with the choir.
A passage in Ælfric's homilies appears to prove that in his
time the *Agnus Dei* was sung in the churches of England:
"Be þam singað Godes þeowas æt ælcere mæssan. Agnus Dei
qui tollis peccata mundi, miserere nobis. þat is on urum
geþeode," &c. *Hom. in di. sanct. pascha.* It was forbidden
on easter eve in that age by the canons of Ælfric (whether
the same Ælfric I cannot say): "On easter eve, let there
not be sung at the mass-offering, neither *Agnus Dei*, nor
'Communio,' but among those who desire the housel, let the
chanter begin: Alleluia," &c. Thorpe, *Antient laws and
institutes*, vol. ii, p. 359.

HERFORD. ROM.

P AX ✠ Domini sit ✠ semper vobis ✠ cum.

E T cum spiritu tuo.

℞.

E T cum spiritu tuo.

Particulam ipsam immittit in calicem, dicens secreto:

H ÆC commixtio et consecratio corporis et sanguinis Domini nostri Jesu Christi, fiat accipientibus nobis in vitam æternam, Amen.

Ad Agnus Dei *dicendum, accedant diaconus et subdiaconus ad sacerdotem uterque a dextris: diaconus propior et subdiaconus remotior: et dicant privatim:*

Cooperit calicem, genuflectit, surgit, et inclinatus sacramento, junctis manibus, et ter pectus percutiens, dicit:

A GNUS Dei,[70] qui tollis peccata mundi, miserere nobis.

---

[68] "Then eft sone tho prist wil saye,
Stande stille and herken him al-waye:
He saies AGNUS thryse or he cese,
Tho last worde he spekis of pese:...
Then is gode of god to crave,
That thou charyte may haue:
There when tho prist pax wil kis,
Knele thou and praye then this."
Layfolks mass book.

[69] The canon of the Leofric missal ends here.

[70] "*In missis pro defunctis, dicitur hoc modo,* Agnus Dei, qui tollis peccata mundi, dona eis requiem: *cum hac additione in tertia repetitione,* sempiternam." *Rubr. Sar.*

"Quare ad missam mortuorum pax non datur, triplex as-

SARUM.	BANGOR.	EBOR.

AGNUS Dei, qui tollis peccata mundi, miserere nobis.[71]

AGNUS Dei, qui tollis peccata mundi, dona nobis pacem.[72]

Hic cruce signando deponat dictam tertiam partem hostiæ in sacramento sanguinis (in sanguine, Bangor.) sic dicendo: *Hic deponat tertiam partem hostiæ in sanguine dicens:*

HÆC sacrosancta commixtio corporis et sanguinis Domini nostri Jesu Christi fiat mihi (nobis, Ebor.)

---

signatur ratio. Prima est quoniam hoc officium triduanam Christi sepulturam significat ubi pax non datur propter osculum Judæ. Secunda quia non communicamus mortuis, quia nobis non respondent : unde est quod corpus nunquam debet esse in ecclesia quamdiu missa de die celebratur. Tertia est quoniam sicut ex multis granis collectis unus panis efficitur et ex multis racemis vinum eliquatur, sic et ex multis fidelibus (quorum quidam boni, quidam mali) una ecclesia constituitur et coadunatur. Quia ergo mortuo homine nescitur utrum sit ipse de conformitate ecclesiæ, et pacem cum creatore suo habeat, ideo pacem non damus, nec *Benedicamus* nec *Deo gratias* nec aliquas laudes referimus pro mortuis, quia non est unde agendæ sint ; non enim apparet eorum requies." *Manuale Sar.*

[71] Probably without sufficient permission the *Agnus Dei* was sometimes treated like the Kyrie eleison and interpolations introduced. For example the following which occurs in some old missal, but I have lost the reference :—

"Agnus Dei, qui tollis peccata mundi, crimina tollis, aspera mollis, agnus honoris, miserere nobis.

"Agnus Dei, qui tollis peccata mundi, vulnera sanas, ardua planas, agnus amoris, miserere nobis.

"Agnus Dei, qui tollis peccata mundi, sordida mundas, cuncta fecundas, agnus odoris, dona nobis pacem."

[72] " Propter denique schisma e medio tollendum, et propter pacem Christi fidelibus a Deo impetrandam, ad hanc usque diem remansit ritus dicendi, *Dona nobis pacem*, in tertio

HERFORD. ROM.

AGNUS Dei, qui tollis peccata mundi, miserere nobis.

AGNUS Dei, qui tollis peccata mundi, dona nobis pacem.

Tunc partem quam tenet in dextera manu ponat in calice dicendo:

HÆC sacrosancta commixtio corporis

Agnus Dei, dum celebratur missa. Antiquitus enim tribus vicibus uniformiter dicebatur; *miserere nobis:* sed ob multas et varias ecclesiæ olim adversitates ecclesia cœpit ad Dominum de tribulatione clamare: *Dona nobis pacem.*" Angelo Rocca, *de campanis,* cap. xviij. He goes on to quote from pope Innocent the practice still observed "in basilica Lateranensi" (as being the most ancient church) of repeating the *miserere nobis* three times: and complains that Durand in his *Rationale,* lib. iv. cap. 25, has spoken of this and of the alteration without acknowledging the authority of Innocent.

At this part of the mass the corporal oath was taken: whether always so may be doubted; but Walsingham gives us an example on a very important occasion, when peace was made in 1360 between Edward the third and Charles the fifth of France. This extract serves also to explain the meaning of corporal oath; on which some remarks are made in the *Mon. ritualia,* vol. 2. p. lj. It is clear that in the present instance Charles touched the paten on which lay the consecrated host, and the missal also, as containing the holy gospels :—

"Parisiis igitur celebrata solenni missa, dictoque ter Agnus Dei, adjecto Dona nobis pacem, dictus Carolus dextram super patenam, cum corpore dominico, et lævam super missale posuit, hæc verba proferens: Nos Carolus juramus ad sacrosancta corpus Domini et evangelia firmiter servare penes nos pacem," &c. *Hist. Angl.* p. 175.

SARUM.   BANGOR.   EBOR.

et omnibus [73] (omnibusque, Sar.) sumentibus salus mentis et corporis : et ad vitam æternam (promerendam et, Sar. et Bangor.) capescendam [74] preparatio salutaris. [75]

PER eundem Christum Dominum nostrum. Amen.

PER eundem Dominum nostrum Jesum Christum Filium tuum. Qui tecum vivit et regnat.

Antequam pax detur dicat sacerdos:

DOMINE, sancte Pater, omnipotens æterne Deus : da mihi hoc sacrosanctum corpus et sanguinem Filii tui Domini nostri Jesu Christi ita digne sumere : ut merear per hoc remissionem omnium peccatorum meorum accipere et tuo sancto Spiritu repleri, et pacem tuam habere. Quia tu es Deus (solus, Bangor.) et non est alius præter te : cujus regnum gloriosum permanet in sæcula sæculorum. Amen.

Hic osculetur sacerdos corporalia in   *Hic detur oscu-*

---

[73] The Bangor pontifical reads " omnibusque."

[74] "Ad vitam æternam capescendam." *Bangor pontifical.*

[75] This prayer is remarkable, retained as it was so long in the English church, after the chalice was no longer given to the laity. It is not in the Roman use in the editions of the fifteenth century. Archbishop Cranmer in his answer to the Devonshire rebels was not forgetful of the argument which this prayer seems to support for communion in both kinds. Vide *Remains*, vol. ii. p. 217.

HERFORD.

ROM.

et sanguinis Domini nostri Jesu Christi fiat mihi et omnibus sumentibus salus mentis et corporis : et ad vitam æternam promerendam et capescendam præparatio salutaris. Per eundem Christum, &c.

Oratio.

Deinde junctis manibus super altare, inclinatus dicit sequentes orationes.

DOMINE Jesu Christe, qui dixisti apostolis tuis : pacem meam do vobis, pacem relinquo vobis : (Pacem relinquo vobis, pacem meam do vobis : Rom.) ne respicias peccata mea, sed fidem ecclesiæ tuæ : eamque secundum voluntatem tuam pacificare et coadunare dignare : (digneris, Rom.) Qui vivis et regnas Deus, per omnia sæcula sæculorum. Amen.

Tunc offerat pacem: sed Si danda est pax, osculatur

The mystical intention of the immission into the chalice is explained by Micrologus : "Ad designandum corporis et animæ conjunctionem in resurrectione Christi." Cap. xvij. And to the same effect pope Innocent : "Commixtio panis et vini designat unionem carnis et animæ, quæ in resurrectione Christi denuo sunt unitæ."

Simeon of Durham relates a miracle which occurred at this part of the mass, and by which a priest was converted from an evil life in the time of St. Cuthbert. *Hist.* p. 35.

SARUM.	BANGOR.	EBOR.

dextera parte et summitatem calicis, et postea diaconum dicens:

lum pacis dicendo:

SARUM: PAX tibi et ecclesiæ.

BANGOR: PAX tibi et ecclesiæ Dei.

EBOR: HABETE vinculum pacis et caritatis, ut apti sitis sacrosanctis mysteriis Dei.

Responsio:

ET cum spiritu tuo.

Responsio diaconi:

ET cum spiritu tuo.

Diaconus a dextris sacerdotis ab eo pacem recipiat [76] *et subdiacono porri-*

---

[76] (*Diaconus pacem recipiat.*) "Pax: instrumentum, quod inter missarum solemnia populo osculandum præbetur." Ducange, gloss. The introduction of the pax instead of the old practice of mutual salutation was not until about the thirteenth century. In a council held at York in the year 1250 under Walter Gray, archbishop, the earliest mention occurs of the pax or *Osculatorium* as used in England. It is named among the ornaments and furniture of the altar which were to be provided by the parishioners. Wilkins, *Concil.* i. 698. Again, in the same collection, ii. 280, we find a similar order to have been made in the province of Canterbury in the year 1305 at the council of Merton: "*tabulas pacis ad osculatorium.*" Both of these constitutions are to be found also in Johnson's *Eccles. laws*, vol. ii. Several figures of the pax are given in works relating to the subject, and in many of the printed editions of the Sarum missal it is represented as part of the furniture of the altar in the woodcut which commonly precedes the service for advent sunday.

The mediæval practice during synods at solemn celebration of mass before the archbishop of Canterbury was that the bishop of Winchester should carry to him the pax. Archbishop Parker says: "Hujus proprium fuit in missis auream

HERFORD.

primo osculetur calicem, deinde altare, dicendo:

Habete vinculum caritatis et pacis, ut apti sitis sacris mysteriis Dei.

Et osculando ministrum dicat:

Pax Christi et sanctæ ecclesiæ tibi et cunctis ecclesiæ filiis.

ROM.

altare, et dans pacem, dicit:

Pax tecum.

℞.

Et cum spiritu tuo.

---

pacem accipere, eandemque ad archiepiscopum osculandam deferre et altari referre." But Parker is careful also to explain that this custom was observed only "in profligatis illis papisticis ritibus pomposis atque solennibus." *De ant. Brit. eccl.* p. 30. Parker's old puritan adversary (quoted above, p. 30) remarks on this, "what a worthye reputacion the bishoppe off Winchester thought yᵗ to bee for a commendacion off honour to carie him the golden pax, for his supersticious lippes to kisse." Sign. D. ij.

Le Brun, tom. 1. p. 292, has an interesting disquisition on the subject of the pax; and in a note states that the reason why it also in its own turn fell into disuse abroad was the quarrels about precedency which it occasioned among the people. Sometimes this jealousy led to great irreverence. In 1496 one Johanna Dyaca, of the parish of All Saints, Stanyng, was presented before the archdeacon of Middlesex, "quod projecit le paxbrede ad terram, in ecclesia, ea occasione quod alia mulier ejusdem parochie osculavit ante eam.' Hale's *Precedents*, cxcj. Chaucer, more than a hundred years before this time, had also spoken of the same matter. He makes the Parson in his Tale say of the proud man that "he awaiteth to sit, or els to go above him in the waie, or kisse

gat: deinde ad gradum chori ipse diaconus pacem portet rectoribus chori: et ipsi pacem choro portent uterque suæ parti incipiens a majoribus. Post pacem datam dicat sacerdos orationes sequentes privatim, antequam se communicet: tenendo hostiam duabus manibus:

Hic inclinet se sacerdos, dicens orationes sequentes antequam communicet, tenendo hostiam duabus manibus:

---

paxe, or be encenced before his neighbour," &c. Notices of the pax are common in monastic and church inventories. In the Rites of Durham abbey we are told that they possessed "a marvelous faire booke, which had the epistles and gospels in it, the which booke had on the outside of the coveringe the picture of our saviour Christ, all of silver—whiche booke did serve for the pax in the masse;" p. 7. A book which an abbot of Glastonbury gave to the high altar might have and possibly did answer the same purpose: "unum textum argenteum et auratum, cum crucifixo, Maria et Johanne, splendidus emalatum." Johan. Glaston. *de rebus Glaston.;* Hearne, p. 265. Examples of paxes are to be seen in many public collections of works of mediæval art. In London some are in the British museum; and more are in the collections at South Kensington, in metal, silver, and ivory. They are generally carved with some scriptural subject, and occasionally have inscriptions. For instance, I have seen on one the appropriate prayer, "Da pacem, Domine, in diebus nostris:" on another, above the annunciation, "Ave Maria:" on a third, representing the nativity with the shepherds, "Gloria in excelsis Deo, et in terra pax." In small or poor parishes it is probable that paxes were often made of wood. None in that mean material are known to exist, but "iij lyttel pax-bredes of tre" belonged to the parish of St. Mary Chepe in 1431. A list of goods destroyed in the diocese of Lincoln by the commissioners in 1566 (printed by Mr. Peacock) tells us

HERFORD. ROM.

●

of "a paxe of wood" burnt at Baston, another at Dunsbie, and another at Haconbie.

One of the latest notices, if not the last, in England of the use of the pax is in the injunctions given in 1548 (2 Edw. VI) to the deanery of Doncaster: "And the clerk in like manner shall bring down the pax, and standing without the church door shall say boldly to the people these words: 'This is a token of joyfull peace, which is betwixt God and men's conscience. Christ alone is the peace-maker, which straitly commands peace between brother and brother.'" *Hierurgia Anglic.* p. 2. The "church door" here spoken of refers to the door in the roodscreen between the nave and chancel of the church. See note in *Monum. ritualia*, vol. i. p. 50.

In some remarks on the pax which I had occasion to make in a dissertation on mediæval carvings in ivory I drew attention to a passage in the third act of Shakspeare's Henry the fifth, scene 5. Bardolph is to be hanged because he "hath stolen a pax," a "pax of little price." Until lately the editors printed the word as "pyx:" but Shakspeare lived too near the time when both were in general use to be ignorant of the distinction between them; although Dr. Johnson (who, after all, could not know everything) informs us that the two words "signified the same thing." I would refer for what I further said to the note itself; *Ivories, ancient and mediæval*, p. lxxxj.

SARUM. BANGOR. EBOR.

OREMUS.

DOMINE, sancte Pater, omnipotens æterne Deus, da nobis hoc corpus et sanguinem Filii tui Domini Dei nostri Jesu Christi ita sumere, ut mereamur per hoc remissionem peccatorum nostrorum accipere et tuo sancto Spiritu repleri: quia tu es Deus, et præter te non est alius nisi tu solus. Qui vivis et regnas Deus.

OREMUS.

DEUS Pater, fons et origo totius bonitatis, qui ductus misericordia Unigenitum tuum pro nobis ad infima mundi descendere, et carnem sumere voluisti: quam ego indignus hic in manibus meis teneo:

Hic inclinet se sacerdos ad hostiam dicens:

TE adoro, te glorifico, te tota cordis (ac mentis meæ, Bangor.) intentione laudo: et precor, ut nos famulos tuos non deseras, sed peccata nostra dimittas: quatenus tibi soli Deo vivo et vero puro corde ac (et, Bangor.) casto corpore servire mereamur (valeamus, Bangor.[77]). Per eundem Christum Dominum nostrum. Amen.

DOMINE Jesu Christe, Fili Dei vivi, qui ex voluntate Patris cooperante Spiritu sancto per mortem tuam mundum vivificasti: libera me (quæso, Bangor.) per hoc sacrosanctum corpus et hunc sanguinem tuum a cunctis iniquitatibus meis, et ab universis malis: et fac me tuis semper obedire mandatis:

---

[77] The Bangor pontifical also reads "valeamus."

HERFORD. ROM.

Oratio.

DOMINE, sancte Pater, omnipotens æterne Deus, da mihi hoc sacrosanctum corpus et sanguinem Filii tui ita digne sumere ut merear per hoc remissionem omnium peccatorum meorum accipere: et tuo sancto Spiritu repleri: quia tu es Deus solus, et præter te non est alius: cujus regnum et imperium sine fine permanet in sæcula sæculorum. Amen.

Alia oratio.

DOMINE Jesu Christe, Fili Dei vivi, qui ex voluntate Patris, cooperante Spiritu sancto, per mortem tuam mundum vivificasti: libera me per hoc sacrosanctum corpus et sanguinem tuum, ab omnibus iniquitatibus meis et (ab, Herford.) universis malis, et fac me tuis semper obedire (inhærere, Rom.) mandatis, et a te nunquam in perpetuum permittas separari (et a te nunquam separari permittas. Rom.).

SARUM.   BANGOR.   EBOR.

et a te nunquam in perpetuum permittas separari : (separari permittas. salvator mundi,[78] Bangor.) Qui cum Deo Patre, et eodem Spiritu sancto, vivis et regnas Deus : per omnia sæcula sæculorum. Amen.

CORPORIS et sanguinis tui, Domine Jesu (Christe, Bangor.), sacramentum quod licet indignus accipio : non sit mihi judicio et condemnationi, sed tua prosit pietate corporis mei et animæ saluti. Amen.

PERCEPTIO corporis et sanguinis tui, Domine Jesu Christe, quam indignus sumere præsumo : non mihi veniat ad judicium nec ad condemnationem, sed pro tua pietate prosit mihi ad tutamentum animæ et corporis. Qui cum Deo Patre et Spiritu sancto vivis et regnas Deus.

OREMUS.

DOMINE Jesu Christe, Fili Dei vivi, qui ex voluntate Patris, cooperante Spiritu sancto, per mortem tuam

---

[78] This is an important variation : with which agrees also the Bangor pontifical.

HERFORD.

QUI vivis et regnas cum Deo Patre in unitate ejusdem, &c.

ROM.

QUI cum eodem Deo Patre et Spiritu sancto vivis et regnas Deus in sæcula sæculorum. Amen.

PERCEPTIO corporis tui, Domine Jesu Christe, quod ego indignus sumere præsumo, non mihi proveniat in judicium et condemnationem : sed pro tua pietate prosit mihi ad tutamentum mentis et corporis, et ad medelam percipiendam. Qui vivis et regnas cum Deo Patre in unitate Spiritus sancti Deus, per omnia sæcula sæculorum. Amen.

Genuflectit, surgit, et dicit :

DEUS Pater, fons et origo totius bonitatis, qui misericordia ductus unigenitum tuum pro nobis ad infima mundi descendere, et carnem sumere voluisti, quem ego

PANEM cœlestem accipiam, et nomen Domini invocabo.
Deinde parum inclinatus, accipit ambas partes hostiæ inter pollicem et indicem sinistræ manus, et patenam

x

SARUM.	BANGOR.	EBOR.
		mundum vivificasti : libera me per hoc sacrosanctum corpus et sanguinem tuum ab omnibus iniquitatibus et universis malis meis : et fac me tuis obedire præceptis et a te nunquam in perpetuum separari permittas. Qui cum Deo Patre et eodem Spiritu sancto vivis et regnas Deus. Per omnia sæcula sæculorum. Amen.

---

[79] In the first edition I was obliged to leave a small portion of this prayer conjecturally supplied in italics: "apud te adjuvari : *et pro defunctis fidelibus* offerimus," &c. As I then

HERFORD.

indignus et miserrimus peccator hic manibus teneo, te adoro, te glorifico, te tota cordis intentione laudo, et precor ut nos famulos tuos non deseras sed peccata nostra deleas: quatenus tibi soli Deo vivo et vero, puro corde et casto corpore semper servire valeamus. Per eundem.

AGIMUS tibi Deo Patri gratias pro jam beatificatis, postulantes eorum interventu apud te adjuvari: pro his autem qui adhuc sunt in purgatoriis locis, offerimus tibi Patri Filium: supplicantes ut per hanc sacrosanctam hostiam eorum pœna levior sit et brevior: pro nobis autem quos adhuc gravant peccata carnis et sanguinis immolamus tibi Patri Filium: obsecrantes ut peccata quæ ex carne et sanguine contraximus caro mundet, sanguis lavet unigeniti Filii tui Domini nostri Jesu Christi. Qui tecum vivit.[70]

ROM.

inter eundem indicem et medium, et dextera percutiens pectus, elevata aliquantulum voce, dicit ter devote et humiliter:

DOMINE non sum dignus, ut intres sub tectum meum: sed tantum dic verbo, et sanabitur anima mea.

---

stated in a note, this was because one of the copies of the Hereford use in the Bodleian library had an erasure which was supplied with those words in an old or contemporary hand,

SARUM.	BANGOR.	EBOR.
Ad corpus dicat[80] *cum humiliatione antequam percipiat:*	*Ad corpus cum inclinatione antequam percipiat dicat:*	*Hic sumat corpus*[81] *cruce prius facta cum ipso corpore ante: deinde ad sanguinem dicens:*

AVE in æternum sanctissima caro Christi: mihi ante omnia et super omnia summa dulcedo. Corpus Domini nostri Jesu Christi sit mihi peccatori via et vita.[82] (Amen. Bangor.)

CORPUS Domini nostri Jesu Christi sit mihi reme-

---

though (as I also remarked) they could not be those which originally had been there; and the other had lost the leaf altogether. I was not then aware (through some error which I cannot now account for) that the copy which I spoke of as being in St. John's college, Oxford, was not a York (see pref. first edit. p. lxxviij) but a Hereford missal. This book upon examination, though very imperfect and mutilated in many places, yet happily supplies the perfect text in this important prayer, as I have given it above.

Since the publication of that edition I have also found this prayer, occupying somewhat the same place in the canon, in the manuscript missal said to have belonged to the church of St. Paul's, London; and of which I have spoken in the preface to the present edition.

[80] It will be observed that the English uses differ in the form at the priest's receiving. When laity communicated there was also a considerable variety in the words used. From St. Ambrose, *de sacramentis*, lib. iv. cap. 5, and from St. Augustine, *serm.* 272, 332, we may conclude that as in the Clementine liturgy the simple words were said, "Corpus Christi:" to which was answered "Amen." Many forms of later ages, in delivering both the Body and the Blood to the people, may be seen collected in Georgius, tom. iii. lib. iv. cap. xix. Several again in the various orders printed by Martene, in his

HERFORD.

Tunc inclinet se supra calicem, et valde devote percipiat corpus Christi, sed ante perceptionem dicat:

ROM.

Postea dextera se signans cum hostia super patenam, dicit:

CORPUS Domini nostri Jesu Christi sit animæ meæ remedium in vitam æternam. Amen.

CORPUS Domini nostri Jesu Christi custodiat animam meam in vitam æternam. Amen.

---

first volume, *de ant. ritibus.* Micrologus gives this: "Corpus et sanguis Domini nostri Jesu Christi proficiat tibi in vitam æternam." Cap. 23.

[81] One of the constitutions of St. Edmund of Canterbury in the thirteenth century directs how priests are to take the host: "Item in celebratione missæ hostiam consecratam daturus sacerdos sibimet ipsi, ne admoveat ori suo, quia ante perceptionem eam ore suo tangere non debet. Si vero de patena, sicut quidam faciunt, eam sumat, post celebrationem missæ tam patenam quam calicem faciat aqua perfundi, vel solum calicem, si eam non sumat de patena: habeat quoque sacerdos juxta altare pannum mundissimum circumdatum undique et honeste et decenter coopertum, in quo, post sumptionem sacramenti salutaris, digitos cum labiis ablutos emundet." *Concil.* tom. i. p. 639.

[82] "Caveat sibi sacerdos post istas orationes dictas a nimia prolixitate tractandi propter cogitationes volubiles aliquorum; tamen in præmissis orationibus debet sacerdos meditari de incarnatione, nativitate, passione et piissima morte domini nostri Jesu Christi et de hujus sacramenti virtute; et tunc cum magna devotione et omni reverentia et timore debet communicari (cruce prius facta, ex ipso corpore scilicet Christi, ante os recipientis) dicens, *In nomine,*" &c. *Manuale Sar.*

SARUM.

IN nomine ✠ Patris, et Filii, et Spiritus sancti.

Hic sumat corpus, cruce prius facta cum ipso corpore ante os.

BANGOR.

Hic debet sacerdos intime meditari de incarnatione, caritate, passione, et de dira morte Jesu Christi, quas pro nobis passus est et etiam voluntarie sustinuit. Et sic cum timore et reverentia magna corpus Christi et sanguinem sumat: cruce de ipso corpore prius facta ante os ejus recipientis.

EBOR.

dium sempiternum in vitam æternam. Amen.

Deinde ad sanguinem cum magna devotione dicens :

AVE in æternum cœlestis potus, mihi ante omnia et super omnia summa dulcedo. Corpus et sanguis Domini nostri Jesu Christi prosint mihi peccatori ad remedium sempiternum in vitam æternam. Amen. In nomine ✠ Patris, et Filii, et Spiritus sancti. Amen.

SANGUIS Domini nostri Jesu Christi conservet me in vitam æternam. Amen.

CORPUS et sanguis Domini nostri Jesu

HERFORD. ROM.

Sumit reverenter ambas partes hostiæ, jungit manus, et quiescit aliquantulum in meditatione sanctissimi sacramenti. Deinde discooperit calicem, genuflectit, colligit fragmenta, si quæ sint, extergit patenam super calicem, interim dicens:

QUID retribuam Domino pro omnibus, quæ retribuit mihi? Calicem salutaris accipiam, et nomen Domini invocabo. Laudans invocabo Dominum, et ab inimicis meis salvus ero.

Ante perceptionem sanguinis dicat:

Accipit calicem manu dextera, et eo se signans, dicit:

SANGUIS Domini nostri Jesu Christi conservet animam meam in vitam æternam. Amen.

SANGUIS Domini nostri Jesu Christi custodiat animam meam in vitam æternam. Amen.

SARUM.	BANGOR.	EBOR.
		Christi : custodiat corpus meum et animam meam in vitam æternam. Amen.
Hic sumat sanguinem : quo sumpto [88] *inclinet*	*Hic sumat totum sanguinem : quo sumpto et calice*	

---

[88] If any were to be communicated during the mass this was the time appointed: as it is still directed in the *Ritus celebrandi missam:* "Si qui sint communicandi in missa, sacerdos post sumptionem sanguinis, antequam se purificet, facta genuflexione, ponat particulas," &c. Tit. x. 6. The *Rubricæ generales* of the Paris missal are particular on one point :—

"Si qui sint sacram communionem accepturi, sacerdos non eos differat post missæ finem sine necessitate. Ordo enim postulat, ut communio populi fiat intra missam, et immediate sequatur communionem sacerdotis." Cap. x.

So, also, the Roman ritual: "Communio autem populi infra missam fieri debet (nisi quandoque ex rationabili causa post missam sit facienda) cum orationes, quæ in missa post communionem dicuntur, non solum ad sacerdotem sed etiam ad alios communicantes spectant."

I need scarcely add that for many ages before the reformation (probably from the eleventh century) communion was given in the church of England in one kind only. We may take the reasons for this from Lyndwood: "Quæ est ratio" (he enquires) "quare laicis non datur eucharistia sub duplici specie?" We may observe that as mere communicants clerics as well as laity were under the same rule: the priest could receive in both kinds only if he also consecrated: "Dic, una ratio est, quia sic possent credere quod totus Christus non esset sub eadem specie. Alia ratio est propter periculum, quia de facili posset effundi sanguis. Tertia est ut veritas respondeat umbræ, quia in lege non habebant offerentes de libamine. Alia potest esse ratio, quia non esset decens nec securum, ut tantum conficeretur de sanguine, quantum suffi-

HERFORD.   ROM.

Sumit totum sanguinem cum particula. Quo sump-to, si qui sunt communi-

ceret uni magnæ parochiæ, in qua sunt quandoque multa millia personarum, nec posset altare tale vas in quo conficeretur recipere." Lib. 1. tit. 1, Altissimus, *verb*. vinum purum.

After receiving the communion people in the middle ages were given unconsecrated wine, of which they took a small portion. Repeated injunctions were laid upon parish priests that they should carefully explain that the wine so given was merely wine, and that the Blood of our Lord had been already received under one kind only.

The rubrics at the beginning of the Roman missal still prescribe the same rule; but in practice, at least everywhere in England, the observance of it has long been forgotten: "Minister autem dextra manu tenens vas cum vino et aqua, sinistra vero mappulam, aliquanto post sacerdotem eis porrigit purificationem, et mappulam ad os abstergendum." *Ritus celebr. missam.* x.

Upon the mode of receiving I need scarcely remind the reader of the famous passage in St. Cyril, *Catech. mystag.* v. cap. xxj: and according to the same feelings the Church has always insisted upon outward gestures of reverence and awe; not merely by way of decency as on less solemn occasions but here as of actual necessity. As St. Augustine declares, "nemo carnem illam manducat nisi prius adoraverit." *Enar. in ps.* xcviii. 5. I shall only add a passage from St. Chrysostom, as cited and translated by an Anglican writer in the seventeenth century: "This Body the wise men reverenced, even when it lay in the manger, and approaching thereto worshipped with great fear and trembling. Let us therefore who are citizens of heaven imitate at least these barbarians... But thou seest this Body not in the manger, but on the altar; not

SARUM.	BANGOR.	EBOR.
se sacerdos, et dicat cum devotione orationem sequentem:	*altari superposito, inclinans se sacerdos cum magna veneratione in*	

held by a woman, but presented by the priest... Let us therefore stir up ourselves, and show far greater reverence than those barbarians, lest by our careless and rude coming we heap fire on our heads." *Homil.* xxiv, cit. Ashwell, *Gestus eucharisticus;* cf. also pp. 46 and 120. And in Lactantius, *de morte persec.*, the vision of St. Perpetua; cited by Gerbert, tom. i. p. 125: "ego accepi junctis manibus."

How long the custom continued of receiving the eucharist into the hands is uncertain. "Primis temporibus (says Mabillon, *Mus. Ital.* 2. lix) eucharistia etiam laicis tribuebatur in manus." There is a canon of the council of Toledo, A.D. 400: "Si quis acceptam a sacerdote eucharistiam non sumpserit, veluti sacrilegus repellatur." But this is directed against the heresy of the Priscillianists. The old form was first given up at Rome, before the age of St. Gregory the great: but for some long time after it was still retained in other churches. We hear of a certain abbess, St. Odilia, into whose hands not only the host but the chalice was delivered in the eighth century; *præfat. in sæc. iii*, Benedict. p. i, observat. x. Georgius, tom. iii. p. 174, from whom I quote the above, cites also St. Cæsar of Arles, who proves that men and women received differently: "viri enim, quando ad altare accessuri sunt, lavant manus suas, et omnes mulieres nitida exhibent linteamina ubi corpus Christi accipiant." See, almost word for word, St. Augustine, *Serm.* 152 (cit. Casalius, p. 91). There is an express canon in the year 578: "Ne liceat mulieri nuda manu eucharistiam accipere." *Concil. Autisiodor.* And another canon of the same council orders that "unaquæque mulier (quando communicat) dominicalem suam habeat." As to what this dominicale was, Baronius, Mabillon, and many others suppose it to be the same as the linteamina above: but Stephen Baluze says it was a covering for the head, resting his opinion upon a council of Angers: "Si mulier communicans dominicale suum super caput suum non habuerit, usque

HERFORD.

ROM.

candi, eos communicet, antequam se purificet. Postea dicit:

---

ad alium diem non communicet." The Anglo-saxon rule was, "mulieribus licet sub nigro velamine eucharistiam accipere." Egbert, *Confessional.* 37. It is difficult to explain a later canon under king Edgar: "We enjoin that no woman come near to the altar while mass is celebrating." Thorpe, vol. i. p. 255. One thing is clear, that women were not permitted to receive with uncovered hands. To return to men: Bede records the death in the year 680 of Cædmon, a monk, who feeling himself dying "interrogavit, si eucharistiam intus haberent... Rursus ille: ' et tamen,' ait, ' afferte mihi eucharistiam.' Qua accepta in manu, interrogavit, si omnes placidum erga se animum haberent," &c. *Hist. eccles.* lib. iv. cap. 24.

Very anciently there seems to have been great difference of practice as to the administration of the chalice by deacons. Martene, *de ant. rit.* lib. i. c. iv, brings many examples by which he proves that it was not only allowed but general: and there is the well-known complaint of St. Laurence to pope Sixtus: "Quo sacerdos sancte sine diacono properas? nunquid degenerem me probasti? experire, utrum idoneum magistrum elegeris, cui commisisti dominici sanguinis dispensationem." As Merati remarks upon Gavantus, tom. i. p. 230, citing this; St. Laurence says not the Body, but the Blood: as if to give the chalice was an especial part of the office of deacons. On the other hand, we have St. Chrysostom, *Hom.* 46. *in Matt.*, declaring that none but a priest can administer the chalice, and the fifteenth canon of the second council of Arles decreeing that when a priest is present a deacon may not administer "the body of the Lord;" which seems still further to limit the canon of the council of Nice, viz. that deacons should not "give the body of Christ" to priests. The sixteenth of the canons of Ælfric allows deacons to "baptize children, and housel the people:" which, if there should be any doubt, is fully explained in the pastoral epistle

*medio altaris et
crucem respiciens*

---

of the same Ælfric: "the deacon may give the bread, and baptize children." Thorpe, *Ancient laws and institutes*, vol. ii. pp. 349, 379.

But this canon of the council of Nice may be reconciled with the others by remembering that deacons were forbidden by it to distribute to priests; in which case there would be conveyed a tacit permission that they might to the laity. There seems to be no ground for supposing that the Nicene fathers intended in any way to oppose the custom of the first and apostolic age when, as St. Justin tells us (*Apolog.* ii.), the deacons carried the eucharist to the absent and the sick. The thirty-eighth canon of the fourth council of Carthage, A.D. 252, is very much to the point: "Præsente presbytero, diaconus eucharistiam corporis Christi populo, si necessitas cogat, jussus eroget." And with this Lyndwood agrees, in his gloss upon the text, *Diaconi baptizare non præsumant, nisi*," &c.: "In casu necessitatis, absente presbytero, potest diaconus suo jure baptizare, et corpus Christi erogare infirmis: sed in ecclesia præsente presbytero non potest, etiamsi necessitas exigat, nisi jussus a presbytero, puta, cum multi sint qui indigent baptismo, et presbyter non potest omnibus sufficere. Similiter, si multi volunt accipere corpus Christi, nec presbyter sufficit omnibus." Lib. iii. tit. 24, Baptisterium habeatur. So that in all these cases an express command from the priest was necessary, that deacons might not presume; and attempt even perhaps to consecrate: as may be inferred from the twenty-fifth chapter of the council of Laodicea, cited by Cassander, *Opera*, p. 73: "Non oportet diacono panem dare, nec calicem benedicere." One word upon the address of St. Laurence to pope Sixtus cited above. I would remind the reader that in the text of the Benedictine edition of the works of St. Ambrose, upon whose authority the tradition mainly rests, the reading is not *dispensationem* but *consecrationem*. *De off*. lib. i. 41, tom. ii. p. 55. If this latter is correct, it can only be understood in a very extended sense. See above, note 12. p. 127.

An abuse seems to have crept in in England about the thirteenth century, which is thus described and forbidden in the constitutions of Walter Cantilupe bishop of Worcester: "Audivimus autem quidem, quod merito credimus reprobandum, quod quidam sacerdotes parochianos suos, cum communicant, offerre compellunt: propter quod simul communicant, et offerunt, per quod venalis exponi videtur corporis et sanguinis Christi hostia pretiosa: hoc, quod execrabile sit, nullus ambigit sanæ mentis: hoc igitur avaritiæ horrendum vitium. interdicimus et execramus." Wilkins, *Concilia*, tom. i. p. 671. So, once more, a canon of a synod of the diocese of Chichester in 1289: "In sacrosancto die paschæ, sine ulla exactione decimæ vel debiti, seu oblationis, liberaliter conferant corpus Christi; ne una manu porrigendo eucharistiam, altera recipiendo pecuniam, nostræ redemptionis mysterium fiat venale. Quod si compertum sit fieri, præcipimus hujusmodi flagitiosum commercium severitate canonica graviter vindicari." *Concil.* tom. 2. p. 170; cf. tom. 3. p. 60.

In the first age of the Church all who were present at the service of the blessed eucharist, except those under discipline, partook of the communion: the prayers alone of the liturgies, even had we no other evidence, abundantly testify that they were drawn up on the supposition of the presence of many communicants. Micrologus in the eleventh century says: "sciendum est, juxta antiquos patres, quod soli communicantes divinis mysteriis interesse consueverunt." Cap. 51. Cardinal Bona adds "hanc consuetudinem diu perstitisse evidens est," and goes on to speak of some churches at Rome where the priest is not permitted to communicate alone at high mass: "In missa solemni retenta est ab aliquibus ecclesiis communio ministrorum, quæ Romæ nunc permanet in insignioribus basilicis, et ubi desierat, apostolicæ visitationis decreto restituta est. Sapientissimo sane consilio, ne in desuetudinem abeat antiquissimus ecclesiæ ritus, sine quo vix possunt intelligi, quæ in liturgicis orationibus quotidie recitantur." *Rerum. liturg.* lib. ii. cap. xvii. 2. Van Espen

SARUM.　　　　BANGOR.　　　　EBOR.

dicat hanc oratio-
nem sequentem.

GRATIAS tibi ago, Domine,
sancte Pater, omnipotens æterne Deus : qui me refecisti de sacratissimo corpore et sanguine Filii tui
Domini nostri Jesu Christi : et precor, ut hoc sacramentum salutis nostræ quod sumpsi indignus peccator,
non veniat mihi ad judicium neque
ad condemnationem pro meritis
meis : sed ad profectum corporis et
animæ in vitam æternam.　Amen.

Qua dicta eat sacerdos ad dexterum
cornu altaris cum calice inter manus,
digitis adhuc conjunctis sicut prius :
et accedat subdiaconus et effundat in
calicem vinum et aquam :[84] *et resin-*
ceret[85] *sacerdos manus suas ne aliquæ*
reliquiæ corporis vel sanguinis rema-
neant, in digitis vel in calice.

Post primam ab-　Hic lavet sacer-　Post primam ab-

---

speaks to the same purpose, and advises that parish priests
should warn their people that they would communicate them
only during the service : and again, "Ulterius populo ex-
ponendum, quod ipsa communio sive participatio sacramenti
partem quodam modo sacrificii constituat : ideoque summopere conveniens esse, ut dum una cum sacerdote sacrificium offerunt, etiam una de sacrificio sacramentaliter com-
municando participent." *Jus ecc. universum,* pars. ii. sect i.
tit. v.

[84] The reader will observe a difference here in the English
uses, and again between them and the Roman : which last
appoints wine for the first ablution, which is rather called
the purification.　Many of the ancient ritualists speak of

HERFORD.   ROM.

.

Postquam communicaverit
eat ad dextrum cornu alta-
ris cum calice, et abluat eum
cum vino, dicendo:

---

wine; and Durand of an ablution "missa finita," which was
then to be thrown away into some clean place; probably
the piscina: "in locum mundum et honestum." Lib. iv.
cap. 55.

    [85] "Loke pater noster thou be sayande,
    I whils tho preste is rynsande:
    When tho preste has rinsynge done,
    Opon thi fete thou stonde up sone:
    Then tho clerke flyttis tho boke,
    Agayne to tho south auter noke:
    Tho preste turnes til his seruyce,
    And saies forthe more of his office."
                 Layfolks mass book.

SARUM.	BANGOR.	EBOR.
lutionem vel effu-sionem, dicitur hæc oratio:	*dos digitos suos in concavitate cali-cis, cum vino in-fuso a subdiacono vel alio ministro: quo hausto, dicat sacerdos:*	*lutionem dicetur hæc oratio:*

QUOD ore sumpsimus,[86] Domine, pura mente capiamus: et de munere temporali fiat nobis remedium sempiternum (in vitam æternam. Amen. Ebor.).

Hic lavet digitos in concavitate ca-licis cum vino in-fuso a subdiacono, quo hausto, sequa-tur oratio:	*Hic etiam subdia-conus vel alius mi-nister infundat vinum vel aquam in calicem: quo hausto, sequatur hæc oratio:*	*Sumat hic cali-cem, et ponat su-per patenam, et postea inclinando se dicat:*

HÆC nos communio, Domine (Domine, communio, Ebor.), purget a crimine: et cœlestis remedii fa-ciat esse consortes. (Per Christum. Ebor. Per Chris-tum Dominum nostrum. Amen. Bangor.)

•

	Finita oratione: eat sacerdos in me-dio altaris, ibi-dem calicem super	
Post perceptionem ablutionum ponat	*patenam jacentem dimittens: et se*	

---

[86] "*Postquam omnes communicaverunt, dicit:* Quod ore sumpsimus," &c. Micrologus, cap. xxiii. Compare what the same old writer says in another place: "Postquam omnes communicaverint dicit sacerdos hanc orationem sub silentio,

HERFORD.   ROM.

QUOD ore sumpsimus, Domine, pura mente capiamus: et de munere temporali fiat nobis remedium sempiternum (in vitam æternam. Amen. Herford.).

Deinde abluat digitos suos supra calicem cum vino vel aqua, dicendo:

HÆC nos communio, Domine, purget a crimine: et cœlestis remedii faciat esse consortes. Per Christum Dominum nostrum. Amen.

Tunc abluat cum aqua, et redeat ad medium altaris cum illa ablutione, et ibi sumat eam et iterum dicat:

Interim porrigit calicem ministro, qui infundit in eo parum vini, quo se purificat: deinde prosequitur:

Quod ore sumpsimus. Qua finita sequitur oratio sive orationes post communionem dicendæ." Cap. 19. Many forms of prayer after receiving are in the collections of Martene, *de ant. ecc. rit.* tom. i. 212, &c.

SARUM.	BANGOR.	EBOR.

sacerdos calicem super patenam: ut si quid remaneat stillet; et postea inclinando se dicat:

cum magna veneratione respiciendum crucem inclinans, dicat in memoria passionis Domini:

ADORAMUS (Adoremus, Bangor.) crucis signaculum, per quod salutis sumpsimus sacramentum.[87]

Deinde lavet manus:[89] *diaconus interim corporalia complicet.*[90]

Tunc cum ista oratione eat sacerdos ad dextrum cornu altaris, et

---

[87] " When this is sayde knele doun sone,
Saye pater-noster til messe be done,
For tho messe is noght sest,
Or tyme of ite, misa est."

Layfolks mass book.

[88] (*Quem potavi.* Herf. and Rom.) This prayer was necessarily altered after the chalice was received by none except the officiating priest. Anciently it was in the plural number; and occurs in the old Gothic liturgy: " Corpus tuum, Domine, quod accipimus (*accepimus?*) et calicem tuum (*calix tuus?*) quem potavimus," &c. Thom. *missale Gothicum*, p. 392. It is in the singular, however, in the old missal edited by Flacius Illyricus: but that can scarcely prove much, as it seems allowed that that famous blunder (as regarded the purpose of its first editor) is rather to be considered as a manual of occasional prayers which might be used by the priest, mixed up in no exact arrangement with the much more ancient

HERFORD.   ROM.

CORPUS tuum, Domine, quod sumpsi, et calix (sanguis, Rom.) quem potavi,[88] adhæreant semper (adhæreat, Rom.) visceribus meis:

HERFORD.	ROM.
et præsta, ut in me non remaneat macula peccati, in quem pura et sancta introierunt sacramenta corporis et sanguinis tui. Qui vivis et regnas.	et præsta, ut in me non remaneat scelerum macula, quem pura et sancta refecerunt sacramenta. Qui vivis et regnas in sæcula sæculorum. Amen.
Tunc ponat calicem jacentem super patenam, et inclinet se ad altare, et eat ad sacrarium et lavet ma-	*Abluit digitos, extergit, et sumit ablutionem: extergit os, et calicem quem operit, et plicato corporali, collocat*

Roman sacramentary. Moreover, according to that order the chalice is to be given also to the assistant clergy: though there appears to be some doubt as to the people.

[88] "Cardinal Wolsey officiated at St. Paul's, where, it seems, some of the principal nobility gave him the basin to wash at high mass. He is charged with intolerable pride for suffering persons of the first quality to do this office: however, the matter is capable of a fairer construction than is generally put upon it. For the holding the basin at high mass may rather be supposed a ministration in religion, and an honour to God Almighty, than any respect to the cardinal; and if the ceremony was thus paid, why might it not be received under the same consideration?" Collier, *Ecc. hist.* vol. ii. p. 18.

[90] (*Corporalia complicet.*) "Quod ita plicari debet ut nec initium nec finis appareat, sicut etiam sudarium in sepulchro Domini inventum est. Sudarium est ligamentum capitis." Alcuin, *de divinis officiis; Bibl. patr. auct.* tom. i. p. 282.

SARUM.	BANGOR.	EBOR.

*Ablutis manibus
et redeunte sacer-
dote ad dexterum
cornu altaris: di-
aconus   calicem
porrigat ori sa-
cerdotis, si quid
infusionis in eo
remanserit resu-
mendum. Postea
vero dicat cum su-
is ministris com-
munionem.*[91]

*abluat   manus.
Post perceptionem
sacramenti sacer-
dote ad manus ab-
luendas veniente,
diaconus corpora-
lia complicet : et
in loculo ponat.
Postea vero ipsa
corporalia,   cum
offertorio vel su-
dario, calici sup-
ponat.   Ablutis
manibus revertat
se   ad   dexterum
cornu   altaris, et
dicat una cum mi-
nistris suis com-
munionem.*

*Deinde facto signo crucis in facie ver-
tat se sacerdos ad populum : elevatisque aliquantulum brachiis et junctis
manibus dicat :*

D OMINUS
vobiscum.

D OMINUS
vobiscum.

*Et iterum revertens se ad altare di-
cat :*

O REMUS.

O REMUS.

---

[91] (*Communionem.*) This was an antiphon or verse taken
usually from a psalm, which varied with the day; and in old
times was sung whilst the people communicated. See Gerbert,
tom. i. p. 458. St. Augustine speaks of it, in his own time
at Carthage : "Ut hymni ad altare dicerentur de psalmorum

HERFORD.

nus suas, et in eundo dicat:

LAVABO inter innocentes manus meas: et circumdabo altare tuum, Domine.

Deinde reversus ad altare dicat communionem.

Qua dicta signet se et vertat se ad populum et dicat:

DOMINUS vobiscum.
Et dicat postcommunionem.

Et ad finem orationis jungat manus, et eat ad medium altaris dicendo:

ROM.

in altari ut prius: deinde prosequitur missam:

---

libro, sive ante oblationem sive cum distribueretur populo quod fuisset oblatum." *Retract.* lib. ii. cap. xj. We have no evidence from the old Gallic liturgies as to what might have been the practice of the British churches before the coming of Augustine of Canterbury.

SARUM.	BANGOR.	EBOR.

Deinde dicat postcommunionem:[92] *juxta numerum et ordinem antedictarum orationum ante epistolam. Finita ultima postcommunione*[93] *factoque signo crucis in fronte, iterum vertat se sacerdos ad populum, et dicat:*

　　　Dominus vobiscum.

Deinde diaconus:

Benedicamus Domino.[94]

In alio vero tempore dicitur:

Ite, missa est.[95]

---

[92] (*Postcommunionem.*) A short prayer which like the communio varied with the office of the day. Some ancient copies of the Gregorian and Gelasian sacramentaries prefix instead the title " *ad complendum :*" which is followed in the Leofric missal. It is to this that St. Augustine alludes, when writing to Paulinus he says, "participato tanto sacramento, gratiarum actio cuncta concludit." It was especially intended for those who had communicated; as Walafrid Strabo, *de rebus ecc.* cap. xxii, declares "ejus petitio maxime pro iis est qui communicant." Micrologus repeats this, and in another place says that in number they ought to correspond with the collects and secret prayers before the preface. See also Radulph. Tungr. prop. 23: "ante ipsas communicare non negligunt, quicunque earundem orationum benedictione foveri desiderant." *De canonum observantia.*

[93] During lent a prayer was appointed in the old English missals to be said after the postcommunion, called the "*super populum :*" and was preceded by the form, "Humiliate capita vestra Deo." This custom was very ancient, as may be seen by an examination of cardinal Thomasius' edition of the Gelasian sacramentary, and was for a long time said during the whole year: but afterwards was restricted to the season of lent, that the people might during their discipline be the

HERFORD.

ROM.

PER Dominum nos-
trum Jesum Chris-
tum Filium tuum. Qui te-
cum vivit.

Iterum signet se et vertat
ad populum et dicat:
Dominus vobiscum.
Antequam revertatur di-
cat, Ite: *in revertendo di-*
cat, missa est.
In missis quando non dici-
tur Gloria in excelsis, *di-*
catur:
Benedicamus Domino.

Dicto, post ultimam oratio-
nem,
Dominus vobiscum.
℞. Et cum spiritu tuo.
dicit, pro missæ qualitate,
vel
Ite missa est, *vel*
Benedicamus Domino.
℞. Deo gratias.

---

better fortified by the prayers and benedictions of the Church
against the malice of the devil. As Amalarius tells us the
intention was, "si omni tempore necesse est paratum esse
bellicosum, adversus insidias sive impetus inimicorum : quanto
magis in procinctu? Quadragesimali tempore scit adversarius
noster a sancta ecclesia singulare certamen commissum esse
contra se. ... Vult sacerdos noster ut nostris armis vestiti
simus : propterea jubet per ministrum, ut humiliemus capita
nostra Deo, et ita tandem infundit super milites protectionem
benedictionis suæ." Lib. iii. cap. 37; compare Micrologus,
cap. 51. These prayers are still retained in the Roman
missal.

[94] (*Benedicamus Domino.*) The reason why sometimes this
form and sometimes the "*Ite missa est*" was used seems to
be that upon the lesser festivals only the more religious and
spiritually disposed would make a practice of being present,
who were not to be so suddenly (as it were) dismissed, but
rather were to give thanks to God. Upon the greater feasts
a large number of people of all occupations would probably
attend, and to these the "*Ite missa est*" would be a licence to
depart. See Micrologus, cap. 46.

[95] "Then when thou heris say ite,
　　Or benedicamus if hit be:

SARUM.	BANGOR.	EBOR.

Quotiescumque enim dicitur, Ite missa est: *semper dicitur ad populum convertendo.*[96] *Et cum dici debeat*, Benedicamus Domino: *convertendo ad altare dicitur.*[97]

His dictis, sacerdos inclinato corpore, junctisque manibus, tacita voce coram altari in medio dicat hanc orationem:

Sacerdos hic inclinato corpore junctisque manibus, tacita voce in medio altaris dicat hanc orationem.

PLACEAT tibi,[98] sancta Trinitas, obsequium servitutis meæ, et præsta: ut hoc sacrificium quod

---

Then is tho messe al done,
Bot yit this prayere thou make right sone:
Aftir hit wele thou may,
In gods name wende thi way."

Layfolks mass book.

[96] This turning towards the people, or towards the altar if " Benedicamus" was said, is noticed by many of the ancient ritualists. Micrologus, cap. 46: " Cum *Ite, missa est*, dicimus, ad populum vertimur, quem discedere jubemus; cum autem, *Benedicamus Domino*, non ad populum sed ad altare, id est, ad Dominum vertimur, nosque ipsos non ad discedendum, sed ad benedicendum Domino adhortamur." So also Durandus, lib. iv. cap. 57; Belethus, cap. 49, &c. Le Brun says that in some churches of France the deacon turned towards the north, but he knows not why.

[97] Micrologus gives us (writing in the eleventh century) the rule which then governed the saying either of the one form or the other: "Semper autem cum *Gloria in excelsis*

HERFORD.   ROM.

Tunc inclinet se cum junc- | *Dicto* Ite missa est, *vel* Be-
tis manibus ad altare, di- | nedicamus Domino, *sacer-*
cens : | *dos inclinat se ante medium*
| *altaris, et manibus junctis*
| *super illud, dicit :*

PLACEAT tibi, sancta Trinitas, obsequium servitutis meæ, et præsta : ut (hoc, Herford.) sacri-

---

etiam, *Te Deum*, et *Ite missa est*, recitamus." Cap. 46. That
is, upon the Lord's day and the greater festivals.

"Ad missas de *Requiem* quod attinet, Stephanus Au-
gustodunensis ex 600 jam annis nos monuit loco *Ite missa
est*, dici *Requiescant in pace*. . . . Non ergo populum per *Ite
missa est* dimitti congrueret, cum fere missam sepultura
precesque consequantur, quæ sane persuadere adstantibus
debent, ut ne recedant." Le Brun, i. 323; and Belethus,
cap. 49.

[98] According to the old English uses the mass ended with
the "Ite missa est" or the "Benedicamus Domino;" and the
people then were at liberty to leave the church : though it
is not likely that many left until they knew that the prayer
" Placeat tibi" had been said. This prayer was in very early
times left to the discretion and devotion of the priest to be
said or not as he thought proper. The reason why the final
blessing was not given to the people in England before the
seventeenth century may probably have been because of the

SARUM. BANGOR. EBOR.

oculis majestatis tuæ (tuæ majestatis, Ebor. et Bangor.) indignus obtuli, tibi sit (sit tibi, Ebor.) acceptabile: mihique et omnibus pro quibus illud obtuli, sit, te miserante, propitiabile. Qui vivis et regnas (Deus. Per omnia sæcula sæculorum. Amen. Sar. et Bangor.). *Qua finita erigat se sacerdos, signans se in facie sua, dicens:*

IN nomine Patris, &c.

IN nomine Patris, et Filii, et Spiritus sancti. Amen.

Et sic inclinatione facta, eo ordine, quo prius accesserunt ad altare in principio missæ, sic induti cum ceroferariis et cæteris ministris redeant. Sacerdos vero in redeundo dicat evangelium:[99] In principio.[1]

episcopal benedictions which were to be said before the Agnus Dei. The date of the addition of the benediction to the Roman use is uncertain: but when first added only a bishop was allowed to give it. Some writers have carried the date up to the tenth or ninth century, because the blessing of the people at the end of the mass is mentioned by early ritualists. But the blessing so spoken of refers to the postcommunion. This is clear from the words of Walafrid Strabo (A.D. 830): "Statutum est, ut populus ante benedictionem sacerdotis non egrediatur de missa. Quæ benedictio intelligitur illa ultima sacerdotis oratio." Cap. 22.

Although this prayer is not in the old ordines Romani it is nevertheless very ancient, and occurs in the manuscript edited

HERFORD.　　　　　　　ROM.

ficium, quod oculis tuæ majestatis indignus obtuli, tibi sit acceptabile: mihique et omnibus pro quibus illud obtuli, sit, te miserante, propitiabile. (Qui vivis. Herford. Per Christum Dominum nostrum. Amen. Rom.)

Et osculetur altare.

Deinde osculatur altare: et elevatis oculis, extendens, elevans, et jungens manus, caputque cruci inclinans, dicit:

BENEDICAT vos omnipotens Deus.
Et versus ad populum, semel tantum benedicens, prosequitur: Pater, et Filius ✠ et Spiritus sanctus. ℟. Amen.

Dum deponit vestimenta sua, vel in eundo ab altari usque ad vestibulum, dicat ant. Trium Puerorum.

Deinde in cornu evangelii, dicto, Dominus vobiscum, *et* Initium, *vel* Sequentia sancti evangelii, *signans altare, vel librum, et se, legit evangelium secundum*

---

by Illyricus, in many others of equal date, and is noticed by Micrologus. Another reason why the ordines omit it possibly is because in fact the service is already over, having concluded with the "Ite missa est." So in many manuscripts it is headed *post missam*, and Micrologus says: "Finita missa dicit, Placeat tibi, sancta Trinitas." Cap. 23.

[99] This lection was the first fourteen verses of the first chapter of the gospel according to St. John. It has been said that it was not obligatory according to the Roman use until the last revision, after the council of Trent; but the rubrics of the Bangor and Sarum missals do not seem to leave a discretion. In some of the churches of France this last gospel is still read not at the altar but as in England anciently in

SARUM.   BANGOR.   EBOR.

---

returning to the sacristy; in others standing at the entrance to it; and again, in some, in the sacristy. Many of the monastic uses omitted this gospel.

The directions when this gospel is now to be omitted according to the Roman liturgy, and another read in its stead, are given in the *Rubr. gen.* xiij. 2.

[1] "*Cum vero sacerdos exuerit casulam et alia indumenta sacerdotalia, dicat psalmos subscriptos: cum antiph.* Trium. puerorum. *ps.* Benedicite sacerdotes: *usque ad finem cantici. ps.* Laudate Dominum in sanctis ejus: *totus psalmus.* Nunc dimittis servum: *cum* Gloria Patri, *et* sicut erat. Deinde *dicitur tota antiph.* Trium puerorum cantemus hymnum, quem cantabant in camino ignis benedicentes Dominum. Kyrie eleyson. Christe eleyson. Kyrie eleyson. Pater noster. Et ne nos. Sed libera nos. Benedicamus Patrem, et Filium, cum sancto Spiritu. Laudemus et superexaltemus eum in sæcula. Benedictus es Domine in firmamento cœli. Et laudabilis et gloriosus in sæcula.

"Benedicat et custodiat nos sancta Trinitas. Amen. Non intres in judicium cum servo tuo, Domine. Quia non justificabitur in conspectu tuo omnis vivens. Domine Deus virtutum converte nos. Et ostende faciem tuam et salvi erimus. Domine exaudi orationem meam. Et clamor meus ad te veniat. Dominus vobiscum. Et cum spiritu tuo. Oremus.

"*Oratio.*

"Deus, qui tribus pueris mitigasti flammas ignium, concede propitius, ut nos famulos tuos non exurat flamma vitiorum.

"*Oratio.* Ure igne sancti Spiritus renes nostros et cor nostrum, Domine: ut tibi casto corpore serviamus, et mundo corde placeamus.

HERFORD.

ROM.

Joannem, In principio erat Verbum, *vel aliud evang. ut dictum est in rubricis generalibus. Cum dicit,* Et verbum caro factum est, *genuflectit : In fine,* ℞. Deo gratias.

"*Oratio.* Actiones nostras quæsumus, Domine, aspirando præveni et adjuvando prosequere : ut cuncta nostra operatio et a te semper incipiat, et per te cœpta finiatur. *Et finiantur hæ tres orationes sic :* Per Christum Dominum nostrum. Amen." *Sar. miss.* edit. 1492.

The Bangor use agrees in the main with the above. The York has also nearly the same verses and responses with one collect only, viz. "Deus, qui tribus :" headed "¶ *Orationes post missam communes.*" The Hereford appoints similar verses and responses and the prayer "Deus, qui tribus," followed by "*Alia oratio.* Protector in te sperantium Deus, sine quo nihil est validum, nihil sanctum : multiplica super nos misericordiam tuam, ut te rectore, te duce, sic transeamus per bona temporalia, ut non amittamus æterna. Per."

On the same page immediately preceding the canon in the Salisbury missal of 1492, upon which is the "*oratio dicenda ante missam*" which I have already given (note 1. p. 2), is the following "*Oratio dicenda post missam.* Omnipotens sempiterne Deus Jesu Christe Domine, esto propitius peccatis meis, per assumptionem corporis et sanguinis tui. Tu enim loquens dixisti : qui manducat meam carnem et bibit meum sanguinem, in me manet et ego in eo, ideo te supplex deprecor : ut in me cor mundum crees, et spiritum rectum in visceribus meis innoves, et spiritu principali me confirmare digneris, atque ab omnibus insidiis diaboli ac vitiis emundes : ut gaudiorum cœlestium merear esse particeps. Qui vivis et regnas Deus, per omnia sæcula sæculorum. Amen."

Many editions contain more prayers to be said at the priest's choice both before and after the service. The Bangor and Hereford missals do not give any : in my copy of the

York use a very long prayer is printed before the ordinary. to be said before the service, "quam sanctus Augustinus composuit:" and the following at the end of the canon :—

"¶ *Oratio dicenda post celebrationem missæ.* Gratias ago tibi, dulcissime Domine Jesu Christe, lux vera, salus credentium, solatium tristium, spesque cunctorum, gaudium angelorum : qui me miserum et magnum peccatorem famulum tuum hodie sacratissimo corpore et sanguine tuo pascere dignatus es. Ideo et ego miserrimus et innumerabilibus criminibus infectus, lachrymosis precibus imploro benignissimam misericordiam tuam, et summam clementiam, ut hæc dulcissima refectio, summa et incomprehensibilis communio, non sit mihi judicium animæ meæ sed prosit mihi in remedium ad evacuandas omnes insidias et nequitias diabolicæ fraudis, ita ut nulla ejus dominetur iniquitas in corde, corpore, anima, et sensibus meis, sed tua clementia me perducat ad superna convivia angelorum, ubi tu es vera beatitudo, clara lux, sempiterna lætitia. Amen."

Additional Note.

Additional Note.

I.

SOME observations still remain which perhaps may fitly be put together in this place, and some extracts and other documents relating to the Liturgy, by way of an additional note; which I trust will not be found altogether without their use.

I. First then, upon the origin of the word *Missa.* Some, with Baronius, have traced it to the Hebrew *Missah*, which signifies an oblation : others to the Greek μύησις : and some few, of whom Albaspinæus is the chief authority, to the German *Mess* or *Mes.* With respect to this last derivation or guess a superficial modern writer, notwithstanding that it has been long exploded among the best learned in the subject, has not hesitated to state that "it can admit of no doubt."[1] Some other derivations, not necessary to be mentioned, have been proposed : and lastly that which, as it appears to me, cardinal Bona has completely established as the true one; that it is a liturgical Latin word, *a mittendo ;* and derived from the usual form by which, first the catechumens and others were dismissed, and secondly

---

[1] Hampson, *Medii ævi Kalendarium*, vol. ii. p. 263. This is a work useful in some points, but cannot be always relied on; the compiler having written in a bigoted spirit of ignorant hostility to Catholic truth. Much is it to be wished that some one really learned would give us a work which the above scarcely makes more than a pretence to be. By far the best at present is the *Chronology of history*, by Sir H. Nicolas.

the faithful at the conclusion of the service: "Ite, missa est."

For further information I shall refer the reader to the following authorities, all of whom treat fully upon the matter and in fact exhaust it: Baronius, *ann.* 34; Bellarmine, *de missa*, lib. v. cap. 1; Bona, *Opera*, tom. i. lib. i. cap. 1, and Sala's additions to his text; Casalius, *de Christian. rit.* cap. 9; Cassander, *Liturgica*, cap. 26 (*Opera*, p. 55); Durant, *de ritibus*, lib. ii. cap. 1; van Espen, tom. i. p. 410; Ducange, *Glossarium;* and Gavantus, *Thesaurus*, tom. i. p. 7. These are works which are more easily to be obtained than are the older ritualists, Micrologus, Alcuin, Isidore, Hugo Victorinus, &c., who agree with them. From a careful examination of these as well as of those who hold the contrary opinion we may reasonably conclude that the question has been settled, and that *Missa* is derived "a mittendo" and from the "Ite, missa est."

II. The word "Missa" especially in the most ancient writers, and in ecclesiastical documents such as monastic statutes and decrees of councils, does not always signify "the Liturgy" or "Office of the Holy Communion." It means sometimes the dismission from any divine office; sometimes the portion of the service at which catechumens were present; sometimes again that to which only the faithful had been admitted: also, as I have had occasion to remark before,[2] it sometimes means collects or lections, or even the canonical hours, and in later ages the feast-day, as our own Christ-mas and Michael-mas. I again refer the student to the authors before named, particularly Bona and Ducange. There is usually little difficulty in deter-

---

[2] Note 8, p. 120.

mining whether the term is to be taken in its strict and more usual or in its improper sense; and instances are not very abundant of its use, even in early writers, in other than its true meaning as applied to the liturgy.

III. As "Missa" is to be understood sometimes as other than the liturgy, so the liturgy had other names than missa. Such, among the Greeks, were mystagogia, synaxis, telete, anaphora, and prosphora: and among the Latins collecta, dominicum, agenda, communio, and oblatio.

IV. The chief kinds of masses were (1) *Missa solemnis;* or, that which was celebrated with the full attendance of the priest and his ministers, deacon, sub-deacon, and acolytes, with the proper solemnities of incensing, &c., and in short all the ceremonies which the full rubrics of the particular church appointed. Under this head were included the *missa pontificia, episcopalis,* and *abbatialis;* when a bishop or mitred abbot officiated *pontificaliter.*

(2) *Missa alta;* or, at it is now commonly called in England, high mass. This is the same as the missa solemnis; and appears to have been a term chiefly in use in this country. We find it as early, at least, as the year 1356 when John Grandison, bishop of Exeter, ordered a procession and special prayers for the king and prince of Wales: " et deinde altam missam, sicut in die sanctæ trinitatis solenniter cum sequenti celebrare." [3] And, again,

---

[3] *Concilia,* tom. 3. p. 37. A few years afterwards a mandate of his successor, bishop Brentingham, was directed against intruding priests, who would say low masses in parish churches on sundays and holidays, which parishioners attended instead of the parochial mass; the "magna missa" as it was also commonly called. One consequence of this was that the people lost the benefit of hearing the accustomed sermon.

nearly two hundred years later, in 1528, there is a canon of the diocese of Ely: "quod clerici parochiales omnes et singuli per totam diœcesim tempore altæ missæ sacerdotibus deserviant reverenter et obedienter in superpelliceis," &c.[4] Gavantus and Ducange cite only from a charter of 1377 in Rymer's *Fœdera*: "usque summum altare ad altam missam celebrandam accesseram."[5] But the term (and also *missa magna*) occurs not unfrequently in the York and Sarum missals.

(3) *Missa publica*: at which persons of either sex were permitted to attend: and was so called from that circumstance and not from the place where it was celebrated, "quia olim" (says Gavantus) "in cryptis et abditis locis celebrabatur." These masses were forbidden in some monasteries for obvious reasons. The *missa communis* seems to have been the same as the *publica*.

(4) *Missa privata* was celebrated by the priest with only one attendant, and is that which is now commonly called in England low mass; or *missa bassa*, or *plana;* that is, as distinguished from missa alta, or solemnis: but as opposed to the missa publica it would seem to mean that at which, whether the people were present or not, the priest alone communicated. The missa privata must not be confounded with the *missa solitaria;* which last, although for a time it was not uncommon in monasteries, was at length altogether forbidden; and was that in which a priest consecrated and performed the divine service not only privately but without any attendant minister or other person present.

The following examples will prove how early care was taken in England to prevent this abuse. At

---

[4] *Concilia*, tom. 3. p. 713.   [5] Tom. vii. p. 139.

a council of York, A.D. 1195, it was decreed, "Cum inter cætera ecclesiæ sacramenta hostia salutaris præemineat, tanto impensior circa eam debet existere devotio sacerdotum, ut cum humilitate conficiatur, cum timore sumatur, cum reverentia dispensetur: ... nec sine ministro literato celebretur."[6] Some centuries earlier there are two remarkable decisions upon this point in the Anglo-saxon ecclesiastical institutes; which would appear to prove that in those days one minister alone present was not sufficient: "At such times when ye attend the gemot of bishops, have ... II priests or III or as many laymen called, that they may reverently celebrate the holy mystery with you." Almost immediately after follows: "Mass-priests shall not on any account celebrate mass alone without other men [butan oðrum mannum] that he may know whom he addresses, and who responds to him. He shall address those standing about him, and they shall respond to him. He shall bear in mind the Lord's saying, which he said in his gospel. He said: ' there, where two or three men shall be gathered in my name, there will I be in the midst of them.'"[7]

(5) Of the same kind as the missa privata were the *missa familiaris* and *peculiaris*,[8] the *specialis* and *singularis*.

---

[6] Wilkins, *Concilia*, tom. i. p. 501. Compare also in the same volume, p. 707, the constitutions of Walter de Kirkham, bishop of Durham, "Ad augendum vero divini," &c.

[7] Thorpe, *Antient laws*, vol. ii. pp. 405, 407.

[8] There is a constitution of John Peckham, "Sacerdotes caveant universi ne missarum peculiarium seu familiarium se celebrationi obligent, quo minus valeant canonico officio commissam sibi officiare ecclesiam, ut tenentur." And see Lyndwood's gloss. lib. iij. tit. 23, De celeb. miss. Sacerdotes caveant. One extract may be made: "*Verb.* canonico officio, i.e. missa de die, quæ non debet omitti propter alias, ut prædictum est.

(6) The *Missa votiva* strictly meant a mass which the priest said at his own option; not agreeing with the office appointed for the day. This, of course, was subject to certain rules. But in a wider sense, those were called votive masses which by a statute of the Church were fixed to be said at certain times; and they were so called with respect to the Church herself, by whose devotion they had been so prescribed. Such was the " Missa pro defunctis" which was to be said upon the second day of November.

(7) The *Missa præsanctificatorum* was a species of imperfect service, in which no consecration was made, and the priest communicated of the oblation which had been consecrated upon a previous day. In the Greek Church during lent these masses only are allowed, except upon saturdays and sundays, and the feast of the annunciation; in the Roman catholic church it is limited to Good Friday.

The thirty-sixth of the canons of Ælfric, in 957, as translated from the Anglo-saxon by Thorpe, shows us the antiquity of the Good Friday service as observed in England a thousand years ago: " Housel may not be hallowed on Good Friday [langa Fɲiȝe-bæȝ, long Friday] because Christ suffered on that day for us: but there must nevertheless be done what appertains to that day: so that two lectures be read, with two expositions,[9] and with two collects, and Christ's passion; and, afterwards, the prayers. And let them pray to the holy rood, so that they all greet the rood of God with kiss. Let the priest then go to the altar of God, with the housel bread that he hallowed on Thursday,

---

Et nota, quod caute dicit, *canonico officio*, ac si per hoc innuat, quod missa sit de officiis canonicis, non tamen de horis canonicis."

[9] Rather "with two tracts"(?): "mið tpam tpactum:" the meaning is not clear.

and with unhallowed wine mixed with water, and conceal it with his corporal, and then immediately say, 'Oremus; præceptis salutaribus moniti' and 'Pater noster' to the end.' And then let him say to himself, 'Libera nos quæso Domine ab omnibus malis,' and aloud 'per omnia sæcula sæculorum.' Let him then put a part of the housel into the chalice, then let him go silently to the housel; and, for the rest, let look who will."[10] The prayers and collects referred to are those which have been especially said on Good Friday for various conditions of men from a very remote age. Lanfranc speaks of them in his constitutions: and that as now "pro cunctis ordinibus flectantur genua, nisi pro Judæis."[11]

(8) With this last mass the *Missa sicca* has been often confounded; but there is an essential distinction: because the missa sicca was not only without consecration but without communion; a mere recitation of part only of the service. Long before the sixteenth century it would seem to have been abolished. Durand's account of it is: " Potest sacerdos accepta stola epistolam et evangelium legere, et dicere orationem dominicam, et dare benedictionem; quinimo si ex devotione, non ex superstitione velit totum officium missæ sine sacrificio dicere, accipiat omnes vestes sacerdotales, et missam suo ordine celebret, usque ad finem offerendæ, dimittens secreta, quæ ad sacrificium pertinent. Præfationem vero dicere potest, licet in eadem videantur

---

[10] *Anglo-Saxon institutes*, vol. i. p. 359. It would seem that in the eleventh century others besides the priest might communicate. The office for Good-Friday ends thus in the Leofric missal: "Pater noster: *ut supra: et adorata cruce, communicent omnes.*"

[11] *Concilia*, tom. i. p. 338. So, in the Leofric MS., there is a distinct order before the prayer "pro perfidis Judæis" that the people should not kneel.

angeli invocari ad consecrationem corporis et sanguinis Christi. De canone vero nihil dicat, sed
orationem dominicam non prætermittat, et quæ ibi
sequuntur sub silentio dicenda non dicat: calicem
et hostiam non habeat: nec de his, quæ super calicem seu eucharistiam dicuntur, vel fiunt, aliquid
dicat, vel faciat. Potest etiam dicere ' Pax Domini
sit semper,' &c., et exinde missæ officium suo ordine
peragat."[12]

There is some doubt after all, although Durand
speaks thus decidedly, whether the missa sicca was
at any time permitted in the western Church.
Quarti and Merati think that it was so: but against
these are even greater ritualists, among whom are
cardinal Bona and Benedict XIV. But there is
evidence certainly that another, the same in fact,
namely the *missa nautica* or *navalis*, was at one
time allowed "tempore navigationis, quando scilicet
ob periculum effusionis non licebat celebrare." Such
an office perhaps might be more reasonably excused
at sea: and it may not be out of place to give the
rubric which refers to it, from an ordo missæ printed
at Rome in 1511:—

"*De missa sicca in mari et fluminibus celebrari
solita.*

" In loco fluctuanti, ut in mari et fluminibus, celebrare non licet alicui. Consuevit tamen in mari,
pro populorum devotione, absque consecratione missa
(quam siccam vocant) dici per sacerdotem hoc ordine. In loco navis ecclesiola nuncupato, parata
est mensa; supra quam ponitur mappa munda, etiam
non benedicta: et in medio partis posterioris ejusdem mensæ crux; hac hinc et inde in cornibus
posterioribus ipsius mensæ duo candelabra cum

---

[12] Lib. iv. cap. i. 23.

duabus candelis ardentibus collocantur : ubi sacerdos missam hujusmodi dicturus, ante dictam mensam stans, accipit superpellicium ; et desuper stolam ab humeris dependentem, quam traversat ante pectus per modum crucis, et cingulo eam firmat. Vel secundum alios, omnibus paramentis sacerdotalibus induitur, ordine superius dato ; omissa sola planeta sive casula, qua non utitur. Sicque paratus stans ante mensam prædictam, facit confessionem cum interessentibus dicens : *In nomine Patris et Filii et Spiritus sancti. Introibo,* &c., prout habetur supra in principio missæ ; usque ad orationem, *Oramus te, Domine, ut per merita,* &c., exclusive ascendit ad mensam prædictam, et omisso illius osculo stans in cornu epistolæ legit illius introitum, *Kyrieleison. Gloria in excelsis Deo ;* si est dicendum. *Dominus vobiscum,* non vertendo se ad populum. *Oremus :* et orationem ordinariam. Deinde si placet, et dici conveniat, facit unam vel duas commemorationes. Legit epistolam ; graduale ; alleluia, si est dicendum ; vel tractum ; portat librum ad cornu evangelii ; dicit in medio mensæ, *Munda,* &c. *Dominus sit in corde,* &c. : deinde ante librum, *Dominus vobiscum. Sequentia,* &c., signando librum et se in fronte, ore, et pectore. Finito evangelio osculatur textum ; dicit *Credo,* si dies et officium requirit : *Dominus vobiscum,* non vertendo se ad populum ; *Oremus ;* Offertorium ; Præsentationem ; *Sanctus,* &c. *Oremus ; Præceptis salutaribus moniti,* &c. *Pater noster, Agnus Dei ;* et dat osculum pacis, si alias officio illius diei quod legit conveniat. Revertitur cum libro ad cornu epistolæ ; dicit communionem in eodem loco. *Dominus vobiscum :* non vertendo se ad populum. Postcommunionem et commemorationes ; si prius fecit ibidem. *Dominus vobiscum,* ut prius : et *Ite missa est :* vel *Benedicamus :* prout convenit, aut *Requiescant in pace:* si legit pro defunctis. Quo dicto, ibidem se vertit ad populum et illi more solito benedicit; si non legit pro defunctis. Pro quibus si legit, benedictionem hujusmodi prætermittit. Tum dicit *Dominus vobiscum,* et signans seipsum in fronte, ore, et pectore, continuat: *Initium sancti evangelii secundum Joannem. In principio,* &c., ut supra: quo finito, vestes sacras quas recepit ibidem deponit. Omnia præmissa in hujusmodi missa dicuntur voce intelligibili: ita quod ab omnibus illi interessentibus audiantur."[13]

Besides the above there are other kinds of masses, the names of which may be found and a full explanation of them in Gavantus, Bona, and other writers. I have very briefly noticed the chief differences, and those which relate to the Church of England before the sixteenth century.

V. I shall not make any attempt at a short account of the various vestments which the priest wore in celebrating the divine mysteries. A good arrangement which without repetition would give us the sum of the information which is dispersed in very numerous volumes is still [1846] to be desired;[14] but for this I have not space. I shall therefore now state the names only, in the order in which they were to be put on. 1. The amice. 2. The alb. 3. The girdle. 4. The maniple. 5. The stole. 6. The chasuble. The result of much enquiry about these as well as other ecclesiastical vestments is to be found in (without mentioning rarer works) Gavantus, cardinal Bona, Durand, Saussajus, Durant, and Ducange.

---

[13] Fol. xxiv.

[14] Some very useful and very learned books, it should now be added, have been published during the last forty years, both in England and abroad, upon ecclesiastical vestments and the furniture of the altar.

There is not enough in the old rubrics to enable us to decide where the priest in parish churches put on his vestments. The orders in the consuetudinaries usually have reference only to the practice in cathedral or abbatial churches. We may not improperly, however, conclude that priests vested in the sacristy, where there was a sacristy or vestry attached to the church. But it might be and perhaps often that parish churches, and especially in country places, had no sacristy. In such cases the priest by special leave might take his vestments from the altar and vest before it. If he had no such licence he would probably take them from the chest in which his vestments were kept and on which we may suppose they were laid ready. Such chests are frequently named in old inventories and other mediæval documents. Canon Simmons interprets the first and last rubrics of the Hereford use[15] to mean that the priest certainly vested at the altar. They do not seem to me to decide the question either way; but, rather, to my mind, against the practice.[16] To add one word more; it appears clear that in the fourteenth and fifteenth centuries a common custom was that the priest (whether or not he vested before the altar) should vest in the sanctuary. In the treatise *Of the manner and mode of the mass* we read thus :—

> "Whon that thou comest the chirche with-inne
> And thou sest the prest bigynne,
>   Take his vestimens on,
> Loke thou do as I sey the,
> Knele a-doun vppon thi kne,
>   Noyse that thou make non."[17]

---

[15] See above, pp. 3, 203.

[16] I would, however, especially refer the reader to canon Simmons' valuable note; *Layfolks mass book*, p. 163.

[17] From the Vernon manuscript in the Bodleian, fol. 302; printed by canon Simmons, p. 128.

The following rubric is taken from the manuscript pontifical of the diocese of Exeter, of which an account is given elsewhere in the dissertation on service books :[18]—

"*fol.* 1. Modus induendi episcopum ad solemniter celebrandum. Primo veniat pontifex ante altare, vel alibi ubi dispositum fuerit, et prostratus breviter oret, et surgens ponat se ad cathedram et statim incipiantur psalmi consueti : ' Quam dilecta :' cum cæteris, ut supra. Interim ministri vel domicelli caligas cum sandalis secrete extenso superiori indumento ei subministret. Deinde manutergium cum aqua ad lavandum deportent. Postea exuat cappam et induat amictum, albam, et stolam, et reliquias circa collum, ac deinceps tunicam, dehinc dalmaticam et manipulum. Et tunc sedendo chirothecas manibus imponat, et annulum pontificalem magnum, una cum uno parvo strictiori annulo ad tenendum fortius super imponat. Et sudarium retortum in manu recipiat ad faciem extergendam. Et sic sedendo post psalmos infra scriptos orationes sequentes consuetas perdicat. Et cum hora fuerit, surgat et casulam induat, et mitram capiti imponat, et baculum pastoralem in manu sua sinistra assumat, curvatura baculi ad populum conversa, cujus contrarium faciant ministri tenendo baculum vel portando. Et sic choro cantando ' Gloria Patri' procedat de sacrario ad altare populum benedicendo."

The psalms and the prayers above mentioned follow on the reverse of the same folio. I have printed them below from the Sarum pontifical, together with the " Modus induendi episcopum" at full length from the same manuscript. The reader will see that it agrees exactly with the order in the pontifical of bishop Lacy.

---

[18] *Monumenta ritualia,* vol. i.

There is one point in the above, valuable as it all is, especially worthy of notice; viz. that the maniple is directed to be put on before the chasuble: whereas the Roman pontifical, and with two exceptions all the pontificals which Georgius (the most learned writer on that subject) had examined, direct bishops, when they officiate, to be vested with the maniple last of all. And, indeed, this Exeter pontifical expressly remarks the distinction. " Et sciendum quod" (it says in the rubric before the prayers) " secundum usum curiæ Romanæ, ultimo omnium datur et ponitur in veniendo ad altare manipulus in brachio sinistro, et post missam primo amoveatur juxta illud: Venientes autem venient cum exultatione, portantes manipulos suos." The remark of Georgius is, " præterea manipulum celebraturi pontifices sumebant post cætera sacra indumenta, . . . sed in pontificali tantum Prudentii Trecensis imponitur post stolam, et in sacramentario Moysacensis monasterii annorum 800 post zonam. Alias liturgiæ antiquæ omnes statuunt, manipulum sumendum post reliqua sacerdotalia indumenta,"[19] &c. Cardinal Bona says that anciently all priests, and not bishops only, received the maniple last of the vestments;[20] and this was rendered necessary by the peculiar shape of the chasuble.[21]

VI. In the first ages of the Christian Church

---

[19] *De lit. Rom. pontificis,* tom. i. p. 270.

[20] Compare also Hugo, *de sacram.* lib. i. cap. 51: " De favone. Ad extremum sacerdos favonem in sinistro brachio ponit, quem et manipulum et sudarium veteres appellaverunt," &c. This author does not especially mention the maniple among the episcopal vestments.

See also Amalarius, lib. ii. cap. 5, " De introitu episcopi ad missam." But Rabanus Maurus speaks of it as a priestly vestment, in its modern order; *De instit. clericorum,* cap. 18.

[21] " Cum planeta totum corpus ambiret," &c.; tom. ii. p. 225.

when persecutions raged, and in some after-times of
like dangers and necessity, the holy eucharist was
celebrated not only in secret places but at any hour
either of the day or night, when the malice of the
enemy might the more probably be escaped. Of
these night-assemblies for the purpose of communion the missa in nocte nativitatis Domini is the
last remnant.

The rubric in the note below[22] states the present
order of the Roman catholic church:[23] and I shall
cite some few authorities upon the ancient custom
of the church of England before the sixteenth
century.

The first from a constitution of archbishop Raynold published in the council of Oxford, A.D. 1322:
" Nullus insuper sacerdos parochialis præsumat missam celebrare, antequam matutinale persolverit officium, et primam et tertiam de die."[24] Lyndwood
in his gloss upon this says that the *matutinale
officium* includes " totum illud, quod continetur in
nocturnis et in laudibus;" and that although this
canon is especially directed towards parish priests,
yet that every priest is bound to say at least
matins before he presumes to celebrate. There are

---

[22] " Missa privata saltem post
matutinum et laudes quacunque
hora ab aurora usque ad meridiem dici potest.

" Missa autem conventualis et
solemnis sequenti ordine dici
debet. In festis duplicibus, et
semiduplicibus, in dominicis, et
infra octavas, dicta in choro
hora tertia. In festis simplici-
bus, et in feriis per annum, dicta
sexta. In adventu, quadragesima, quatuor temporibus,
etiam infra octavam pentecostes,

et vigiliis quæ jejunantur, quamvis sint dies solemnes, missa de
tempore debet cantari post nonam.

" Missa autem defunctorum
dici debet post primam diei."
Rubr. generales, xv. Some few
exceptions follow to these general rules.

[23] Compare Amalarius, lib. iii.
cap. 42, " De consueto tempore
missae."

[24] Wilkins, *Concilia*, tom. ii.
p. 513.

other canons which respect parochial masses, and
these equally insist upon the third hour also being
previously said: because, says Lyndwood, about
the third hour our blessed Lord was crucified, and
the Holy Ghost descended upon the apostles. In
considering these and similar constitutions, the
reader must remember that the *missa parochialis*
was not necessarily a *missa solemnis*: but that if
it was "sine cantu" it would be of the nature
of a low mass, and therefore not limited by the
same strict rules as were the services of greater
solemnity.[25]

In the synod of Norwich, A.D. 1257, it was ordered
"quod nullus sacerdos celebret, quousque prima canonice sit completa."[26] And again, by the constitutions of Cantilupe bishop of Worcester, A.D. 1240,
to the same effect; but on account of the reason
which is given I shall quote the canon at length:
"Et quia, sicut accepimus, quidam capellani, ad
annualia vel ad officium beatæ virginis assumpti,
interdum matutinis præpositis, aut seorsum, a choro
vel ab ecclesia, per se dictis, missas celebrant im-
mature, per campos vel per villas postmodum dis-
currentes: præcipimus, ut omnes capellani, qui in
una parochia commorantur, simul intersint et conveniant matutinis et vesperis, et aliis horis ca-

---

[25] We must not forget however
that the third hour admitted of
some considerable variation from
that which naturally and strictly
was the corresponding hour of
the day. Hence, we find it laid
down by van Espen: "Insuper
ut populus ad missam parochialem frequentandam incitetur, de-
cretum est, ut parochi statuta
eaque populo commodiori hora

missam parochialem diebus præsertim dominicis et festis cele-
brent." *Jus eccles.* pars ii. sect.
i. tit. v. And he goes on to cite
councils which forbid the fixed
hour to be put off or hastened
for the sake of rich neighbours;
and others, directing that bells
should be rung to call the people
together.

[26] *Concilia*, tom. i. p. 735.

nonicis, in ecclesiis celebrandis, et missis: et maxime de die, nisi causa rationabili fuerint impediti: nec aliquis celebret, quousque prima fuerit canonice completa."[27]

There seems no necessity upon this point to add many examples; and we need therefore only refer to two more from monastic statutes. The one, of the hospital of Elsing Spital, London: this relates also to the time before which mass should end; " circa horam tertiam cujuslibet diei pulsatis primitus campanis, ... missam de die, prout diei solemnitas requirit, decantent; ita quod hujusmodi missa singulis diebus circiter horam nonam finiatur."[28] The other, from the rule of the hospital of St. John baptist at Nottingham: " insuper statuimus, ut omnes fratres simul surgant ad matutinas, ... cantatisque consequenter prima et tertia, celebretur missa."[29]

It has been held from very early times that the holy eucharist should not be celebrated unless the office of one of the hours had been previously recited; whether of tierce, sext, or the ninth hour. So that Lyndwood says: "potest colligi, quod in festo natalis Domini celebraturus primam missam, quæ solet cantari ante laudes, debet prius perficere matutinas et primam."[30] With whom agrees a more modern ritualist: " missa solemnis semper dicitur post aliquam horam, etiam in nocte nativitatis Domini: ut horæ canonicæ sint quasi quædam ad missam præparatio."[31]

---

[27] *Concilia*, tom. i. p. 668.

[28] Dugdale, *Monast. Anglic.* vol. vi. p. 706.

[29] *Monast. Anglic.* vol. vi. p. 679. See also *Rites of the Church of Durham:* "At ix of the clocke, ther rong a bell to masse, called the chapter masse." p. 82.

[30] Lib. iii. tit. 23, Linteamina corporalia, *verb.* Primam.

[31] Gavantus, *Thes. sacr. rit.* tom. i. p. 112.

I must add the following from *Piers Plowman:*—

" The kyng and hise knyghtes,
To the kirk wente,

VII. There can be no doubt that in the first beginnings of the Christian Church the holy eucharist was offered not only in such places but at such times and opportunities as would be the most likely, in periods of violent persecution, to escape observation ; and therefore, chiefly taking care as St. Austin tells us not to omit celebration if possible upon the Lord's day, it was subject occasionally to longer intervals than were permitted afterwards. Long before, however, the date of the council of Nice the practice of priests consecrating daily became common in most churches.[32] St. Cyprian's testimony is sufficient upon this point, who says, " episcopatus nostri honor grandis et gloria est pacem dedisse martyribus, ut sacerdotes, qui sacrificia Dei quotidie celebramus, hostias Deo et victimas præparemus."[33]

This custom was not likely for many reasons to become, as time went on, less observed : and it is recorded of Alcuin that, at the request of archbishop Boniface, he drew up services for each day

---

To here matyns of the day,
And the masse after."
Passus quintus.
So the "parson" says in the dialogue between him and the ploughman: a blasphemous publication by one of the extreme reformers in the early years of Edward the sixth. The parson is explaining the service for Corpus Christi day :—
"But nowe if thou wilt marke me welle,
From begynning to endynge I wyl the tell,
Of the godly seruice that shall be tomorrowe.

. . . .
We shal firste haue matins, is it not a godly hereynge ?"
Jon Bon and Mast Person.

[32] We may well believe that in the early days of the apostles no opportunity was lost of receiving the consecrated elements: when "the multitude of them that believed were of one heart and of one soul," they continued " daily breaking bread from house to house." But the persecutions had not begun.
[33] *Epist.* 54, Ad Cornelium.

Q

in the week; which might be used when otherwise
the days would have been vacant, or have had no
proper office. Or again, as Micrologus says: "et
hoc ideo, ut presbyteri illius temporis nuper ad
fidem conversi, nondum ecclesiasticis officiis instructi,
nondum etiam librorum copia præditi, vel aliquid
haberent, cum quo officium suum qualibet die possent explere."[34] And in the very ancient manuscript
which Illyricus edited the priest after the communion is directed to say this prayer: "Obsecro etiam
te piissime omnium auxiliator, ne ad damnationem
æternam mihi proveniat, quod quotidie cum con-
scientia polluta . . . corpus Christi Filii tui et sanguinem indignus audeo accipere." But before the
tenth century more than one canon of councils are
to be found, not exactly directing so much as
strongly exhorting all priests to celebrate daily.[35]
I shall not however add other testimonies upon this
point except one of Bede, cited by Gabriel Biel;[36]
which, whatever difference of opinion there might be
as to the weight of all his arguments, certainly declares the reason on which in his day the necessity
of this practice was supposed to rest: "Sacerdos
non legitime impeditus celebrare omittens, quantum
in ipso est, privat sanctissimam Trinitatem laude et
gloria, angelos lætitia, peccatores venia, justos sub-
sidio et gratia, in purgatorio existentes refrigerio,
ecclesiam speciali Christi beneficio, et seipsum me-
dicina et remedio."

There is no proof that in the old Church of England the practice of daily consecrating the holy
eucharist or of the daily communion of the clergy
was enforced by any council or rested upon other

---

[34] Cap. lx.

[35] Mabillon, *Annal. Benedict.*,

præf. iv. 36; Gavantus, tom. i. p. 21.

[36] *Lect.* 87, In canonem.

obligation than individual piety or the statutes of some deceased benefactor. In the council of Cloveshoo, A.D. 747, it was decreed, canon 14, " Ut dominicus dies legitima veneratione a cunctis celebretur, sitque divino tantum cultui dedicatus, omnes abbates ac presbyteri isto sacratissimo die in suis monasteriis atque ecclesiis maneant, missarumque solennia agant." And the end of the same canon extends the like obligation, in nearly as strong terms, to the people : " Hoc quoque decernitur, quod eo die sive per alias festivitates majores, populus per sacerdotes Dei ad ecclesiam sæpius invitatus, ad audiendum verbum Dei conveniat : missarumque sacramentis ac doctrinæ sermonibus frequentius adsit."[37]

More than five hundred years after we find no other order than the following : I quote from Lyndwood, on account of his gloss upon it : " Statuimus insuper, ut quilibet sacerdos, quem canonica necessitas non excusat, conficiat omni hebdomada, saltem semel."[38]

Upon the *canonica necessitas* Lyndwood observes that an impediment would exist if the priest were suspended, or excommunicate, or in mortal sin ; or, if he could not obtain access to a consecrated place : " nam in loco non sacrato, non est celebrandum sine licentia episcopi." Or, if he has not the sacred vestments : or even " quia non habet stolam et manipulum." Or, if he has not an assistant : " et breviter, in omni casu ubi non potest habere requisita ad missæ celebrationem, et confectionem eucharistiæ, præsertim ea quæ sunt de materia hujus sacramenti." Upon the words *saltem semel* his gloss

---

[37] Wilkins, *Concilia*, tom. i. p. 96.
[38] Lib. iii. tit. 23, Altissimus.

is, "et hoc fiat die dominica, si fieri poterit, juxta illud *Aug.* 'Quotidie eucharisticam communionem accipere nec laudo, nec vitupero : omnibus tamen dominicis diebus ad communicandum hortor.' Et ista constitutio facta est ad invitandum presbyteros frequentius celebrare, qui forsan vix quater in anno consueverunt celebrare."[39]

VIII. The great stress which was laid for some centuries upon the propriety of every priest celebrating the holy Service once every day led for many reasons, which will naturally occur to the reader, to a great abuse. Priests consecrated more than once, and indeed many times, upon the same day. This in some instances was the result only of a mistaken piety and devotion unmixed with any baser motive. Walafrid Strabo records that pope Leo the third sometimes celebrated nine times in one day : " Fidelium relatione virorum in nostram usque pervenit notitiam, Leonem papam (sicut ipse fatebatur) una die vij. vel ix. missarum solennia sæpius celebrasse."[40]

But measures were very early taken in England to check (at least) the excess into which this practice,

---

[39] He goes on to speak of another case : "Et hic nota, quod licet quidam dicant sacerdotem non peccare, qui dimittit celebrationem missæ, nisi habeat populum sibi commissum, vel ex obedientia teneatur celebrare : tamen quia, ut *Grego.* dicit, cum crescunt dona, rationes crescunt donorum. Ideo cum sacerdoti sit data potestas nobilissima, reus est negligentiæ nisi utatur ea ad honorem Dei et salutem animæ suæ, et aliorum vivorum et mortuorum : secundum illud, 1 *Petri* 4, *Unusquisque, sicut accepit gratiam, alterutrum illam administret*, &c. Sacerdos enim tenetur Deo sacrificium reddere, licet nulli homini teneatur. Sacerdotibus enim præceptum est, *Hoc facite in meam commemorationem.*"

[40] *De rebus eccles.* cap. 21. But it has been said that this was owing to the multitude whom he was desirous to communicate, and for all of whom he wished himself to celebrate. See Fleury, *hist. eccl.* tom. x. p. 158.

so very objectionable, was likely to extend. The fifty-fifth of the excerpts of archbishop Egbert in the eighth century declares: "et sufficit sacerdoti unam missam in una die celebrare, quia Christus semel passus est, et totum mundum redemit."[41] The thirty-seventh of the canons enacted under king Edgar enjoins "that no priest, on one day, celebrate mass oftener than thrice, at the very utmost."[42] The eighteenth of the laws of the Northumbrian priests is to the same purpose: "If a priest in one day celebrate mass oftener than thrice, let him pay xij ores."[43] In almost the same words as in Egbert's excerptions Ælfric speaks in his pastoral epistle: "it is much that mass may be celebrated once in one day, though it be not celebrated oftener."[44] These bring us nearly to the period of the Norman conquest, up to which time we find no more than repeated attempts to check (as I have said) the evil which existed: but soon after that event there were very frequent orders, and more determinate, made in the provincial and diocesan synods. Take the second canon of the council of London, A.D. 1200: "Non liceat presbytero bis in die celebrare, nisi necessitate urgente; et tunc idem cum in die bis celebrat, post primam celebrationem et sanguinis sumptionem nil infundatur calici."[45] These cases of necessity seem explained more fully, a few years later, in a provincial constitution of archbishop Langton: "Bis in die celebrare nullus præsumat, nisi in diebus nativitatis et resurrectionis dominicæ: et quando corpus in propria ecclesia fuerit tumulandum: et tunc in prima missa ablutio

[41] Wilkins, *Concilia*, tom. i. p. 104.

[42] Thorpe, *Ancient laws*, &c., vol. ii. p. 253.

[43] *Ibid.* vol. ii. p. 293.

[44] *Ibid.* vol. ii. p. 377.

[45] Wilkins, *Concilia*, tom. i. p. 505.

digitorum vel calicis a celebrante non sumatur."[44]
The council of Durham, A.D. 1220, makes a like
order, "ne quis celebret bis in die:" with the same
exceptions, or if "aliqua evidens urgeat necessitas."
So also the council of Oxford about the same time;
and some synodal constitutions (of an uncertain
diocese) A.D. 1237.[47] In the year 1230 one of the
articles of enquiry for the archdeacons of the diocese
of Lincoln asks: "An aliquis sacerdos bis celebret
in die, nisi in casibus concessis, et in propria persona in propria ecclesia?"[48] And to quote no
others, we find the same order in some of the last
injunctions published in England: "Item, that no
prest say two masses in one day, except Chrystmas
day, without express licens."[49] Gavantus or rather
Merati in his additions states that the first order
to the effect of the above canons was made by pope
Alexander the second, A.D. 1070. The words used
by archbishop Egbert and by Ælfric, already cited,
are those which are in the decree of Gratian.[50]

The injunctions added to the canons which have
just been mentioned, that the ablution should not
be taken in the first mass if, for any lawful cause,
the priest was about to celebrate again, were in
consequence of the strict rule laid down that none
should consecrate or communicate except fasting:[51]

---

[44] Wilkins, *Con.* tom. i. p. 531.

[47] *Ibid.* tom. i. pp. 579, 586, 574, 657.

[48] *Ibid.* tom. i. p. 628.

[49] *Ibid.* tom. iv. p. 145.

[50] "Sufficit sacerdoti unam missam in die una celebrare, quia Christus semel passus est, et totum mundum redemit. Non modica res est unam missam facere; et valde felix est, qui

unam missam dignam celebrare potuit." *De consecrat.* distinct. i. can. 53.

[51] Walafrid Strabo, cap. xix, allows that anciently there was no rule to this effect: "sed a sequentibus honesta et rationa- bili deliberatione statutum esse cognoscitur; ut omni tempore a jejunis, sacrosancta celebren- tur mysteria." *De rebus eccle-*

which fast would not be broken by the communion
of the consecrated chalice, although of course by
the subsequent ablution. Hence on the day of the
nativity when priests might lawfully consecrate three
times, the ablution was ordered to be taken only at
the third and last mass. And to such an exactness
was this to be observed, that if by mistake or accident the priest should have taken the ablution at
the first of these, he was not then allowed to perform the other two.[52] Lyndwood says: " Ratio est,
quia si faceret, non esset jejunus, et celebratio missæ
debet fieri jejuno stomacho." Again, no priest might
under any necessity consecrate[53] upon good Friday:
his fast moreover would be broken by the unconsecrated wine which he must take with the reserved
host. In this case the exception of two parishes or
large populations (which I shall speak of presently)
would not hold, because there was no obligation
upon the people to attend the service on good
Friday.[54]

The constitution above, of archbishop Langton,
allows not only an exception upon the day of the
nativity but of the resurrection. Lyndwood says,

---

siasticis. Pope Benedict however denies this: " Nemo nes-
cius est sanctos apostolos tunc
jejunos non fuisse, cum eucharistiam acceperunt, tamen ob
tanti sacramenti reverentiam ab
apostolicis usque temporibus statutum fuit semperque in ecclesia
observatum, ne quisquam nisi
jejunus eucharistiam sumeret."
Opera, tom. ix. p. 328. But the
pope does not (the canon excepted) support his dictum with
any authorities. See Bingham,
book xv. cap. vij; and, especially,

Fell's note upon St. Cyprian,
epist. lxiij. p. 156.

[52] Thom. iii. par. quæst. 80.
art. 8.

[53] By an oversight this was
misprinted in the second edition
" consecrate twice." Evident as
it was from the context that it was
a mere misprint, an over-eager
controversialist thought it worth
his while to draw particular attention to the statement as if it
arose from ignorance.

[54] Benedict XIV, *Opera,* tom.
ix. p. 286.

"*Resurrectionis dominicæ*: i.e. in die paschæ: de isto die, quod in eo possit bis celebrari, non invenio textum alicujus juris vel canonis. Sed istud ideo fortassis hic ordinatur, quia contingit sæpius, quod in una magna parochia non est nisi unus presbyter, qui commode illo die non posset in missa solenniori de die omnes parochianos suos communicare, et oportet quod servientes illo die ministrent et præparent ea quæ ad ipsorum servitia spectant erga adventum dominorum suorum et magistrorum: unde tales communicari possunt et debent in prima missa."[55] There are nevertheless some examples, which may be seen in Bona,[56] of two celebrations with their full and different services upon easter day: and it is possible that in the twelfth century some remains of the old custom were still left in England, and not intended to be forbidden in the archbishop's constitution.

But the gloss of Lyndwood at any rate teaches us what was the practice of his own time : and that upon easter day equally with all other days, excepting always of the nativity, one mass only was to be celebrated by the same priest. For the exception which he allows, and supposes in the archbishop's constitution to be intended, does not seem to meet the case; because not only upon Easter day, but on other great festivals, the bishop could always give licence to a parish priest who had large populations under his charge to celebrate for their convenience, and to meet the necessities of their case, more than once. The same was permitted if he had two parishes under him.[57]

---

[55] *Provinc.* lib. iij. tit. 23, Ad excitandos.

[56] *Rerum lit.* lib. i. cap. xviij. 6.

[57] Sotus, in 4 *Sent.* dist. 13. *quæst.* 2. art. 2 ; Gonzalez, in cap. *Consuluisti de celeb. missar.*

The cases of necessity which are spoken of in the canons, as exceptions, are agreed generally to have been, lest a sick man should die without the viaticum and there was no host consecrated : if a bishop or prince should arrive at a place after the service was over : if a person was to be buried ; but this, in places only where it was always the custom not to bury except with the celebration of the holy eucharist. Lyndwood, in the same place before cited, says that in all excepted cases they availed only if no other priest happened to be at hand ; and that, upon any account whatsover, it was not permitted to celebrate more than twice : "quod in nullo casuum prædictorum licet ultra duas missas celebrare, excepto die nativitatis Domini."

The day of the nativity having been so often mentioned, as the only exception, I cannot think it will be out of place to add Lyndwood's reasons why three services were not only permitted but ordered for that day : he does not offer them as his own, but from earlier canonists :—

"Significat prima missa tempus ante legem et ideo celebratur in tenebris. Secunda significat tempus sub lege, quo tempore incipiebat sciri Christus, sed non clare, et ideo celebratur inter diem et noctem. Tertia significat tempus gratiæ, et cantatur in plena luce, ad designandum Christum venisse, *qui est lux vera, et illuminat omnem hominem venientem in hunc mundum.* Vel dic, secundum *Jo. An.* quod prima missa significat generationem Christi æternam quæ occulta est, et ideo celebratur in nocte. Secunda significat nativitatem Christi, partim naturalem quia ex muliere, et partim occultam

---

num. 2 ; Belletus, *Disquisit. cle-* *de eucharist.* disput. 20. 1. num.
ric. 2. 29. 3 ; Cardinal de Lugo, 46.

quia ex virgine: ideo celebratur in mane. Tertia significat generationem spiritualem, quæ fit per gratiam, et illa celebratur in tertia, quia clarescit secundum veritatem." [68]

IX. I shall conclude this with some observations upon the Cautelæ missæ, or, as they were commonly called, " The cautells of the mass."

Scarcely was the conversion of the Anglo-saxons begun and Christian missionaries for a second time sent into England, before the same care was insisted upon to be observed by all the priests of the English Church in the celebration of the divine mysteries, which was enforced as much as possible in other parts of the world. Some persons who have not catholic faith may probably think that these precautions were carried into excess. But it would be idle uncharitableness to deny that they sprang solely from a pious and right regard towards the great sacrament of the gospel: and in such a matter, concerning the highest mysteries, concerning that bread and wine, that Body and Blood, every one will allow that it is difficult to say where reverence

---

[68] Lib. iii. tit. 23, Ad excitandos. Compare also Durand, lib. vj. cap. 13, and Gavantus, tom. 1. p. 374.

I may add that two communions were provided for by the first common Prayer book of king Edward the sixth, and a proper introit, collect, epistle, and gospel appointed for each. Why the third office was not added I am ignorant. But at the next review, in 1552, only one communion office was allowed on Christmas-day.

There is a curious entry in some churchwardens' accounts for the parish of St. Helen, at Abingdon, which is not easy to explain, except by supposing that in some places the old custom was still (though illegally) kept up so late even as the third year of queen Elizabeth: "Payde for four pounde of candilles upon Christmas-day in the morning for the masse, os. 12d." *Archæologia*, vol. i. p. 15. We know from the same accounts that the new "communion boke" of 1559 had been bought two years before.

ceases to be within the bounds of a due moderation; but not so difficult to say where irreverence begins.[59]

I shall take first some extracts from the penitential of archbishop Theodore. His thirty-ninth chapter is " de negligentia eucharistiæ," and to each offence or accident a certain penalty is attached, proportioned to the greatness at which it was then esteemed : " Si quis eucharistiam negligentiæ causa perdiderit. . . . . Si sacrificium in terra ceciderit, causa negligentiæ. . . . . Qui non bene custodierit sacrificium. . . . . Qui autem perdiderit, et non inventum fuerit. . . . . Qui neglexerit sacrificium, ut vermes in eo sint, aut colorem non habeat saporemque. . . . . Si ceciderit sacrificium de manibus offerentis terra tenus, et non inveniatur, omne quodcunque inventum fuerit in loco quo ceciderit comburatur igni, et cinis ejus sub altare abscondatur. Si vero inventum fuerit sacrificium, locus scopa mundetur, et stramen igni comburatur, cinisque, ut supra dictum est, abscondatur. . . . . Si de calice per negligentiam aliquid stillaverit in terra, lingua lam-

[59] About the middle of the sixteenth century a Genevan puritan, named Peter Viret, wrote in French a book of considerable length, in which he translated the ordinary and canon of the mass, with "certaine annotations." An English translation dedicated to Lord Burleigh was published in 1584. At the beginning the writer examines and discusses the " cawtelles;" and probably there is no publication of the sixteenth century which exceeds this in violence and blasphemy. There is little argument, or rather none, in the book from beginning to end; nothing but abuse and foul language. It is a remarkable example of the extent to which the liberty of what was in those days called religious controversy was allowed to go. Coarse and disgraceful as were some of the writings of the English reformers in king Edward's time—for example, those of bishop Bale—they fall far short of this. I know nothing which can be compared with it except some of the tracts of the later puritans in Elizabeth's reign, against the bishops of the reformed English church. Happily, the book of M. Peter Viret is extremely rare.

batur, terraque radatur. . . . . Si super altare stillaverit calix, sorbeat minister stillam," &c. . . . .[60]
Other orders to the same effect may be found in
the same archbishop's capitula.[61]

In the next century archbishop Egbert of York,
in his confessional, appoints a penance, " si sacerdos calicem effundat postquam missam cantaverit."[62]
In his penitential we find several canons to the same
effect: " Si quis ex incuria sua eucharistiam perdiderit. . . . . Si sacrificium ex incuria in terram ceciderit. . . . . Si quis neglexerit consecratam eucharistiam, ita ut nimis diu servata sordes in ea sit, vel
colorem suum non habeat. . . . . Omne sacrificium
quod sordidum est, vel vetustate corruptum, comburatur. . . . . Qui effuderit calicem suum inter missam suam," &c.[63]

We will pass on to the canons of Ælfric. " The
priest shall purely and carefully do God's ministries
(ᴦoᴅeᵹ þenunᵹa) with clean hands and with clean
heart; and let him see that his oblations be not old
baken, nor ill seen to. . . . . Great honours they
merit who minister to God with zeal and devotion :
and also it is written, that he is accursed who doth
God's ministry with carelessness. We may by this
know, that a man who has not his sight should not
dare to celebrate mass, when he sees not what he
offers to God, whether it be clean or foul."[64] Archbishop Lanfranc in his statutes has one chapter, " de
negligentia circa corpus Domini."[65] But, lastly, to
come down nearer to the date of the cautels themselves, a canon of the constitutions of W. de Kirk-

---

[60] Thorpe, *Ancient laws and institutes*, vol. ii. p. 46.
[61] *Ibid.* p. 75.
[62] *Ibid.* p. 141.
[63] Thorpe, vol. ii. p. 218;

Wilkins, *Concilia*, tom. i. p. 139.
[64] Thorpe, vol. ii. p. 361.
[65] *Opera Lanfranci*, p. 282. cap. x.

ham bishop of Durham in the thirteenth century orders : " ut si per negligentiam aliquid de sanguine Christi stillaverit super terram lambatur lingua; tabula radatur, super quam stillaverit : . . . . si autem super altare: . . . . si super linteum," &c. :[66] and to each of these a penalty is attached, for the carelessness owing to which it must have occurred.

We do not know by whom these "cautelæ missæ" were drawn up and arranged from the decrees of councils and the opinions of doctors and canonists, nor by whose authority they were introduced into the missal. Gavantus says that the earliest edition of the Roman use in which he had seen cautions of this kind was in that printed at Venice, 1557. They have since been always added to the Roman missal, but arranged differently from the cautelæ and headed " De defectibus circa missam occurrentibus." In the Hereford missal they are styled " De casibus et periculis quæ possunt evenire circa altare." These differ somewhat from the Sarum; but equally with those in the present Roman missal have the same object in view, and make very similar arrangements and rules. In the York missal, 4to. 1517 (which has been followed in the present volume), the " cautelæ ad missam celebrandam " are placed at the end of the book, and are exactly the same as those which I am now about to give from the Salisbury use. In this last (the Salisbury missal) they are to be found in almost all editions after 1500: sometimes in the beginning after the calendar, sometimes at the end of the book; and more commonly either before the ordinary or after the canon. I shall take them from an edition by Regnault, Paris, 1529.

---

[66] Wilkins, *Concilia*, tom. i. p. 707.

II.

Cautelae Missae.

❡ *Sequuntur informationes et cautelæ observandæ presbytero volenti divina celebrare.*

PRIMA cautela est: ut sacerdos missam celebraturus, conscientiam suam per puram confessionem optime præparet, sacramentum vehementer desideret, et confiteri intendat. Notulam de modo agendi officium memoriter et bene sciat. Gestus valde compositos ac devotos habeat. Cum enim quilibet teneatur Deum diligere ex toto corde, ex tota anima, et ex totis viribus suis. Hic Deum diligere non probatur, qui in mensa altaris ubi rex regum et dominus omnium tractatur et sumitur, irreligiosus, indevotus, impudicus, distractus, vagus, aut desidiosus apparuerit. Attendat igitur unusquisque quod ad mensam magnam sedeat. Cogitet qualiter eum præparari oporteat. Sit cautus et circumspectus. Stet erectus, non jacens in altari. Cubitos jungat lateribus. Manus exaltet, ut extremitates digitorum modicum super humeros videantur.

Intellectum signis et verbis coaptet, quoniam magna latent in signis, majora in verbis, maxima in intentione. Tres digitos jungat quibus signa faciat, reliquos duos in manu componat. Signa faciat directe non oblique, alte satis ne calicem evertat. Non circulos pro crucibus. Cum vero inclinandum erit, non oblique sed directe ante altare, toto curvatus corpore, se inclinet.

Secunda est, ut non putet, sed certo sciat se debitas materias habere, hoc est, panem triticeum, et vinum cum aqua modica. De vino et aqua sic poterit certificari. Exigat a ministro, ut gustet tam vinum quam aquam. Ipse autem presbyter gustare non debet. Guttam fundat in manum, digito terat et odoret, sic erit certior. Non credat ampullæ signatæ, non colori; quoniam sæpius fallunt. Videat calicem ne sit fractus. Consideret vinum; si est corruptum, nullo modo celebret: si acetosum, dissimulet. Si nimis aquosum, abstineat, nisi sciat vinum aquæ prævalere. Et in omni casu si contingat dubitari; vel propter acedinem, vel propter mixturam vel illimpiditatem utrum possit confici, consulimus abstinere: quia in hoc sacramento nihil sub dubio est agendum, ubi certissime est dicendum; *Hoc est enim corpus meum*, et, *Hic est enim calix sanguinis mei*. Item oblatas convenientes eligat, et vinum competenter infundat, quia hoc sacramentum debet sensibus deservire ad videndum, tangendum, et gustandum, ut sensus reficiatur ex specie, et intellectus ex re contenta foveatur. Aqua etiam in parvissima quantitate infundatur, ut a vino absorbeatur, et saporem vini recipiat. Non est enim periculum quantumcunque modicum apponatur de aqua, est autem periculum si multum. Apponitur etiam aqua solum ad significandum, sed una gutta tantum significat, quantum mille. Ideo caveat sacerdos ne cum impetu infundat, ne nimis cadat.

Tertia est, ut canonem morosius legat quam cætera. Et præcipue ab illo loco: *Qui pridie quam pateretur accepit.* Tunc enim respirans attendere debet, et se totum colligere (si prius non potuit) singulis verbis intendens. Et dum dixerit: *Accipite et manducate ex hoc omnes;* respiret et uno spiritu tractim dicat, *Hoc est enim corpus meum:* sic non immiscet se alia cogitatio. Non enim videtur esse rationabile discontinuare formam tam brevem, tam arduam, tam efficacem, cujus tota virtus dependet ab ultimo verbo, scilicet, *meum*, quod in persona Christi dicitur. Unde non debet cuilibet verbo punctus imponi. Cum id nulla ratione valeat ut dicatur: *Hoc est enim, corpus meum.* Sed totum simul proferat. Pari modo hoc idem in forma consecrationis sanguinis observetur.

Item proferendo verba consecrationis circa quamlibet materiam, sacerdos semper intendat conficere id quod Christus instituit, et ecclesia facit.

Quarta est, ut si plures hostias habet consecrare, debet harum unam elevare, quam sibi deputaverat a principio ad missam; et teneat illam penes alias, ita quod visum et intentionem ad omnes simul dirigat. Et signando et dicendo: *Hoc est enim corpus meum:* omnes cogitet quas demonstrat.

Consulimus quoque ut canonem presbyter memoriter sciat, quia devotius dicitur; semper tamen liber habeatur, ut ad ipsum memoriter recurratur.

Quinta est, ut dum sumat, nunquam uno haustu calicem sumat, ne propter impetum tussis inopinate occurrat, sed bis vel ter caute sumat ut impedimentum non habeat. Si vero plures hostias debet sumere, ut quando hostia est renovanda, primo sumat eam quam confecit et sanguinem: post hæc alias quæ supersunt. Suam prius sumat quam alias, quia de suis credit et scit, de aliis credit et nescit. Demum desuper ablutiones, et non prius.

Sexta est, ut paucorum nominibus se astringat in canone; nec perpetuo, sed quamdiu velit faciat, quando velit omittat, quia canon de multitudine nominum prolixatur, et per hoc cogitatio distrahitur. Dignum tamen est ut pater, mater, frater, soror ibi nominentur. Et si qui pro tempore commendantur;

et specialiter pro quibus missa celebratur. Non tamen ibi fiat vocalis expressio, sed mentalis.

Septima est, ut ante missam non os vel dentes lavet; sed tantum labia exterius ore clauso si indiget, ne forte aquæ gustum cum saliva immittat. Post missam etiam caveat excreationes quantum potest, donec comederit et biberit, ne forte aliquid inter dentes remanserit, aut in faucibus, quod excreando ejiceretur. Quamvis autem missa devotissime sit celebranda contemplationis causa, est tamen modus habendus, ne protractione vel acceleratione fiat homo notabilis. Nam acceleratio signum est incuriæ. Protractio est occasio detractionis. Sed medio tutissimus ibit. Eo autem affectu est quælibet missa habenda et dicenda a quocumque sacerdote, quasi prima dicatur et nunquam amplius sit dicenda: tam magnum enim donum, semper debet esse novum.

Habeat itaque sacerdos diligentiam ad conficiendum: reverentiam ad tangendum: et devotionem ad sumendum. Sic sentiendo et agendo digne tractabitur sacramentum, rite peragetur officium, atque pericula et scandala evitabuntur.

Item, in collectis dicendis semper impar numerus observetur. Una propter unitatem Deitatis. Tres propter trinitatem Personarum. Quinque propter quinque partitam passionem Christi. Septem, propter septiformem gratiam Spiritus sancti. Septenarium numerum excedere non licet.

Item, quandocumque oratio dirigitur solum ad Patrem, in fine dicatur. *Per Dominum nostrum Jesum Christum.* Si vero dirigitur ad Patrem et mentio fit Filii in ipsa, in fine dicatur. *Per eundem Dominum nostrum Jesum Christum.* Si autem oratio dirigitur solum ad Filium, in fine dicatur: *Qui cum eodem Patre et Spiritu sancto.* Et si mentio Spiritus sancti in quacumque oratione fiat, in fine dicatur; *ejusdem Spiritus sancti Deus, per omnia sæcula sæculorum. Amen.*

℃ *Incipiunt cautelæ servandæ, quid agendum sit circa defectus, vel casus, qui oriri possunt in missa, et præsertim circa consecrationem eucharistiæ.*

Primo quid sit agendum cum sacerdos deficit.

℃ Si sacerdos deficiat sive moriatur ante canonem, non est necesse ut alius missam compleat. Si tamen alius vult celebrare, debet ab initio missam reincipere, et totum rite peragere.

Si autem in canone deficiat, factis jam aliquibus signis, tamen ante transubstantiationem et consecrationem sacramenti, tunc alius sacerdos ab illo loco ubi ille dimisit, debet reincipere, et tantum illud supplere quod omissum est.

Si autem sacerdos in actu consecrationis deficiat, verbis aliquibus jam in parte prolatis, sed in toto non completis, secundum Innocentium, alius sacerdos debet incipere ab illo loco, *Qui pridie.*

Si tamen sacerdos deficiat consecrato corpore, sed non sanguine, alius sacerdos compleat consecrationem sanguinis, incipiens ab illo loco, *Simili modo.* Si consecrato corpore, percipiat vinum non esse in calice, debet hostia munde reponi in corporali, et calice rite præparato, incipiat ab illo loco, *Simili modo.*

Si ante consecrationem sanguinis, percipiat aquam non esse in calice, debet statim apponere, et conficere.

Si autem post consecrationem sanguinis, percipiat quod aqua desit in calice, debet nihilominus procedere, nec debet miscere aquam cum sanguine, quia pro parte sequeretur corruptio **sacramenti**: debet tamen sacerdos dolere et puniri.

Si post consecrationem sanguinis percipiat quod

vinum non fuerit positum, sed aqua tantum in calice, siquidem hoc percipit ante sumptionem corporis, debet aquam deponere et imponere vinum cum aqua, et resumere consecrationem sanguinis ab illo loco, *Simili modo*.

Si percipiat hoc post sumptionem corporis, debet apponere de novo aliam hostiam, iterum cum sanguine consecrandam, secundum doctores in sacra pagina, debet autem resumere verba consecrationis ab illo loco, *Qui pridie*. In fine autem iterum debet sumere hostiam illam ultimo consecratam, non obstante si prius sumpsit aquam et etiam illum sanguinem. Innocentius tamen dicit quod si ex prolongatione sacerdos timet scandalum, quo sufficiunt tantum illa verba per quæ consecratur sanguis, scilicet *Simili modo*, et sic sumere sanguinem.

Quid autem faciet cum aquam, sumpto corpore, jam habet in ore, et jam primo sentit quod sit aqua; utrum debeat eam deglutire vel emittere. Require in summa Hostiensis in titulo de celebr. missæ. Tutius tamen est eam deglutire quam emittere; et hoc ideo ne aliqua particula corporis cum aqua exeat.

Item si sacerdos post consecrationem recordetur se non esse jejunum, vel commisisse aliquod peccatum, vel esse excommunicatum: debet nihilominus procedere, cum proposito satisfaciendi, et absolutionem impetrandi.

Si autem ante consecrationem recordetur prædictorum, tutius est missam inceptam deserere et absolutionem petere, nisi inde grave scandalum oriatur.

Item si musca vel aranea vel aliquid talium ante consecrationem in calicem ceciderit, vel etiam venenum immissum fore deprehenderit, vinum debet effundi quod est in calice, et abluto calice aliud vinum cum aqua poni ad consecrandum. Sed si aliquid horum post consecrationem acciderit, debet musca vel aranea vel aliquid talium caute capi, et diligenter inter digitos pluries lavari; et vermis comburi; et ablutio cum cineribus combustis in sacrario reponi. Venenum autem nullo modo debet sumi, sed cum reliquiis debet sanguis talis cui venenum est immissum in vasculo mundo reservari. Et ne sacramentum maneat imperfectum, debet calicem denuo rite præparare, et resumere consecrationem sanguinis ab illo loco, *Simili modo.* Et nota quod secundum doctores, nihil abominabile sumi debet occasione hujus sacramenti.

Item si sacerdos non recolit se dixisse aliquod horum quæ debuit dicere, non debet mente turbari; non enim qui multa dicit, semper recolit quæ dixit. Etiam si sibi pro certo constat quod aliqua omiserit, si talia non sunt de necessitate sacramenti, sicut sunt secretæ, vel aliqua verba canonis, ultra procedat, nec aliquid resumat. Si tamen probabiliter sibi constat quod omisit aliquid, quod sit de necessitate sacramenti, sicut forma verborum per quam consecratur, omnia verba consecrationis super suam materiam resumere debet, quia consecratio facta non esset. Quod tamen non oportet si prætermissa esset conjunctio *enim* vel alia verba quæ præcedunt vel sequuntur formam; quæ non sunt de ipsius substantia.

Si autem sacerdos dubitaret an aliquod verbum pertinens ad substantiam formæ omisisset vel non, nullatenus debet servare formam conditionalem; sed sine temeraria assertione formam totam super suam propriam materiam debet resumere, cum hac intentione: quod si consecratio esset facta, nullo modo voluisset consecrare; sed si consecratio non esset facta, vellet corpus et sanguinem consecrare.

Item si quis tempore consecrationis, ab actuali

intentione et devotione distractus fuerit, nihilominus consecrat; dummodo intentio habitualis in eo remanserit; summo sacerdote, scilicet Christo, supplente ejus defectum.

Si autem per nimiam distractionem habitualis intentio cum actuali tolleretur, videtur quod deberet verba consecrationis cum actuali intentione resumere, sic tamen quod nollet consecrare, si consecratio facta esset.

Item si hostia consecrata propter frigus, vel alia de causa, labitur sacerdoti in calicem, sive ante divisionem hostiæ, sive post; non debet eam de sanguine extrahere, nec aliquid propter hoc reiterare, vel immutare circa celebrationem sacramenti; sed procedat in signis et in aliis, ac si haberet eam in manibus.

Si eucharistia ad terram ceciderit, locus ubi jacuit radatur, et incineretur per ignem, et cinis juxta altare recondatur.

℞ Item si per negligentiam aliquid de sanguine stillaverit, super tabulam quæ terræ adhæret, stilla per sacerdotem cum lingua lambatur, et locus tabulæ radatur, et rasura igni comburatur, et cinis juxta altare cum reliquiis recondatur, et quadraginta diebus pœniteat cui hoc accidit.

Si vero super altare stillaverit calix, sorbeatur stilla, et tribus diebus pœniteat.

Si vero super linteum et ad aliud stilla pervenerit, quatuor diebus pœniteat. Si usque ad tertium, novem diebus pœniteat. Si usque ad quartum stilla sanguinis pervenerit, viginti diebus pœniteat, et linteamina quæ stilla tetigerit tribus vicibus lavet sacerdos, vel diaconus, calice supposito, et ablutio cum reliquiis recondatur.

Item si quis aliquo casu gulæ eucharistiam evomuerit, vomitus ille debet incinerari, et cineres juxta altare debent recondi. Et si fuerit clericus, monachus, presbyter, vel diaconus, quadraginta diebus pœniteat, episcopus septuaginta, laicus triginta.

Si vero ex infirmitate evomuerit, quinque diebus pœniteat.

Qui vero non bene custodit sacramentum, ita quod mus vel aliud animal comederit, quadraginta diebus pœniteat.

Qui autem perdiderit illud, vel pars ejus ceciderit et non fuerit inventa, triginta diebus pœniteat. Eadem pœnitentia videtur dignus sacerdos, per cujus negligentiam putrescunt hostiæ consecratæ. Dictis autem diebus pœnitens debet jejunare, et a communione, et a celebratione abstinere. Pensatis tamen circumstantiis delicti et personæ, potest minui vel augeri pœnitentia prædicta, secundum arbitrium discreti confessoris. Hoc autem tenendum est, quod ubicunque inveniuntur species sacramenti integræ, reverenter sumendæ sunt: quod si sine periculo fieri non potest, sunt tamen pro reliquiis reservandæ.

Item si hostia, vel pars hostiæ inventa fuerit sub palla vel corporali, et dubitatur si est consecrata vel non, debet eam post sumptionem sanguinis reverenter sumere, ut in titulo de celebratione missarum plenius invenies.

Item circa materiam sanguinis vide ne sit agresta, vel vinum ita debile, quod nullo modo habeat speciem vini. Ne sit aqua rubea expressa de panno intincto in vino rubeo. Ne sit acetum, vel vinum omnino corruptum; ne sit claretum, vel vinum de moris aut malogranatis confectum; quia veram speciem vini non retinent.

Conficiens cum vino quod est in via corruptionis, vel ad corruptionem tendens, gravissime peccat (licet conficiat) quoniam non retinet speciem vini.

Item cavendum est, ne apponatur nisi modicum de aqua, quia si tantum poneretur quod speciem vini tolleret, non conficeretur.

Item si qua hic desunt, requirantur in summa et lectura Hostien. in titulo de celebr. missarum.

III.

De modo exequendi Officium dominica prima in Adventu, ad missam: et de Officiis singulorum ministrorum.[67]

DOMINICA prima in adventu, peracta processione, dum tertia cantatur, executor officii et sui ministri ad missam dicendam se induant, et si episcopus fuerit, tres habeat diaconos et totidem subdiaconos ad minus, sicut in omni festo novem lectionum, quando ipse exequitur officium. In die vero pentecostes, et in die cœnæ, septem diaconos et septem subdiaconos et tres acolytos. In aliis vero duplicibus, quinque tantum. Die vero parasceve, unum solum diaconum, et unum solum subdiaconum.

Cantata vero tertia et officio missæ inchoato, dum post officium " Gloria patri " inchoatur, executor officii cum suis ministris ordinate presbyterium intrent, et ad altare accedant: diacono et subdiacono casulis indutis, manus tamen ad modum sacerdotis extra casulam non tenentibus. Cæteris ministris in albis existentibus: quibus vero temporibus, diaconi et subdiaconi casulis, dalmaticis, et tunicis, et albis uti debeant, in ordinali plene describitur. Ad gra-

---

[67] From the Consuetudinarium of Sarum, in the manuscript *Registrum S. Osmundi*, fol. xv. Preserved among the muniments of the bishop of Salisbury; and of which I have given some account at the end of the dissertation on service books, *Monumenta ritualia*, vol. i. p. ccxxiv, with some other extracts.

dum autem altaris sacerdos ipse confessionem dicat: diacono ei assistente a dextris, subdiacono a sinistris: et sciendum quod quisque sacerdos officium exequatur, semper episcopus si præsens fuerit ad gradum altaris, "Confiteor" dicat. Dicta vero absolutione, sacerdos diaconum deosculetur; deinde subdiaconum: quod semper observatur, nisi missa pro fidelibus fuerit dicenda, et exceptis tribus ultimis diebus in passione Domini. His peractis, ceroferarii candelabra cum cereis ad gradum altaris demittant. Post humiliationem vero sacerdotis ad altare factam, ipsum altare sacerdos thurificet, diaconi ministerio: deinde ab ipso diacono ipse sacerdos thurificetur; et postea textum ministerio subdiaconi deosculetur. His peractis, in dextro cornu altaris, cum diacono et subdiacono, officium missæ usque ad orationem prosequatur, sive usque ad "Gloria in excelsis," quando "Gloria in excelsis" dicitur. Quo facto sacerdos, cum suis ministris, in sedibus ad hoc paratis se recipiant, usque ad orationem dicendam, vel in alio tempore, usque ad "Gloria in excelsis" incipiendum. Dum vero sacerdos ad officium exequendum stat ad altare, diaconus post eum stet in primo gradu ante altare: deinde subdiaconus ordinate, ita quod quoties sacerdos ad populum se convertit, diaconus similiter se convertat: subdiacono interim ipsi sacerdoti de casula aptanda subministrante. Sciendum autem quod quicquid a sacerdote dicitur ante epistolam, in dextro cornu altaris expletur. Similiter post perceptionem sacramenti: cætera omnia in medio altaris fiunt. Post introitum vero missæ, unus ceroferariorum panem, et vinum, et aquam, in pixide et phiolis solemniter ad locum ubi panis, vinum, et aqua, ad eucharistiæ ministrationem disponuntur, deferat. Reliquus vero ceroferarius pelves cum aqua et manutergio. Incepta vero ultima oratione ante epistolam, casula interim deposita, subdiaconus per medium chori ad legendam epistolam ad pulpitum accedat, et dum epistola legitur, duo pueri in superpelliciis facta inclinatione ad altare ad gradum chori, in pulpito ipso se ad cantandum gradale præparent. Interim etiam veniant duo ceroferarii obviam acolyto ad ostium presbyterii, cum veneratione ipsum calicem ad locum prædictæ administrationis deferenti, offertorio et corporalibus ipsi calici superpositis: est autem acolytus in albis, et mantello serico, ad hoc parato. Calice itaque in loco debito reposito, corporalia ipse acolytus super altare solemniter deponat, ipsum altare in recessu deosculando. Quo facto ceroferarii candelabra cum cereis, ad gradum altaris demittant. Lecta epistola, subdiaconus panem et vinum, post manuum ablutionem, ad eucharistiæ ministrationem in loco ipsius administrationis præparet ministerio acolyti. Dum gradale canitur, duo de superiore gradu ad cantandum "Alleluia" cappis sericis se induant, et ad pulpitum accedant. Dicto vero gradali, pueri cantores ad gradum altaris inclinaturi redeant. Post quoque epistolam unus ceroferariorum cum aliquo puero de choro aquilam in pulpito ad legendum evangelium ornando præparet. Dum "Alleluia" canitur, diaconus prius ablutis manibus, casula humerum sinistrum modo stolæ succinctus, corporalia super altare disponat. Dum prosa canitur, diaconus ipse altare thurificet; deinde ad commonitionem puerorum ministrantium a choro ad ministeria sua redientium, accepto texto evangeliorum et data ei humiliato a sacerdote benedictione, cum ceroferariis et thuribulo præcedente, subdiacono librum lectionis evangelicæ deferente per medium chori, ad pulpitum accedat. Textum ipsum super sinistram manum solemniter gestando: et cum ad locum legendi pervenerit, textum ipsum subdiaconus accipiat; et a sinistris ipsius diaconi, ipsum dum evangelium legitur teneat. Et lecto evangelio, ipsum deosculandum ipsi diacono porrigat a dextra parte ipsius. In redeundo tamen, textum ipsum ad altare ex directo pectore deferat. Post inceptionem "Credo in unum," sacerdos ipse ministerio diaconi thurificetur, et postea, ministerio subdiaconi, textum deosculetur. Quo peracto, chorus, ministerio pueri, more solito incensetur, sequente subdiacono textum deosculandum singulis eo ordine quo incensantur porrigente. His peractis, acolyto ministrante subdiacono, subdiacono ipsi diacono, sacerdos prius hostiam super patenam, deinde calicem a manu diaconi accipiat. Diacono manum ipsius sacerdotis, utraque vice, deosculante. Postea ordinato sacrificio et debito modo deposito sacerdos sacrificium, ministerio diaconi, ter in signum crucis thurificet; deinde ter in circuitu; postea ex utraque parte sacrificii. Quo peracto sacerdos manus abluat, ministerio subdiaconi et aliorum ministrorum. Diacono interim ipsum altare in sinistro cornu incensante, et reliquias, more solito, in circuitu. Accedente autem sacerdote ad divinum obsequium exequendum, diaconus et subdiaconus suis gradibus ordinate se teneant. Et si episcopus celebraverit, omnes diaconi in eodem gradu diaconorum consistant: principali diacono medium locum inter eos obtinente. Simili modo subdiaconi in gradu subdiaconorum se habeant. Cæteris omnibus diaconis et subdiaconis gestum principalis diaconi, et principalis subdiaconi imitantibus. Excepto quod principalis subdiaconus sacerdoti ad populum convertenti solus ministret. Sacerdote vero " Per omnia sæcula" incipiente, subdiaconus offertorium et patenam a manu diaconi accipiat, et ipsam tenendam, quousque oratio dominica dicatur, acolyto

offertorio coopertam committat in gradu post subdiaconum interim constituto. Sciendum autem quod
pueri ministrantes, dum secretum missæ tractatur,
in choro moram faciunt exteriorem locum primæ
formæ tenentes, quousque sacerdos, cancellatis manibus, ad altare se inclinet. Tunc enim ad altare
accedunt ad ministrandum diacono in manuum ablutione cum subdiacono. Sacerdote vero corpore Domini calicem in modum crucis signante, diaconus ei
a dextris assistat, eique in corporalibus sustinendis
subministret. Inchoata vero oratione dominica, diaconus patenam a manu subdiaconi recipiat, et post
dictam orationem dominicam eam sacerdoti porrigat:
post tertium "Per omnia" si episcopus celebraverit,
diaconus ad populum conversus, baculum episcopi in
dextra tenens, curvatura baculi ad se conversa, dicat
"Humiliate vos ad benedictionem." Deinde episcopus, eucharistia interim super patenam reposita, super
populum faciat benedictionem. Ad "Agnus Dei" dicendum, ascendat diaconus et subdiaconus ad sacerdotem uterque a dextris; diaconus propior, subdiaconus remotior. Pacem vero diaconus a sacerdote accipiat: deinde primo subdiaconum; deinde ad gradum
chori rectorem ex parte decani; dehinc alium ex
parte cantoris, osculetur: qui duo pacem choro re-
portent, incipientes a decano et cantore, vel ab his
qui stallis eorum stant proximiores. Post perceptionem sacramenti, sacerdote ad manus abluendas
veniente, diaconus corporalia complicet et in loculo
reponat. Postea vero ipsa corporalia calici cum
offertorio superponat; ipsumque calicem, dum postcommunio dicitur, ipsi acolyto committat, qui dum
"Per omnia" dicitur post orationem, ea solemnitate
qua eum apportavit reportet. Post "Benedicamus"
dictum a diacono, iterum casula induto, ad populum converso, et post inclinationem a se factam,

sacerdos cum suis ministris, modo quo accessit, abscedat.

Vitalis presbyter,[68] vicarius perpetuus de Suning,

----

[68] These examinations of illiterate priests, presented to a dean of Salisbury at a visitation of his peculiars in the early part of the thirteenth century, viz. A.D. 1222, are taken from the same manuscript, the *Registrum S. Osmundi*, fol. xliij, and are written in a contemporary hand, probably being the authentic record at the time. Certainly they have little else to do with my present subject, beyond the canon being made the test of a competent knowledge, but they are extremely curious.

A year or two before this very time the provincial constitutions of archbishop Stephen Langton had been published; and, probably, increased care was taken at visitations to correct illiterate priests. All archdeacons were directed to ascertain " quod sacerdotes rite noverint proferre verba canonis et baptismatis; et quod in hac parte sanum habeant intellectum." On which Lyndwood thus glosses : " *Canonis.* Et dic canonis, i. e. sacramentalium verborum. Vel *canonis*, i.e. omnium quæ sequuntur præfationem usque ad orationem Dominicam. *Sanum intellectum*, i.e. fidelem intellectum, sive catholicum." Lib. 1. tit. 10, Ut archidiaconi.

I have omitted other examinations, after which those presented were declared to be sufficiently learned. Undoubtedly these examples show a large amount of ignorance in more than one case of the clergy who were examined ; but equally beyond doubt they prove the care which was taken by those who were in authority to check the evil. We must remember, moreover, that the early part of the thirteenth century included many years of the reign of probably the worst monarch who ever wore the English crown; when everything seemed for a time to be given up to tyranny, cruelty, and confusion.

It would be highly improper for me to presume to offer any opinion upon the general state of theological learning among Anglican clergy of our own day. One fact, I think, cannot be disputed. During the last fifty years there has been a great improvement. But looking further back, it may very fairly be a question whether the illiterate priests of the thirteenth century might not easily have been overmatched in numbers by the rectors and curates of the eighteenth; and most certainly the penalty for ignorance was not so sharply and carefully administered by bishops or deans in their visita-

præsentavit capellanum, quem secum habet, nomine Simonem, quem modo retinuit usque ad festum B. Michaelis. Requisitus idem Simon de suis ordinibus; dicit, quod apud Oxoniam recepit ordinem subdiaconi, a quodam episcopo Yberniæ, Albino nomine, tunc vicario episcopi Lincolniensis. Item ab eodem recepit ordinem diaconi. Item ordinem presbyteratus ab Hugone modo Lincolniensi episcopo : transactis quatuor annis. Probatus fuit de evangelio Dominicæ primæ in adventu et inventus est minus habens, nec intelligens quod legeret. Item probatus fuit de canone missæ : " Te igitur, clementissime Pater," &c. Nescivit cujus casus esset " Te" nec a qua parte regeretur. Et cum dictum esset ei, ut diligenter inspiceret quæ pars posset competentius regere " Te," dixit, quod Pater, qui omnia regit. Requisitus quid esset " clementissime," vel cujus casus, vel qualiter declinaretur ; nescivit. Requisitus quid esset " Clemens ;" nescivit. Item idem Simon nullam differentiam antiphonarum novit, nec cantum hymnorum, nec etiam de illo, " Nocte surgentes :" nec aliquid scit de officio divino, vel psalterio cordetenus. Dixit etiam, quod indecens ei videbatur quod probaretur coram decano, cum jam esset ordinatus. Requisitus super quo fuisset probatus quando ordinem presbyteratus accepit: dicit quod non meminit. Sufficienter illiteratus est.

Johannes de Herst præsentavit capellanum suum Ricardum nomine, natum apud Rosam. Juvenis quidem est, et nihil scit. Dicit quod ordinem subdiaconi recepit London. a Willielmo episcopo. Ab epi-

---

tions. To mention one example within my own memory. The rector of a small and remote parish in Dorset, a neighbour of mine about the year 1838, reading the second evening lesson, told his congregation that St. Paul besought Philemon for his " son, one Simus, whom he had begotten in his bonds."

scopo Petro, Winton. ordinem diaconi, transactis sex annis : a Willielmo vero episcopo Cestrensi eodem anno ordinem presbyteratus. Probatus de hac collecta adventus : ·" Excita quæsumus Domine ;" dixit quod nihil voluit respondere. Requisitus de canone, dixit, quod nihil voluit super hoc respondere. Postquam enim suus presbyter primo exierat ab ecclesia post examinationem, et venisset ad alios, omnes inierunt consilium unum quod non responderent. Aliqui tamen eorum in articulo responderunt postea ad magnam instantiam decani. Postea requisitus noluit in ultimo capitulo examinari, et remansit suspensus.

Johannes de Erburge præsentavit capellanum Reginaldum, natum apud Windelshoram. Ordinatus sicut ipse dicit, ad ordinem subdiaconi apud Sarum. diaconi vero et presbyt. apud Winton. transactis jam iiij annis. Probatus de hac oratione " Excita," &c., et de hoc textu canonis, " Te igitur, clementissime Pater;" nihil prorsus voluit respondere. Postea venit et obtulit se examinationi et nihil scivit, vel legere vel canere.

Capellanus de Sandhurst Johannes de Sireburñ. dicit quod ordinatus fuit subdiaconum apud Cicestriam : diaconum apud Winton. ab episcopo Godefrido, in Ybernia : et jam ministravit in prædicta capella per iiij annos. Probatus de hac oratione " Excita," &c., et de " Te igitur," nihil scit respondere. Probatus de cantu, de offertorio dominicæ adventus, scilicet : " Ad te levavi;" nescivit cantare.

Item Vitalis presbyter præsentavit ad capellam de Rotiscamp Jordanum presbyterum, natum apud Stratton in Dorset. Ordinatus ut dicit subdiaconum et diaconum apud Sarum ab episcopo Herberto. Presbyterum autem ab episcopo Roffensi Gilberto de Glanvill. ante generale interdictum. Probatus ut alii supra, de oratione " Excita," et " Te igitur;" nihil scit. Proposito ei libro ut cantaret, noluit cantare. Præceptum est Vitali, ut bonos capellanos inveniat et ibi et apud Sunning; vel decanus capiet beneficia in manus suas.

Item apud Erberge fuit quidam veteranus in domo Ricardi Bulloc, presbyter quidam de Radinḡ; et cum probaretur a decano, utrum videret [60] et utrum verba integra proferret, inventum est quod nullum verbum evangelii vel canonis integrum potuit proferre. Et ideo præcepit decanus Johanni de Erburge ne ulterius permitteret eum ministrare in capella illa.

---

[60] See above, p. 236, the canon of Ælfric.

IV.

Modus induendi Pontificem.[70]

MODUS induendi pontificem ad solemniter celebrandum. Primo veniat pontifex ante altare, vel alibi, ubi dispositum fuerit: et prostratus breviter oret. Et surgens ponet se ad cathedram, et statim incipiantur psalmi consueti: "Quam dilecta" &c., ut infra. Interim ministri vel domicelli caligas cum sandalis secrete extenso superiori indumento ei subministrent. Deinde manutergium cum aqua ad lavandum deportent. Postea exuat cappam et induat amictum, albam, et stolam: et reliquias circa collum, ac deinceps tunicam, dehinc dalmaticam, et manipulum. Et tunc consedendo chirothecas manibus imponat, et annulum pontificalem magnum una cum uno parvo strictiori annulo ad tenendum fortius superimponat. Et sudarium retortum in manu recipiat, ad faciem extergendam. Et sic sedendo post psalmos infra scriptos orationes sequentes consuetas perdicat. Et cum hora fuerit, surgat et casulam induat, et mitram capiti imponat, et baculum pastoralem in manu sua sinistra assumat, curvatura baculi ad populum conversa, cujus contrarium faciant ministri tenendo baculum vel portando. Et sic, choro canente "Gloria Patri" vel alias officium incipiente, procedat de sacrario ad altare populum benedicendo. Et veniens ante altare, deposita mitra, dicat confessionem. Qua dicta, repo-

---

[70] From the manuscript pontifical *ad usum Sarum* in the library of the university of Cambridge. (Mm. 3. 21, folio, fol. xi.)

natur mitra usque ad principium primæ collectæ de die, ita quod salutando populum ante principalem orationem dicat versus populum: " Pax vobis." Et deponatur mitra dum dicitur collecta, et post collectam, dicto " Jesum Christum Filium tuum," ad hæc verba, " Qui tecum," reponatur mitra usque ad evangelium, et tunc amoveatur, recepto baculo, usque inceperit "Credo in unum." Et tunc utatur mitra usque postquam verterit se ad populum, dicendo " Orate fratres." Et hoc dicto conversus ad altare, removeat minister mitram et ponat eam super cornu altaris, quasi stando, quousque fiat benedictio super populum: missam quoque totam sicut cæteri sacerdotes dicat. Et post " per omnia" ante pacem faciat benedictionem solemnem super populum, diacono baculum in manibus tenente, et ad chorum converso, dicendo alta voce, " Humiliate vos ad benedictionem."

Chorus respondeat. " Deo gratias."

Et sic eucharistia super patenam reposita, acceptaque mitra, et baculo in manu sinistra, et manu dextra super populum elevata, dicat benedictionem prout tempus exigit et requirit. Et postea remotis mitra et baculo, reversus ad altare dicat: "Et pax ejus." Et cætera sequentia sicut alii sacerdotes, nisi quod lotis manibus reponat mitram et resumat chirothecas et annulos, et postquam se verterit ad populum, dicat: " Dominus vobiscum," et reversus amoveatur mitra, dum dicitur postcommunio. Et iterum post orationem resumatur, ut supra in prima oratione. Et sic mitratus recedat, dicendo evangelium: " In principio," cum psalmo, " Benedicite sacerdotes."

V.

Quae sunt dicenda induendo et exuendo episcopum.[n]

*C*ELEBRATURUS *pontifex missarum sol-*
lemnia, quosdam psalmos et orationes ex in-
stitutione Celestini papæ primo præmittit,
quos interim dum caligis et sandalis ornatur dicet
secundum exhortationem psalmistæ dicentis.

Præoccupemus faciem ejus in confessione, et in
psalmis jubilemus ei.

Hi quinque psalmi sunt qui dici debent, viz.

Quam dilecta tabernacula tua, Domine. Ps.
lxxxiij.

Benedixisti, Domine, terram tuam. Ps. lxxxiv.

Inclina, Domine, aurem tuam et exaudi me. Ps.
lxxxv.

Credidi propter quod locutus sum. Ps. cxv.

De profundis clamavi. Ps. cxxix.

Ant. Veni, Domine, visitare nos in pace, ut læte-
mur coram te corde perfecto.

Kyrie eleison. Christe eleison. Kyrie eleison.

Pater noster. Et ne nos.

Repleatur os meum laude.

Resp. Ut cantem.

Vers. Domine, averte faciem tuam a peccatis
meis.

Resp. Et omnes.

Vers. Cor mundum crea in me, Domine.

Resp. Et spiritum.

[n] From the same manuscript.

S 2

Vers. Ne projicias me a facie tua.

Resp. Et spiritum.

Vers. Redde mihi lætitiam salutaris tui.

Resp. Et spiritum.

Vers. Sacerdotes tui induantur justitiam.

Resp. Et sancti.

Vers. Domine Deus, converte nos.

Resp. Et ostende.

Vers. Domine exaudi orationem meam.

Resp. Et clamor.

Vers. Dominus vobiscum.

Resp. Et cum spiritu tuo.

     Oremus.

℃ *Oratio.* Aures tuæ pietatis, mitissime Deus, inclina precibus meis, et gratia sancti spiritus illumina cor meum, ut tuis mysteriis digne ministrare merear. Per Christum.

Actiones nostras, quæsumus Domine, aspirando præveni et adjuvando prosequere, ut cuncta nostra operatio a te semper incipiat, et per te cœpta finiatur.

Fac me, quæso Deus, ita justitia indui, ut in electorum tuorum merear exultatione lætari, quatenus exutus ab omnibus sordibus peccatorum consortium adipiscar tibi placentium sacerdotum, meque tua misericordia a vitiis omnibus exuat quem reatus propriæ conscientiæ gravat. Per Christum.

Caligis et sandalis impositis, pontifex priusquam sibi amictum imponat, caput peccinat, manus et faciem lavat, et dum lavit dicat episcopus hanc orationem.

℃ Largire sensibus nostris, omnipotens Pater, ut sicut hic abluuntur inquinamenta manuum, ita a te mundentur interius pollutiones mentis, et crescat semper in nobis augmentum sanctarum virtutum. Per Christum.

℃ *Ad amictum imponendum capiti suo.*

Spiritus sanctus superveniet in me, et virtus altissimi obumbrabit caput meum.

℃ *Ad albam.*

· Miserere mei, Deus, miserere mei : et munda me a reatibus cunctis, et cum illis qui dealbaverunt stolas suas in sanguine Agni mereamur perfrui gaudiis perpetuis.

℃ *Ad zonam.*

Præcinge me, Domine, zona justitiæ, et constringe in me dilectionem Dei et proximi.

℃ *Ad stolam.*

Stola justitiæ circumda, Domine, cervicem meam, et ab omni corruptione peccati purifica mentem meam.

℃ *Ad tunicam.*

Indue me, Domine, vestimento salutis, et indumento lætitiæ circumda me semper.

℃ *Ad dalmaticam.*

Da mihi, Domine, sensum et vocem, ut possim cantare laudem tuam ad hanc missam.

℃ *Ad fanonem.*

Indue me, Pater clementissime, novum hominem, deposito veteri cum actibus suis, qui secundum Deum creatus est in justitia et sanctitate veritatis.

℃ *Ad casulam.*

Indue me, Domine, lorica fidei, et galea salutis, ac gladio Spiritus sancti. Amen.

Deinde dicat episcopus antequam accedat ad altare:

Ant. Introibo ad altare, &c., *ut continetur in missale.*

Cum vero episcopus exuerit casulam, et alia indumenta episcopalia, dicat hos psalmos sub uno Gloria Patri, *cum hac antiphona:* Trium puerorum.

Ps. Benedicite sacerdotes, *usque ad finem.*

Ps. Laudate Dominum in sanctis.

Ps. Nunc dimittis. Gloria Patri. Sicut.

Deinde dicatur antiphona : Trium puerorum.

Sequatur : Kyrie eleison. Christe eleison. Kyrie eleison. Pater noster. Et ne nos.

Benedicamus Patrem, et Filium, cum sancto Spiritu.

Resp. Laudemus.

Benedictus es, Domine, in firmamento cœli.

Benedicat et custodiat.

Non intres.

Domine Deus virtutum.

Domine, exaudi.

Dominus vobiscum.

    Oremus.

Oratio. Deus qui tribus pueris.

Oratio. Ure igne.

Oratio. Actiones.

Et finiatur sic : Per Christum Dominum nostrum. Amen.

VI.

Praefationes per totum annum.[72]

SEQUUNTUR præfationes.
  *Et primo præfatio nativitatis Domini; quæ
  præfatio dicitur in die nativitatis Domini
ad omnes missas, et quotidie per hebdomadam, et in die
circumcisionis, et in omnibus missis de sancta Maria,
ab hac die usque ad purificationem, et etiam in die
purificationis. Dicatur etiam in festo Corporis Christi
et in octava ejusdem et infra: quando de eo fit servitium. Dicitur etiam in commemoratione ejusdem.*
Communicantes *vero dicitur tantum usque ad cir-
cumcisionem et in die circumcisionis.*

Æterne Deus. Quia per incarnati Verbi mysterium, nova mentis nostræ oculis lux tuæ claritatis
infulsit: ut dum visibiliter Deum cognoscimus, per
hunc in invisibilium amorem rapiamur. Et ideo cum
angelis, &c.

*Nota, quod infra canonem, ad primam missam in
nocte nativitatis Domini, dicitur* Communicantes: et
noctem sacratissimam, &c. *Ad omnes alias missas
dicitur:* Diem sacratissimum, *quandocunque dicitur.*

Infra canonem.

Communicantes, et diem sacratissimum (*et noctem
sacratissimam*) celebrantes, quo beatæ Mariæ inte-
merata virginitas huic mundo edidit salvatorem: sed
et memoriam venerantes, in primis ejusdem gloriosæ
semper virginis Mariæ, genitricis ejusdem Dei et

---

[72] From *Missale ad usum Sarum*, Paris, fol., Regnault, 1529.

Domini nostri Jesu Christi, sed et beatorum apostolorum ac martyrum tuorum, Petri, . . . et Damiani,
et omnium sanctorum tuorum, quorum meritis precibusque concedas, ut in omnibus protectionis tuæ
muniamur auxilio. Per eumdem Christum Dominum
nostrum. Amen.

❡ *Sequens præfatio dicitur in die epiphaniæ, et per*
octavam et in octava, et Communicantes *similiter.*

Æterne Deus. Quia cum Unigenitus tuus in
substantia nostræ carnis apparuit, in novam nos
immortalitatis suæ lucem reparavit. Et ideo cum
angelis, &c.

Infra canonem.

Communicantes, et diem sacratissimum celebrantes,
quo unigenitus tuus in tua tecum gloria coæternus,
in veritate carnis nostræ visibiliter corporalis apparuit: sed et memoriam venerantes, in primis gloriosæ semper virginis Mariæ genitricis ejusdem Dei
et Domini nostri Jesu Christi: sed et beatorum
apostolorum ac martyrum tuorum, Petri, . . . et Damiani: et omnium sanctorum tuorum, quorum meritis precibusque concedas, ut in omnibus protectionis
tuæ muniamur auxilio. Per eumdem, &c.

❡ *Sequens præfatio dicitur feria iiij. in capite*
jejunii, et in omnibus missis de jejunio, nisi in domi-
nicis ab hinc usque ad cœnam Domini.

Æterne Deus. Qui corporali jejunio vitia com-
primis, mentem elevas, virtutem largiris et præmia:
per Christum Dominum nostrum. Per quem. *Nota*
quod in dominicis per quadragesimam dicitur præ-
fatio quotidiana. In cœna Domini etiam præfatio
quotidiana dicitur. Infra canonem Communicantes,
et Hanc igitur, *et* Qui pridie, *tam ab episcopo quam a*
sacerdote dicuntur.

Infra canonem.

Communicantes, et diem sacratissimum celebrantes,

quo Dominus noster Jesus Christus pro nobis tra-
ditus est: sed et memoriam venerantes, in primis
gloriosæ semper virginis Mariæ genitricis ejusdem
Dei et Domini nostri Jesu Christi: sed et beatorum
apostolorum ac martyrum tuorum, Petri, ... et
Damiani: et omnium sanctorum tuorum, quorum
meritis precibusque concedas: ut in omnibus protectionis tuæ muniamur auxilio.   Per eumdem
Christum Dominum nostrum.   Amen.

Item. Hanc igitur oblationem servitutis nostræ, sed
et cunctæ familiæ tuæ, quam tibi offerimus ob diem
in quo Dominus noster Jesus Christus tradidit discipulis suis corporis et sanguinis sui mysteria celebranda, quæsumus Domine, ut placatus accipias,
diesque nostros in tua pace disponas, atque ab
æterna damnatione nos eripi, et in electorum tuorum
jubeas grege numerari.   Per Christum Dominum
nostrum.   Amen.

Qui pridie quam pateretur pro nostra omniumque
salute, hoc est hodie; accepit panem in sanctas ac
venerabiles manus suas, et elevatis oculis in cœlum
ad te Deum, &c.

❡ *Sequens præfatio dicitur in die paschæ, et per
totam hebdomadam, et in omnibus dominicis, usque
ad ascensionem, quando de dominica sive de pascha dicitur missa.   Sed in vigilia paschæ tantum dicitur
in præfatione,* Sed in hac potissimum nocte. *Quandocunque vero alias dicitur; dicitur,* Sed in hac potissimum die. Communicantes *vero, et* Hanc igitur *per
hebdomadam, et in octava paschæ tantum dicuntur:
ita quod in vigilia paschæ tantum dicitur,* noctem
sacratissimam.   *In die vero paschæ, et alias quando
dicitur,* diem sacratissimum, *dicatur,*

Æterne Deus.   Et te quidem omni tempore, sed
in hac potissimum die (nocte) gloriosius prædicare,
cum pascha nostrum immolatus est Christus.   Ipse

enim verus est agnus, qui abstulit peccata mundi. Qui mortem nostram moriendo destruxit, et vitam resurgendo reparavit. Et ideo cum angelis, &c.

Infra canonem.

Communicantes, et diem sacratissimum (*noctem sacratissimam*) celebrantes resurrectionis Domini nostri Jesu Christi, secundum carnem : sed et memoriam venerantes, in primis gloriosæ semper virginis Mariæ genitricis ejusdem Dei et Domini nostri Jesu Christi : sed et beatorum apostolorum ac martyrum tuorum, Petri . . . . . et Damiani : et omnium sanctorum tuorum, quorum meritis precibusque concedas, ut in omnibus protectionis tuæ muniamur auxilio. Per eumdem Christum Dominum nostrum. Amen.

Item. Hanc igitur oblationem servitutis nostræ, sed et cunctæ familiæ tuæ, quam tibi offerimus pro his quoque, quos regenerare dignatus es ex aqua et Spiritu sancto, tribuens eis remissionem omnium peccatorum, quæsumus Domine, ut placatus accipias, diesque nostros in tua pace disponas, atque ab æterna damnatione nos eripi, et in electorum tuorum jubeas grege numerari. Per Christum Dominum nostrum. Amen.

❡ *Sequens præfatio dicitur in die ascensionis Domini: et per octavam et in octava, et in dominica infra octavam quando de dominica agitur: et* Communicantes.

Æterne Deus : per Christum Dominum nostrum. Qui post resurrectionem suam omnibus discipulis suis manifestus apparuit; et ipsis cernentibus est elevatus in cœlum, ut nos divinitatis suæ tribueret esse participes. Et ideo cum angelis.

Infra canonem.

Communicantes, et diem sacratissimum celebrantes, quo Dominus noster Jesus Christus unigenitus Filius tuus, unitam sibi fragilitatis nostræ substantiam in gloriæ tuæ dextera collocavit. Sed et memoriam venerantes, in primis gloriosæ semper virginis Mariæ genitricis ejusdem Dei et Domini nostri Jesu Christi : sed et beatorum apostolorum ac martyrum tuorum Petri, ... et Damiani : et omnium sanctorum tuorum quorum meritis precibusque concedas, ut in omnibus protectionis tuæ muniamur auxilio. Per eumdem.

℟ *Sequens præfatio dicitur in die pentecostes, et per hebdomadam, et in omnibus missis de sancto Spiritu.* Communicantes, *et* Hanc igitur *in die pentecostes et ab hinc usque ad festum sanctæ Trinitatis dicuntur tantum.*

Æterne Deus : per Christum Dominum nostrum. Qui ascendens super omnes cœlos, sedensque ad dexteram tuam, promissum Spiritum sanctum hodierna die in filios adoptionis effudit. Quapropter profusis gaudiis, totus in orbe terrarum mundus exultat : sed et supernæ virtutes atque angelicæ potestates hymnum gloriæ tuæ concinunt, sine fine dicentes.

Infra canonem.

Communicantes, et diem sacratissimum pentecostes celebrantes, quo Spiritus sanctus apostolis in igneis linguis apparuit. Sed et memoriam venerantes, in primis gloriosæ semper virginis Mariæ genitricis ejusdem Dei et Domini nostri Jesu Christi ; sed et beatorum apostolorum ac martyrum tuorum Petri, ... et Damiani : et omnium sanctorum tuorum quorum meritis precibusque concedas, ut in omnibus protectionis tuæ muniamur auxilio. Per eumdem Christum Dominum nostrum. Amen.

Item. Hanc igitur oblationem servitutis nostræ, sed et cunctæ familiæ tuæ, quam tibi offerimus pro his quoque, quos regenerare dignatus es ex aqua et Spiritu sancto, tribuens eis remissionem omnium peccatorum, quæsumus Domine, ut placatus accipias, diesque nostros in tua pace disponas, atque ab æterna damnatione nos eripi, et in electorum tuorum jubeas grege numerari. Per eumdem Christum Dominum nostrum. Amen.

℄ *Sequens præfatio dicitur in die sanctæ Trinitatis, et in omnibus dominicis usque ad adventum Domini, quando de dominica dicitur missa, licet in capella dicatur, et in omnibus commemorationibus sanctæ Trinitatis per totum annum, et in omni missa sponsalium.*

Æterne Deus. Qui cum unigenito Filio tuo et Spiritu sancto unus es Deus, unus es Dominus : non in unius singularitate personæ, sed in unius Trinitate substantiæ. Quod enim de tua gloria, revelante te, credimus, hoc de Filio tuo, hoc de Spiritu sancto, sine differentia discretionis sentimus. Ut in confessione veræ sempiternæque Deitatis, et in personis proprietas, et in essentia unitas, et in majestate adoretur æqualitas. Quam laudant angeli atque archangeli, cherubin quoque ac seraphin, qui non cessant clamare una voce dicentes.

℄ *Sequens præfatio dicitur in omnibus festis apostolorum, et evangelistarum, et per octavas apostolorum Petri et Pauli, atque Andreæ, quando de octava dicitur missa, præterquam in festo sancti Johannis apostoli et evangelistæ, in hebdomada nativitatis Domini. In octava vero ejusdem dicetur, et in festo ejus in tempore paschali.*

Æterne Deus : et te Domine suppliciter exorare, ut gregem tuum, pastor æterne, non deseras : sed per beatos apostolos tuos continua protectione custodias. Ut iisdem rectoribus gubernetur, quos operis tui vicarios eidem contulisti præesse pastores. Et ideo cum angelis et archangelis, cum thronis et dominationibus, cumque omni militia cœlestis exercitus hymnum gloriæ tuæ canimus, sine fine dicentes.

℃ *Sequens præfatio dicitur, in utroque festo sanctæ crucis, et in commemorationibus ejusdem, per totum annum.*

Æterne Deus. Qui salutem humani generis in ligno constituisti, ut unde mors oriebatur, inde vita resurgeret: et qui in ligno vicerat, in ligno quoque vinceretur: per Christum Dominum nostrum. Per quem majestatem tuam laudant angeli, adorant dominationes, tremunt potestates. Cœli, cœlorumque virtutes, ac beata seraphin socia exultatione concelebrant. Cum quibus et nostras voces ut admitti jubeas deprecamur, supplici confessione dicentes.

℃ *Sequens præfatio dicitur in omni festo beatæ Mariæ virginis, nisi in purificatione ejusdem. Dicatur etiam per octavas assumptionis et nativitatis beatæ Mariæ et in commemoratione ejusdem, per totum annum: nisi a die nativitatis Domini, usque ad purificationem beatæ Mariæ.*

Æterne Deus: et te in conceptione, et te in annunciatione, et te in assumptione, et te in nativitate, et te in visitatione, et te in veneratione beatæ et gloriosæ semper virginis Mariæ exultantibus animis, laudare, benedicere, et prædicare. Quæ et unigenitum tuum sancti Spiritus obumbratione concepit: et virginitatis gloria permanente, huic mundo lumen æternum effudit, Jesum Christum Dominum nostrum. Per quem majestatem tuam laudant angeli, adorant dominationes, tremunt potestates. Cœli, cœlorumque virtutes, ac beata seraphin socia exultatione concelebrant. Cum quibus et nostras voces ut admitti jubeas deprecamur, supplici confessione dicentes.

VII.

Benedictiones Episcopales.[73]

The following selections will enable the reader to judge of the general character of the episcopal benedictions, which were anciently given during the canon of the mass when a bishop officiated. They are referred to in the Sarum manual, and probably were continued in the English church until the alteration of the service in the reign of Edward the sixth, although they had been long disused elsewhere. The reader will find more information about them in my dissertation on the service books (*Mon. rit.* vol. 1), to which I must venture to refer him. The Sarum benedictions do not agree with those in the pontifical of the church of Bangor, nor with many of those in the Exeter pontifical of bishop Lacy; but rather with the benedictional of St. Æthelwold,[74] and, though there are considerable variations, with the benedictions at the end of the Junta Roman pontifical of 1520, the only printed edition in which they are contained.

The benedictions in the Exeter manuscript are stated to have been edited and published by John Peckham, archbishop of Canterbury.

DOMINICA prima adventus Domini benedictio.

    Omnipotens Deus, cujus unigeniti adventum et præteritum creditis et futurum expectatis,

---

[73] From the manuscript pontifical *ad usum Sarum*, before described.

[74] Published in the *Archæologia*, vol. 24.

ejusdem adventus vos illustratione sanctificet, et sua benedictione locupletet.   Amen.

In præsentis vitæ stadio vos ab omni adversitate defendat, et se vobis in judicio placabilem ostendat. Amen.

Quo a cunctis peccatorum contagiis liberati, in præsentis vitæ curriculo cum sanctis animabus tanto intercessore inveniamini digni, et illius tremendi examinis diem expectetis interriti.   Amen.

Ista benedictio sequens dicatur in fine cujuslibet benedictionis per annum.

Quod ipse præstare dignetur, cujus regnum et imperium sine fine permanet in sæcula sæculorum. Amen.

Benedictio Dei omnipotentis, Pa ✠ tris, et Fi ✠ lii, et Spiritus ✠ sancti, descendat super vos, et maneat semper.   Amen.

Benedictio in festo sancti Stephani protomartyris.

Deus, qui beatum Stephanum protomartyrem et confessione fidei et agone coronavit martyrii, mentes vestras circumdet in præsenti sæculo corona justitiæ, et in futuro perducat ad coronam gloriæ sempiternæ. Amen.

Illius obtentu tribuat vobis Dei et proximi caritate semper fervere, qui hanc studuit etiam inter lapidantium impetus feliciter obtinere.   Amen.

Quo ejus et exemplo roborati, et intercessione muniti, ab eo quem ille a dextris Dei vidit stantem mereamini benedici.   Amen.

Quod ipse, &c.

In die paschæ.   Benedictio.

Benedicat vos omnipotens Deus, hodierna interveniente paschali solemnitate : et ab omni miseratus dignetur defendere pravitate.   Amen.

Ut qui ad æternam vitam in unigeniti sui resurrectione vos reparat : in ipsius adventu immortalitatis vos gaudiis vestiat.   Amen.

Ut qui expletis jejuniorum sive passionis dominicæ diebus paschalis festi gaudia celebratis: ad
ea festa quæ non sunt annua sed continua, ipso
opitulante exultantibus animis veniatis.   Amen.

Quod ipse, &c.

In festo sanctæ Trinitatis.

Omnipotens Trinitas, unus et verus Deus, Pater
et Filius, et Spiritus sanctus, det vobis eum desi-
derare feliciter, agnoscere veraciter, diligere since-
riter.   Amen.

Æqualitatem atque incommutabilitatem suæ es-
sentiæ ita vestris mentibus infigat, ut ab eo nunquam vos quibuscumque phantasiis aberrare per-
mittat.   Amen.

Sicque vos in sua fide et caritate perseverare con-
cedat, ut per ea postmodum ad sui manifestationem
visionemque interminabilem introducat.   Amen.

Quod ipse, &c.

In celebratione nuptiarum.

Summæ providentiæ Dominus qui post lapsum
protoplastorum per bona matrimonii usum carnalis
desiderii excusabilem existere decrevisti, sanctificare
digneris conjugale propositum in quo præsentes con-
juges abdicatis tori illiciti maculis nectere voluisti.
Amen.

Da eis sub præsentis commercii indulgentia inquinamenta cætera devitare: ut fructum tricenum
ex verbi tui semine valeant obtinere.   Amen.

Quo sicut conjugium magis magnum existat
Christi et ecclesiæ sacramentum, sic unitati corporum præponderet caritas animarum, et magis tole-
rantes quam amantes carnale commercium ad illud
mentaliter suspendantur gaudium, ubi similitudo
felicitatis angelicæ excludit omne contagium mor-
talium nuptiarum.   Amen.

Quod ipse, &c.

VIII.

The following prayers are taken from a manuscript missal in my possession, of the thirteenth century; it formerly belonged to some English Benedictine monastery. I do not remember to have seen these prayers in any other missal; they are placed immediately before the prefaces, after the ordinary. Martene, among the numerous orders which he gives in the first volume of his collections, has printed an ancient one preserved in the Colbertine library, in which some similar prayers may be found; *De ant. ecc. rit.* tom. i. p. 194.

AD miscendum. Ex latere Christi sanguis et aqua exisse perhibetur, et ideo pariter commiscemus: ut omnipotens et misericors Deus utrumque ad medelam animarum nostrarum sanctificare dignetur. Qui vivit.

Ad corporale sternendum. In tuo conspectu, Domine, quæsumus hæc nostra munera tibi placita sint, ut nos tibi placere valeamus. Per Dominum.

Ad hostiam. Grata tibi sit, Domine, hæc oblatio, quam tibi offerimus pro nostris delictis, et pro ecclesia tua sancta catholica. Per.

Ad calicem. Offerimus tibi, Domine, hæc munera in memoriam Jesu Christi, Filii tui, humiliter deprecantes clementiam tuam: ut ante conspectum Divinæ majestatis tuæ, cum odore suavitatis ascendant. Per eundem.

Super hostiam impositam. Suscipe, Domine sancte,

T

Pater omnipotens, æterne Deus, hanc hostiam oblationis, quam ego indignus et peccator tibi Deo
meo vivo et vero humiliter offero : et mittere dignare Spiritum sanctum tuum de cœlis, qui sua ad-
mixtione sanctificet hoc munus tibi oblatum. Per
ejus.

IX.

Missa pro rege.

The "missa pro rege" is included among the votive or occasional masses in many editions of the Sarum missal. The office which follows is taken from a remarkable little volume printed on vellum, in the Bodleian library (Gough, 160), of which no other copy is known. Unfortunately the title is wanting and there is no colophon.

The first page contains the collect, secret, and postcommunion for Henry the seventh. The second page has the "Præparatio ad missam," with the form of confession for the priest who is about to celebrate if he wishes to confess at that time. This form is commonly to be found in editions of the Sarum missal.

❦ *VOLENS confiteri dicat sacerdos:* Benedicite, pater.

Sacerdos. Dominus sit in corde tuo et in labiis tuis ad confitendum omnia peccata tua. In nomine ✠ Patris et Filii, &c.

Tunc dicat peccata sua: quibus dictis dicat sacerdos: Misereatur tui omnipotens Deus, &c.

Indulgentiam et absolutionem, &c.

Meritum passionis Domini nostri Jesu Christi, suffragia sanctæ matris ecclesiæ, bona quæ fecisti et quæ per Dei gratiam facies sint tibi in remissionem peccatorum tuorum: *injungat penitentiam dicens*, et pro penitentia speciali dices hoc et hoc, vel facies hoc et hoc.

T 2

Tunc absolvat, dicens:

Dominus noster Jesus Christus qui est summus pontifex per suam piissimam misericordiam te absolvat. Et ego auctoritate mihi concessa absolvo te primo a sententia minoris excommunicationis si indigeas. Deinde absolvo te ab omnibus peccatis tuis, in nomine Patris, &c.

Then follow the prayers before putting on the vestments; after which are the ordinary and canon of the mass. The remainder of the volume contains some eight or ten votive masses. Among them are those for the cross; for our lady; for the dead; for the five wounds; and for fevers.

The book seems to have been printed by Wynkyn de Worde or Pynson, about the year 1500. Possibly this collection of short masses was intended to be used in royal chapels only; and very few copies were printed.

The "missa pro rege" in the Sarum missals includes other portions of the service.

"*Officium.* Protector noster aspice Deus, et respice in faciem Christi tui : quia melior est dies una in atriis tuis super millia.

In tempore paschali: Alleluia, alleluia.

Ps. Quam dilecta tabernacula tua, Domine virtutum : concupiscit et deficit anima mea in atria Domini.

Oratio. Quaesumus omnipotens Deus, . . superare ; et ad te qui via, &c.

Epistola. Orationem faciebant sacerdotes.

Grad. Salvum fac servum tuum, Deus meus, sperantem in te.

Versus. Auribus percipe, Domine, orationem meam. Alleluia.

Versus. Eripe me de inimicis meis, Deus meus : et ab insurgentibus in me libera me.

Secundum Marcum. In illo tempore : Dixit Jesus discipulis suis ; Amen, dico vobis, quod quicunque dixerit huic monti . . . peccata vestra. (c. xj.)

Offertorium. Exaudi, Deus, orationem meam, et ne despexeris deprecationem meam : intende in me, et exaudi me.

Secreta. Munera quæsumus, &c.

Postcommunio. Hæc, Domine, salutaris sacramenti . . . quatenus et ecclesiasticæ pacis obtineat tranquillitatem, et post istius temporis decursum ad æternam perveniat hereditatem. Per Dominum."

The same collect, secret, and postcommunion are written on the blank leaf preceding the title in the vellum copy of the Hereford missal in the Bodleian; headed, " Oratio pro rege et regina."

The collect begins, " Quæsumus, omnipotens et misericors Deus, ut famulus rex noster Henricus octavus, in terris ecclesiæ Anglicanæ supremum caput . . . et famula tua Anna regina nostra virtutum omnium," &c.

The words " in terris ecclesiæ Anglicanæ supremum caput " have been almost erased by some contemporary hand.

A manuscript in the British museum contains the benedictions proper to the mass for the king, which up to the reformation were given according to English use, before the Agnus Dei,[75] when a bishop said the mass :—

"*Ben. pro rege.* O sempiterne Deus, qui omnium jura regum immobiliter gubernas, benedic et protege regem nostrum et custodi eum ab omni impedimento æmulorum. Amen.

"Ab omni eum perturbatione libera et in veræ pacis fundamento consolida. Amen.

---

[75] See above, p. 160.

"Talique eum benedictione sanctifica ut sublimitatis sceptrum munitus atque illæsus possideat, per plurima sæculorum spatia. Amen." MS. Cotton, Tiberius B. iij. f. 131.

Missa pro rege.

Sequuntur orationes in missis dicendæ pro bono felici ac prospero statu Christianissimi atque excellentissimi regis nostri Henrici septimi.

Quæsumus, omnipotens et misericors Deus, ut rex noster Henricus septimus, qui tua miseratione regni suscepit gubernacula, virtutum omnium percipiat incrementa, quibus decenter ornatus vitiorum voraginem devitare, corporis incolumitate gaudere, hostes superare, et in tranquilla pace dum in humanis aget tam feliciter possit sua tempora pertransire, ut post hujus vitæ decursum ad te qui via, veritas, et vita es, gratiosus valeat pervenire. Per.

Secretum.

Munera, quæsumus, Domine, oblata sanctifica, ut nobis unigeniti tui corpus et sanguis fiant, et famulo tuo Henrico septimo regi nostro obtinendum animæ corporisque salutem: et ad peragendum in firma fide et solida pace injunctum sibi officium, te largiente, usquequaque proficiat. Per.

Postcommunio.

Hæc quæsumus, Domine, salutaris sacramenti perceptio famulum tuum Henricum septimum regem nostrum ab omnibus tueatur adversis, quatenus diuturnam et prosperam vitam in tranquillitate ecclesiasticæ pacis obtineat: et post hujus vitæ decursum ad æternam beatitudinem tua gratia cooperante perveniat. Per.

Liturgia S. Clementis.

ΕΙΤΩΤΣ ὁ διάκονος λέγῃ· "μή τις τῶν κατηχουμένων.
μή τις τῶν ἀκροωμένων· μή τις τῶν ἀπίστων. μή
τις τῶν ἑτεροδόξων. οἱ τὴν πρώτην εὐχὴν εὐχόμενοι
προέλθετε. τὰ παιδία προσλαμβάνεσθε αἱ μητέρες. μή
τις κατά τινος. μή τις ἐν ὑποκρίσει. ὀρθοὶ πρὸς κύριον 5
μετὰ φόβου καὶ τρόμου ἑστῶτες ὦμεν προσφέρειν." ὧν γε-
νομένων οἱ διάκονοι προσαγέτωσαν τὰ δῶρα τῷ ἐπισκόπῳ
πρὸς τὸ θυσιαστήριον· καὶ οἱ πρεσβύτεροι ἐκ δεξιῶν αὐτοῦ
καὶ ἐξ εὐωνύμων στηκέτωσαν, ὡς ἂν μαθηταὶ παρεστῶτες
διδασκάλῳ. δύο δὲ διάκονοι ἐξ ἑκατέρων τῶν μερῶν τοῦ 10
θυσιαστηρίου κατεχέτωσαν ἐξ ὑμένων λεπτῶν ῥιπίδιον, ἢ
πτερῶν ταῶνος, ἢ ὀθόνης· καὶ ἠρέμα ἀποσοβείτωσαν τὰ
μικρὰ τῶν ἱπταμένων ζώων, ὅπως ἂν μὴ ἐγχρίμπτωνται
εἰς τὰ κύπελλα. εὐξάμενος οὖν καθ' ἑαυτὸν ὁ ἀρχιερεὺς
ἅμα τοῖς ἱερεῦσι, καὶ λαμπρὰν ἐσθῆτα μετενδύς, καὶ στὰς 15
πρὸς τῷ θυσιαστηρίῳ, τὸ τρόπαιον τοῦ σταυροῦ κατὰ τοῦ
μετώπου τῇ χειρὶ ποιησάμενος εἰς πάντας, εἰπάτω· "ἡ
χάρις τοῦ παντοκράτορος Θεοῦ, καὶ ἡ ἀγάπη τοῦ κυρίου
ἡμῶν Ἰησοῦ Χριστοῦ, καὶ ἡ κοινωνία τοῦ ἁγίου πνεύματος,
ἔστω μετὰ πάντων ὑμῶν." καὶ πάντες συμφώνως λεγέ- 20
τωσαν, "ὅτι καὶ μετὰ τοῦ πνεύματός σου." καὶ ὁ ἀρχιε-
ρεύς· "ἄνω τὸν νοῦν." καὶ πάντες· "ἔχομεν πρὸς τὸν
κύριον." καὶ ὁ ἀρχιερεύς· "εὐχαριστήσωμεν τῷ κυρίῳ."
καὶ πάντες· "ἄξιον καὶ δίκαιον." καὶ ὁ ἀρχιερεὺς εἰ-
πάτω· "ἄξιον ὡς ἀληθῶς καὶ δίκαιον, πρὸ πάντων ἀν- 25

ὑμνεῖν σε τὸν ὄντως ὄντα Θεόν, τὸν πρὸ τῶν γενητῶν ὄντα, ἐξ
οὗ πᾶσα πατριὰ ἐν οὐρανῷ καὶ ἐπὶ γῆς ὀνομάζεται· τὸν
μόνον ἀγέννητον, καὶ ἄναρχον, καὶ ἀβασίλευτον, καὶ ἀδέ-
σποτον, τὸν ἀνενδεῆ· τὸν παντὸς ἀγαθοῦ χορηγόν, τὸν πάσης
5 αἰτίας καὶ γενέσεως κρείττονα, τὸν πάντοτε κατὰ τὰ αὐτὰ
καὶ ὡσαύτως ἔχοντα· ἐξ οὗ τὰ πάντα, καθάπερ ἔκ τινος
ἀφετηρίας, εἰς τὸ εἶναι παρῆλθεν. σὺ γὰρ εἶ ἡ ἄναρχος
γνῶσις, ἡ ἀΐδιος ὅρασις, ἡ ἀγέννητος ἀκοή, ἡ ἀδίδακτος
σοφία· ὁ πρῶτος τῇ φύσει, καὶ νόμος τῷ εἶναι, καὶ κρείτ-
10 των παντὸς ἀριθμοῦ. Ὁ τὰ πάντα ἐκ τοῦ μὴ ὄντος εἰς τὸ
εἶναι παραγαγὼν διὰ τοῦ μονογενοῦς σου υἱοῦ· αὐτὸν δὲ
πρὸ πάντων αἰώνων γεννήσας βουλήσει, καὶ δυνάμει, καὶ
ἀγαθότητι, ἀμεσιτεύτως, υἱὸν μονογενῆ, λόγον Θεόν, σοφίαν
ζῶσαν, πρωτότοκον πάσης κτίσεως, ἄγγελον τῆς μεγάλης
15 βουλῆς σου, ἀρχιερέα σόν, βασιλέα δὲ καὶ κύριον πάσης
νοητῆς καὶ αἰσθητῆς φύσεως, τὸν πρὸ πάντων, δι' οὗ τὰ
πάντα. σὺ γὰρ θεὲ αἰώνιε, δι' αὐτοῦ τὰ πάντα πεποίηκας,
καὶ δι' αὐτοῦ τῆς προσηκούσης προνοίας τὰ ὅλα ἀξιοῖς.
δι' οὗ γὰρ τὸ εἶναι ἐχαρίσω, δι' αὐτοῦ καὶ τὸ εὖ εἶναι
20 ἐδωρήσω. ὁ Θεὸς καὶ πατὴρ τοῦ μονογενοῦς υἱοῦ σου· ὁ
δι' αὐτοῦ πρὸ πάντων ποιήσας τὰ Χερουβὶμ καὶ τὰ Σεραφίμ, αἰῶνάς τε καὶ στρατίας, δυνάμεις τε καὶ ἐξουσίας,
ἀρχάς τε καὶ θρόνους, ἀρχαγγέλους τε καὶ ἀγγέλους· καὶ
μετὰ ταῦτα πάντα, ποιήσας δι' αὐτοῦ τὸν φαινόμενον τοῦ-
25 τον κόσμον, καὶ πάντα τὰ ἐν αὐτῷ· σὺ γὰρ εἶ ὁ τὸν οὐρα-
νὸν ὡς καμάραν στήσας, καὶ ὡς δέῤῥιν ἐκτείνας, καὶ τὴν
γῆν ἐπ' οὐδενὸς ἱδρύσας γνώμῃ μόνῃ· ὁ πήξας στερέωμα,
καὶ νύκτα καὶ ἡμέραν κατασκευάσας· ὁ ἐξαγαγὼν φῶς
ἐκ θησαυρῶν, καὶ τῇ τούτου στολῇ ἐπαγαγὼν τὸ σκότος,
30 εἰς ἀνάπαυλαν τῶν ἐν τῷ κόσμῳ κινουμένων ζώων· ὁ τὸν
ἥλιον τάξας εἰς ἀρχὰς τῆς ἡμέρας, ἐν οὐρανῷ, καὶ τὴν
σελήνην εἰς ἀρχὰς τῆς νυκτός, καὶ τὸν χορὸν τῶν ἀστέρων
ἐν οὐρανῷ καταγράψας, εἰς αἶνον τῆς σῆς μεγαλοπρε-
πείας· ὁ ποιήσας ὕδωρ πρὸς πόσιν καὶ κάθαρσιν, ἀέρα

ζωτικὸν πρὸς εἰσπνοὴν καὶ φωνῆς ἀπόδοσιν διὰ γλώττης
πληττούσης τὸν ἀέρα, καὶ ἀκοὴν συνεργουμένην ὑπ' αὐτοῦ
ὡς ἐπαίειν εἰσδεχομένην τὴν προσπίπτουσαν αὐτῇ λαλιάν·
ὁ ποιήσας πῦρ πρὸς σκότους παραμυθίαν, πρὸς ἐνδείας
ἀναπλήρωσιν, καὶ τὸ θερμαίνεσθαι ἡμᾶς καὶ φωτίζεσθαι 5
ὑπ' αὐτοῦ· ὁ τὴν μεγάλην θάλασσαν χωρίσας τῆς γῆς,
καὶ τὴν μὲν ἀναδείξας πλωτήν, τὴν δὲ ποσὶ βάσιμον ποιήσας, καὶ τὴν μὲν ζώοις μικροῖς καὶ μεγάλοις πληθύνας,
τὴν δὲ ἡμέροις καὶ ἀτιθάσσοις πληρώσας, φυτοῖς τε δια-
φόροις στέψας, καὶ βοτάναις στεφανώσας, καὶ ἄνθεσι 10
καλλύνας, καὶ σπέρμασι πλουτίσας· ὁ συστησάμενος
ἄβυσσον, καὶ μέγα κύτος αὐτῇ περιθείς, ἁλμυρῶν ὑδάτων
σεσωρευμένα πελάγη, περιφράξας δὲ αὐτὴν πύλαις ἄμμου
λεπτοτάτης· ὁ πνεύματί ποτε μὲν αὐτὴν κορυφῶν εἰς ὀρέων
μέγεθος, ποτὲ δὲ στρωννύων αὐτὴν ὡς πεδίον, καὶ ποτὲ μὲν 15
ἐκμαίνων χειμῶνι, ποτὲ δὲ πραΰνων γαλήνῃ, ὡς ναυσιπόροις
πλωτῆρσιν εὔκολον εἶναι πρὸς πορείαν· ὁ ποταμοῖς δια-
ζώσας τὸν ὑπὸ σοῦ διὰ Χριστοῦ γενόμενον κόσμον, καὶ
χειμάρροις ἐπικλύσας, καὶ πηγαῖς ἀεννάοις μεθύσας, ὄρεσι
δὲ περισφίγξας εἰς ἕδραν ἀτρεμῆ γῆς ἀσφαλεστάτην. 20
ἐπλήρωσας γάρ σου τὸν κόσμον, καὶ διεκόσμησας αὐτὸν
βοτάναις εὐόσμοις καὶ ἰασίμοις· ζώοις πολλοῖς καὶ δια-
φόροις, ἀλκίμοις καὶ ἀσθενεστέροις, ἐδωδίμοις καὶ ἐνεργοῖς,
ἡμέροις καὶ ἀτιθάσσοις· ἑρπετῶν συριγμοῖς, πτηνῶν ποικί-
λων κλαγγαῖς· ἐνιαυτῶν κύκλοις, μηνῶν καὶ ἡμερῶν ἀριθ- 25
μοῖς, τροπῶν τάξεσι. νεφῶν ὀμβροτόκων διαδρομαῖς, εἰς
καρπῶν γονάς, καὶ ζώων σύστασιν, σταθμὸν ἀνέμων δια-
πνεόντων ὅτε προσταχθῶσι παρὰ σοῦ, τῶν φυτῶν καὶ τῶν
βοτανῶν τὸ πλῆθος. καὶ οὐ μόνον τὸν κόσμον ἐδημιούρ-
γησας· ἀλλὰ καὶ τὸν κοσμοπολίτην ἄνθρωπον ἐν αὐτῷ 30
ἐποίησας, κόσμου κόσμον αὐτὸν ἀναδείξας. εἶπας γὰρ τῇ
σῇ σοφίᾳ· Ποιήσωμεν ἄνθρωπον κατ' εἰκόνα ἡμετέραν, καὶ
καθ' ὁμοίωσιν· καὶ ἀρχέτωσαν τῶν ἰχθύων τῆς θαλάσσης,
καὶ τῶν πετεινῶν τοῦ οὐρανοῦ. Διὸ καὶ πεποίηκας αὐτὸν

ἐκ ψυχῆς ἀθανάτου καὶ σώματος σκεδαστοῦ· τῆς μὲν ἐκ
τοῦ μὴ ὄντος, τοῦ δὲ ἐκ τῶν τεσσάρων στοιχείων· καὶ
δέδωκας αὐτῷ, κατὰ μὲν τὴν ψυχήν, τὴν λογικὴν διάγνω-
σιν, εὐσεβείας καὶ ἀσεβείας διάκρισιν, δικαίου καὶ ἀδίκου
5 παρατήρησιν· κατὰ δὲ τὸ σῶμα τὴν πένταθλον ἐχαρίσω
αἴσθησιν, καὶ τὴν μεταβατικὴν κίνησιν. σὺ γὰρ Θεὲ παντοκράτορ, διὰ Χριστοῦ παράδεισον ἐν Ἐδὲμ κατὰ ἀνατολὰς
ἐφύτευσας, παντοίων φυτῶν ἐδωδίμων κόσμῳ, καὶ ἐν αὐτῷ
ὡς ἂν ἐν ἑστίᾳ πολυτελεῖ εἰσήγαγες αὐτόν· κἂν τῷ ποιεῖν
10 νόμον δέδωκας αὐτῷ ἔμφυτον, ὅπως οἴκοθεν καὶ παρ' ἑαυτοῦ
ἔχοι τὰ σπέρματα τῆς θεογνωσίας. εἰσαγαγὼν δὲ εἰς τὸν
τῆς τρυφῆς παράδεισον, πάντων μὲν ἀνῆκας αὐτῷ τὴν ἐξουσίαν
πρὸς μετάληψιν, ἑνὸς δὲ μόνου τὴν γεῦσιν ἀπεῖπας ἐπ'
ἐλπίδι κρειττόνων, ἵνα ἐὰν φυλάξῃ τὴν ἐντολήν, μισθὸν ταύ-
15 της τὴν ἀθανασίαν κομίσηται. ἀμελήσαντα δὲ τῆς ἐντολῆς,
καὶ γευσάμενον ἀπηγορευμένου καρποῦ ἀπάτῃ ὄφεως καὶ
συμβουλίᾳ γυναικός, τοῦ μὲν παραδείσου δικαίως ἐξῶσας
αὐτόν, ἀγαθότητι δὲ εἰς τὸ παντελὲς ἀπολλύμενον οὐχ
ὑπερεῖδες· σὸν γὰρ ἦν δημιούργημα· ἀλλὰ καθυποτάξας
20 αὐτῷ τὴν κτίσιν, δέδωκας αὐτῷ οἰκείοις ἱδρῶσι καὶ πόνοις
πορίζειν ἑαυτῷ τὴν τροφήν, σοῦ πάντα φύοντος καὶ αὔξοντος
καὶ πεπαίνοντος· χρόνῳ δὲ πρὸς ὀλίγον αὐτὸν κοιμίσας,
ὅρκῳ εἰς παλιγγενεσίαν ἐκάλεσας· ὅρον θανάτου λύσας,
ζωὴν ἐξ ἀναστάσεως ἐπηγγείλω. καὶ οὐ τοῦτο μόνον· ἀλλὰ
25 καὶ τοὺς ἐξ αὐτοῦ εἰς πλῆθος ἀνάριθμον χέας, τοὺς ἐμμεί-
ναντάς σοι ἐδόξασας, τοὺς δὲ ἀποστάντας σου ἐκόλασας·
καὶ τοῦ μὲν Ἀβέλ, ὡς ὁσίου προσδεξάμενος τὴν θυσίαν,
τοῦ δὲ ἀδελφοκτόνου Κάϊν ἀποστραφεὶς τὸ δῶρον, ὡς ἐνα-
γοῦς. καὶ πρὸς τούτοις τὸν Σήθ, καὶ τὸν Ἐνὼς προσελά-
30 βου, καὶ τὸν Ἑνὼχ μετατέθεικας. σὺ γὰρ εἶ ὁ δημιουργὸς
τῶν ἀνθρώπων, καὶ τῆς ζωῆς χορηγός, καὶ τῆς ἐνδείας
πληρωτής· καὶ τῶν νόμων δοτήρ, καὶ τῶν φυλαττόντων
αὐτοὺς μισθαποδότης, καὶ τῶν παραβαινόντων αὐτοὺς ἔκ-
δικος. ὁ τὸν μέγαν κατακλυσμὸν ἐπαγαγὼν τῷ κόσμῳ

διὰ τὸ πλῆθος τῶν ἀσεβησάντων, καὶ τὸν δίκαιον Νῶε
ρυσάμενος ἐκ τοῦ κατακλυσμοῦ ἐν λάρνακι σὺν ὀκτὼ ψυχαῖς, τέλος μὲν τῶν παρῳχηκότων, ἀρχὴν δὲ τῶν μελλόντων
ἐπιγίνεσθαι. ὁ τὸ φοβερὸν πῦρ κατὰ τῆς Σοδομηνῆς πεν-
ταπόλεως ἐξάψας, καὶ γῆν καρποφόρον εἰς ἅλμην θέμενος 5
ἀπὸ κακίας τῶν κατοικούντων ἐν αὐτῇ, καὶ τὸν ὅσιον Λὼτ
ἐξαρπάσας τοῦ ἐμπρησμοῦ. σὺ εἶ ὁ τὸν Ἀβραὰμ ρυσάμενος προγονικῆς ἀσεβείας, καὶ κληρονόμον τοῦ κόσμου κατα-
στήσας, καὶ ἐμφανίσας αὐτῷ τὸν Χριστόν σου· ὁ τὸν
Μελχισεδὲκ, ἀρχιερέα τῆς λατρείας προχειρισάμενος. ὁ 10
τὸν πολύτλαν θεράποντά σου Ἰὼβ νικητὴν τοῦ ἀρχεκάκου
ὄφεως ἀναδείξας. ὁ τὸν Ἰσαὰκ ἐπαγγελίας υἱὸν ποιησάμενος. ὁ τὸν Ἰακὼβ πατέρα δώδεκα παίδων, καὶ τοὺς ἐξ
αὐτοῦ εἰς πλῆθος χέας, καὶ εἰσαγαγὼν εἰς Αἴγυπτον ἐν
ἑβδομήκοντα πέντε ψυχαῖς. σὺ κύριε, Ἰωσὴφ οὐχ ὑπερεῖ- 15
δες· ἀλλὰ μισθὸν τῆς διὰ σὲ σωφροσύνης ἔδωκας αὐτῷ
τὸ τῶν Αἰγυπτίων ἄρχειν. σὺ κύριε, Ἑβραίους ὑπὸ Αἰγυπτίων καταπονουμένους οὐ περιεῖδες, διὰ τὰς πρὸς τοὺς
πατέρας αὐτῶν ἐπαγγελίας· ἀλλ᾽ ἐρρύσω, κολάσας Αἰγυπτίους. παραφθειράντων δὲ τῶν ἀνθρώπων τὸν φυσικὸν 20
νόμον, καὶ τὴν κτίσιν, ποτὲ μὲν αὐτόματον νομισάντων,
ποτὲ δὲ πλεῖον ἢ δεῖ τιμησάντων, καὶ σοὶ τῷ Θεῷ τῶν
πάντων συντατόντων· οὐκ εἴασας πλανᾶσθαι, ἀλλὰ ἀναδείξας τὸν ἅγιόν σου θεράποντα Μωϋσῆν, δι᾽ αὐτοῦ πρὸς
βοήθειαν τοῦ φυσικοῦ τὸν γραπτὸν νόμον δέδωκας, καὶ τὴν 25
κτίσιν ἔδειξας σὸν ἔργον εἶναι, τὴν δὲ πολύθεον πλάνην
ἐξώρισας. τὸν Ἀαρὼν καὶ τοὺς ἐξ αὐτοῦ ἱερατικῇ τιμῇ
ἐδόξασας· Ἑβραίους ἁμαρτόντας ἐκόλασας, ἐπιστρέφοντας
ἐδέξω· τοὺς Αἰγυπτίους δεκαπλήγῳ ἐτιμωρήσω· θάλασσαν
διελών, Ἰσραηλίτας διεβίβασας· Αἰγυπτίους ἐπιδιώξαντας 30
ὑποβρυχίους ἀπώλεσας· ξύλῳ πικρὸν ὕδωρ ἐγλύκανας·
ἐκ πέτρας ἀκροτόμου ὕδωρ ἀνέχεας· ἐξ οὐρανοῦ τὸ μάννα
ὕσας· τροφὴν ἐξ ἀέρος ὀρτυγομήτραν· στῦλον πυρὸς τὴν
νύκτα πρὸς φωτισμόν, καὶ στῦλον νεφέλης ἡμέραν πρὸς

σκιασμὸν θάλπους. τὸν Ἰησοῦν στρατηγὸν ἀναδείξας, ἑπτὰ
ἔθνη Χαναναίων δι᾽ αὐτοῦ καθεῖλες, Ἰορδάνην διέρρηξας, τοὺς
ποταμοὺς Ἠθὰμ ἐξήρανας, τείχη κατέρριψας ἄνευ μηχα-
νημάτων καὶ χειρὸς ἀνθρωπίνης. ὑπὲρ ἁπάντων σοι ἡ δόξα,
5 δέσποτα παντοκράτορ. σὲ προσκυνοῦσιν ἀνάριθμοι στρατιαὶ
ἀγγέλων, ἀρχαγγέλων, θρόνων, κυριοτήτων, ἀρχῶν, ἐξουσιῶν,
δυνάμεων, στρατιῶν, αἰώνων· τὰ Χερουβίμ, καὶ τὰ ἑξαπτέ-
ρυγα Σεραφίμ, ταῖς μὲν δυσὶ κατακαλύπτοντα τοὺς πόδας,
ταῖς δὲ δυσὶ τὰς κεφαλάς, ταῖς δὲ δυσὶ πετόμενα, καὶ
10 λέγοντα, ἅμα χιλίαις χιλιάσιν ἀρχαγγέλων, καὶ μυρίαις
μυριάσιν ἀγγέλων, ἀκαταπαύστως καὶ ἀσιγήτως βοώ-
σαις· καὶ πᾶς ὁ λαὸς ἅμα εἰπάτω· "ἅγιος, ἅγιος,
ἅγιος κύριος Σαβαώθ· πλήρης ὁ οὐρανὸς καὶ ἡ γῆ τῆς
δόξης αὐτοῦ· εὐλογητὸς εἰς τοὺς αἰῶνας. ἀμήν." καὶ ὁ
15 ἀρχιερεὺς ἑξῆς λεγέτω· "ἅγιος γὰρ εἶ ὡς ἀληθῶς, καὶ
πανάγιος, ὕψιστος καὶ ὑπερυψούμενος εἰς τοὺς αἰῶνας.
ἅγιος δὲ καὶ ὁ μονογενής σου υἱὸς ὁ κύριος ἡμῶν καὶ Θεὸς
Ἰησοῦς ὁ Χριστός· ὃς εἰς πάντα ὑπηρετησάμενός σοι τῷ
Θεῷ αὐτοῦ καὶ πατρί, εἴς τε δημιουργίαν διάφορον, καὶ
20 πρόνοιαν κατάλληλον, οὐ περιεῖδε τὸ γένος τῶν ἀνθρώπων
ἀπολλύμενον, ἀλλὰ μετὰ φυσικὸν νόμον, μετὰ νομικὴν
παραίνεσιν, μετὰ προφητικοὺς ἐλέγχους, καὶ τὰς τῶν
ἀγγέλων ἐπιστασίας, παραφθειρόντων σὺν τῷ θετῷ καὶ τὸν
φυσικὸν νόμον, καὶ τῆς μνήμης ἐκβαλλόντων τὸν κατακλυ-
25 σμόν, τὴν ἐκπύρωσιν, τὰς κατ᾽ Αἰγυπτίων πληγάς, τὰς
κατὰ Παλαιστηνῶν σφαγάς, καὶ μελλόντων ὅσον οὐδέπω
ἀπόλλυσθαι πάντων, εὐδόκησεν αὐτὸς γνώμῃ σῇ ὁ δημιουργὸς ἀνθρώπου, ἄνθρωπος γενέσθαι, ὁ νομοθέτης ὑπὸ νόμους,
ὁ ἀρχιερεὺς ἱερεῖον, ὁ ποιμὴν πρόβατον, καὶ ἐξευμενίσατό σε
30 τὸν ἑαυτοῦ Θεὸν καὶ πατέρα, καὶ τῷ κόσμῳ κατήλλαξε,
καὶ τῆς ἐπικειμένης ὀργῆς τοὺς πάντας ἠλευθέρωσε, γενόμενος ἐκ παρθένου, γενόμενος ἐν σαρκί, ὁ Θεὸς λόγος, ὁ
ἀγαπητὸς υἱός, ὁ πρωτότοκος πάσης κτίσεως, κατὰ τὰς
περὶ αὐτοῦ ὑπ᾽ αὐτοῦ προρρηθείσας προφητείας ἐκ σπέρ-

ματος Δαβίδ, καὶ Ἀβραάμ, καὶ φυλῆς Ἰούδα· καὶ γέγονεν
ἐν μήτρᾳ παρθένου ὁ διαπλάσσων πάντας τοὺς γενωμένους,
καὶ ἐσαρκώθη ὁ ἄσαρκος, ὁ ἀχρόνως γεννηθεὶς ἐν χρόνῳ
γεγένηται· πολιτευσάμενος ὁσίως καὶ παιδεύσας ἐνθέσμως,
πᾶσαν νόσον καὶ πᾶσαν μαλακίαν ἐξ ἀνθρώπων ἀπελάσας, 5
σημεῖά τε καὶ τέρατα ἐν τῷ λαῷ ποιήσας· τροφῆς καὶ
ποτοῦ καὶ ὕπνου μεταλαβών, ὁ τρέφων πάντας τοὺς χρή-
ζοντας τροφῆς, καὶ ἐμπιπλῶν πᾶν ζῶον εὐδοκίας· ἐφανέ-
ρωσέ σου τὸ ὄνομα τοῖς ἀγνοοῦσιν αὐτό, τὴν ἄγνοιαν
ἐφυγάδευσε, τὴν εὐσέβειαν ἀνεζωπύρωσε, τὸ θέλημά σου 10
ἐπλήρωσε, τὸ ἔργον ὃ ἔδωκας αὐτῷ ἐτελείωσε· καὶ ταῦτα
πάντα κατορθώσας, χερσὶν ἀνόμων κατασχεθείς, ἱερέων καὶ
ἀρχιερέων ψευδωνύμων καὶ λαοῦ παρανόμου, προδοσίᾳ τοῦ
τὴν κακίαν νοσήσαντος, καὶ πολλὰ παθὼν ὑπ᾽ αὐτῶν, καὶ
πᾶσαν ἀτιμίαν ὑποστὰς σῇ συγχωρήσει, παραδοθεὶς Πι- 15
λάτῳ τῷ ἡγεμόνι, καὶ κριθεὶς ὁ κριτής, καὶ κατακριθεὶς
ὁ σωτήρ, σταυρῷ προσηλώθη ὁ ἀπαθής, καὶ ἀπέθανεν ὁ
τῇ φύσει ἀθάνατος, καὶ ἐτάφη ὁ ζωοποιός, ἵνα πάθους
λύσῃ καὶ θανάτου ἐξέληται τούτους δι᾽ οὓς παρεγένετο, καὶ
ῥήξῃ τὰ δεσμὰ τοῦ διαβόλου, καὶ ῥύσηται τοὺς ἀνθρώπους 20
ἐκ τῆς ἀπάτης αὐτοῦ· καὶ ἀνέστη ἐκ νεκρῶν τῇ τρίτῃ
ἡμέρᾳ· καὶ τεσσαράκοντα ἡμέρας ἐνδιατρίψας τοῖς μαθηταῖς, ἀνελήφθη εἰς τοὺς οὐρανούς, καὶ ἐκαθέσθη ἐκ δεξιῶν
σου τοῦ Θεοῦ καὶ πατρὸς αὐτοῦ. μεμνημένοι οὖν ὧν δι᾽
ἡμᾶς ὑπέμεινεν, εὐχαριστοῦμέν σοι, Θεὲ παντοκράτορ, οὐχ 25
ὅσον ὀφείλομεν, ἀλλ᾽ ὅσον δυνάμεθα, καὶ τὴν διάταξιν
αὐτοῦ πληροῦμεν. ἐν ᾗ γὰρ νυκτὶ παρεδίδοτο, λαβὼν ἄρτον
ταῖς ἁγίαις καὶ ἀμώμοις αὐτοῦ χερσί, καὶ ἀναβλέψας
πρὸς σὲ τὸν Θεὸν αὐτοῦ καὶ πατέρα, καὶ κλάσας, ἔδωκε
τοῖς μαθηταῖς, εἰπών· τοῦτο τὸ μυστήριον τῆς καινῆς δια- 30
θήκης· λάβετε ἐξ αὐτοῦ, φάγετε· τοῦτό ἐστι τὸ σῶμά
μου, τὸ περὶ πολλῶν θρυπτόμενον εἰς ἄφεσιν ἁμαρτιῶν·
ὡσαύτως καὶ τὸ ποτήριον κεράσας ἐξ οἴνου καὶ ὕδατος, καὶ
ἁγιάσας, ἐπέδωκεν αὐτοῖς, λέγων· πίετε ἐξ αὐτοῦ πάντες·

τοῦτό ἐστι τὸ αἷμά μου, τὸ περὶ πολλῶν ἐκχυνόμενον εἰς
ἄφεσιν ἁμαρτιῶν· τοῦτο ποιεῖτε εἰς τὴν ἐμὴν ἀνάμνησιν.
ὁσάκις γὰρ ἐὰν ἐσθίητε τὸν ἄρτον τοῦτον, καὶ πίνητε τὸ
ποτήριον τοῦτο, τὸν θάνατον τὸν ἐμὸν καταγγέλλετε, ἄχρις
5 ἂν ἔλθω. μεμνημένοι τοίνυν τοῦ πάθους αὐτοῦ, καὶ τοῦ
θανάτου, καὶ τῆς ἐκ νεκρῶν ἀναστάσεως, καὶ τῆς εἰς οὐ-
ρανοὺς ἐπανόδου, καὶ τῆς μελλούσης αὐτοῦ δευτέρας πα-
ρουσίας, ἐν ᾗ ἔρχεται μετὰ δόξης καὶ δυνάμεως κρῖναι
ζῶντας καὶ νεκρούς, καὶ ἀποδοῦναι ἑκάστῳ κατὰ τὰ ἔργα
10 αὐτοῦ, προσφέρομέν σοι τῷ βασιλεῖ καὶ Θεῷ, κατὰ τὴν
αὐτοῦ διάταξιν, τὸν ἄρτον τοῦτον, καὶ τὸ ποτήριον τοῦτο,
εὐχαριστοῦντές σοι δι᾽ αὐτοῦ, ἐφ᾽ οἷς κατηξίωσας ἡμᾶς
ἑστάναι ἐνώπιόν σου, καὶ ἱερατεύειν σοι· καὶ ἀξιοῦμέν
σε, ὅπως εὐμενῶς ἐπιβλέψῃς ἐπὶ τὰ προκείμενα δῶρα
15 ταῦτα ἐνώπιόν σου, σὺ ὁ ἀνενδεὴς Θεός, καὶ εὐδοκήσῃς
ἐπ᾽ αὐτοῖς εἰς τιμὴν τοῦ Χριστοῦ σου, καὶ καταπέμψῃς
τὸ ἅγιόν σου Πνεῦμα ἐπὶ τὴν θυσίαν ταύτην, τὸν μάρ-
τυρα τῶν παθημάτων τοῦ κυρίου Ἰησοῦ, ὅπως ἀποφήνῃ
τὸν ἄρτον τοῦτον σῶμα τοῦ Χριστοῦ σου, καὶ τὸ πο-
20 τήριον τοῦτο αἷμα τοῦ Χριστοῦ σου, ἵνα οἱ μεταλαβόντες
αὐτοῦ, βεβαιωθῶσι πρὸς εὐσέβειαν, ἀφέσεως ἁμαρτημάτων
τύχωσι, τοῦ διαβόλου καὶ τῆς πλάνης αὐτοῦ ῥυσθῶσι, Πνεύματος ἁγίου πληρωθῶσιν, ἄξιοι τοῦ Χριστοῦ σου γένωνται,
ζωῆς αἰωνίου τύχωσι, σοῦ καταλλαγέντος αὐτοῖς, δέσποτα
25 παντοκράτορ. ἔτι δεόμεθά σου, κύριε, καὶ ὑπὲρ τῆς ἁγίας
σου ἐκκλησίας τῆς ἀπὸ περάτων ἕως περάτων, ἣν περι-
ποιήσω τῷ τιμίῳ αἵματι τοῦ Χριστοῦ σου, ὅπως αὐτὴν
διαφυλάξῃς ἄσειστον καὶ ἀκλυδώνιστον, ἄχρι τῆς συντε-
λείας τοῦ αἰῶνος· καὶ ὑπὲρ πάσης ἐπισκοπῆς τῆς ὀρθοτο-
30 μούσης τὸν λόγον τῆς ἀληθείας. ἔτι παρακαλοῦμέν σε καὶ
ὑπὲρ τῆς ἐμῆς τοῦ προσφέροντός σοι οὐδενίας, καὶ ὑπὲρ
παντὸς τοῦ πρεσβυτερίου, ὑπὲρ τῶν διακόνων καὶ παντὸς
τοῦ κλήρου, ἵνα πάντας σοφίσας, Πνεύματος ἁγίου πληρώ-
σῃς. ἔτι παρακαλοῦμέν σε, κύριε, ὑπὲρ τοῦ βασιλέως,

καὶ τῶν ἐν ὑπεροχῇ καὶ παντὸς τοῦ στρατοπέδου, ἵνα εἰρηνεύωνται τὰ πρὸς ἡμᾶς, ὅπως ἐν ἡσυχίᾳ καὶ ὁμονοίᾳ
διάγοντες τὸν πάντα χρόνον τῆς ζωῆς ἡμῶν, δοξάζωμέν
σε διὰ Ἰησοῦ Χριστοῦ τῆς ἐλπίδος ἡμῶν. ἔτι προσφέρομέν
σοι καὶ ὑπὲρ πάντων τῶν ἀπ᾽ αἰῶνος εὐαρεστησάντων σοι 5
ἁγίων, πατριαρχῶν, προφητῶν, δικαίων, ἀποστόλων, μαρτύρων, ὁμολογητῶν, ἐπισκόπων, πρεσβυτέρων, διακόνων,
ὑποδιακόνων, ἀναγνωστῶν, ψαλτῶν, παρθένων, χηρῶν, λαϊ-
κῶν, καὶ πάντων ὧν αὐτὸς ἐπίστασαι τὰ ὀνόματα. ἔτι
προσφέρομέν σοι ὑπὲρ τοῦ λαοῦ τούτου, ἵνα ἀναδείξῃς αὐτὸν 10
εἰς ἔπαινον τοῦ Χριστοῦ σου βασίλειον ἱεράτευμα, ἔθνος
ἅγιον· ὑπὲρ τῶν ἐν παρθενίᾳ καὶ ἁγνείᾳ, ὑπὲρ τῶν χηρῶν
τῆς ἐκκλησίας, ὑπὲρ τῶν ἐν σεμνοῖς γάμοις καὶ τεκνογο-
νίαις, ὑπὲρ τῶν νηπίων τοῦ λαοῦ σου, ὅπως μηδένα ἡμῶν
ἀπόβλητον ποιήσῃς· ἔτι ἀξιοῦμέν σε καὶ ὑπὲρ τῆς πόλεως 15
ταύτης καὶ τῶν ἐνοικούντων, ὑπὲρ τῶν ἐν ἀρρωστίαις, ὑπὲρ
τῶν ἐν πικρᾷ δουλείᾳ, ὑπὲρ τῶν ἐν ἐξορίαις, ὑπὲρ τῶν ἐν
δημεύσει, ὑπὲρ πλεόντων καὶ ὁδοιπορούντων· ὅπως ἐπίκουρος
γένῃ πάντων, βοηθὸς καὶ ἀντιλήπτωρ. ἔτι παρακαλοῦμέν
σε καὶ ὑπὲρ τῶν μισούντων ἡμᾶς καὶ διωκόντων ἡμᾶς 20
διὰ τὸ ὄνομά σου, ὑπὲρ τῶν ἔξω ὄντων καὶ πεπλανημένων
ὅπως ἐπιστρέψῃς αὐτοὺς εἰς ἀγαθόν, καὶ τὸν θυμὸν αὐτῶν
πραΰνῃς. ἔτι παρακαλοῦμέν σε καὶ ὑπὲρ τῶν κατηχουμένων τῆς ἐκκλησίας, καὶ ὑπὲρ τῶν χειμαζομένων ὑπὸ τοῦ
ἀλλοτρίου, καὶ ὑπὲρ τῶν ἐν μετανοίᾳ ἀδελφῶν ἡμῶν· ὅπως 25
τοὺς μὲν τελειώσῃς ἐν τῇ πίστει, τοὺς δὲ καθαρίσῃς ἐκ τῆς
ἐνεργείας τοῦ πονηροῦ, τῶν δὲ τὴν μετάνοιαν προσδέξῃ, καὶ
συγχωρήσῃς καὶ αὐτοῖς καὶ ἡμῖν τὰ παραπτώματα ἡμῶν.
ἔτι προσφέρομέν σοι καὶ ὑπὲρ τῆς εὐκρασίας τοῦ ἀέρος καὶ
τῆς εὐφορίας τῶν καρπῶν· ὅπως ἀνελλειπῶς μεταλαμ- 30
βάνοντες τῶν παρὰ σοῦ ἀγαθῶν, αἰνῶμέν σε ἀπαύστως,
τὸν διδόντα τροφὴν πάσῃ σαρκί. ἔτι παρακαλοῦμέν σε καὶ
ὑπὲρ τῶν δι᾽ εὔλογον αἰτίαν ἀπόντων· ὅπως ἅπαντας ἡμᾶς
διατηρήσας ἐν τῇ εὐσεβείᾳ, ἐπισυναγάγῃς ἐν τῇ βασιλείᾳ

U

τοῦ Χριστοῦ σου, τοῦ Θεοῦ πάσης αἰσθητῆς καὶ νοητῆς
φύσεως, τοῦ βασιλέως ἡμῶν, ἀτρέπτους, ἀμέμπτους, ἀ-
εγκλήτους· ὅτι σοὶ πᾶσα δόξα, σέβας καὶ εὐχαριστία,
τιμὴ καὶ προσκύνησις, τῷ πατρί, καὶ τῷ υἱῷ, καὶ τῷ ἁγίῳ
5 πνεύματι, καὶ νῦν, καὶ ἀεί, καὶ εἰς τοὺς ἀνελλειπεῖς καὶ
ἀτελευτήτους αἰῶνας τῶν αἰώνων." καὶ πᾶς ὁ λαὸς λεγέτω·
"ἀμήν." καὶ ὁ ἐπίσκοπος εἰπάτω· "ἡ εἰρήνη τοῦ Θεοῦ εἴη
μετὰ πάντων ὑμῶν." καὶ πᾶς ὁ λαὸς λεγέτω· "καὶ μετὰ
τοῦ πνεύματός σου." καὶ ὁ διάκονος κηρυσσέτω πάλιν.

10 "Ἔτι καὶ ἔτι δεηθῶμεν τοῦ Θεοῦ διὰ τοῦ Χριστοῦ αὐτοῦ,
ὑπὲρ τοῦ δώρου τοῦ προσκομισθέντος κυρίῳ τῷ Θεῷ, ὅπως ὁ
ἀγαθὸς Θεὸς προσδέξηται αὐτὸ διὰ τῆς μεσιτείας τοῦ
Χριστοῦ αὐτοῦ εἰς τὸ ἐπουράνιον αὐτοῦ θυσιαστήριον, εἰς
ὀσμὴν εὐωδίας. ὑπὲρ τῆς ἐκκλησίας ταύτης καὶ τοῦ λαοῦ
15 δεηθῶμεν, ὑπὲρ πάσης ἐπισκοπῆς, παντὸς πρεσβυτερίου,
πάσης τῆς ἐν Χριστῷ διακονίας καὶ ὑπηρεσίας, παντὸς τοῦ
πληρώματος τῆς ἐκκλησίας δεηθῶμεν· ὅπως ὁ κύριος
πάντας διατηρήσῃ καὶ διαφυλάξῃ. ὑπὲρ βασιλέων καὶ
τῶν ἐν ὑπεροχῇ δεηθῶμεν· ἵνα εἰρηνεύωνται τὰ πρὸς ἡμᾶς,
20 ὅπως ἤρεμον καὶ ἡσύχιον βίον ἔχοντες, διάγωμεν ἐν πάσῃ
εὐσεβείᾳ καὶ σεμνότητι. τῶν ἁγίων μαρτύρων μνημονεύ-
σωμεν· ὅπως κοινωνοὶ γενέσθαι τῆς ἀθλήσεως αὐτῶν κατ-
αξιωθῶμεν. ὑπὲρ τῶν ἐν πίστει ἀναπαυσαμένων δεηθῶμεν.
ὑπὲρ τῆς εὐκρασίας τῶν ἀέρων καὶ τελεσφορίας τῶν
25 καρπῶν δεηθῶμεν. ὑπὲρ τῶν νεοφωτίστων δεηθῶμεν, ὅπως
βεβαιωθῶσιν ἐν τῇ πίστει. πάντες ὑπ' ἄλλων παρακαλέ-
σθωσαν. ἀνάστησον ἡμᾶς ὁ Θεὸς ἐν τῇ χάριτί σου· ἀνα-
στάντες ἑαυτοὺς τῷ Θεῷ διὰ τοῦ Χριστοῦ αὐτοῦ παραθώμεθα." καὶ ὁ ἐπίσκοπος λεγέτω· "ὁ Θεὸς ὁ μέγας καὶ
30 μεγαλώνυμος, ὁ μέγας τῇ βουλῇ, καὶ κραταιὸς τοῖς ἔργοις,
ὁ Θεὸς καὶ πατὴρ τοῦ ἁγίου παιδός σου Ἰησοῦ τοῦ σωτῆρος
ἡμῶν, ἐπίβλεψον ἐφ' ἡμᾶς καὶ ἐπὶ τὸ ποίμνιόν σου τοῦτο,
ὃ δι' αὐτοῦ ἐξελέξω εἰς δόξαν τοῦ ὀνόματός σου, καὶ
ἁγιάσας ἡμῶν τὸ σῶμα καὶ τὴν ψυχὴν καταξίωσον καθα-

ροὺς γενομένους ἀπὸ παντὸς μολυσμοῦ σαρκὸς καὶ πνεύματος, τυχεῖν τῶν προκειμένων ἀγαθῶν, καὶ μηδένα ἡμῶν
ἀνάξιον κρίνῃς, ἀλλὰ βοηθὸς ἡμῶν γενοῦ, ἀντιλήπτωρ, ὑπερ-
ασπιστής, διὰ τοῦ Χριστοῦ σου· μεθ᾽ οὗ σοὶ δόξα, τιμή,
αἶνος, δοξολογία, εὐχαριστία, καὶ τῷ ἁγίῳ πνεύματι, εἰς 5
τοὺς αἰῶνας. ἀμήν." καὶ μετὰ τὸ πάντας εἰπεῖν, ἀμήν· ὁ
διάκονος λεγέτω· "πρόσχωμεν" καὶ ὁ ἐπίσκοπος προσ-
φωνησάτω τῷ λαῷ οὕτω. "τὰ ἅγια τοῖς ἁγίοις." καὶ ὁ
λαὸς ὑπακουέτω· "εἷς ἅγιος, εἷς κύριος, εἷς Ἰησοῦς Χριστος,
εἰς δόξαν Θεοῦ πατρός, εὐλογητὸς εἰς τοὺς αἰῶνας. ἀμήν. 10
δόξα ἐν ὑψίστοις Θεῷ, καὶ ἐπὶ γῆς εἰρήνη, ἐν ἀνθρώποις
εὐδοκία. Ὡσαννὰ τῷ υἱῷ Δαβίδ· εὐλογημένος ὁ ἐρχό-
μενος ἐν ὀνόματι κυρίου, Θεὸς κύριος, καὶ ἐπεφάνη ἡμῖν·
Ὡσαννὰ ἐν τοῖς ὑψίστοις." καὶ μετὰ τοῦτο μεταλαμ-
βανέτω ὁ ἐπίσκοπος, ἔπειτα οἱ πρεσβύτεροι, καὶ οἱ διάκονοι, 15
καὶ ὑποδιάκονοι, καὶ οἱ ἀναγνῶσται, καὶ οἱ ψάλται,
καὶ οἱ ἀσκηταί, καὶ ἐν ταῖς γυναιξὶν αἱ διακόνισσαι,
καὶ αἱ παρθένοι, καὶ αἱ χῆραι, εἶτα τὰ παιδία, καὶ
τότε πᾶς ὁ λαὸς κατὰ τάξιν μετὰ αἰδοῦς καὶ εὐλα-
βείας ἄνευ θορύβου. καὶ ὁ μὲν ἐπίσκοπος διδότω τὴν προσ- 20
φοράν, λέγων· "σῶμα Χριστοῦ." καὶ ὁ δεχόμενος λεγέτω·
"ἀμήν." ὁ δὲ διάκονος κατεχέτω τὸ ποτήριον, καὶ ἐπιδιδοὺς
λεγέτω· "αἷμα Χριστοῦ, ποτήριον ζωῆς" καὶ ὁ πίνων λε-
γέτω· "ἀμήν." ψαλμὸς δὲ λεγέσθω τριακοστὸς τρίτος,
ἐν τῷ μεταλαμβάνειν πάντας τοὺς λοιπούς. καὶ ὅταν 25
πάντες μεταλάβωσι καὶ πᾶσαι, λαβόντες οἱ διάκονοι
τὰ περισσεύσαντα, εἰσφερέτωσαν εἰς τὰ παστοφόρια. καὶ
ὁ διάκονος λεγέτω, παυσαμένου τοῦ ψάλλοντος.

"Μεταλαβόντες τοῦ τιμίου σώματος, καὶ τοῦ τιμίου
αἵματος τοῦ Χριστοῦ, εὐχαριστήσωμεν τῷ καταξιώσαντι 30
ἡμᾶς μεταλαβεῖν τῶν ἁγίων αὐτοῦ μυστηρίων, καὶ παρα-
καλέσωμεν, μὴ εἰς κρίμα, ἀλλ᾽ εἰς σωτηρίαν ἡμῖν γενέσθαι,
εἰς ὠφέλειαν ψυχῆς καὶ σώματος, εἰς φυλακὴν εὐσεβείας,
εἰς ἄφεσιν ἁμαρτιῶν, εἰς ζωὴν τοῦ μέλλοντος αἰῶνος.

ἐγειρώμεθα. ἐν χάριτι Χριστοῦ ἑαυτοὺς τῷ Θεῷ, τῷ μόνῳ
ἀγεννήτῳ Θεῷ, καὶ τῷ Χριστῷ αὐτοῦ παραθώμεθα." καὶ
ὁ ἐπίσκοπος εὐχαριστείτω.

"Δέσποτα ὁ Θεὸς ὁ παντοκράτορ, ὁ πατὴρ τοῦ Χριστοῦ
5 σου τοῦ εὐλογητοῦ παιδός, ὁ τῶν μετ᾽ εὐθύτητος ἐπικαλου-
μένων σε ἐπήκοος, ὁ καὶ τῶν σιωπώντων ἐπιστάμενος τὰς
ἐντεύξεις· εὐχαριστοῦμέν σοι, ὅτι κατηξίωσας ἡμᾶς μεταλαβεῖν τῶν ἁγίων σου μυστηρίων, ἃ παρέσχου ἡμῖν, εἰς πληρο-
φορίαν τῶν καλῶς ἐγνωσμένων, εἰς φυλακὴν τῆς εὐσεβείας,
10 εἰς ἄφεσιν πλημμελημάτων· ὅτι τὸ ὄνομα τοῦ Χριστοῦ σου
ἐπικέκληται ἐφ᾽ ἡμᾶς, καὶ σοὶ προσῳκειώμεθα. ὁ χωρίσας
ἡμᾶς τῆς τῶν ἀσεβῶν κοινωνίας, ἕνωσον ἡμᾶς μετὰ τῶν
καθωσιωμένων σοι, στήριξον ἡμᾶς ἐν τῇ ἀληθείᾳ τῇ τοῦ
ἁγίου πνεύματος ἐπιφοιτήσει, τὰ ἀγνοούμενα ἀποκάλυψον,
15 τὰ λείποντα προσαναπλήρωσον, τὰ ἐγνωσμένα κράτυνον.
τοὺς ἱερεῖς ἀμώμους διαφύλαξον ἐν τῇ λατρείᾳ σου· τοὺς
βασιλεῖς διατήρησον ἐν εἰρήνῃ, τοὺς ἄρχοντας ἐν δικαιοσύνῃ,
τοὺς ἀέρας ἐν εὐκρασίᾳ, τοὺς καρποὺς ἐν εὐφορίᾳ, τὸν
κόσμον ἐν παναλκεῖ προνοίᾳ. τὰ ἔθνη τὰ πολεμικὰ πράϋνον·
20 τὰ πεπλανημένα ἐπίστρεψον· τὸν λαόν σου ἁγίασον. τοὺς
ἐν παρθενίᾳ διατήρησον· τοὺς ἐν γάμῳ διαφύλαξον ἐν
πίστει· τοὺς ἐν ἁγνείᾳ ἐνδυνάμωσον· τὰ νήπια ἄδρυνον·
τοὺς νεοτελεῖς βεβαίωσον· τοὺς ἐν κατηχήσει παίδευσον,
καὶ τῆς μυήσεως ἀξίους ἀνάδειξον· καὶ πάντας ἡμᾶς ἐπι-
25 συνάγαγε εἰς τὴν τῶν οὐρανῶν βασιλείαν, ἐν Χριστῷ Ἰησοῦ
τῷ κυρίῳ ἡμῶν· μεθ᾽ οὗ σοὶ δόξα, τιμὴ καὶ σέβας, καὶ τῷ
ἁγίῳ πνεύματι, εἰς τοὺς αἰῶνας. ἀμήν." καὶ ὁ διάκονος
λεγέτω· "τῷ Θεῷ διὰ τοῦ Χριστοῦ αὐτοῦ κλίνατε, καὶ
εὐλογεῖσθε." καὶ ὁ ἐπίσκοπος ἐπευχέσθω, λέγων· "ὁ Θεὸς
30 ὁ παντοκράτωρ, ὁ ἀληθινὸς καὶ ἀσύγκριτος, ὁ πανταχοῦ ὢν
καὶ τοῖς πᾶσι παρὼν καὶ ἐν οὐδενὶ ὡς ἐνόν τι ὑπάρχων, ὁ
τόποις μὴ περιγραφόμενος, ὁ χρόνοις μὴ παλαιούμενος, ὁ
αἰῶσι μὴ περατούμενος, ὁ λόγοις μὴ παραγόμενος, ὁ γε-
νέσει μὴ ὑποκείμενος, ὁ φυλακῆς μὴ δεόμενος, ὁ φθορᾶς

ἀνώτερος, ὁ τροπῆς ἀνεπίδεκτος, ὁ φύσει ἀναλλοίωτος, ὁ
φῶς οἰκῶν ἀπρόσιτον, ὁ τῇ φύσει ἀόρατος, ὁ γνωστὸς
πάσαις ταῖς μετ᾽ εὐνοίας ἐκζητούσαις σε λογικαῖς φύσεσιν,
ὁ καταλαμβανόμενος ὑπὸ τῶν ἐν εὐνοίᾳ ἐπιζητούντων σε·
ὁ Θεὸς Ἰσραήλ, τοῦ ἀληθινῶς ὁρῶντος, τοῦ εἰς Χριστὸν 5
πιστεύσαντος λαοῦ σου· εὐμενὴς γενόμενος ἐπάκουσόν μου
διὰ τὸ ὄνομά σου, καὶ εὐλόγησον τούς σοι κεκλικότας τοὺς
ἑαυτῶν αὐχένας, καὶ δὸς αὐτοῖς τὰ αἰτήματα τῶν καρδιῶν
αὐτῶν τὰ ἐπὶ συμφέροντι, καὶ μηδένα αὐτῶν ἀπόβλητον
ποιήσῃς ἐκ τῆς βασιλείας σου· ἀλλὰ ἁγίασον αὐτούς, 10
φρούρησον, σκέπασον, ἀντιλαβοῦ, ῥῦσαι τοῦ ἀλλοτρίου,
παντὸς ἐχθροῦ, τοὺς οἴκους αὐτῶν φύλαξον, τὰς εἰσόδους
αὐτῶν καὶ τὰς ἐξόδους φρούρησον· ὅτι σοὶ δόξα, αἶνος,
μεγαλοπρέπεια, σέβας, προσκύνησις, καὶ τῷ σῷ παιδὶ
Ἰησοῦ τῷ Χριστῷ σου τῷ κυρίῳ ἡμῶν καὶ Θεῷ καὶ βασιλεῖ, 15
καὶ τῷ ἁγίῳ πνεύματι, νῦν καὶ ἀεὶ καὶ εἰς τοὺς αἰῶνας
τῶν αἰώνων. ἀμήν." καὶ ὁ διάκονος ἐρεῖ· "ἀπολύεσθε ἐν
εἰρήνῃ."

Constitutionum Apost. lib. 8; *Cotelerius, Amst.* 1724, fol.

The Order of the Communion.[1]

*Fyrste the personne, uicar or curat, the next Son-
day or holy day, or at the least one day before he
shall minister the Communion, shal geue warnyng
to his parysshioners, or those whyche be present, that
they prepare them selfes therto, saiyng to them openlie
and plainlie as herafter followeth, or such lyke.*

Dere frendes, and you especially, upon whose
soules I haue cure and charge, upon   daye
next I doe intende by Godes grace to offer to all
suche as shalbe therto godlie dysposed, ye most
comfortable Sacrament of the body and bloude of
Chryste, to be taken of them in the remembrance
of his most fruictfull and gloryous passion. By the
which passion we have obteined remission of our
synnes, and be made partakers of the kyngdom of
heuen; wherof we be assured and asserteyned yf
we come to the sayd Sacrament, with hartye repent-
ance for our offences, stedfast faith in Godes mercye,
and earnest mynde to obey godes wyll, and to
offend no more : wherfore our duety is, to come to
these holy misteries with most harty thankes to be
geuen to almightye God, for his infinite mercy
and benefites, geuen and bestowed upon vs, his
vnworthye seruauntes, for whome he hath not only

---

[1] From one of the copies in the British museum; press mark,
C 25, f. 12. Printed by Grafton, 1548.

geuen his body to death and shed his bludde, but
also dothe vouchesaufe in a Sacrament, and mysterye,
to geue vs his said body and bloud spiritually, to
fede and drynke vpon. The whych Sacrament,
being so diuine and holy a thynge, and so comfortable to them whych receaue it worthelye, and so
daungerous to them that will presume to take the
same vnworthely: my duty is to exhorte you, in
the meane season, to consyder the greatnes of the
thynge, and to searche and examyne your awne
consciences, and that not lightlie, nor after the
maner of dyssimulers wyth god; But as they which
should come to a most godly and heauenlie banket:
not to come, but in the maryage garment, requyred
of God in scripture, that you maye so much as lyeth
in you, be founde worthie to come to suche a table:
The wayes and meanes therto is.

Fyrst, that you be truly repentaunte of your
former euell life, and that you confesse wyth an
vnfayned harte to almyghtie god your synnes and
vnkindnes to wardes his Maiestye committed eyther
by wil, worde or dede, infirmitie or ignoraunce, and
that wyth inwarde sorowe and teares, you bewayle
your offences, and requier of almightye god, mercy,
and pardon, promising to him, from the botome of
your hartes, thamendment of your former life. And
emonges all others, I am commaunded of God,
especially to moue and exhorte you, to reconcile
your selfs to your neyghbours, whome you haue
offended, or who hath offended you, puttynge out
of your hartes, al hatered and malyce against them,
and to be in loue and charyte wyth all the worlde,
and to forgeue other, as you would that God should
forgeue you. And if there be any of you, whose
conscience is troubled and greued in any thing, lack-
ing comforte or counsaile, let him come to me, or

to some other dyscrete and learned priest taught in
the lawe of God, and confesse and open his synne
and grief secretlie, that he maye receaue suche
ghostlie counsaile, aduise, and comforte, that his
conscience maye be releued, and that of vs as a minister of God and of the church, he may receaue
comfort and absolution to the satisfaction of his
mynde and auoyding of al scruple and doubtfulnes :
requyring suche as shalbe satisfied with a generall
confession, not to be offended with them that doth
vse, to their further satisfiyng, thauriculer and secret
confession to the priest, nor those also, which think
nedeful or conuenient for the quyetnes of their awne
consciences, particulerly to open their synnes to
the priest, to be offended, with them whiche are
satisfyed wyth their humble confession to god, and
the general confession to the church : But in al
these thinges, to folowe and kepe the rule of charitie : and euery man to be satisfyed with his awne
conscience, not iudginge other mens myndes or
actes, wher as he hathe no warrant of Godes
worde for the same.

The tyme of the communion, shalbe immediatlie
after that the priest himself hath receaued the Sacra-
ment, without the variyng of any other rite or cere-
mony in the masse (vntil other order shalbe prouided)
but as heretofore vsuallie the priest hath done wyth
the Sacramente of the body, to prepare, blesse and
consecrate so muche as wyll serue the people: so it
shall yet contynue still after the same maner and
fourme, saue that he shall blesse and consecrate the
byggest chalice or some fayr and conuenient cup or
cuppes ful of wyne wyth some water put vnto it.
And that daye, not drynke it vp all hym self, but
takyng one onlye suppe or draught, leue the rest vpon
the aultare couered, and turne to them that are dis-

*posed to be partakers of the communion, and shall
thus exhorte them as followeth.*

Derely beloued in the Lord, ye commyng to thys
holy communion, must consyder what S. Paule
wryteth to the Corinthians, how he exhorteth al
personnes diligentlie to trye and examine them
selues, or euer they presume to eate of this bread
and drink of this cuppe, for as the benefite is greate,
if with a truely penitent harte, and lyuely faith, we
receiue this holy sacrament (for then we spiritually
eate the fleshe of Christ, and drynk his blood:
Then we dwell in Christe and Christ in vs, wee
be made one with Christ and Christ with vs) so is
the daunger greate, if we receyue the same vn-
worthelie; for then we become gilty of the body
and bloud of Christ, our sauiour, we eate and drynke
our awne dampnation, because we make no difference
of the Lordes body, wee kyndle Godes wrath ouer
vs, we prouoke him to plage vs with dyuerse dyseases
and sondry kyndes of death. Judge therfore your
selfes (brethren) that ye be not iudged of the Lord.
Let your mynd be without desier to synne. Repent
you trulie for your sinnes past, haue an earnest and
lyuely faith in Christ, our sauiour, be in perfect
charytie wyth all men, so that ye be mete partakers
of these holy misteries. But aboue all thynges you
muste geue most humble and hartye thankes to
God the father, the sonne, and the holy ghost, for
the redemption of the world, by the deathe and
passion of our sauiour Christ, both God and man,
who dyd humble himself euen to the deathe vpon
the crosse for vs miserable synners, liying in darknes and the shadowe of death, that he might make
vs the children of God, and exalte vs to euerlasting
life. And to thende that wee shoulde alwaye remember the excedyng loue of our master and onlie

sauiour Jesus Christ thus doing for vs, and the
innumerable benefites which by his precyous bloud
shedyng he hath obteyned to vs, he hath lefte in
these holy misteries as a pledge of hys loue, and
a contynuall remembraunce of the same, his awne
blessed body and precyous bloud, for vs spiritually
to fede vpon, to our endles comforte and consolation.
To hym therefore wyth the father and the holy
ghost, let vs gene, as wee are most bounden, con-
tynual thankes, submittyng our selfes wholy to his
holy wyl and pleasure, and studiyng to serue hym
in true holynes and righteousnes all the dayes of
our life.　Amen.

*Then the priest shall say to them which be redy to
take the Sacrament.*

If any man here be an open blasphemer, aduouterer, in malice, or enuy, or any other notable cryme,
and be not truly sory therefore, and earnestlye
mynded to leaue the same vyces, or that doth not
trust himself to be reconcyled to almightye God,
and in charyte with all the worlde, let him yet a
whyle bewayle his synnes and not come to thys
holy table, least after the taking of this moste
blessed breade, the deuell enter into him, as he
dyd into Judas, to fulfill in him all iniquite, and to
bring him to destruction, bothe of body and soule.

*Heare the priest shal pawse a while, to see yf any
man will wythdrawe hym selfe: and if he perceaue
any so to do, then let hym common wyth hym pryuely
at conuenient leasure, and see whether he can wyth
good exhortacion, bring him to grace: and after a
lytle pause, the priest shal say.*

You that do trulie and earnestlie repent you of
your synnes, and offences, commytted to almyghtie
God, and be in loue and charytie wyth your neyghbours, and entende to leade a newe life and hartelye

to followe the commaundements of God, and to
walke from hensforthe in his holye waies, drawe
nere, and take this holy Sacrament to your comforte,
make your humble confession to almightie God, and
to his holy church, here gathered together, in hys
name, mekely kneling vpon your knees.

*Then shall a generall confession be made in the
name of al those that are mynded to receyue the holy
Communion, either by one of them, or els by one of
the ministers, or by the priest hymself, all kneelyng
humbly vpon their knees.*

Almyghtie God, father of our lord Jesus Christe,
maker of all thinges, iudge of all men, wee knowlege and bewayle our manyfolde synnes and wyckednes, whyche we from tyme to tyme most greuouslie
haue commytted by thought, worde, and dede, against
thy diuine maiestie, prouoking most iustlye thy
wrath and indignacion against vs: wee doe earnestlie repent, and be hartely sory, for these our
mysdoinges: The remembraunce of them is gre-
uouse vnto vs, the burthen of them is intollerable;
haue mercy vpon vs, haue mercy vpon vs, moste mer-
cyfull father, for thy sonne our Lord Jesus Christes
sake. Forgeue vs al that is past, and graunt that
we maye euer hereafter, serue and please the in
newnes of life, to the honour and glorye of thy
name, through Jesus Christ our Lorde.

*Then shall the priest stand vp, and turnyng hym
to the people, say thus.*

Our blessed Lord, who hath left power to his
churche to absolue penitent synners from their
synnes, and to restore to the grace of the heauenlye
father suche as trulie beleue in Christ, haue mercy
vpon you, pardon and delyuer you from al synnes,
confyrme and strength you in al goodnes, and
bryng you to euerlastyng life.

Then shall the priest stande vp, and turnynge him toward the people, say thus:

Here what comfortable woordes our sauiour Christ saith to all that trulie turne to hym.

Come vnto me al that trauail and be heauy loden, and I shall refreshe you. So God loued the world that he gaue his onlie begotten sonne, to thend that all that beleue in hym shoulde not peryshe, but haue life euerlasting.

Here also what S. Paule sayth.

This is a true saiyng, and worthy of all men to be embraced and receaued, that Jesus Christ came into this world to saue synners.

Heare also what S. John sayth.

Yf any man synne, wee haue an aduocate wyth the father, Jesus Christ the righteous, he it is that obteyned grace for our sinnes.

Then shall the priest kneele doune and saye in the name of all them that shall receaue the Communion, this prayer followyng.

We do not presume to come to this thy table (O mercyful Lord) trusting in our awne righteousnes, but in thy manifold and greate mercyes; we be not worthie so muche as to gather by the crommes vnder the table. But thou arte the same Lord, whose propertye is alwayes to haue mercy: Graunt vs therefore gracious Lorde so to eate the fleshe of thy dere sonne Jesus Christ, and to drynk his bloud in these holy misteries, that we maye continually dwell in hym, and he in vs, that oure synfull bodyes maye be made cleane by his body, and our soules washed through his most precious bloud. Amen.

Then shall the priest rise, the people still reuerentlie knelyng, and the prieste shall deliuer the communion, first to the ministers, if any be there present, that thai maie be redy to helpe the priest, and after to the other.   And when he dooth deliuer the Sacrament of the body of Christe, he shall say to euery one these wordes following.

The bodye of oure Lorde Jesus Christ, whiche was geuen for the, preserue thy body vnto euerlastyng life.

And the priest delyuering the Sacrament of the bloud, and geuyng euery one to drynke once and no more, shall saye.

The bloude of oure Lorde Jesus Christ, which was shed for the, preserue thy soule vnto euerlastyng life.

If there be a deacon or other priest, then shall he followe with the chalyce, and as the priest ministreth the breade, so shall he for more expedicion minister the wine, in forme before wrytten.

Then shal the priest, turnyng him to ye people, let the people depart with this blessynge.

The peace of God whiche passeth all vnderstandyng, kepe your hartes and myndes in the knowlege and loue of God, and of his sonne Jesus Christe, our Lorde.

To the whiche the people shall answere Amen.

Note, that the breade that shalbe consecrated shalbe suche as heretofore hath bene accustomed.   And euery of the sayd consecrated breades, shalbe broken in twoo peces at the least, or more, by the discretion of the ministre, and so distributed.   And men must not thynke lesse to be receiued in part then in the whole, but in eche of theim the whole body of our sauiour Jesu Chryst.

Note, that yf it dothe so chaunce, that the wyne halowed and consecrate dooth not suffice or bee ynough for theim that dooe take the Communion, the prieste ·
after the firste cuppe or chalice be emptied, may go

again to the aulter, and reuerentlie and deuoutlie prepare and consecrate an other, and so the thirde, or more lykewyse, begynnyng at these woordes, Simili modo, postquam cenatum est, *and endyng at these woordes*, qui pro uobis et pro multis effundetur in remissionem peccatorum, *and wythout any leuacion or lyftyng vp.*

The Supper of the Lorde,

AND THE HOLY COMMUNION,

COMMONLY CALLED THE MASSE.

(According to the first Common Prayer Book of Edward VI, 1549.)

*S*O *many as intende to bee partakers of the holy Communion, shall sygnifie their names to the Curate, ouer night: or els in the morning, afore the beginning of Matins, or immediatly after.*

And if any of those be an open and notorious euill liuer, so that the congregacion by hym is offended, or haue doen any wrong to his neighbours, by worde, or dede: The Curate shall call hym, & aduertise hym, in any wise not to presume to the lordes table, vntil he haue openly declared hym-selfe, to haue truly repented, and amended his former naughtie life: that the congregacion maie thereby be satisfied, whiche afore were offended: and that he haue recompensed the parties, whom he hath dooen wrong vnto, or at the least bee in full purpose so to doo, as sone as he conueniently maie.

❡ *The same ordre shall the Curate vse, with those betwixt whom he perceiueth malice and hatred to reigne, not suffering them to bee partakers of the Lordes table, vntill he knowe them to bee reconciled. And yf one of the parties so at variaunce be con-tent to forgeue from the botome of his harte, all that the other hath trespaced against hym, and to make amendes, for that he hymself hath offended:*

and the other partie will not bee perswaded to a godly vnitie, but remaigne still in his frowardnes and malice: The Minister in that case ought to admit the penitent persone to the holy Communion, and not hym that is obstinate.

℣ *Upon the daie, and at the tyme appoincted for the ministracion of the holy Communion, the Priest that shal execute the holy ministery shall put vpon hym the vesture appoincted for that ministracion, that is to saye: a white Albe plain, with a vestement or Cope. And where there be many Priestes, or Decons, there so many shalbe ready to helpe the Priest, in the ministracion, as shalbee requisite: And shall haue vpon theim lykewise, the vestures appointed for their ministery, that is to saye, Albes, with tunacles. Then shall the Clerkes syng in Englishe for the office, or Introite (as they call it), a Psalme appointed for that daie.*

The Priest standing humbly afore the middes of the Altar, shall saie the Lordes praier, with this Collect.

ALMIGHTIE GOD, vnto whom all hartes bee open, and all desyres knowen, and from whom no secretes are hid: clense the thoughtes of our heartes, by the inspiracion of thy holy spirite : that we may perfectly loue thee, and worthely magnifie thy holy name : Through Christ our Lorde. Amen.

Then shall he saie a Psalme appointed for the introite: whiche Psalme ended, the Priest shall saye, or els the Clerkes shal syng.

iij. Lorde haue mercie vpon us.
iij. Christ haue mercie vpon vs.
iij. Lorde haue mercie vpon vs.

Then the Prieste standyng at Goddes borde shall begin.

Glory be to God on high.

The Clerkes.

And in yearth peace, good will towardes men.

We praise thee, we blesse thee, we worship thee, we glorifie thee, wee geue thankes to thee for thy greate glory, O Lorde GOD, heauenly kyng, God the father almightie.

O Lorde the onely begotten sonne Jesu Christe, O Lorde God, Lambe of GOD, sonne of the father, that takest awaye the synnes of the worlde, haue mercie vpon vs : thou that takest awaye the synnes of the worlde, receiue our praier.

Thou that sittest at the right hande of GOD the father, haue mercie vpon vs : For thou onely art holy, thou onely art the Lorde. Thou onely (O Christ) with the holy Ghoste, art moste high in the glory of God the father. Amen.

Then the priest shall turne him to the people and saye.

The Lorde be with you.

The aunswere.

And with thy spirite.

The Priest.

Let vs praie.

Then shall folowe the Collect of the daie, with one of these two Collectes folowyng, for the Kyng.

ALMIGHTIE God, whose kingdom is euerlasting, and power infinite, haue mercie vpon the whole congregacion, and so rule the heart of thy chosen seruaunt Edward the sixt, our kyng and gouernour : that he (knowyng whose minister he is) maie aboue

al thinges seke thy honour and glory, & that we his.
subiectes (duely consydering whose auctoritie he
hath) maye faithfully serue, honour, and humbly
obeye him, in thee, and for thee, according to thy
blessed word, and ordinaunce: Through Jesus
Christe oure Lorde, who with thee, and the holy
ghost, liueth, and reigneth, euer one God, worlde
without ende. Amen.

ALMIGHTIE and euerlasting GOD, we bee
taught by thy holy worde, that the heartes of
Kynges are in thy rule and gouernaunce, and that
thou doest dispose, and turne them as it semeth
best to thy godly wisedom: We humbly beseche
thee, so to dispose and gouerne the hart of Edward
the sixt, thy seruaunt, our Kyng and gouernour,
that in all his thoughtes, wordes, and workes, he
maye euer seke thy honour and glory, and study to
preserue thy people, committed to his charge, in
wealth, peace, and Godlynes: Graunt this, O mercifull father, for thy dere sonnes sake, Jesus Christ
our Lorde. Amen.

The Collectes ended, the priest, or he that is appointed,
shall reade the Epistle, in a place assigned for the
purpose, saying.

The Epistle of sainct Paule written in the
Chapiter of   to the   .

The Minister then shall reade thepistle. Immediatly
after the Epistle ended, the priest, or one appointed
to reade the Gospel, shall saie.

The holy Gospell written in the   Chapiter of .

The Clearkes and people shall aunswere.

Glory be to thee, O Lorde.

The priest or deacon then shall reade the Gospel: after the Gospell ended, the priest shall begin.

I belieue in one God.

The Clerkes shall syng the rest.

The father almightie, maker of heauen and yearth, and of all thinges visible and inuisible: And in one Lorde Jesu Christ, the onely begotten sonne of GOD, begotten of his father before all worldes, God of GOD, light of light, very God of very God, begotten, not made, beeyng of one substaunce with the father, by whom all thinges were made, who for vs men, and for our saluacion, came doune from heauen, and was incarnate by the holy Ghoste, of the Virgin Mary, and was made manne, and was Crucified also for vs vnder Poncius Pilate, he suffered and was buried, and the thirde daye he arose again according to the scriptures, and ascended into heauen and sitteth at the right hande of the father: And he shall come again with glory, to iudge both the quicke and the dead.

And I belieue in the holy ghost, the Lorde and geuer of life, who procedeth from the father and the sonne, who with the father and the sonne together is worshipped and glorified, who spake by the Prophetes. And I beleue one Catholike and apostolike Churche. I acknowlege one Baptisme, for the remission of synnes. And I loke for the resurreccion of the deade: and the lyfe of the worlde to come. Amen.

After the Crede ended, shall folowe the Sermon or Homely, or some porcion of one of the Homelyes, as thei shalbe hereafter deuided: wherin if the people bee not exhorted, to the worthy receiuyng of the holy Sacrament, of the bodye & bloude of our sauior Christ: then shal the Curate geue *this exhortacion, to those y^t be minded to receiue ye same.*

DERELY beloued in the Lord, ye that mynde
to come to the holy Communion of the bodye
& bloude of our sauior Christe, must considre what
S. Paule writeth to the Corinthians, how he exhorteth all persones diligently to trie & examine
themselues, before they presume to eate of that
breade, and drinke of that cup: for as the benefite
is great, if with a truly penitent heart, and liuely
faith, we receiue that holy Sacrament: (for then we
spiritually eate the fleshe of Christ, & drinke his
bloude, then we dwell in Christ & Christ in vs,
wee bee made one with Christ, and Christ with vs)
so is the daunger great, yf wee receyue the same
vnworthely, for then wee become gyltie of the body
and bloud of Christ our sauior, we eate and drinke
our owne damnacion, not considering the Lordes
bodye. We kyndle Gods wrathe ouer vs: we prouoke him to plague vs with diuerse dyseases, and
sondery kyndes of death. Therefore if any here be
a blasphemer, aduouterer, or bee in malyce or enuie,
or in any other greuous cryme (except he bee truly
sory therefore, and earnestly mynded to leaue the
same vices, and do trust him selfe to bee reconciled
to almightie God, and in Charitie with all the
worlde) lette him bewayle his synnes, and not come
to that holy table, lest after the taking of that most
blessed breade, the deuyll enter into him, as he dyd
into Judas, to fyll him full of all iniquitie, and brynge
him to destruccion, bothe of body and soule. Judge
therfore your selfes (brethren) that ye bee not
iudged of the lorde. Let your mynde be without
desire to synne, repent you truely for your synnes
past, haue an earnest and lyuely faith in Christ our
sauior, be in perfect charitie with all men, so shall

ye be mete partakers of those holy misteries. And
aboue all thynges : ye must geue moste humble and
hartie thankes to God the father, the sonne, and the
holy ghost, for the redempcion of the worlde, by the
death and passion of our sauior Christ, both God
and man, who did humble him self euen to the death
vpon the crosse, for vs miserable synners, whiche
laie in darknes and shadowe of death, that he
myghte make vs the children of God : and exalt vs
to euerlasting life. And to thend that wee should
alwaye remembre the excedyng loue of oure master,
and onely sauior Jesu Christe, thus diyng for vs,
arid the innumerable benefites (whiche by his precious bloudshedyng) he hath obteigned to vs, he
hath lefte in those holy Misteries, as a pledge of his
loue, and a continual remembraunce of the same his
owne blessed body, and precious bloud, for vs to
fede vpon spiritually, to our endles comfort and
consolacion. To him therfore with the father and
the holy ghost, let vs geue (as we are most bounden)
continual thankes, submittyng our selfes wholy to
hys holy will and pleasure, and studying to serue
hym in true holines and righteousnes al the daies
of our life. Amen.

*In Cathedral churches or other places where there is
dailie Communion, it shal be sufficient to reade
this exhortacion aboue written, once in a moneth.
And in parish churches, vpon the weke daies it
may be lefte vnsayed.*

C *And if vpon the Sunday or holy daye, the people
be negligent to come to the Communion: Then
shall the Priest earnestly exhorte his parishoners, to dispose themselfes to the receiuing of
the holy communion more diligently, saying these
or like wordes vnto them.*

DERE frendes, and you especially vpon whose soules I haue cure and charge, on next I do intende, by Gods grace, to offre to all suche as shalbe godlye disposed, the moste comfortable Sacrament of the body and bloud of Christ, to be taken of them, in the remembraunce of his moste fruitfull and glorious Passyon : by the whiche passion, we haue obteigned remission of our synnes, and be made partakers of the kyngdom of heauen, whereof wee bee assured and asserteigned, yf wee come to the sayde Sacrament, with hartie repentaunce for our offences, stedfast faithe in Goddes mercye, and earnest mynde to obeye Goddes will, and to offende no more. Wherefore our duetie is, to come to these holy misteries, with moste heartie thankes to bee geuen to almightie GOD, for his infinite mercie and benefites geuen and bestowed vpon vs his vnworthye seruauntes, for whom he hath not onely geuen his body to death, and shed his bloude, but also doothe vouchsaue in a Sacrament and Mistery, to geue vs his sayed bodye and bloud to feede vpon spiritually. The whyche Sacrament beyng so Diuine and holy a thyng, and so comfortable to them whiche receyue it worthilye, and so daungerous to them that wyll presume to take the same vnworthely: My duetie is to exhorte you in the meane season, to consider the greatnes of the thing, and to serche and examine your owne consciences, and that not lyghtly nor after the maner of dissimulers with GOD: But as they whiche shoulde come to a moste Godly and heauenly Banket, not to come but in the mariage garment required of God in scripture, that you may (so muche as lieth in you) be founde worthie to come to suche a table. The waies and meanes therto is.

First that you be truly repentaunt of your former
euill life, and that you confesse with an vnfained
hearte to almightie God, youre synnes and vnkynd-
nes towardes his Maiestie committed, either by will,
worde or dede, infirmitie or ignoraunce, and that
with inwarde sorowe and teares you bewaile your
offences, and require of almightie god, mercie, and
pardon, promising to him (from the botome of your
hartes) thamendment of your former lyfe. And
emonges all others, I am commaunded of God, especially to moue and exhorte you, to reconcile your
selfes to your neighbors, whom you haue offended,
or who hath offended you, putting out of your
heartes al hatred and malice against them, and to
be in loue and charitie with all the worlde, and to
forgeue other, as you woulde that God should forgeue you. And yf any man haue doen wrong to any
other : let him make satisfaccion, and due restitucion
of all landes and goodes, wrongfully taken awaye or
with holden, before he come to Goddes borde, or at
the least be in ful minde and purpose so to do, as-
sone as he is able, or els let him not come to this
holy table, thinking to deceyue God, who seeth al
mennes hartes. For neither the absolucion of the
priest, can any thing auayle them, nor the receiuyng
of this holy sacrament doth any thing but increase
their damnacion. And yf there be any of you,
whose conscience is troubled and greued in any
thing, lackyng comforte or counsaill, let him come
to me, or to some other dyscrete and learned priest,
taught in the law of God, and confesse and open
his synne and griefe secretly, that he maye receiue
suche ghostly counsaill, aduyse and comfort, that
his conscience maye be releued, and that of vs (as
of the Ministers of GOD and of the churche) he
may receiue comfort and absolucion, to the satis-

faccion of his mynde, and auoyding of all scruple and doubtfulnes: requiryng suche as shalbe satisfied with a generall confession, not to be offended with them that doo vse, to their further satisfiyng, the auriculer and secret confession to the Priest: nor those also whiche thinke nedefull or conuenient, for the quietnes of their awne consciences particuliarly to open their sinnes to the Priest: to bee offended with them that are satisfied, with their humble confession to GOD, and the generall confession to the churche. But in all thinges to folowe and kepe the rule of charitie, and euery man to be satisfied with his owne conscience, not iudgyng other mennes myndes or consciences: where as he hath no warrant of Goddes word to the same.

❡ *Then shall folowe for the Offertory, one or mo, of these Sentences of holy scripture, to bee song whiles the people doo offer, or els one of theim to bee saied by the minister, immediatly afore the offeryng.*

Math. v. Let your light so shine before men, that they maye see your good woorkes, and glorify your father whiche is in heauen.

Math. vi. Laie not vp for your selfes treasure vpon the yearth, where the rust and mothe doth corrupt, and where theues breake through and steale: But laie vp for your selfes treasures in heauen, where neyther ruste nor mothe doth corrupt, and where theues do not breake through nor steale.

Math. vii. Whatsoeuer you would that menne should do vnto you, euen so do you vnto them, for this is the Law and the Prophetes.

Math. vii. Not euery one that saieth vnto me, lorde, lorde, shall entre into the kyngdom of heauen, but he that doth the will of my father whiche is in heauen.

Zache stode furthe, and saied vnto the Lorde : be- Luc. xix. holde Lorde, the halfe of my goodes I geue to the poore, and if I haue doen any wrong to any man, I restore foure fold.

Who goeth a warfare at any tyme at his owne i. Cor. ix. cost ? who planteth a vineyarde, and eateth not of the fruite thereof ? Or who fedeth a flocke, and eateth not of the milke of the flocke ?

If we haue sowen vnto you spirituall thinges, is it a i. Cor. ix. great matter yf we shall reape your worldly thynges ?

Dooe ye not knowe, that they whiche minister i. Cor. ix. aboute holy thinges, lyue of the Sacrifice ? They whiche waite of the alter, are partakers with the alter ? euen so hath the lorde also ordained : that they whiche preache the Gospell should liue of the Gospell.

He whiche soweth litle, shall reape litle, and he ii. Cor. ix. that soweth plenteously, shall reape plenteously. Let euery manne do accordyng as he is disposed in his hearte, not grudgyngly, or of necessitie, for God loueth a cherefull geuer.

Let him that is taught in the woorde, minister Gala. vi. vnto hym that teacheth, in all good thinges. Be not deceiued, GOD is not mocked. For whatsoeuer a man soweth, that shall he reape.

While we haue tyme, let vs do good vnto all men, Gala. vi. and specially vnto them, whiche are of the houshold of fayth.

Godlynes is greate riches, if a man be contented i. Timo. vi. with that he hath : For we brought nothing into the worlde, neither maie we cary any thing out.

Charge theim whiche are riche in this worlde, that i. Timo. vi. they bee ready to geue, and glad to distribute, laying vp in stoare for theimselfes a good foundacion, against the time to come, that they maie attain eternall lyfe.

Hebre. vi. GOD is not vnrighteous, that he will forget youre woorkes and labor, that procedeth of loue, whiche loue ye haue shewed for his names sake, whiche haue ministred vnto the sainctes, and yet do minister.

Hebre. xiii. To do good, and to distribute, forget not, for with suche Sacrifices God is pleased.

i. Jhon. iii. Whoso hath this worldes good, and seeth his brother haue nede, and shutteth vp his compassion from hym, how dwelleth the loue of God in him?

Toby. iiii. Geue almose of thy goodes, and turne neuer thy face from any poore man, and then the face of the lorde shall not be turned awaye from thee.

Toby. iiii. Bee mercifull after thy power: if thou hast muche, geue plenteously, if thou hast litle, do thy diligence gladly to geue of that litle, for so gathereste thou thy selfe a good reward, in the daie of necessitie.

Prouerbes xix. He that hath pitie vpon the poore, lendeth vnto the Lorde: and loke what he laieth out, it shalbe paied hym again.

Psal. xli. Blessed be the man that prouideth for the sicke and nedy, the lorde shall deliuer hym in the tyme of trouble.

Where there be Clerkes, thei shal syng one, or many of the sentences aboue written, accordyng to the length and shortnesse of the tyme, that the people be offeryng.

In the meane tyme, whyles the Clerkes do syng the Offertory, so many as are disposed, shall offer vnto the poore mennes boxe euery one accordynge to his habilitie and charitable mynde. And at the offeryng daies appoynted: euery manne and woman shall paie to the Curate, the due and accustomed offerynges.

Then so manye as shalbe partakers of the holy Com-

munion, shall tary still in the quire, or in some conuenient place, nigh the quire, the men on the one side, and the women on the other syde. All other (that mynde not to receiue the said holy Communion) shall departe out of the quire, except the ministers and Clerkes.

Then shall the minister take so muche Bread and Wine, as shall suffice for the persons appoynted to receiue the holy Communion, laiyng the breade vpon the corporas, or els in the paten, or in some other comely thyng, prepared for that purpose. And puttyng the wyne into the Chalice, or els in some faire or conueniente cup, prepared for that vse (if the Chalice will not serue) puttyng therto a litle pure and cleane water : And settyng both the breade and wyne vpon the Alter : Then the Prieste shall saye.

The Lorde be with you.

Aunswere.

And with thy spirite.

Priest.

Lift vp your heartes.

Aunswere.

We lift them vp vnto the Lorde.

Priest.

Let vs geue thankes to our Lorde God.

Aunswere.

It is mete and right so to do.

The Priest.

IT is very mete, righte, and our bounden dutie that wee shoulde at all tymes, and in all places, geue thankes to thee, O Lorde, holy father, almightie euerlastyng God.

❧ *Here shall folowe the proper preface, accordyng to the tyme (if there bee any specially appoynted) or els immediatly shall folowe,* Therefore with Angelles, &c.

PROPRE PREFACES.

❧ Upon Christmas daie.

BECAUSE thou diddeste geue Jesus Christe, thyne onely sonne to bee borne, as this daye for vs, who by the operacion of the holy ghoste, was made very man, of the substaunce of the Virgin Mari his mother, and that without spot of sinne, to make vs cleane from all synne. Therfore, &c.

❧ Upon Easter daie.

BUT chiefly are we bound to praise thee, for the glorious resurreccion of thy sonne Jesus Christe, our Lorde, for he is the very Pascall Lambe, whiche was offered for vs, and hath taken awaie the synne of the worlde, who by his death hath destroyed death, and by his risyng to life againe, hath restored to vs euerlastynge life. Therefore, &c.

❧ Upon the Ascencion daye.

THROUGH thy most dere beloued sonne, Jesus Christ our Lorde, who after his moste glorious resurreccion manifestly appered to all his disciples, and in their sight ascended vp into heauen, to prepare a place for vs, that where he is, thither mighte we also ascende, and reigne with hym in glory. Therfore, &c.

❧ Upon Whitsondaye.

THROUGH Jesus Christ our Lorde, accordyng to whose moste true promise, the holy

Ghoste came doune this daye from heauen, with a
sodain great sound, as it had been a mightie wynde,
in the likenes of fiery toungues, lightyng vpon the
Apostles, to teache them, and to leade them to all
trueth, geuyng them bothe the gifte of diuerse lan-
guages, and also boldnes with feruent zeale, con-
stantly to preache the Gospell vnto all nacions,
whereby we are brought out of darkenes and error,
into the cleare light and true knowlege of thee, and
of thy sonne Jesus Christ. Therfore, &c.

℃ Upon the feast of the Trinitie.

IT is very meete, righte, and oure bounden duetie,
that we should at al tymes, and in al places,
geue thankes to thee O Lorde, almightye euerlasting
God, whiche arte one God, one Lorde, not one onely
person, but three persones in one substaunce : For
that which we beleue of the glory of the father, the
same we beleue of the sonne, and of the holy ghost,
without any difference, or inequalitie, whom the
Angels, &c.

After whiche preface shall folowe immediatly.

Therfore with Angels and Archangels, and with
all the holy companye of heauen : we laude and
magnify thy glorious name, euermore praisyng thee,
and saying :
Holy, holy, holy, Lorde God of Hostes : heauen
and earth are full of thy glory : Osanna in the
highest. Blessed is he that commeth in the name of
the Lorde : Glory to thee O lorde in the highest.
This the Clerkes shal also syng.

℃ *When the Clerkes haue dooen syngyng, then shall
the Priest, or Deacon, turne hym to the people and
saye.*

Let vs praie for the whole state of Christes churche.

❦ Then the Priest turnyng hym to the Altar, shall saye or syng, playnly and distinctly, this prayer folowyng.

ALMIGHTIE and euerliuyng God, whiche by thy holy Apostle haste taught vs to make prayers and supplicacions, and to geue thankes for al menne : We humbly beseche thee moste mercy-fully to receiue these our praiers, which we offre vnto thy diuine Maiestie, beseching thee to inspire continually the vniversal churche, with the spirite of trueth, vnitie and concorde : And graunt that al they that do confesse thy holy name, maye agree in the trueth of thy holye worde, and liue in vnitie and godly loue. Speciallye we beseche thee to saue and defende thy seruaunt, Edwarde our Kyng, that vnder hym we maye be Godly and quietly gouerned. And graunt vnto his whole counsaile, and to all that be put in aucthoritie vnder hym, that they maye truely and indifferently minister iustice, to the pun-ishemente of wickednesse and vice, and to the main-tenaunce of Goddes true religion and vertue. Geue grace (O heauenly father) to all Bishoppes, Pastors, and Curates, that thei maie bothe by their life and doctrine set furthe thy true and liuely worde, and rightely and duely administer thy holy Sacramentes. And to al thy people geue thy heauenly grace, that with meke heart and due reuerence, they may heare and receiue thy holy worde, truely seruyng thee in holynes and righteousnes, all the dayes of their life : And we most humbly beseche thee of thy goodnes (O Lorde) to coumfort and succour all them, whyche in thys transytory life be in trouble, sorowe, nede, syckenes, or any other aduersitie. And especially

we commend vnto thy mercifull goodnes, this congregacion which is here assembled in thy name, to
celebrate the commemoracion of the most glorious
death of thy sonne: And here we do geue vnto
thee moste high praise, and hartie thankes for the
wonderfull grace and vertue, declared in all thy
sainctes, from the begynning of the worlde: And
chiefly in the glorious and moste blessed virgin
Mary, mother of thy sonne, Jesu Christe our Lorde
and God, and in the holy Patriarches, Prophetes,
Apostles and Martyrs, whose examples (o Lorde)
and stedfastnes in thy fayth, and kepyng thy holy
commaundementes: graunt vs to folowe. We commend vnto thy mercye (O Lorde) all other thy seruauntes, which are departed hence from vs, with the
signe of faith, and nowe do reste in the slepe of
peace: Graunt vnto them, we beseche thee, thy
mercy, and euerlasting peace, and that at the day
of the generall resurreccion, we and all they which
bee of the misticall body of thy sonne, may altogether be set on his right hand, and heare that his
most ioyfull voyce: Come vnto me, O ye that be
blessed of my father, and possesse the kingdom,
whiche is prepared for you, from the begynning of
the worlde: Graunt this, O father, for Jesus Christes
sake, our onely mediatour and aduocate.

O God heauenly father, which of thy tender
mercie, diddest geue thine only sonne Jesu Christ,
to suffre death vpon the crosse for our redempcion,
who made there (by his one oblacion once offered)
a full, perfect, and sufficient sacrifyce, oblacion, and
satysfacyon, for the synnes of the whole worlde, and
did institute, and in his holy Gospell commaund vs,
to celebrate a perpetuall memory, of that his precious
death, vntyll his comming again: Heare vs (o mer-
ciful father) we besech thee: and with thy holy

spirite and worde, vouchsafe to bl✠esse and sanc-
✠tifie these thy gyftes and creatures of bread and
wyne, that they maie be vnto vs the bodye and
bloude of thy moste derely beloued sonne Jesus
Here the   Christe. Who in the same nyght that he was be-
prieste
must take trayed : tooke breade, and when he had blessed,
the bread
into his and geuen thankes : he brake it, and gaue it to his
handes.
disciples, saiyng : Take, eate, this is my bodye
which is geuen for you, do this in remembraunce
of me.

Here the   Likewyse after supper he toke the cuppe, and
priest shall
take the when he had geuen thankes, he gaue it to them,
Cuppe into
his handes. saiyng : drynk ye all of this, for this is my bloude
of the newe Testament, whyche is shed for you and
for many, for remission of synnes : do this as oft as
you shall drinke it in remembraunce of me.

*These wordes before rehersed are to be saied, turning
still to the Altar, without any eleuacion, or shew-
ing the Sacrament to the people.*

WHEREFORE, O Lorde and heauenly father,
accordyng to the Instytucyon of thy derely
beloued sonne, our sauiour Jesu Christ, we thy
humble seruauntes do celebrate, and make here
before thy diuine Maiestie, with these thy holy
giftes, the memoryall whyche thy sonne hath wylled
vs to make, hauing in remembraunce his blessed
passion, mightie resurreccyon, and gloryous ascen-
cion, renderyng vnto thee most hartie thankes, for
the innumerable benefites procured vnto vs by
the same, entierely desiryng thy fatherly goodnes,
mercifully to accepte this our Sacrifice of praise and
thankes geuing : most humbly beseching thee to
graunt, that by the merites and death of thy sonne
Jesus Christ, and through faith in his bloud, we and
al thy whole churche, may obteigne remission of our

sinnes, and all other benefites of hys passyon. And here wee offre and present vnto thee (O Lorde) oure selfe, oure soules, and bodies, to be a reasonable, holy, and liuely sacrifice vnto thee : humbly besechyng thee, that whosoeuer shalbee partakers of thys holy Communion, maye worthely receiue the moste precious body and bloude of thy sonne Jesus Christe : and bee fulfilled with thy grace and heauenly benediccion, and made one bodye with thy sonne Jesu Christe, that he maye dwell in them, and they in hym. And although we be vnworthy (through our manyfolde synnes) to offre vnto thee any Sacryfice : Yet we beseche thee to accepte thys our bounden duetie and seruice, and commaunde these our prayers and supplicacions, by the Ministery of thy holy Angels, to be brought vp into thy holy Tabernacle before the syght of thy dyuine maiestie : not waiyng our merites, but pardonyng our offences, through Christe our Lorde, by whome, and with whome, in the vnitie of the holy Ghost : all honour and glory be vnto thee, O father almightie, world without ende. Amen.

Let vs praye.

AS our sauiour Christe hath commaunded and taught vs, we are bolde to saye. Our father whyche art in heauen, halowed be thy name. Thy Kyngdome come. Thy wyll be doen in yearth, as it is in heauen. Geue vs this daye our dayly breade. And forgeue vs our trespaces, as wee forgeue them that trespasse agaynst vs. And leade vs not into temptacion.

The aunswere.

But deliuer vs from euill. Amen.

Then shall the priest saye.

The peace of the Lorde be alwaye with you.

The Clerkes.

And with thy spirite.

The Priest.

CHRIST our Pascall lambe is offred vp for vs, once for al, when he bare our sinnes on hys body vpon the crosse, for he is the very lambe of God, that taketh away the sinnes of the worlde : wherfore let vs kepe a ioyfull and holy feast with the Lorde.

Here the priest shall turne hym toward those that come to the holy Communion, and shall saye.

YOU that do truly and earnestly repent you of your synnes to almightie God, and be in loue and charitie with your neighbors, and entende to lede a newe life, folowyng the commaundementes of God, and walkyng from hencefurth in his holy wayes : drawe nere and take this holy Sacrament to your comforte, make your humble confession to almightie God, and to his holy church here gathered together in hys name, mekely knelyng vpon your knees.

Then shall thys generall Confession bee made, in the name of al those that are minded to receiue the holy Communion, eyther by one of them, or els by one of the ministers, or by the prieste hymselfe, all kneling humbly vpon their knees.

ALMYGHTIE GOD, father of oure Lord Jesus Christ, maker of all thynges, iudge of all men, we knowlege and bewaile our manyfold synnes and wyckednes, which we from tyme to tyme, most greuously haue committed, by thought, word and dede, agaynst thy diuine maiestie, prouoking moste iustly thy wrath and indignacion against vs, we do earnestly repent and be hartely sory for these our misdoinges, the remembraunce of them is greuous vnto vs, the burthen of them is intollerable: haue mercye vpon vs, haue mercie vpon vs, moste mercifull father, for thy sonne our Lorde Jesus Christes sake, forgeue vs all that is past, and graunt that we may euer hereafter serue and please thee in neunes of life, to the honor and glory of thy name: Through Jesus Christe our Lorde.

Then shall the Prieste stande vp, and turnyng hymselfe to the people, say thus.

ALMIGHTIE GOD our heauenly father, who of his great mercie, hath promysed forgeuenesse of synnes to all them, whiche with hartye repentaunce and true fayth, turne vnto him: haue mercy vpon you, pardon and delyuer you from all youre sinnes, confirme and strengthen you in all goodnes, and bring you to euerlasting lyfe: through Jesus Christ our Lord.   Amen.

Then shall the Priest also say.

Heare what coumfortable woordes our sauiour Christ sayeth to all that truely turne to him.

Come vnto me all that trauell and bee heauy laden, and I shall refreshe you. So God loued the worlde that he gaue his onely begotten sonne, to the ende that al that beleue in hym shoulde not perishe, but haue lyfe euerlasting.

Heare also what saint Paul sayeth.

This is a true saying, and woorthie of all men to bee receiued, that Jesus Christe came into thys worlde to saue sinners.

Heare also what saint John sayeth.

If any man sinne, we haue an aduocate with the father, Jesus Christ the righteous, and he is the propiciation for our sinnes.

Then shall the Priest turnyng him to gods boord knele down, and say in the name of all them, that shall receyue the Communion, this prayer folowing.

WE do not presume to come to this thy table (o mercifull lord) trusting in our owne righteousnes, but in thy manifold and great mercies : we be not woorthie so much as to gather vp the cromes vnder thy table, but thou art the same lorde whose propertie is alwayes to haue mercie : Graunt vs therfore (gracious lorde) so to eate the fleshe of thy dere sonne Jesus Christ, and to drynke his bloud in these holy Misteries, that we may continuallye dwell in hym, and he in vs, that oure synfull bodyes may bee made cleane by his body, and our soules washed through hys most precious bloud. Amen.

Then shall the Prieste firste receiue the Communion in both kindes. himselfe, and next deliuer it to other Ministers, if any be there presente (that they may bee ready to helpe the chiefe Minister) and after to the people.

And when he deliuereth the Sacramente of the body of Christe, he shall say to euery one these woordes.

The body of our Lorde Jesus Christe whiche was geuen for thee, preserue thy bodye and soule vnto euerlasting lyfe.

And the Minister deliuering the Sacrament of the bloud, and geuing euery one to drinke once and no more, shall say.

The bloud of our Lorde Jesus Christe which was shed for thee, preserue thy bodye and soule vnto euerlasting lyfe.

If there be a Deacon or other Priest, then shal he folow with the Chalice: and as the priest ministreth the Sacrament of the body, so shal he (for more expedicion) minister the Sacrament of the bloud, in fourme before written.

In the Communion tyme the Clarkes shall syng.

ii. O lambe of god that takeste away the sinnes of the worlde : haue mercie vpon vs.

O lambe of god that takeste away the synnes of the worlde : graunt vs thy peace.

Beginning so soone as the Prieste doeth receyue the holy Communion: and when the Communion is ended, then shall the Clarkes syng the post Communion.

Sentences. of holy scripture, to be sayd or song euery daye one, after the holy Communion, called the post Communion.

If any man will folowe me, let him forsake hym- Math xvi. selfe, and take vp his crosse and folowe me.

Whosoeuer shall indure vnto thende, he shalbe Mar. xiii. saued.

Praysed be the Lorde god of Israell, for he hath Luc. i. visited and redemed hys people : therefore let vs serue hym all the dayes of our lyfe, in holines and righteousnes accepted before hym.

Happie are those seruauntes, whome the Lord Luc. xii. (when he cummeth) shall fynde waking.

Be ye readye, for the sonne of manne will come, Luc. xii. at an hower when ye thinke not.

The seruaunte that knoweth hys maisters will, Luc. xii. and hath not prepared himself, neither hath doen according to his will, shalbe beaten with many stripes.

John. iiii.   The howre cummeth and now it is, when true woorshippers shall wurship the father in spirite and trueth.

John. v.   Beholde, thou art made whole, sinne no more, lest any wurse thing happen vnto thee.

Iohn. viii.   If ye shall continue in my woorde, then are ye my very disciples, and ye shall knowe the truth, and the truth shall make you free.

John. xii.   While ye haue lighte, beleue on the lyght, that ye may be the children of light.

Iohn. xiiii.   He that hath my commaundementes, and kepeth them, the same is he that loueth me.

Ihon. xiiii.   If any man loue me, he will kepe my woorde, and my father will loue hym, and wee will come vnto hym and dwell with hym.

Iohn. xv.   If ye shall byde in me, and my woorde shall abyde in you, ye shall aske what ye will, and it shall bee doen to you.

Iohn. xv.   Herein is my father gloryfyed, that ye beare muche fruite, and become my disciples.

Iohn. xv.   This is my commaundement, that you loue togeether as I haue loued you.

Roma. viii.   If God be on our syde, who can be agaynst vs ? which did not spare his owne sonne, but gaue him for vs all.

Rom. viii.   Who shall lay anything to the charge of Goddes chosen ? it is GOD that iustifyeth, who is he that can condemne ?

Rom. xiii.   The nyght is passed, and the day is at hande, let vs therfore cast away the dedes of darkenes, and put on the armour of light.

i. Corin. i.   Christe Jesus is made of GOD, vnto vs wisedome, and righteousnes, and sanctifying, and redempcion, that (according as it is written) he whiche reioyceth shoulde reioyce in the Lorde.

i. Corin. iii.   Knowe ye not that ye are the temple of GOD,

and that the spirite of GOD dwelleth in you? if
any manne defile the temple of GOD, him shall
God destroy.

Ye are derely bought, therfore glorifye God in i. Corin. vi.
your bodies, and in your spirites, for they belong
to God.

Be you folowers of God as deare children, and Ephes. v.
walke in loue, euen as Christe loued vs, and gaue
hymselfe for vs an offeryng and a Sacrifyce of a
sweete sauoure to God.

Then the Priest shall geue thankes to God, in the
name of all them that haue communicated, turn-
ing him first to the people, and saying.

The Lorde be with you.

The aunswere.

And with thy spirite.

The priest.

Let vs pray.

ALMIGHTYE and euerlyuyng GOD, we moste
hartely thanke thee, for that thou hast vouch-
safed to feede vs in these holy Misteries, with the
spirituall foode of the moste precious body and
bloud of thy sonne, our sauiour Jesus Christ, and
hast assured vs (duely receiuing the same) of thy
fauour and goodness toward vs, and that we be very
membres incorporate in thy Misticall bodye, whiche
is the blessed companye of all faythfull people : and
heyres through hope of thy euerlasting kingdome,
by the merites of the most precious death and passion, of thy deare sonne. We therfore most humbly
beseche thee, O heauenly father, so to assist vs
with thy grace, that we may continue in that holy
felowship, and doe all suche good woorkes, as thou
hast prepared for vs to walke in, through Jesus

Christe our Lorde, to whome with thee, and the holy goste, bee all honour and glory, world without ende.

Then the Priest turning hym to the people, shall let them depart with this blessing.

The peace of GOD (whiche passeth all vnderstandyng) kepe your heartes and mindes in the knowledge and loue of GOD, and of hys sonne Jesus Christe our lorde. And the blessing of God almightie, the father, the sonne, and the holy gost, be emonges you, and remayne with you alway.

Then the people shall aunswere.

Amen.

Where there are no clerkes, there the Priest shall say al thinges appoynted here for them to sing.

When the holy Communion is celebrated on the worke-day, or in priuate howses : Then may be omitted, the Gloria in excelsis, the Crede, the Homily, and the exhortacion, beginning.

Dearely beloued, &c.

❧ *Collectes to bee sayed after the Offertory, when there is no Communion, euery such day one.*

ASSIST vs mercifully, O Lord, in these our supplicacions and praiers, and dispose the way of thy seruauntes, toward the attainement of euerlasting saluacyon, that emong all the chaunges and chaunces of thys mortall lyfe, they may euer bee defended by thy moste gracious and readye helpe: throughe Christe our Lorde. Amen.

O ALMIGHTIE Lorde and euerlyuyng GOD, vouchesafe, we beseche thee, to direct, sanctifye and gouerne, both our heartes and bodies, in the

wayes of thy lawes, and in the workes of thy commaundementes : that through thy most mightie pro-
teccion, both here and euer, we may be preserued in
body and soule : Through our Lorde and sauiour
Jesus Christ. Amen.

GRAUNT we beseche thee almightie god, that
the wordes whiche we haue hearde this day
with our outwarde eares, may throughe thy grace,
bee so grafted inwardly in our heartes, that they
may bring foorth in vs the fruite of good liuing, to
the honour and prayse of thy name : Through Jesus
Christe our Lorde. Amen.

PREUENT vs, O lorde, in all our doinges,
with thy most gracious fauour, and further vs
with thy continuall helpe, that in al our woorkes
begonne, continued and ended in thee : we may
glorifye thy holy name, and finally by thy mercy
obteine euerlasting life. Through, &c.

ALMIGHTIE God, the fountayn of all wisdome,
which knowest our necessities beefore we aske,
and our ignoraunce in asking : we beseche thee to
haue compassion vpon our infirmities, and those
thynges whiche for our vnwoorthines we dare not,
and for our blindnes we can not aske, vouchsaue to
geue vs for the woorthines of thy sonne Jesu
Christ our Lorde. Amen.

ALMIGHTIE god, which hast promised to heare
the peticions of them that aske in thy sonnes
name, we beseche thee mercifully to inclyne thyne
eares to vs that haue made nowe our prayers and
supplicacions vnto thee, and graunte that those
thynges whiche we haue faythfullye asked accordyng to thy will, maye effectually bee obteyned to
the reliefe of oure necessitye, and to the settyng

foorth of thy glorye: Through Jesus Christ our Lorde.

For rayne.

O GOD heauenly father, whiche by thy sonne Jesu Christ hast promised to al them that seke thy kingdom, and the righteousnes thereof, al thinges necessary to the bodely sustenaunce: send vs (we beseche thee) in this our necessitie, such moderate rayne and showers, that we may receiue the fruites of the earth, to our comfort and to thy honor: Through Jesus Christ our Lord.

For fayre wether.

O LORDE God, whiche for the sinne of manne didst once drowne all the worlde, except eight persons, and afterwarde of thy great mercye, didste promise neuer to destroy it so agayn: We humbly beseche thee, that although we for oure iniquities haue woorthelye deserued this plague of rayne and waters, yet vpon our true repentaunce, thou wilt sende vs suche wether wherby we may receiue the fruites of the earth in due season, and learne both by thy punishment to amende our liues, and by the graunting of our peticion, to geue thee prayse and glory: Through Jesu Christ our Lorde.

❧ *Upon wednesdaies and frydaies, the English Letany shalbe said or song in all places, after suche forme as is appoynted by the kynges maiesties Iniunccions: Or as is or shal bee otherwyse appoynted by his highnes. And thoughe there be none to communicate with the Prieste, yet these dayes (after the Letany ended) the Priest shall put vpon hym a playn Albe or surplesse, with a cope, and say al thinges at the Altar (appoynted to bee sayde at the celebracyon of the lordes supper) vntill after the offertory. And then shall adde one or two of the Collectes afore written, as occasion shall serue by his discrecion. And then turning him to the people shall let them depart, with the accustomed blessing.*

And the same order shall be vsed all other dayes, whensoeuer the people be customably assembled to pray in the churche, and none disposed to communicate with the Priest.

Lykewyse in Chapelles annexed, and all other places, there shalbe no celebracion of the Lordes supper, except there be some to communicate with the Priest. And in suche Chapelles annexed where ye people hath not bene accustomed to pay any holy bread, there they must either make some charitable prouision for the bering of the charges of the Communion, or elles (for receyuyng of the same) resort to theyr Parish Churche.

For aduoyding of all matters and occasyon of dyscencyon, it is mete that the breade prepared for the Communion bee made through all thys realme after one sort and fashion: that is to say, vnleauened, and rounde, as it was afore, but without all maner of printe, and some thyng more larger and thicker then it was, so that it may be aptly deuided in diuers pieces: and euery one shall be deuided in two pieces, at the leaste, or more, by the discrecion of the minister, and so distributed. And menne muste not thynke lesse to be receyued in parte, then in the whole, but in eache of them the whole body of our sauiour Jesu Christ.

And forsomuche as the Pastours and Curates within thys realme shal continually fynd at theyr costes and charges in theyr cures, sufficient Breade and

Wyne for the holy Communion (as oft as theyr Parishioners shalbe disposed for theyr spiritual comfort to receyue the same) it is therefore ordred, that in recompence of suche costes and charges, the Parishoners of euerye Parishe shall offer euery Sonday, at the tyme of the Offertory, the iuste valour and price of the holy lofe (with all suche money, and other thinges as were wont to be offered with the same) to the vse of theyr Pastours and Curates, and that in suche ordre and course, as they were woont to fynde and pay the sayd holy lofe.

Also, that the receiuing of the Sacrament of the blessed body and bloud of Christ, may be most agreable to the institucion therof, and to the vsage of the primatiue Churche: In all Cathederall and Collegiate Churches, there shal alwaies some Communicate with the Prieste that ministreth. And that the same may bee also obserued euery where abrode in the countrey: Some one at the least of that house in euery Parishe, to whome by course after the ordinaunce herein made, it apperteyneth to offer for the charges of the Communion, or some other whom they shall prouide to offer for them, shall receiue the holye Communion with the Prieste: the whiche may be the better doen, for that they knowe before, when theyr course commeth, and maie therfore dispose themselues to the worthie receiuyng of the Sacramente. And with hym or them who doeth so offre the charges of the Communion: all other, who be then Godly disposed thereunto, shall lykewyse receiue the Communion. And by this meanes the Minister hauyng alwaies some to communicate with him, maie accordingly solempnise so high and holy misteries, with all the suffrages and due ordre appoynted for the same.

And the Priest on the weke daie shall forbeare to celebrate the Communion, except he haue some that will communicate with hym.

Furthermore, euery man and woman to be bound to heare and be at the diuine seruice, in the Parishe churche where they be resident, and there with deuout prayer, or Godlye silence and meditacion, to occupie themselues. There to paie their dueties, to communicate once in the yeare at the least, and there to receyue, and take all other Sacramentes and rites, in this booke appoynted. And whoso-euer willyngly vpon no iust cause, doeth absent themselues, or doeth vngodly in the Parishe churche occupie themselues: vpon proffe therof, by the Ecclesiasticall lawes of the Realme to bee excommu-nicate, or suffre other punishement, as shall to the Ecclesiastical iudge (accordyng to his discrecion) seme conuenient.

And although it bee redde in aunciente writers, that the people many yeares past, receiued at the priestes handes, the Sacrament of the body of Christ in theyr owne handes and no commaundement of Christ to the contrary: Yet forasmuche as they many tymes conueyghed the same secretelye awaye, kept it with them, and diuersly abused it to super-sticion and wickednes: lest any suche thyng here-after should be attempted, and that an vniformitie might be vsed, throughoute the whole Realme: it is thought conuenient the people commonly receiue the Sacrament of Christes body, in their mouthes, at the Priestes hande.

From the edition of the first Common Prayer Book, "Imprinted at London in Fletestrete by Edward Whitchurche, the seventh daye of Marche, 1549." Folio.

Lightning Source UK Ltd.
Milton Keynes UK
19 May 2010

154358UK00001B/107/P